A BODY BROKEN FOR
A BROKEN PEOPLE

BODY BROKEN
for a BROKEN PEOPLE

THIRD EDITION

Divorce, Remarriage, and the Eucharist

Francis J. Moloney, SDB

Foreword by Xavier Léon-Dufour, SJ

PAULIST PRESS
New York / Mahwah, NJ

Edited by Kevin Mark
Interior design by Lynne Muir
Cover art by [to come]
Cover design by Lightly Salted Graphics
Indexed by Aili Carlson

First published as *A Body Broken for a Broken People: Eucharist in the New Testament* in Australia in 1990 by Collins Dove.
Second edition published in Australia in 1997 by HarperCollins Religious.

This revised and expanded third edition published in Australia in 2015 by
Garratt Publishing
32 Glenvale Crescent
Mulgrave VIC 3170
www.garrattpublishing.com.au

Library of Congress Cataloging-in-Publication Data
Names: Moloney, Francis J.
Title: A body broken for a broken people : divorce, remarriage, and the Eucharist / Francis J. Moloney.
Description: Third Edition. | New York : Paulist Press, 2016. | Includes bibliographical references and index.
Identifiers: LCCN 2015035264 | ISBN 9780809149711 (pbk. : alk. paper)
Subjects: LCSH: Lord's Supper—Biblical teaching. | Bible. New Testament—Criticism, interpretation, etc. | Lord's Supper—History—Early church, ca. 30-600. | Catholic Church—Doctrines.
Classification: LCC BS2545.L58 M65 2016 | DDC 234/.16309015—dc23 LC record available at http://lccn.loc.gov/2015035264

ISBN 978-0-8091-4971-1 (paperback)

Published in the United States in 2016 by
Paulist Press, Inc.
997 Macarthur Boulevard
Mahwah, NJ 07430
www.paulistpress.com

Printed and bound in the
United States of America

In gratitude for
the long and eucharistic lives
of my parents:
Denis (1899-1922) and Mary (1905-1996) Moloney

…io mi rendei,
piangendo, a quei che volentier perdona.
Orribil furon li peccati miei;
ma la bontà infinita ha sì gran braccia,
che prende ciò che si rivolge a lei.

* * *

I gave myself up,
weeping, to Him who willingly pardons.
My sins were horrible;
but infinite goodness has such wide arms,
that it takes what turns to it.

Dante, *Il Purgatorio iii* 119-23

Contents

Abbreviations

I have given complete titles for journals and series within the text. On a few occasions I have used the following recognized abbreviations.

1QS	*The Community Rule* (Qumran)
11QTemple	*The Temple Scroll* (Qumran)
ACFEB	Association Catholique Française pour les Études Bibliques
AT	Author's translation
BDAG	Walter Bauer, William F. Arndt, and Frederick W. Gingrich. *A Greek-English Lexicon of the New Testament and Other Early Christian Literature.* 3rd ed. Revised by Frederick W. Danker. Chicago: University of Chicago Press, 2000
BCE	Before the Common Era
BDF	Friedrich Blass, Albert Debrunner, and Robert W. Funk. *A Greek Grammar of the New Testament.* Chicago: University of Chicago Press, 1961
CCSL	Corpus Christianorum Series Latina
CE	Common Era
CD	*The Damascus Document* (Qumran)
DS	Henricus Denzinger and Adolfus Schönmetzer. *Enchridion Symbolorum: Definitionum et Declarationum de Rebus Fidei et Morum.* 33rd ed. Freiburg: Herder, 1965
JSOT	Journal for the Study of the Old Testament
LXX	The Septuagint
NT	New Testament
OT	Old Testament
PL	*Patrologiae cursus completus, series latina.* Edited by J.-P. Migne. 217 vols. Paris, 1857-1886
RSV	Revised Standard Version of the Bible
SBL	Society for Biblical Literature
SNTS	Society for New Testament Studies
s.v.	Sub voce ("under the word" in a dictionary)
WUNT	Wissenschaftliche Untersuchungen zum Neuen Testament

Foreword

I n reading these pages I have heard the sound of the Good News. Wonderful, but infrequently heard. Jesus lived the gospel of mercy and he proclaimed it without faltering. What is more, he spoke first of all to the poor, the broken. In Jesus' vision of things, what matters is not righteousness in the observance of the commandments, but unconditional commitment to his person, love of God, and love of others. Applied to the contemporary celebration of the eucharistic liturgy, is this preferential love of Jesus still visible? Has Jesus' call to joy been stifled by the detailed indications concerning who might or might not participate in the mystery? Has the Good News been carefully stored away in silos, in an attempt to preserve it better? So that it may never be deprived of its youth, it needs to be let loose into the open air. Francis Moloney guides us to listen carefully to the ever-clear voice of a Living Word.

He has approached the difficult problem of the authentic gospel message over against a tendency that restricts eucharistic practice to a closed circle of "the pure." This is an ancient tendency. Paul himself gave rules of discernment for access to the sacred mysteries. It was a concern of the second and third century Church that did not feel able to hold to its bosom certain "sinners," such as those who had fallen away into apostasy. This self-defensive reflex action of the institutionalized body of the Church ought, nevertheless, to be always counterbalanced by a profound reflection upon the attitude of Jesus of Nazareth. Here, beside many others, the exegete exercises his office in the Church; he must, in season and out of season, assist ecclesial practice ceaselessly to renew itself.

Will one ever be able to say the last word on this question? Such a hope appears somewhat naïve to me, both from the side of the institutionalized Church and from the side of the exegetes. Thus my opinion differs from that of the author on some minor issues: I do not think that Matthew depended directly upon Mark, nor do I accept his structure of John 13, nor his suggestion that the morsel of bread offered by Jesus to Judas was eucharistic. But the essential point lies not in certain exegetical presuppositions, but in one clearly given fact: the institution of the Eucharist is always linked to a mention of Judas the traitor and the prophecy of the denials and failure of the disciples. All exegetes agree on that point. Francis Moloney has pushed this evidence one step further, suggesting that the Eucharist was understood by the early Church as instituted for the broken. This is a stimulating hypothesis that deserves consideration.

I rejoice to see an exegete taking a courageous look at a pastoral problem. He has performed a task too often abandoned by the specialist who imagines that he has completed his work when he thinks that he has determined the meaning of the texts. The exegete should do more. The specialist should always be concerned with the pastoral impact of scholarly affirmations, particularly when explaining the contexts within which the most important actions of Jesus of Nazareth took place. Indeed, we have become accustomed to speaking of the institution of the Eucharist without taking into account the existential context within which this institution took place.

It is here that we have a tendency to simplify the data. Which one of us is able to regard himself or herself as "worthy" to approach the Eucharist? Do I practice all the demands of the Sermon on the Mount? It is thus that I approach the Table of the Lord with a contrite heart? Yes, the Eucharist is there for the broken. This book that I am introducing to you shows that clearly. One question remains. What are we to think of the situation of that person who clearly offends the present laws of the Church and who is unable, for all sorts of reasons, to renounce that situation judged by the Church, quite rightly, as irregular? Has the Church the right to ban these broken people from eucharistic practice?

The answer to this difficult question cannot come from a purely exegetical study. Only the consensus of the Church can correctly appreciate its interior resistance to the poison that unlimited eucharistic access of one or other member whom it considers "guilty" may generate. But exegetical endeavor is indispensable to prevent the Church from resting sleepily on past practices. The critical function of those who have been entrusted by the Church to spell out the immediate meaning of the biblical texts must go on without ceasing. Ecclesial behavior is determined by two factors:

1. The Church's place in each epoch.
2. Its need to be critical of that epoch.

Who does not go forward falls back, as the ancient Fathers of the Desert used to say. However, to go forward it is necessary to momentarily lose the balance one had in the previously acquired situation. It is necessary to keep putting one's foot forward, and in this way eventually regain the balance that had been briefly lost.

Francis Moloney invites us not to settle for acquired positions of strength. They must always be challenged with the demands of the gospel message.

Xavier Léon-Dufour, SJ
Paris (Centre Sèvres)
1990

INTRODUCTION

"The Lord Jesus on the night when he was betrayed took bread, and when he had given thanks, he broke it, and said, 'This is my body, broken for you. Do this in remembrance of me … This cup is the new covenant in my blood. Do this … in remembrance of me.' For as often as you eat this bread and drink the cup, you proclaim the Lord's death until he comes" (see 1 Cor 11:24-26).[1] Paul has called his erring Corinthian converts to task by telling them the story of Jesus' words and actions "on the night when he was betrayed" (v. 23). That same story has been told and retold for almost two thousand years. Christians have experienced the eucharistic story, enshrined within the liturgy, in the Church's response to the command of Jesus: "Do this in memory of me" (Luke 22:19; 1 Cor 11:24, 25). However, this story has not only been told in the liturgy. It has been narrated just as significantly in the lives of Christians who have been prepared to break their own bodies and spill their own blood in a deeply eucharistic way, proclaiming "the Lord's death until he comes" (1 Cor 11:26). Rooted in the broken body and the spilt blood of Jesus himself, the Eucharist has always been the story of a body broken for a broken people. This is the aspect of the central mystery of the Christian life that I would like to highlight through the New Testament study that follows. Above all, I wish to show that the Eucharist is the celebrated and lived expression of a love so great that we have never been able to match it.

Such love, however, raises some difficult questions to its institutionalization. As a twenty-first century Christian Church looks back upon its history, it should repeatedly test whether it has lost touch with its founding story. I wish to raise some questions that arise from a contemporary reading of that inspired story. Through my years of teaching the New Testament I have been increasingly surprised by an overwhelming impression that the eucharistic passages in the New

Testament proclaim the presence of the love of God, made visible in Jesus, to a broken people. This "brokenness," of course, is articulated in different ways by the New Testament authors, but the sense of the Eucharist as God's gift to those in need is all-pervading. I began to articulate this impression in various lectures from 1986 to 1988. I eventually published some preliminary results of my research into this question in a scholarly article in 1989, and a book appeared in 1990.[2] A foreword from Xavier Léon-Dufour, SJ, was part of that first edition; it is retained here because of its importance. That edition was published by a Catholic publishing house in Australia, but had come to the notice of publishers in the United States of America. A second, slightly rewritten edition appeared with an American publisher in 1997.[3] That edition attempted to reach beyond the original Roman Catholic audience, to speak to as many people as possible so that they may more deeply appreciate both the beauty and the risk of celebrating Eucharist. Given some of the entrenched traditions that surround the understanding and practice of the Eucharist in many of the established Christian Churches, some found my study uncomfortable. What follows could be regarded as a third edition of *A Body Broken for a Broken People*, but that hardly represents the agenda of the present publication.

It is inspired by the courageous openness manifested by Pope Francis, and responds to his charismatic presence as the head of the Roman Catholic Church. Following the first session of the Synod of Bishops on the Family (October 2014), Pope Francis (and many Bishops across the world) asked, in continuation of the practice of the return to the sources of our faith (*ressourcement*), so central to the Second Vatican Council, that time and effort be devoted to a study of the biblical and theological traditions that impinge upon marriage and family in the Catholic Church.

The German Bishops have been the most outspoken. They have formally stated that "only a minority think that present Church teaching is theologically correct and pastorally appropriate."[4] What follows will appear between the two sessions of the Synod on the Family, due to resume in October 2015, and its focus is caught by the sub-title: "Divorce, Remarriage, and the Eucharist." It thus reaches beyond the earlier studies, and I trust will serve all Christians who celebrate and live the Eucharist. But it is written expressly to guide Roman Catholics, and especially Catholic leaders, in our attempt to rethink some traditions in the light of the difficult questions that contemporary Catholic life has posed to the Synod. It is also a response to the request of Vatican II: "The sacred scriptures contain the word of God, and, because they are inspired, they truly are the word of God; therefore the study of the Sacred page should be the very soul of sacred theology" (*Dei Verbum*, 24).[5] The Word of God must be unleashed, to be in the Church "living and active, sharper than any two-edged sword, piercing to the division of soul and spirit, of joints and marrow, and discerning the thoughts and intentions of the heart" (Heb 5:12).

I first look at the place of a biblical study of the New Testament material that questions the well-established tradition of "exclusion" from the Table of the Lord in the Christian Churches (Chapter One). Chapter Two devotes attention to 1 Corinthians 11:17-34, long used to distance so-called sinners from the eucharistic table. Especially important, over the centuries, for this end, has been 11:27: "Whoever, therefore, eats the bread or drinks the cup of the Lord in an unworthy manner will be guilty of profaning the body and blood of the Lord." However, as always in a study of the Pauline literature, we must attempt to rediscover the precise situation in the Corinthian Church that led Paul to quote from his tradition of the words of Jesus (see vv. 23-25) in his debate with his converts. This rediscovery calls for a consideration of 1 Corinthians 10:14-22 and its wider context. The practice of the blessing of the cup and the breaking of the bread is used to exhort the Corinthians to a more committed Christian form of life in a pagan world. This study attempts to discover the original and originating Christian Traditions that produced the New Testament texts, as we have them. The Tradition existed prior to the written Word; the Word articulates the Tradition. It is thus important to follow the historical development of that Word in our reflections. The Letter to the Corinthians is one of the earliest pieces of Christian writing we possess. It appeared about 54 CE, only some twenty years after the death and resurrection of Jesus of Nazareth.

Chapter Three is dedicated to Mark 6:31-44 and 8:1-10 (the feeding miracles) and Mark 14:17-31 (the Last Supper). My concern is to rediscover what the Gospel of Mark (which appeared about 70 CE) attempted to say to a Christian community about the celebration of the Eucharist through telling of the story of Jesus. Each eucharistic text is set within the wider context of the narrative flow of the Gospel. I presuppose that we can best find what Mark (or Matthew, Luke, or John) is telling his readers or listeners by looking at the entire story, not merely the part that appears most immediately relevant to our search for eucharistic thought and practice. Although at first sight very similar, there is need to study Matthew's re-telling of the same stories (Matt 14:13-21 and 15:32-39 [the feeding miracles] and 26:20-35 [the Last Supper]). Matthew's account, which appeared in the second half of the 80's CE, is not an unconsidered copying of his source, Mark.[6] Attention must be given to Matthew's pastoral concern for his particular community through his well-considered use of these accounts. Chapter Four locates these passages within their narrative contexts.

Chapter Five is devoted entirely to the Lukan material: Luke 9:10-17 (the feeding miracle), 22:14-38 (the supper), and 24:13-35 (Emmaus), read in close association with the final meal with the eleven apostles (24:36-49). Of all the authors of the Synoptic Gospels, Luke is the most original. He has only one feeding miracle, while Mark and Matthew have two. He also adds the story of the walk to Emmaus. This significant narrative is found nowhere else in the New Testament.[7] Luke's ability to "tell a good story" is reflected in his very personal use of the traditional material of the feeding miracle and the Last Supper.[8]

In his story of Jesus' last encounter with his disciples, the Fourth Evangelist gives no explicit account of a meal tradition containing words of institution. Scholars often miss this Evangelist's contribution to eucharistic theology in 13:1-38, and important eucharistic teachings in John 6:51c-58 and 19:34 must not be ignored.[9] Through a detailed study of John 13:1-38 (Chapter Five) I suggest that, while the Eucharist is not at the center of the narrative found in the first section of the Gospel's account of Jesus' final evening with his disciples, there is much to learn from the story of Jesus' gift of the morsel on the night he was betrayed.

Only on the basis of the data I have assembled from the inspired pages of the New Testament itself do I have any right to raise theological and pastoral questions of divorce, remarriage, and the Eucharist. Pope Francis and many of the Bishops made clear after the first session of October 2014, that critical questions need to be asked about the Church's understanding of divorce, remarriage, and admission to the eucharistic table. Such questions must be informed by a critical reading of the early Church's teaching on divorce and remarriage.[10] As Xavier Léon-Dufour indicated in 1990, this critical reading must be conducted from the heart of the Church. It is from there that I ask about Jesus' own table practice, and the eucharistic practices of the early Church revealed to us in the authoritative Word of God in the Scriptures.

Since 1990 I have often been asked about the impact my work on the eucharistic texts in the New Testament might make upon the problem of the full participation of divorced Catholics in the eucharistic table. This question was hotly debated at the first session of the Synod on the Family, and left the Bishops undecided. The position of the German Bishops is clear: "The Eucharist is not a reward for the perfect but a magnanimous remedy and nourishment for the weak."[11] The debate will resume in the second session. Earlier editions of *A Body Broken for a Broken People* raised the issue but made no attempt to respond to it. I face this shortcoming in the present study. In a new final chapter I summarize what the New Testament and its contemporary interpreters say about Jesus' and the early Church's teachings on divorce. Once that is in place, I may be in a better position to consider how the "Word of God" might or might not raise questions for the Catholic Church's current practice in the admission of divorced and remarried Catholics to the eucharistic table. This is a delicate matter. At the Second Vatican Council the Church taught that Scripture and Tradition should not be regarded as "two sources" for revelation. In some fashion they are one single source, coming from the same divine well-spring (*Dei Verbum* 9). Just how they relate to one another remains an issue to be investigated, and this study raises the question sharply. How does the teaching of Scripture on God's gift of the Eucharist, and the early Church's struggle to come to terms with Jesus' teaching on divorce, also found in our Sacred Scriptures, relate to current Roman Catholic practices? Once some well-researched responses are given to that question, then will I be in a position to make some firm suggestions concerning the authentic Catholic Tradition (Chapter Seven).

This is not only a book for scholars, even though it has notes that situate my reflections within the broader scholarly discussion of these questions. The current notes retain much of my earlier documentation, but update its breadth and depth considerably. They can be ignored! I have attempted to write in a way that is accessible to all people interested in celebrating and living the Eucharist in the Christian Churches. I am dedicating it to my deceased parents, whose eucharistic lives continue to impact upon my own.[12] The dedication, therefore, indicates my gratitude and my "memory" of them. This memory continues to proclaim the Lord's death to me ... until he comes again.

I would like to record my thanks to a group of fellow-scholars and friends who have been part of this long journey: Brendan Byrne, SJ, Mark Coleridge (now Archbishop of Brisbane, Australia), Peter Cross (RIP), Rod Doyle, CFC, Michael FitzPatrick, OFM (RIP), and Nerina Zanardo, FSP. I am particularly grateful for the lively interest that Xavier Léon-Dufour, SJ, took in the first edition, despite our differences of opinion on the relationships between the three Synoptic Gospels, and the understanding of John 13. His own book on the eucharistic texts in the New Testament remains a classic and a major point of reference for what follows.[13] His valuable Foreword is included in this 2015 edition, despite his passing in 2007.

I am very grateful to Fr Paul Prassert, SDB, Provincial of the Thai Province of the Salesians of Don Bosco. He made possible a lengthy stay at the resort *Talay Dao*, in the royal city of Hua Hin, where I was graciously and generously cared for by my hosts Sukkum and Jarissri Shrimahachota. I began this rethinking and rewriting in those peaceful surroundings, aided only by my New Testament and my Thai friends. It was an excellent way to generate renewed enthusiasm. I am equally grateful to the Postdoctoral Fellows within the Institute for Religion and Critical Inquiry at Australian Catholic University: Dr Stephen Carlson, Dr Toan Do, and Dr Ben Edsall. They have provided expert and informed critical readings of the penultimate version this study. My colleague, Dr Mary Coloe, PBVM, read the entire script as it neared completion. Her sharp eye and scholarly expertise have rendered my readers a significant service.

Although I am responsible for all that follows, these people have shown me that the Eucharist is not only cult; it is life.

Francis J. Moloney, SDB, AM, FAHA
Institute for Religion and Critical Inquiry
Australian Catholic University
Fitzroy VIC 3065, Australia

NOTES

1   The words "broken for you" are widely attested in early manuscripts, but doubts remain about their originality. See John T. Carroll, *Luke: A Commentary*, The New Testament Library (Louisville: Westminster John Knox, 2012), 430-32, for its rejection (although he sees it as a very early [second century] liturgical addition). In support of its inclusion, see François Bovon, *Luke*, Hermeneia, 3 vols., trans. Christine M. Thomas, Donald S. Deer, and James Crouch (Minneapolis: Fortress, 2002-2012), 3:154-56, 158-60. For further detail, see Bruce M. Metzger, *A Textual Commentary on the Greek New Testament* (London/New York: United Bible Societies, 1971), 562. The RSV places them in a note.

2   Francis J. Moloney, "The Eucharist as the Presence of Jesus to the Broken," *Pacifica* 2 (1989), 151-74; idem, *A Body Broken for a Broken People: Eucharist in the New Testament* (Melbourne: Collins-Dove, 1990).

3   Peabody, MA: Hendrickson Publications, 1997.

4   Christa Pongratz-Lippitt, "Remarried Divorcees Issue a Test Case for Church's Credibility, German Bishops Convinced," *National Catholic Reporter*, December 29 (2014), 1. The article is a summary of the statement from the Bishops' working party preparing for the second session of the Synod in October, 2015, issued on December 22, 2014. These sentiments were reinforced by Cardinal Reinhard Marx, Archbishop of Munich and Friesing, Head of the German Bishop's Conference, and a member of the Council of Cardinals advising Pope Francis on the renewal of the Curia, in an interview with Luke Hansen, SJ, in the Memorial Church, Stanford University, January 18, 2015.

5   See Francis J. Moloney, "Vatican II and 'The Study of the Sacred Page'"

as 'The Soul of Theology' (*Dei Verbum* 24)," in *God's Word and the Church's Council: Vatican II and Divine Revelation*, ed. Mark O'Brien and Christopher Monaghan (Adelaide: ATF Theology, 2014), 19-40.

6   I presuppose that Matthew and Luke both used Mark and a further common source, usually called "Q" (from the German word *Quelle* = source). For a very clear presentation of this widely-help hypothesis, see John S. Kloppenborg, *Q, the Earliest Gospel: An Introduction to the Original Stories and Sayings of Jesus* (Louisville, KY: Westminster John Knox, 2008), 1-40. However, neither Mark, Matthew, nor Luke can be understood in terms of their "sources." They grew within a context of a living tradition that will never be entirely subject to scholarly analysis.

7   There is a hint of it in the "longer ending" of Mark in Mark 16:12-13. This passage does not belong to Mark's Gospel, but is a later scribal addition. See Francis J. Moloney, *The Gospel of Mark: A Commentary* (Grand Rapids: Baker Academic, 2012), 355-62; Adela Y. Collins, *Mark*, Hermeneia (Minneapolis: Fortress, 2007), 802-18.

8   The originality of Luke's Gospel is a good example of that "living tradition" mentioned above, in note 6.

9   See, for example, R. Kysar, *The Fourth Evangelist and His Gospel: An Examination of Contemporary Scholarship* (Minneapolis: Augsburg, 1975), 249-59. He concludes his (excellent) survey of current scholarship: "The fourth gospel represents a maverick form of Christianity, to be sure, in which the sacraments, at first at least, were not known or practiced" (259).

10   On the importance of such an approach, see Francis J. Moloney, *Reading the New Testament in the Church: A Primer for Pastors, Religious Educators, and Believers* (Grand Rapids: Baker Academic, 2015), 1-21. This chapter has the title: "Catholic and Critical: The Challenge of Scripture in the Catholic Tradition."

11   Pongratz-Lippitt, "Remarried Divorcees Issue a Test Case…," 1.

12   For further reflection on this, see Francis J. Moloney, *Love in the Gospel of John: An Exegetical, Theological, and Literary Study* (Grand Rapids: Baker Academic, 2013), 214 note 12.

13   Xavier Léon-Dufour, *Sharing the Eucharistic Bread: The Witness of the New Testament*, trans. Matthew J. O'Connell (New York: Paulist, 1987).

CHAPTER ONE

Raising Questions

It can be said, without too much fear of error, that each major period of the history of the Christian Church's life has been marked by its own particular eucharistic theology and practice.[1] Many factors have led to the predominant understanding and practice of Eucharist in the various Christian traditions. While some of these factors are inevitably cultural and thus historically conditioned, the story of Jesus' celebration of the final meal with his disciples has always guided the eucharistic thought and practice of the Christian Churches. Celebrations of the Lord's Supper are highlighted by the use of biblical readings and—in most Christian traditions—the use of the words of Jesus over the bread and wine at the Last Supper, as they are recorded in the Gospels and in St Paul.[2] These practices, and especially the latter, indicate the significance of the story of Jesus' words and actions on the night before he died for the faith and practice of the Christian Churches. They regard the celebration of the Lord's Supper as a response to Jesus' command: "Do this in remembrance of me" (Luke 22:19; see also 1 Cor 11:24-25).

In the light of the New Testament, an answer should be sought to an important and delicate question: what are we doing in memory of Jesus? A further question emerges from Paul's early teaching and a reading of the later New Testament Gospel narratives: for whom was this memory evoked? Centuries of eucharistic practice in almost all Christian traditions suggest that the celebration of the Eucharist, and especially the sharing of the eucharistic species (normally consecrated bread and wine), is only open to an inner-circle of worthy believers. Is this firm tradition an accurate reflection of the eucharistic teachings of the New Testament? These are questions that touch all the Christian cultures and Churches of various denominations that celebrate the Lord's Supper. One of the principles used in the administration of the Eucharist in the Christian Churches is that they should permit this encounter with the Lord only to those whom, as far as they can judge, are worthy of such intimacy. There may be many differences in the way the various Christian cultures celebrate Eucharist. Yet, however far apart we may be in the cultural expression of our eucharistic faith, we are at one in our practice of "excluding" certain people from the Table of the Lord. Is this what Jesus means when he commands his followers: "Do this in memory of me"?

The practice of excluding certain people from full participation in the celebration of the Eucharist has long been part of the sacramental discipline of the Christian Churches. As we will see in the final chapter of this book, the Church has an important duty and responsibility to exercise such discipline.[3] My own Roman Catholic tradition has codified this discipline in the official book of the Church's legislation, *The Code of Canon Law*. This so-called "Code" (Latin: *Corpus*) has a long history, originating in the practice of the earliest ecumenical Councils, which settled matters of uncertainty and dispute by solemn pronouncements on questions of doctrine and discipline.[4] Over the centuries other authoritative pronouncements were made and accepted by the Church catholic. A decisive stage was reached about 1140 when Gratian issued his *Decretum,* which collected the "canons." A variety of other collections led to the eventual post-Tridentine promulgation of a single printed "corpus" in general use after 1580. This was thoroughly revised and promulgated for the Catholic Church in 1917.[5] The Second Vatican Council asked for a further revision (see *Christus Dominus* 44; *Apostolicam Actuositatem* 1; *Ad Gentes* 14).[6] It was promulgated in its revised form as recently as 25 January 1983. The Canons dealing with the admission of people to the eucharistic table read as follows:

> Those who are excommunicated or interdicted after the imposition or declaration of the penalty and others who obstinately persist in manifest grave sin are not to be admitted to Holy Communion. (*Canon* 915)

> A person who is conscious of grave sin is not to celebrate Mass or to receive the body of the Lord without prior sacramental confession

unless a grave reason is present and there is no opportunity of confessing; in this case the person is to be mindful of the obligation to make an act of perfect contrition, including the intention of confessing as soon as possible. (*Canon* 916)[7]

The Second Vatican Council speaks of the importance of the regular and total participation of the faithful in the celebration of the Eucharist (see especially *Sacrosanctum Concilium* 48, 55), but offers no suggestions on the discipline of "exclusion" from full participation. Thus, it was left to the legislative arm of the Church to look to these important questions. Indeed, a careful reading and interpretation of the Canons (especially *Canon* 916) indicates a sensitive understanding of the committed believer who is not conscious of his or her sinfulness, or unable, for grave reasons, to have access to sacramental reconciliation prior to the reception of the Sacrament.[8]

This legislation, with its long standing in Christian practice, leads to the reception of the Eucharist being denied to an increasing number of Catholics. Faced with the complexity of modern secular society, there are now many Catholics whose marriages are not in accord with official teaching.[9] In Western society there are situations where almost fifty percent of Catholic marriages—regarded by the Church as belonging to its sacramental participation in the divine life—end in a breakdown in the relationship and subsequent divorce. In the majority of these situations, divorce leads to remarriage. For psychological, emotional, and financial reasons, especially when there are children from the initial marriage, remarriage is an important further step in a life-story. Remarriage is the road to the peace, happiness, and sometimes financial stability of the woman or man in question. But a divorced Catholic who has remarried is regarded as living in a situation of permanent sinfulness, and thus can never participate fully in the celebration of the Eucharist.[10]

This is such a widespread phenomenon that bishops, priests, and believing people from all corners of the world have been seeking some easing of this prohibition. It is one of the questions that has received considerable attention from those participating in the 2014–2015 Synod of Bishops, as well as the millions who are following these debates with great interest and concern. There is also a residual group of deeply committed Catholics who struggle with the Church's teaching on birth control. Although this latter issue is a more private concern, it appears that many practicing Catholics no longer observe this legislation. Yet there are also some who do all in their power to live lives in which every act of sexual intercourse must be potentially open to the conception of new life, despite the emotional and financial pressures that such choices may generate. Such people will be understandably concerned as to why the Church would reconsider its teaching on something they would consider as important as divorce and remarriage.

One could add the ecumenical question of intercommunion with non-Catholic Christians, in certain circumstances, to this already long list of questions.[11] The Catholic Church's present legislation hinges upon whether a person is considered not fully prepared for the reception of the eucharistic Lord.[12] There are many other situations, better known to the individuals themselves and their pastors, that could be added to this list of well-known reasons for separation of a person, or even a community, from the eucharistic table.[13]

Such a disciplinary practice reflects a eucharistic theology that has its own history and tradition in the Western Church. I have used the present legislation of the Roman Catholic Church to exemplify this practice among the Christian Churches.[14] All the Christian Churches have their own traditions concerning who should or should not be permitted access to the Lord's Table. Does anyone have a right to question this widespread discipline? As Xavier Léon-Dufour indicated in his 1990 foreword to an earlier version of this volume, St Paul already expressed his mind on the matter in the early 50's of the first century: there is some behavior that is intolerable at a Christian community's celebration of the supper of the Lord (see 1 Cor 11:27-34). May one compare this practice, enshrined in the official legislation of the Church, with various other cultural and historical practices that were examined by the great renewal process set in motion by the Second Vatican Council in the Roman Catholic Church? The issue of access to the eucharistic meal was raised in the formative days of Christianity, as was the question of divorce and remarriage. Should we not look back to those Spirit-filled teachings to question the practice of excluding the broken people—those we judge as sinners—from the eucharistic table?

While never denying its crucial importance for the life of the Church, one must not divinize legislation. There are certainly laws that are "written on our hearts" (see Rom 2:14), but most of our laws are also the result of the need to formulate legislation to govern a community of human beings living within the constraints imposed by a particular history and culture. Most people today are aware that there are laws in both the Church and society that are more oppressive than creative. The very existence of an official body for the ongoing interpretation of the new Code of Canon Law is an indication of the Catholic Church's awareness of this fact.[15]

There is nowadays a widespread grass-roots feeling that our current traditions concerning the admission of people to the eucharistic table need to be questioned and possibly re-thought and re-taught.[16] I have been told by more than one Pastor that they act on the basis of pastoral sense. This means that, at the level of practice, people traditionally excluded from the Eucharist are now simply admitted, without further ado.[17] However, it is methodologically unsound to go ahead, either theologically or pastorally, on the basis of "a widespread grass-roots feeling."[18] Many of the important renewal movements in the history of the Church often appear to have come from such "maverick" practices, but these are not sufficient in themselves. Such pastoral practices are based on one's "feeling" about the issue. No matter how finely tuned a particular Pastor may be to the ways of the Spirit in the Church, the biblical and theological motivations for or against such practice must be considered. The Catholic Tradition cannot be renewed only on the basis of the rules of "best practice." Christianity's claim to be a revealed religion is central to its very being. The normative and formative roles of Scripture and Tradition for Christian theology and practice cannot be brushed aside in the face of an urgent pastoral problem. As such, the pastoral—as well as the spiritual—renewal of the Christian traditions must also have its roots in a continual reflection on the richness of the Word of God in the Bible and the great Traditions of the Church. In the light of these factors the teaching offices of the Christian Churches, adopting an attitude of listening and learning, should eventually guide their faithful as they attempt to address the increasingly complex interface between what may only be a Christian *tradition* and the challenges of contemporary Christian *life*.

A Return to the Original Design

The Christian Church, which lays claim to be the community of the followers of Jesus of Nazareth, is called to a patient reflection upon the Christian Tradition in order to gain new insights into its responsibilities and challenges in an ever-changing world. An authoritative spokesman of the Catholic Christian Tradition, Pope Paul VI, stated his understanding of the process of making the Christian Church conform more closely to its original design, and yet present a relevant face to the world:

> We should always wish to lead her [the Church] back to her perfect form corresponding, on the one hand to her original design and, on the other, fully consistent with the necessary development which, like a seed grown into a tree, has given to the Church her legitimate and concrete form in history. (*Ecclesiam Suam* 83)[19]

It is against the background of the authentic *Tradition*, which comes from a serious and critical reflection upon the Christian story, that the Christian Churches must search for a solid basis upon which to position their feet, as they wish to raise a questioning finger to *traditions* that find their way into the Church's official legislation.[20] Part of the Church's responsibility is continually to search out, reflect upon, and respond to its "original design." Any suggestion that the authentic Christian Tradition has in some way been "distorted" over the centuries must be carefully scrutinized by reaching back to a period and a situation before those distortions. As Rosemary Ruether has indicated:

> To look back to some original base of meaning and truth before corruption is to know that truth is more basic than falsehood. … One cannot wield the lever of criticism without a place to stand.[21]

My concern for this "original base of meaning" motivates this study of the eucharistic traditions in the New Testament, especially with regard to the situation of divorced and remarried Catholics. My attention was first drawn to the issue because of the many pastoral concerns that have troubled dedicated Christians over recent years, from the simplest to the highest in the land. There is hardly a family, a pastor, a bishop, or a pope, who does not feel the pain of the long-standing Christian tradition of "exclusion" from the eucharistic table.

However, the question at stake, the "original base of meaning," is much deeper than the pastoral questions, important as they may be. In all Churches, practice and legislation always look to the situation of the believer who, in some way, is judged unworthy to share in this most holy of meals, and the exclusion of the sinful from such celebrations follows logically. The discussion generated by the letter of the German Bishops and the response from the Congregation of the Doctrine of the Faith in 1994 takes it for granted that the sinfulness of Christians in an unacceptable marriage excludes them from the eucharistic table. Commentary upon the discussion between the German Bishops and the Vatican is also based upon the same premise, describing the reception of the Eucharist by a divorced and remarried person as "something illicit."[22] Anxiety over this matter, and intense discussion of it, dominated the first session of the Synod of Bishops on the Family in October 2014. It has only intensified since then, as the Catholic Church prepares for the resumption of the Synod in October 2015.

It has long been unquestioned that Catholic Tradition regards the Eucharist as a unique gift of Jesus Christ to his Church, celebrated in a sacred ritual for worthy recipients of this gift. But has Eucharist always been understood as the holy celebration of a holy Church, to which only the perfect have privileged access? My concern for the pastoral question remains; but deeper questions need to be faced. Subsequent to the first session of the Synod on the Family, opposing voices have been heard. As we have seen, the German Bishops have affirmed that such teaching and practice is theologically and pastorally wrong.[23] Cardinal Walter Kasper was called upon by Pope Francis to address the Cardinals in preparation for the Synod; then and since, he has urged a more serious consideration of the biblical, theological, Christological, and Christian virtue of mercy and compassion.[24] On the other hand, major Vatican figures have been reported as arguing strenuously that any change in this teaching would be a betrayal of the authentic Tradition (Cardinal Raymond Burke) or, more pastorally, that suggestions of possible change should be avoided, as it will only give some people false hopes (Cardinal George Pell). Such affirmations (the German Bishops) and counter-affirmations (other leading Church figures) do not aid quality theological and pastoral reflection. Only a carefully researched analysis of what should be regarded as authentic Catholic Tradition can aspire to discover a satisfying solution to the immediate needs of people who suffer exclusion from the eucharistic table that they long to share.

The logical starting-place in any search for the "original base of meaning" is the authoritative and revealed "Word of God" of the Bible. Yet, as Xavier Léon Dufour indicated in his Foreword, the biblical scholar alone cannot hope to provide the final solution to this difficult theological and pastoral problem. The *entire Tradition* must be subjected to a careful and critical analysis. The study that follows presents itself as a first stage in any such investigation. Christian Tradition, which flows from the traditions enshrined in Israel's sacred books, has its explicit beginnings in the life, teaching, death, and resurrection of Jesus, as they have been reported in the Gospels, and the original reflection upon the Christ-event in the other literature of the New Testament, especially in the letters of Paul. As this study will show—especially in my analysis of the New Testament teaching on divorce—within the inspired pages of the New Testament itself one finds clear evidence of pastoral and theological development.[25] But it is not simply a question of looking back to the given of the past, as we find it in the biblical texts. Any serious Christian scholar must interpret the Bible within the Christian Tradition. Here we face one of the more serious difficulties of contemporary Christian theology and theologians. How does one creatively read the Word of God as it is revealed to us in the Scriptures while remaining loyal to the authentic Tradition of the Christian Church?[26] Continuing the practice of the Second Vatican Council, the way forward for the Catholic Church is a return to its sources, famously described as the process of *ressourcement* that inspired the Council.[27]

The issue I am investigating through this study is on the cutting edge of the questions that necessarily emerge in a study that looks back to the sources of the Church's life and practice, and measure that practice in the light of those origins. The Law of the Church is quite clear on the matter. Anyone who is in a state of sin must not approach the Eucharist. This situation is considered "illicit" in current Catholic practice. At the level of practice, while compassion may be shown to the person objectively judged as "living in sin," the reception of the Eucharist is forbidden. In the Catholic Christian tradition, the final articulation of this "tradition" through the Code of Canon Law, however, is not the result of the whims of the Canon lawyers. On the contrary, what they have attempted to incorporate through clear legislation is a long-respected tradition in the Catholic Church. While the majority of the other Christian Churches do not have such a clear articulation of their tradition on this matter, and the question of the divorced and remarried has long been resolved in favor of the believing Christian, most have practices to ensure that the unworthy are excluded from the eucharistic table. Does this widespread tradition reflect what the New Testament has to say about Jesus' presence to his disciples in the Eucharist? Is this *tradition* part of the authentic Christian *Tradition*? Most text books that respond positively to that question look to Paul's teaching on the Eucharist in 1 Corinthians 10 and 11. But for some centuries the traditional reading of those passages as an exclusion of the unworthy has been questioned. I am raising a theological and pastoral question worthy of serious attention, but also with a great deal of care. Before any further analysis of the New Testament material, some clarification of the role the Word of God must play in its relationship with the Tradition of the Church is called for.[28]

The difficult balance between the word of Scripture and the living Tradition of the Church can only be preserved when full consideration and respect are given to each in its uniqueness, made evident in our respect for the importance of both, in their mutuality. To use Scripture brutally in an attempt to demolish later doctrines and piety, or to use later pious practices and doctrines brutally to create forced interpretations of the New Testament, damages the Church's presence as the sign and bearer of God's love. Exaggerations in either direction lead to a blinkered, and therefore impoverished, understanding of the richness of the Christian Tradition in its wholeness. Such methods offend against the essential and delicate mutuality of Scripture and Tradition that, together, both create and nourish the Christian faith. A critical look at many of the Churches' use and abuse of the Bible, the poverty of much preaching, and the imposition of religious customs that are the product of a given time, place, and culture, shows that much still remains to be done.[29] To paraphrase the Second Vatican

Council, the Christian Church remains at once holy and always in need of purification, following constantly the path of penance and renewal (see *Lumen Gentium* 8).

A New Testament reflection upon one of the mysteries and central practices of our faith must always reflect the mutuality that exists between Scripture and Tradition. At no stage should it presuppose later dogmas, as it must always attempt to respect the literary and historical contexts of the documents and passages analyzed, whilst keeping a critical eye on the traditions that have been formed at a later stage. To ignore them would be to fail as a scholar working within the Christian Tradition. What, then, is the task of the scholar who must reflect upon data that sometimes might question widely accepted ideas and practices?[30] It is essential that the Christian Churches pursue the challenge to learn from the source that nourishes their faith: Scripture and Tradition, which flow from the same divine well-spring (*Dei Verbum* 9). The temptation is always with us to lean more heavily on *either* Scripture *or* Tradition for an assessment of our life and practice of the Christian faith. Rather than looking to Scripture *and* Tradition, we tend to unwittingly set up a conflict between choosing Scripture *or* Tradition.

The Second Vatican Council's Dogmatic Constitution on Divine Revelation spoke eloquently on the importance of this question:

> In the supremely wise arrangement of God, sacred Tradition, sacred Scripture and the Magisterium of the Church are so connected and associated that one of them cannot stand without the others. Working together, each in its own way under the action of the Holy Spirit, they all contribute effectively to the salvation of souls. (*Dei Verbum* 10. See paras. 7-10.)

While the principles stated in *Dei Verbum* 10 are clear, the exact nature of the relationship that should exist between Scripture and Tradition has never been easy to define or practice. The Council addressed the question, calling for interaction and mutuality in the following important statement:

> Sacred Tradition and Sacred Scripture, then, are bound closely together, and communicate one with the other. For both of them, flowing from the same divine well-spring, come together *in some fashion* to form one thing and move towards the same goal. (*Dei Verbum* 9. Emphasis mine.)

As the emphasized words in my citation indicate, the fact of the mutuality is affirmed, but what precisely is meant by "come together in some fashion" (Latin original: *in unum quodammodo coalescunt*)? This formula was deliberately left vague in the light of possible future ecumenical developments, but it leads to difficulties in understanding how Scripture and Tradition relate to one another. Rudolf Schnackenburg, the celebrated Catholic biblical scholar, has written of this Conciliar statement:

> This formulation was a compromise which was devised to keep the way to ecumenical dialogue open, but it is quite unsatisfactory. The expression requires a much broader theological treatment.[31]

The Council document reflects the difficulties and tensions that have always existed between Scripture and Tradition. Yet Vatican II, despite the difficulties it had in finding the exact formula, has taught that Scripture and Tradition need one another, even though neither is totally at ease with the other. Tradition alone is insufficient,[32] but Scripture alone can also lead us down the misleading path of a biblical fundamentalism where the Tradition is never given a voice.[33] The exact nature of the relationship between them remains the subject of theological debate, and no doubt the difficulties that the Conciliar statement has created will eventually produce a more precise understanding of this delicate relationship. Theology, however, must look to the experience of the centuries. Experience teaches us that we have Christian Scriptures today because Tradition has kept them alive. Tradition leads us to proclaim the Word of God in our liturgies, to use it for prayer and to find in it a program for authentic Christian living. This happens today because it has happened in the Christian Churches for almost two thousand years. As is well known, Christian Tradition was alive before there was ever a New Testament. It was precisely the desire to "write" some of the living Tradition that led to the formation of the New Testament. Thus, Tradition gave birth to the letters of Paul and the four Gospels, and Tradition keeps them alive and proclaimed in the heart of the Church. What is found in the New Testament is our earliest written articulation of the primitive and formative Christian Tradition.[34]

Experience also teaches that those who are entrusted with the handing down of the Tradition can fall into the temptation of making it an end unto itself. Such an attitude runs the danger of rendering absolute a particular cultural expression of the faith or a particular historical period in the life of the Christian Church. This understandable tendency attempts to lock the Christian Churches' life and practice into *traditions* that may have had their value in a given time and place, but which should never be equated with *the Tradition*. Such an equation (i.e., a tradition = the Tradition) stands behind many of the current difficulties from the more radically conservative side of the Church today that, in one way or another, refuses to live in a Church that is responding to the commission to preach the Gospel to all nations, guided and supported till the end of time by the presence of the risen Lord (see Mark 13:10; Matt 28:16-20). For example, Archbishop Marcel Lefebvre would not accept that the Roman Catholic Church could understand itself or present itself to the world in any other way than that regulated by the teachings of the Councils of Trent and Vatican I. He made particular historical and cultural expressions into an absolute. The double-edged sword of the Word of God "piercing to the division of soul and spirit, of joints and marrow, and discerning the thoughts and intentions of the heart" (Heb 4:12) has always been used to remind the institution of the Church why she was instituted in the first place. Although Tradition gave birth to Scriptures, and keeps the Bible alive in the Church, Scripture has the task of acting like a "double-edged sword," bringing comfort to the afflicted and affliction to the comfortable, when the Tradition has been exaggeratedly domesticated into historically and culturally conditioned traditions.

One instructive example of this "thorn in the side" presence of the challenge of the Word of God, found in the very early emerging world-wide Church, was the phenomenon of so-called "monks" in Egypt. They followed the lead of Antony who responded to Jesus' words as they are recorded in the Gospel of Matthew: "If you would be perfect, go sell what you possess and give to the poor, and you will have treasure in heaven" (Matt 19:21. See also Mark 10:21).[35] Antony began a movement that, in the fourth century, led remarkable numbers of simple peasant people into the desert in an attempt to live the life that had been described in the early chapters of the Acts of the Apostles (see Acts 2:43-47; 4:32-37; 5:12-16). This movement was, among many other things, a "protest," based on the Word of God, against the gradual assimilation of the Christian Church into the bosom of Roman Imperial society after Constantine. Although something of an overstatement, a contemporary historian of the early Church, William Frend, has described Antony's movement into the desert: "Almost for the first time in three centuries the Lord's commands were being accepted literally by Christ's followers."[36]

In the midst of the continuing theological discussions of this important question, the experience of how Scripture and Tradition have in fact related over the centuries teaches an important lesson. While the Tradition keeps the Scripture alive in the Christian Church, Scripture keeps the Tradition honest.[37]

Is our current tradition of the admission only of the "worthy" to our eucharistic celebrations an "honest" representation of what was handed down to the earliest Church in its Sacred Scriptures? I am posing a question to an important aspect of the Christian Churches' pastoral practice that has become a part of the Roman Catholic Church's life, encoded in its legal tradition (Canon Law). Does this practice of excluding those judged as being sinful, for whatever reason, reflect an understanding of the Church celebrating Eucharist that is faithful to the authoritative word of God as it has come down to us in the Scriptures? What follows is an attempt to reach into the earliest written articulation of the Christian Tradition in Letters of St Paul and the narratives of Matthew, Mark, Luke, and John to ask: is our present practice an honest continuation of the origins of the Catholic Tradition?[38]

POSING QUESTIONS
TO THE TRADITION

Crucial to my understanding of the mutuality that exists between Scripture and Tradition is the corrective role that a critical reading of the word of the Scriptures plays in the heart of the Church.[39] This is only one of the many functions of the Word of God in the Church, and certainly not its most important role. First of all, the Word of God nourishes, inspires, and guides us. As the Second Vatican Council has accurately stated, articulating a belief that is shared, each in its own way, by all the Christian communions:

> The Church has always venerated the divine Scriptures as she venerated the Body of the Lord, in so far as she never ceases, particularly in the sacred liturgy, to partake of the bread of life and to offer it to the faithful from the one table of the Word of God and the Body of Christ. (*Dei Verbum* 21)

The "corrective" role of the Scriptures that I will bring into play throughout the following study must be seen and understood within the wider and more positive terms stated in the teaching of the Second Vatican Council. First and foremost, the Scriptures are a word of life and joy for all Christians.[40] As Vatican II pointed out, Christians are nourished by the mutuality of the Word of God and the gift of the Eucharist. They come from the one Table of the Lord (*Dei Verbum*, 21, 24). From that privileged position in the life of the Church, the Word of God found in the Sacred Scriptures raises questions to a tradition from which it has been long separated. What follows by no means exhausts what could be said about the relationship between the Word of God and the Eucharist, but it may guide us to deepen and enrich our contemporary understanding and practice of the Eucharist in a way that will prove helpful at this critical moment in the Church's history, set off by the Pope Francis' calling of the process that is the current Synod on the Family. Careful and respectful *ressourcement*—a return to the sources of our faith and practice—can only seek to guide the Church in its rediscovery of the original and originating Tradition that is articulated in the books of the New Testament.[41]

The analysis of the Pauline material from 1 Corinthians 10-11 that opens the exegetical chapters of this study is crucial. Paul's Letter to the Corinthians was most likely written about 54 CE. Paul's explicit use of an institution narrative (1 Cor 11:23-26), surrounded by reflections that depend upon the community's understanding of "the body of the Lord," are thus the earliest witness to the Christian tradition and practice of celebrating the meal that we have come to call "the Eucharist."[42] As well as its intrinsic importance as the earliest New Testament reflection upon the early Church's celebration of Eucharist, 1 Corinthians 11:27-29 is widely used to insist on a process of "exclusion" from the eucharistic table (see v. 28: "Examine yourselves, and only then eat of the bread and drink of the cup"). This recommendation from Paul to the Corinthians calls for special attention. Care needs to be devoted to a better understanding of whom Paul was addressing, and why he was so severe in chastising their performance at their eucharistic meals.

I will subsequently devote my attention to the narratives of the two feeding miracles in the Gospel of Mark and Matthew (Mark 6:31-44; 8:1-9; Matt 14:13-21; 15:32-38), and to Luke's remodeling of the two miracle stories into one single account (Luke 9:10-17). I will necessarily study the accounts of the last meal between Jesus and his disciples found in all three Synoptic Gospels (Mark 14:17-31; Matt 26:20-35; Luke 22:14-38) and to the special Lukan story of the walk to Emmaus (Luke 24:13-35).

Beyond the Synoptic tradition, there is need to look at how the Johannine practice and understanding of the Eucharist reflected John's special use of traditions surrounding the meal that Jesus celebrated with his disciples. Many scholars find evidence of the Johannine community's use of words of Jesus at their eucharistic celebrations in 6:51c ("The bread which I shall give for the life of the world is my flesh"). The community's celebration of the Eucharist no doubt lies behind the Johannine version of the multiplication of the loaves and fishes (John 6:1-15), and the final section on the discourse that follows (6:51c-58).[43] But it is often claimed that John surprisingly omits any reference to the Eucharist in his account of Jesus' final evening with his disciples. Chapter Six will suggest that, for the purposes of this study, John 13:1-38—the account of Jesus' meal, footwashing, and gift of the morsel—is dominated by an understanding in the Christian community of these actions as symbolic presentations of Jesus' gifts of Baptism and Eucharist.

Many studies of the eucharistic material in the New Testament have attempted historical reconstructions of Jesus' original meal with his disciples. Oceans of ink have been spent attempting to rediscover exactly what happened on that night. Was it a Passover meal? What were the exact words that Jesus said over the bread and then over the cup (if he used a cup)? Which of the two major traditions: Mark and Matthew (sometimes called the Jerusalem tradition) or Luke and Paul (sometimes called the Antiochene tradition), is the more primitive?[44] These, and many similar questions, have never been finally resolved. Indeed, there is a trend in some contemporary study of the historical Jesus to claim that the reports of a final meal, during which Jesus did and said certain things with bread and wine, pointing forward to his self-gift in love, and to the future kingdom (see Mark 14:22-25; Luke 22:17-20; 1 Cor 11:24-26) were created by the liturgical life of the early Church, and do not go back to something that happened during the life of Jesus of Nazareth. John D. Crossan, for example, points to the early instructions in the shared meal in the *Didache* 9-10 as an indication that the most primitive traditions of this meal had no knowledge of Jesus' words and actions over bread and cup.[45] The study that follows presupposes much of the work done on the historical background to our eucharistic texts, but is not concerned with the *history* of those events. Our concern throughout is the *meaning* that the early Church gave to the traditions it received concerning Jesus' self-gift in love, celebrated in their Eucharists. It takes as given that an impressive "last supper" took place, and does not delve any further into historical questions.[46]

This study is, therefore, deliberately limited to a consideration of the theological and religious message of the present literary and narrative structure of 1 Corinthians 10-11 and the Gospels. I am asking what we can learn from the rediscovery of the eucharistic thought and practice of the Christians at Corinth, the Markan Church, the Matthean Church, the Lukan Church, and the Johannine Church. This is not the only way one can approach these texts; it may not even be the best way. But within the contemporary context of the Catholic Church it is important to ask these questions of the foundational New Testament Churches. The Evangelists and the Apostle Paul "received" traditions concerning the meal that Jesus shared with his disciples on the night before he died (see especially 1 Cor 11:23, where this is explicitly stated). Not one of them repeated a single fixed text in which every word was sacred and irreplaceable. They knew that they must speak the living word in a way that "translated" its deepest message to the needs of the various ecclesial communities.[47]

Research into what may have been the original event that took place between Jesus and his disciples must base itself on these texts "translated" to meet the needs of the various ecclesial communities. Without doubt, when the meal took place, the exact words and gestures used on that occasion, and the subsequent transmission of this data would be important, if ever discovered. But an indication of the speculative nature of this difficult task is found in the fact that the two great experts in this area, Joachim Jeremias and Heinz Schürmann (now both deceased), had given up their life-long attempts to establish this data definitively.[48] Less speculative, and at least equally as important, is the task of reading what each New Testament author proclaims to his audience by means of a story. In fact, when it comes to the Eucharist, all the New Testament authors, including Paul, tell the story of Jesus' sharing a meal. This study turns its attention, almost exclusively, to the message of Paul, and each of the Evangelists.[49] A surprising unity of narrative purpose found across these different authors from the early Church raises an historical question. If the same theme is expressed in a variety of ways across the New Testament, it may have had its origins in the many meals the disciples of Jesus shared with their master, culminating in a final meal that became the first of many other meals shared by the communities of the risen Lord. Behind the narratives found in Paul and the Four Gospels lies the *Tradition* of the earliest Church. The Tradition existed before the written word; the New Testament is the earliest inspired written witness to the Tradition. These historical considerations indicate the importance of the teaching of Vatican II: there cannot be two sources of Revelation; Scripture and Tradition come from the same divine well-spring (*Dei Verbum* 9).

CONCLUSION

On the basis of 1 Corinthians 11:27-30, most Christian Churches have developed an understanding of the Eucharist as the place of encounter between Jesus and the worthy. They differ in their legislation concerning who is or is not "worthy." The study that follows, limited to an analysis of a biblical tradition that all the Christian Churches regard as Revelation—as the Word of God—will indicate that Jesus' eucharistic presence is for his failed and failing disciples. As we will see, surprisingly, this also applies to Paul's audience in Corinth, although this audience is made up of disciples of a later generation. A study of the disciples of Jesus at the Eucharist forms part of the broader theology of discipleship in the New Testament. The authors of the New Testament used their theologies of discipleship to address the Christian community as such. The presentation of the disciples at the Eucharist does not primarily focus its interest upon an encounter between Jesus and the broken, sinful *individual* Christian. In Mark, Matthew, Luke, John, and Paul it is with a *broken Church* that the Lord breaks the bread of his body. "Disciples" in the Gospel stories are not just founding figures from the distant past. For the original authors of the Gospels they were characters in the story of Jesus who addressed the members of early Christian communities. As we continue to read the story of Jesus, the use of these characters will continue to address the Church throughout its history. It is in the experience of the disciples of the Gospel stories that the disciples of the twentieth and twenty-first centuries will discover their own experience of faith and sinfulness.

Studies of this nature can be an exhilarating rediscovery of the breadth, depth, and richness of our Christian tradition. The process of returning to the sources of our faith, asking questions on the basis of what this uncovers, is an aspect of the continued vitality of the Church. Without it we fail in our response to the commission of the risen Jesus (see Matt 20:16-20; Luke 24:44-49; John 20:21-23), and subsequently run the risk of falling into a stagnant dogmatism that may have a glorious past but may not address the challenges of our present and our immediate future. As Raymond Brown has written: "Even when finally fixed in a formula, tradition does not stifle further insight derived from a deeper penetration of Scripture."[50]

The questioning of traditional practices through a careful use of the Scriptures is a delicate but necessary task in a human institution that always runs the risk of "distorting" its original Tradition. In his 1969 commentary on the difficult paragraph of *Dei Verbum* already mentioned (*Dei Verbum* 9), Joseph Ratzinger raises the urgency of the need to face these "distortions" with the correcting role of the Scriptures:

> We shall have to acknowledge the truth of the criticism that there is, in fact, no explicit mention of the possibility of a distorting tradition and of the place of Scripture as an element within the Church that is also critical of tradition, which means that a most important side of the problem, as shown by the history of the Church—and perhaps the real crux of the *ecclesia semper reformanda*—has been

overlooked. ... That this opportunity has been missed can only be regarded as an unfortunate omission.[51]

In a later article in the same volume, commenting on *Dei Verbum* 23, which deals with the use of the Scriptures in the life of the Church, the then Professor Ratzinger wrote:

> A reference to the ecclesial nature of exegesis, on the one hand, and to its methodological correctness on the other, again expresses the inner tension of Church exegesis, which can no longer be removed, *but must be simply accepted as tension.*[52]

It is within this tension that we must stand, not trying to ease away its pain by either a rigid and unbending dogmatism or by an uncritical and unfounded "change for the sake of change" approach.[53] The exegete cannot resolve this difficult problem. It is a task that the entire Christian Church, each community under the guidance of its own teaching authority, and all the Christian communities in deep dialogue with one another, must face.

Under the leadership of Pope Francis, the Roman Catholic Church is courageously examining its conscience on this matter as I write. There is a deep sense within the Catholic Church that something must be done for people whose marriages have failed, who have remarried, and who are subsequently excluded from participating fully in the eucharistic celebration. The study of Paul and the Four Gospels may indicate that Jesus' eucharistic presence is well described as *A Body Broken for a Broken People.* The Word of God, as we have it in the Scriptures of the New Testament, also has important instructions on the question of marriage and divorce in the teaching of Jesus, and in the subsequent assimilation of that teaching within the Church's earliest communities (1 Cor 7:8-14; Mark 10:1-12; Matt 19:1-12; Luke 16:18).

Is there any correlation between the Eucharist as "for the broken" and the marginalized—as we will attempt to uncover it in a study of the relevant texts—and the response of the contemporary Church to the divorced and the remarried? This question touches a fundamental aspect of today's Christian, and especially Catholic, life and practice. Does the Christian Tradition concerning the presence of the Lord to the broken and marginalized in our celebration of the Eucharist have anything to say to those whose marital situations generate "exclusion"?

Has their need for communion with the Lord (vertical) and with the Christian community (horizontal) in the eucharistic celebration been "distorted" (Ratzinger) by contemporary Catholic practice? A concluding chapter will offer a study of the relevant passages in Paul and in the Gospels, providing a pondered, and I trust helpful, response to that urgent question.

NOTES

1   For a study of the historical development of the theology and celebration of the Eucharist in the Western tradition, see Josef Jungmann, *The Mass of the Roman Rite: Its Origin and Development*, trans. Francis A. Brunner, Christian Classics (New York: Thomas More Publishing, 1986). For a broader study of the early period, see Andrew B. McGowan, *Ancient Christian Worship: Early Church Practices in Social, Historical, and Theological Perspective* (Grand Rapids: Baker Academic, 2014).

2   However much such practice is taken for granted nowadays, there is evidence that such was not always and everywhere the case. See Michael Theobald, "Eucharist and Passover: the two 'loci' of the liturgical commemoration of the Last Supper in the early Church," in *Engaging with C.H.Dodd on the Gospel of John: Sixty Years of Tradition and Interpretation*, ed. Tom Thatcher and Catrin H. Williams (Cambridge: Cambridge University Press, 2013), 231-54.

3   See below, pp. 228-232.

4   Behind current canonical legislation on marriage and access to the eucharistic table lies a complex history surrounding the sacramentality of marriage, which came late in Christian history, and the question of the individual's suitability for the reception of the eucharistic species. Although they had an earlier history, both were defined by the Catholic Church, in response to the Protestant Reform, at the Council of Trent in the 16th century. These questions will be briefly documented later in this study.

5   For a concise historical survey, with further bibliography, see the articles "Canon Law," and "*Corpus Iuris Canonici*," in *The Oxford Dictionary of the Christian Church*, ed. Frank L. Cross and Elizabeth A. Livingstone, 2nd ed. (Oxford: Oxford University Press, 1974), 231, 349.

6   I will use the Latin titles for documents of the Second Vatican Council.

A list of the English titles and the corresponding original Latin titles may be found in Austin Flannery, ed., *Vatican Council II: Constitutions, Decrees, Declarations: A Completely Revised Translation in Inclusive Language* (Northport, NY: Costelloe, 1995), v-vi.

7   The translation of the Canons is taken from Canon Law Society of America, *Code of Canon Law: Latin-English Edition* (Washington, DC: Canon Law Society of America, 1983), 343.

8   I am not well-acquainted with contemporary canonical scholarship and discussion, but it surprises me that more has not been made in current discussions among Catholics of what is meant to be "conscious of grave sin" (*qui conscius est peccati gravis*), and what conditions might surround "no opportunity of confessing" (*deficiat opportunitas cofitendi*). The 1994 letter from the German Bishops, and subsequent discussion of it (see below, note 14) did not attend to the detail of the canonical legislation. The discussion generally focuses upon "pastoral" questions, and the need for compassion. In dealing with this long-held position in the Catholic tradition such motivation, although laudable, is insufficient.

9   For the subsequent discussion of this issue in the Roman Catholic tradition, especially at the 1980 Synod on the Family and the resulting Apostolic Exhortation of Pope John Paul II, *Familiaris Consortio* (Città del Vaticano: Editrice Vaticana, 1981), see John M. Huels, *One Table, Many Laws: Essays on Catholic Eucharistic Practice* (Collegeville, MN: Liturgical Press 1986), 74-84. For the reaffirmation of the tradition of exclusion, see *Familiaris Consortio*, 84.

10   There is a widespread misunderstanding among Catholics that divorce itself means that the divorced person, even an innocent person who has been offended against in the breakdown of the relationship, is barred from receiving the eucharistic species. This is incorrect. It is only after remarriage, without a canonical annulment of the first marriage, that the divorced Catholic is not permitted to participate fully in the eucharistic table.

11   The present position of the Catholic Church is described in Huels, *One Table, Many Laws*, 85-97.

12   I am well aware that there is much more to the ecumenical question, especially as regards ecclesiology and the theology of ministry, particularly the latter. An uncritical and indiscriminate "intercommunion" without regard for one's theology of ministry can lead to serious ecumenical problems. For that reason I chose the expression "not fully prepared," as its vagueness can cover a multitude of difficulties.

13   Anecdotally, it appears that the Catholic Church's rigid stance on these matters is one of several major reasons for the current mass departure of Catholics from the life of the Church, especially Sunday Mass. It has been claimed that the largest single Christian denomination in the USA is former practicing Catholics.

14   This legislation was re-stated by the Sacred Congregation for the Doctrine of the Faith in 1994, after its revision had been requested by three German Bishops from the Province of the Upper Rhine. For the text of the letter from the Sacred Congregation and the subsequent letter of the Bishops to their pastors, see "Einspruch und Bekräftigung. Schreiben der Glaubenskongregation und Brief der Bischöfe von Freiburg, Mainz und Rottenburg-Stuttgart zu wiederverheiraten Geschiedenen," *Herder-Korrespondenz* 48 (1994), 565-71. After direction from Pope Francis that further reflection must be given to this matter, the German Conference of Bishops has recently (December 22, 2014) indicated that they regard the current teaching and practice as both pastorally and theologically questionable. The Holy Father, and many participants at the Synod, have asked that consideration be given to the biblical and theological background to this issue. This book is an attempt to do so.

15   The Pontifical Commission for the Interpretation of Canon Law.

16   This is most evident in the letter from the Bishops of the Upper Rhine, asking the Holy See to reassess its legislation. For the text, see *Herder-Korrespondenz* 47 (1993), 460-64.

17   See M. Barth, *Rediscovering the Lord's Supper: Communion with Israel, with Christ, and Among the Guests* (Atlanta: John Knox Press, 1988), 2: "It is a public scandal that many Christian communities exploit the doctrine and the celebration of the communion as a means of excommunication. This scandal persists, even though brave and risky steps are taken by pastors and priests, by student groups and scholars, by deacons and so-called laypeople, to redress this situation in several countries, especially in the framework of local congregations." Barth's provocative book, playing down all concept of real presence, or ministerial priesthood and high sacramentality, is one-sided, but makes some excellent exegetical and pastoral points.

18   I am aware that some Catholic priests and bishops work on the principle of "internal forum" in the question of admitting the divorced to the Eucharist, in the light of a letter of Cardinal Seper (April 11, 1973). For a careful approving study of this approach, see Huels, *One Table, Many Laws,* 74-84. Declarations from leading figures from the Sacred Congregation for the Doctrine of the Faith, especially from its Cardinal Joseph Ratzinger, prior

to his election as Pope Benedict XVI, have made it clear that the Vatican does not approve of this approach to the problem.

19 *Encyclical Letter* Ecclesiam Suam *with a Discussion Aid Outline* (Homebush: St Paul Publications, 1964), 25.

20 At the risk of confusing the issue, I will use the expression "Tradition," with a capital letter, to indicate the articulation of Christian belief and practice that has emerged over the centuries, and which forms a central part of the faith and practice of Christianity. I will use the expression "tradition" and "traditions," with a small letter, to indicate beliefs and practices that come and go in particular places and particular times, but which are not part of the Church's core faith and practice, however important they may have been— or still are—to some people and in some places. The fundamental work on this remains Yves M.-J. Congar, *Tradition and Traditions: A Historical Essay and a Theological Essay* (London: Burns & Oates, 1966). For more recent reflections see Moloney, *Reading the New Testament in the Church*, 191-201.

21 Rosemary R. Ruether, *Sexism and God-Talk: Towards a Feminist Theology* (London: SCM Press, 1983), 18.

22 See John S. Grabowski, "Divorce, Remarriage and Reception of the Sacrament," *America* (October 8, 1994), 20-24. The citation comes from p. 24.

23 Report from Pongratz-Lippirt, "Remarried Divorcees Issue a Test Case…," 1.

24 See now, Walter Kasper, *Mercy: The Essence of the Gospel and the Key to Christian Life*, trans. William Madges (New York/Mahwah, NJ: Paulist Press, 2014).

25 I am grateful to Dr Ben Edsall for raising this important question. This process of pastoral and theological development *within the New Testament* has been clearly shown in his as yet unpublished paper, Benjamin Edsall, "Watching Jesus do Theology: Debating the Sadducees over Resurrection," delivered to the Seattle School of Theology and Psychology, June 2, 2014.

26 There are, of course, many other complex hermeneutical questions that could be raised in a discussion of the Christian Church's use of texts from the *past* to guide its *present* thought and practice. This critical question lies behind so many contemporary debates in the Christian churches: women Priests and Bishops, gay marriage, artificial birth control, etc. See, among several possible studies of this issue, Anthony C. Thiselton, *New Horizons in Hermeneutics: The Theory and Practice of Transforming Biblical Reading* (London: Harper Collins, 1992).

27   See John W. O'Malley, *What Happened at Vatican II* (Cambridge, MA: Harvard University Press, 2008), 40-43, 300-302.

28   Much has been written on this question, which, as we will see was deliberately left vague at Vatican II. Those interested should consult the fine essay of David N. Power, "The Holy Spirit: Scripture, Tradition and Interpretation," in *Keeping the Faith: Essays to Mark the Centenary of Lux Mundi*, ed. Geoffrey Wainwright (London: SPCK, 1989), 152-78. See also Moloney, *Reading the New Testament in the Church*, 191-201.

29   See, for example, the earlier critical, but somewhat iconoclastic study of Dennis Nineham, *The Use and Abuse of the Bible: A Study of the Bible in an Age of Rapid Cultural Change*, Library of Contemporary Philosophy and Religion (London: Macmillan, 1976), and the more creative, simpler study of Henry Wansbrough, *The Use and Abuse of the Bible* (London: T. & T. Clark, 2010). Much has happened in the world of biblical studies in those years, and this is reflected in the tone of the two volumes.

30   On this question, see the brief but helpful reflections of Ignace de la Potterie, "Principles for the Christian Interpretation of Sacred Scripture," in *The Hour of Jesus: The Passion and Resurrection of Jesus according to John: Text and Spirit* (Slough: St Paul Publications, 1989), 182-90. See also Raymond E. Brown, "Critical Biblical Exegesis and the Development of Doctrine," in *Biblical Exegesis and Church Doctrine* (New York: Paulist Press, 1985), 26-53; Francis J. Moloney, "Whither Catholic Biblical Studies?" *The Australasian Catholic Record* 66 (1989), 83-93.

31   Rudolf Schnackenburg, "Die Funktion der Exegese in Theologie und Kirche," in *Maßstab des Glaubens: Fragen heutiger Christen im Licht des Neuen Testaments* (Freiburg: Herder, 1978), 20. See, for a fuller critical discussion of this carefully articulated statement, Joseph Ratzinger, "The Transmission of Divine Revelation," in *Commentary on the Documents of Vatican II*, ed. Herbert Vorgrimler, 5 vols. (London: Burns & Oates/Herder & Herder, 1967-69), 3:190-96. More recently, see Moloney, *Reading the New Testament in the Church*, 16-19.

32   In a memorable moment Alessandro Manzoni, the author of a famous Italian novel whose beauty depends upon its rich assessment of traditional values, has his "storyteller" wisely comment: "And you know that traditions alone, unless you help them, always say too little" (*I Promessi Sposi: Storia Milanese del Secolo XVII*, ed. Fausto Ghisalberti [Milano: Ulrico Hoepli, 1973], XXXVIII:48).

33   Important contributions on the limitations of *sola Scriptura* are nowadays made by Protestant scholars. See, for example, Ernst Käsemann, "Thoughts on the Present Controversy about Scriptural Interpretation," in *New Testament Questions of Today* (London: SCM Press, 1969), 268-85; Peter Stuhlmacher, *Historical Criticism and Theological Interpretation of Scripture* (London: SPCK, 1977); James Barr, *The Scope and Authority of the Bible*, Explorations in Theology 7 (London: SCM Press, 1980). On fundamentalism see James Barr, *Fundamentalism* (London: SCM Press, 1977).

34   On the process that produced the books of the New Testament and established a New Testament Canon, see Moloney, *Reading the New Testament in the Church*, 45-63.

35   See Robert C. Gregg, ed., *Athanasius: The Life of Antony and the Letter to Marcellinus*, The Classics of Western Spirituality (London: SPCK, 1980), 30-32.

36   William H. C. Frend, *The Rise of Christianity* (London: Darton, Longman & Todd, 1984), 423.

37   For a more detailed study of the question, leading to this conclusion, see Moloney, *Reading the New Testament in the Church,* 196-201.

38   As Power, "The Holy Spirit: Scripture, Tradition and Interpretation," 167, comments: "In attending to what is proclaimed from the Bible, or to what is celebrated in liturgy, or to what is passed on in tradition, the Church needs to listen keenly for a word that speaks from a deeper experience of redemption than to the paradigmatic patterns of speech adopted from patriarchal, hierarchical or technological cultures."

39   See especially, Moloney, *Reading the New Testament in the Church*, 196-201.

40   See especially, Pope Francis, *Evangelii Gaudium* (Città del Vaticano: Libreria Editrice Vaticana, 2013), paras. 110-75.

41   de la Potterie, *The Hour of Jesus*, 157, puts it very well: "Faithfulness to tradition does not consist in merely repeating what has already been said, but in following and extending the dynamic of a movement. With the new means at our disposal it is a question of carrying the tradition still further. Every epoch is a link in the chain of a living tradition, in a process that will continue right to the parousia."

42   The Gospel narratives appeared much later: Mark in about 70 CE, Matthew and Luke in the mid to late 80's CE, and John toward the end of the first century CE. For a brief introduction to each Gospel, see Moloney, *Reading the New Testament in the Church*, 113-39.

43   See Francis J. Moloney, "John 6 and the Celebration of the Eucharist," *The Downside Review* 93 (1975), 243-51, and idem, "The Function of Prolepsis in the Interpretation of John 6," in *The Interpretation of John 6*, ed. R. Alan Culpepper, Biblical Interpretation Series 22 (Leiden: Brill, 1997), 129-48.

44   The classical study along these lines remains that of Joachim Jeremias, *The Eucharistic Words of Jesus* (London: SCM Press, 1966). A more satisfactory approach to the same questions is adopted by Xavier Léon-Dufour, *Sharing the Eucharistic Bread*, 183-202. For a questioning of the "Jerusalem" and "Antioch" classification of the two traditions, see the essay of Theobald, "Eucharist and Passover: the two 'loci' of the liturgical commemoration," 231-54. See also Joseph A. Fitzmyer, *First Corinthians*, The Anchor Yale Bible 32 (New Haven: Yale University Press, 2008), 435-44.

45   John D. Crossan, *The Historical Jesus: The Life of a Mediterranean Jewish Peasant* (Edinburgh: T. & T. Clark, 1991), 360-67. Apart from Crossan's many prejudices about what Jesus would or would not have done as a Galilean peasant, no account is taken of the difference in literary form between the exhortation of the *Didache*, and the narratives of the New Testament accounts. But Crossan is not alone. See also Paul F. Bradshaw, *The Search for the Origin of Christian Worship* (Oxford/New York: Oxford University Press, 2002), 47-55, 131-43; Francis Watson, "I Received from the Lord: Paul, Jesus, and the Last Supper," in *Jesus and Paul Reconnected*, ed. Todd Still (Grand Rapids: Eerdmans, 2007), 103-24. Michael Theobald, "Eucharist and Passover: the two 'loci' of the liturgical commemoration," 231-54, suggests that *two* traditions, one containing Jesus' words and actions, and another that recalled the paschal events as a whole, are behind the New Testament's eucharistic traditions. In defense of the historicity of the meal, see Ed Parish Sanders, *The Historical Figure of Jesus* (Harmondsworth: Penguin Books, 1993) 263-64; Gerd Theissen and Annette Merz, *The Historical Jesus: A Comprehensive Guide*, trans. John Bowden (Minneapolis: Fortress, 1998), 405-39; Fitzmyer, *First Corinthians*, 430-31.

46   For a useful overview of the study of the historical question from the beginnings of the century until 1986 see Jerome Kodell, *The Eucharist in the New Testament*, Zacchaeus Studies: New Testament (Wilmington: Michael Glazier, 1989), 22-37.

47   For a theoretical underpinning of the value of a narrative approach to texts that the New Testament authors have compiled from their sources see Francis J. Moloney, "Narrative Criticism of the Gospels," *Pacifica* 4 (1991), 181-201. See also Léon-Dufour, *Sharing the Eucharistic Bread*, 181-82. This

approach does not ignore history, but its main interest is the theological "point of view" communicated by the narrative.

48   For detail, see Léon-Dufour, *Sharing the Eucharistic Bread*, 77-78 and 336 note 1. Gustave Martelet, *The Risen Christ and the Eucharistic World* (London: Collins, 1976), 97: "It is in practice impossible to put forward a convincing genealogy of the texts." However, see the summary of proposals, and a speculative attempt to discover an original text in Theissen and Merz, *The Historical Jesus*, 420-23.

49   For the theological importance of a "narrative approach" to the Scriptures, see Power, "The Holy Spirit: Scripture, Tradition and Interpretation," 168-70.

50   Brown, "Critical Biblical Exegesis and the Development of Doctrine," 33.

51   Joseph Ratzinger, "The Transmission of Divine Revelation," in *Commentary on the Documents of Vatican II*, ed. Vorgrimler, 3:192-93.

52   Joseph Ratzinger, "Sacred Scripture in the Life of the Church," in *Commentary on the Documents of Vatican II*, ed. Vorgrimler, 3:268. Emphasis mine.

53   I agree with Raymond Brown, "Critical Biblical Exegesis," 52: "Neither a fundamentalist interpretation of the NT, which finds later dogmas with great clarity in the NT era, nor a liberal view, which rejects anything which goes beyond Jesus, is faithful to Catholic history."

CHAPTER TWO

THE EUCHARIST AT CORINTH

I n order to follow an historical sequence in our analysis of the New Testament, a study of Paul's discussion of the celebration of the Lord's table at Corinth (1 Cor 11:17-34) must be our first concern. The difficult situation Paul addressed in Corinth generated the earliest written document reflecting the practice of a Christian community's celebration of the Eucharist. While there are accounts of such meals celebrated in the Jerusalem Church in the early chapters of the Acts of the Apostles (see Acts 2:42-47; 20:7-11; 27:33-36), these reports were written by Luke in the 80-90's of the first century.[1] Paul's discussion with his Corinthian converts speaks to a very real situation early in the 50's.[2] This passage therefore is the first *written witness* to the Christian Tradition of the practice of the Eucharist. A eucharistic tradition was in place in the life and practice of Christian communities before any written testimony. It reaches back to Jesus' meal with his disciples, the night before he died, as Paul informs us (1 Cor 11:23).[3] Paul's words to the Corinthians articulate this fundamental early Christian Tradition.

Chronological considerations, on the basis of the probable antiquity of the Gospel or Pauline letter in which these eucharistic texts appear, are only partially useful. Such texts, and particularly the words used by Jesus at the Last Supper, came to the various early Christian authors from traditions older than themselves.[4] It is very difficult to be certain about the antiquity of these various traditions. The present study attempts to trace the theological and pastoral point of view of New Testament authors as they used older eucharistic traditions to address their audiences. Our particular interest, which by no means exhausts the theological and pastoral richness of these passages, will focus special attention on the biblical authors' understandings of those to whom the eucharistic Jesus is present at the Lord's Table.

The authors of the Gospels consistently present the disciples as key players in their reporting of the bread miracles and the meal they shared with Jesus the night before he died. Although the Gospels are directed to Christian communities in the early Church, the story is about Jesus and his presence to the disciples. In the Pauline tradition the situation is quite different. In 1 Corinthians 10-11, Paul writes to his troublesome Corinthian converts about their participation in both the Table of the Lord and the feasts that were part of pagan cult (10:14-22), and about a form of eucharistic celebration where those who had nothing were humiliated (11:17-34).[5]

Paul's attention is directed primarily toward new Christians who were having difficulty in living the Christian life they had accepted. The Apostle's only reference to Jesus' original loving gift of himself is found in the reported words of Jesus in 11:24: "This is my body which is for you." Nevertheless, even though 1 Corinthians 10-11 does not have a full narrative setting that illuminates Jesus' gift of himself to his disciples in the Eucharist, this Tradition is presupposed throughout.[6] Paul's primary concern is with abuses that have crept into the Corinthians' celebrations of the Lord's Supper. In addressing these problems, he turns to the foundation and driving force of his life and preaching: the saving death of Jesus (see Gal 1:10; Phil 3:7-11).

With this witness from Paul, we have a "test case" from the earliest decades of the Church's life and practice. A study of Paul's instructions to his Corinthian converts is crucial, as without sufficient attention to its literary and historical context, 1 Corinthians 11:27-28 is regularly cited as biblical support for the Christian Churches' practice of the "exclusion" of some from full participation in the eucharistic table.[7] Indeed, a Pauline passage, when lifted from its historical and literary context within the overall argument of 1 Corinthians 10-11, reads as a strong defense of such practice:

> Whoever therefore eats the bread or drinks the cup of the Lord in an unworthy manner will be guilty of profaning the body and blood of the Lord. Let a man examine himself and so eat of the bread and drink of the cup. (1 Cor 11:27-28)[8]

Over the centuries this passage alone has generated an understanding that Paul endorsed the reservation of participation in the Eucharist for "the worthy," whatever that may have meant in practice. It is found in Augustine, and no doubt was in place before his time.[9] Without any attempt to place the passage in its Pauline literary and theological context, the Council of Trent relies on this text alone to insist upon the need for Confession before the reception of the Eucharist, for anyone who may be guilty of grave sin. Chapter Seven of Trent's Decree on the Eucharist deals with the necessary preparation called for in order to receive the Sacrament "worthily" (*ut digne quis sacram Eucharistiam percipiat*). It describes these warnings from Paul as words of the Apostle that are "full of terror" (*plena formidinis*) (DS 1646).[10] Since then, 1 Corinthians 11:27-28 is found in the traditional moral and dogmatic theology manuals used for the formation of clergy and Bishops as a biblical "proof-text" against the presence of the broken and the sinful at the eucharistic table.[11]

As a practicing Christian, and a Roman Catholic priest, I read the Word of God within the Tradition (see *Dei Verbum* 10, 12), and Paul gives us the first indications of that Tradition. We must, nevertheless, read the message articulated by Paul in 1 Corinthians 10-11 critically. The determining context for the correct interpretation of 1 Corinthians 11:27-28 is not the Council of Trent's Decree on the Eucharist (DS 1646), but the First Letter of Paul to the Corinthians. In 11:27-28, did Paul wish to utter words against all sinners that are "full of terror," or did he have something more specific in mind? This may be a place where the Tradition that lies behind Paul's teaching has been "distorted" (Ratzinger) by disciplinary practices that have grown over the centuries. As we read the Word of God in the Tradition, we must allow the Word of God to question the distortions that may have developed across the history of Christian and Catholic practice.[12]

THE CONTEXT

Paul's concerns with the Corinthian Church's celebration of the Lord's Table must be located within their overall historical, literary, and theological context.[13] Throughout 1 Corinthians, Paul addresses problems that have arisen in the community at Corinth. There are divisions among members of the Christian community (chapters 1-4, see 1:11), misuse of the body that does not respect the new situation generated by the death and resurrection of Jesus (5:1-6:20), problems concerning sexual relations in marriage (7:1-9), divorce (7:10-16), and changes in social and sexual status (7:17-40). Living in a pagan world, the Corinthian Christians have divided opinions about which food one should or should not eat (chapters 8-9). Some are over-confident in their abilities to judge what is of value or not in joining pagan cultic celebrations, and thus they are offending the scruples of the weak (10:1-11:1).

Having dealt with problems that arise from participation in the cultic celebrations of the pagans (chapters 8-10), in chapters 11-14 Paul addresses a series of divisive problems that were arising within the Corinthians' liturgical assemblies: dress (11:2-16), the Lord's Supper (11:17-34), and the use and abuse of the gifts of the Spirit (chapters 12-14). Paul finally looks to the problem of the resurrection of the body, also apparently causing difficulties in this early Christian community (see 15:1-2). In each of these cases Paul writes to a community that he founded, and that he knows well. He hopes that his authority will be accepted there (see chapter 16), and he has no hesitation in writing to his Corinthian Church, addressing the very real problems of this early Christian community's enthusiastic beginnings.[14]

Although Paul moves from one problem to another, and deals with each one in turn, a common theme can be traced through all the various issues dealt with in 1 Corinthians 8-14. There are some who see themselves as specially gifted in their new found "religion," generated by the "new creation" established by the death and resurrection of Jesus Christ (see 2 Cor 5:17; Gal 6:15).[15] This leads them to adopt, and subsequently manifest, an attitude of superiority. Some tend to despise, belittle, override, or ridicule the others. Paul reacts to this false "enthusiasm" in order to protect the people who are treated as inferior.[16]

Paul deals with the question of eating food that has been sacrificed to idols throughout chapter 8. There are some Corinthian Christians who are strong in faith and rich in knowledge, and they are content to go ahead and eat such meat. They *correctly* claim that idols are meaningless. Paul asks these "strong people" to renounce the liberty that their faith and knowledge—their living in the new freedom made possible by the death and resurrection of Jesus Christ (see Gal 5:1)—have given them. Christ also died for "the weak"; they must be respected and cared for. To offend them through eating meat that had been produced by a ritual slaughtering would be to offend Christ (see 8:11-12). Paul presents himself as an example to the Corinthians in chapter 9. He has been given great privileges and gifts by God, who has called him to be an Apostle, but it would be better for Paul to die rather than insist upon privilege. His role is to take the part of the weak, to be a servant: "To the weak I became weak, that I might win the weak" (9:22). He uses the image of himself as a long-distance runner, not punishing others to attain the victory, but punishing himself (vv. 24-27). This is the Pauline paradigm for the protection and care of the so-called "inferior": self-oblation.[17]

The question of those who regard themselves as spiritually superior when sharing in food sacrificed to idols is still in Paul's mind as he opens 1 Corinthians 10 by reminding the Corinthians what happened to Israel, despite its many privileges as God's people (vv. 1-13). Paul then turns to the specific issue of idol-worship. The "strong" seem to see no problem, in their new-found freedom, in taking part in meals that were associated with pagan sacrifices. "The strong" *correctly* regard such sacrifices as senseless. However, this approach can lead to hurtful arrogance, as it pays no attention to "the weak." God is praised by conduct that builds up the whole body, not by the arrogant assertion of one's own strength and knowledge of what is right or wrong (see 10:31-33).

Having dealt with problems that arise over the sharing in the assemblies and the table of the pagans—meals shared *outside* the Christian community—Paul next turns to the community's own assemblies and the Lord's table. One of the more remarkable features of the newness of Christianity was the place of women in the life and worship of the Church. Paul himself, with reference to a restoration of the original creative plan of God, has declared:

> For as many of you as were baptized into Christ have put on Christ. There is neither Jew nor Greek, there is neither slave nor free, there is neither male nor female; for you are all one in Christ Jesus. (Gal 3:27-28)[18]

But is it permissible that this should lead some women to demonstrate their new-found emancipation by adopting a "manly" pose in the assembly? Paul does not minimize the right of women to pray and prophesy, but he demands that it be done with humility and decency. Women must remain women (11:2-16).[19] They must be groomed as women, and men must be groomed as men, with no confusion as to sexual identity, or imitation of some of the pagan mystery religions. A similar concern for unity and right order is at the heart of 11:17-34, where the eucharistic words of Jesus himself will be called upon to remind the wealthy that Jesus died for all (vv. 23-25). To celebrate Eucharist in an arrogant and superior fashion that discriminates against the poor and the weak would be a denial of all that was Christian in the celebration.

The same concern for the more fragile members of the community lies behind the discussions of chapters 12-14, where some more charismatically gifted people seem to be claiming superiority. While there are many gifts, they should never divide the believers. The community must be marked by the quality of its love (see 13:1-13), not its division into the more and the less gifted (chapter 12). The basic reason for this "enthusiastic" form of Christianity is found in chapter 15. The Corinthians need to be reminded of the central place of Jesus' death and resurrection. They do not yet live the risen life. That is still to come.

This brief overview of the evolving argument of 1 Corinthians indicates a polarized Corinthian community. While some scholars have attempted to unite all of these divisions around one common group that opposed the Pauline vision,[20] there were probably many factions, each one living a new-found freedom in its own way. The two occasions in the Letter to the Corinthians where Paul makes reference to the community's eucharistic celebrations both appear within this context of hurtful division that needs to be overcome. The factions cannot agree over their approach to idol-worship (chapters 8-10), their freedom to behave as they like at community services (chapters 11-14), and their use of charismatic gifts (chapters 12-14). Within the context of this overall rhetoric Paul presents the eucharistic table as a place of union, summoning believers to "remember" the story of Jesus' gift of himself for them.[21] How, asks Paul, can the Corinthian community, which was founded upon the preaching of the cross and resurrection (1 Cor 11:23-25; 15:3-8), and which "remembers" that cross at its eucharistic celebrations, be divided between "the strong" and "the weak," the "haves" and the "have nots"?

Our former selves have been crucified with Christ in the experience of the death of baptism (see Rom 6:3-6; Gal 2:19), but the symbol of the cross that Paul raises up over against the "old world" has its roots in the bloody reality of the experience of Jesus. Are the Corinthians prepared to live that reality in their lives?

This called for respect for the weak, for whom Christ died (chapters 8-10, esp. 1 Cor 8:11), a welcome to all at the eucharistic table (11:27-34).[22] They had to understand that no matter what gifts had been given, all were one (chapter 12) and called to a remarkable quality of love (chapter 13), so that the quality of their Christian fellowship would bring outsiders to faith (chapter 14).

1 CORINTHIANS 10:14-22

1 Corinthians 8-10 deals with problems that arose amongst the Corinthian believers because they lived within a pagan environment.[23] The dangers of injuring the weak through an insensitive use of superior knowledge and understanding—in eating meat sacrificed to idols—were dealt with in 8:1-13. Although 9:1-27 concentrates on the experience of Paul himself, it is used as an example for the community (see especially vv. 19-22). Paul often uses this method. It is pointless only to preach. The preached word must be seen as a lived reality in the life of the preacher. Paul has no hesitation in telling the Corinthians: "Be imitators of me, as I am of Christ" (11:1. See also 4:16-17; 1 Thess 1:6; Gal 1:16, 24; 4:12; Phil 4:9).[24]

In an introductory passage Paul deals with the disastrous results of the over-confidence of the fathers of Israel (10:1-13). He is warning the Corinthians that there is a parallel between the situation of the chosen people—the Israelites in the desert—and that of "the strong" in Corinth. Indeed, writing to a Christian community he claims that the Israelites ate a "spiritual food" and drank a "spiritual drink" from a "spiritual Rock." And the Rock was Christ (vv. 2-4).[25] Paul is drawing a parallel between the experience of Israel, which passed through the waters of a baptism in its passage through the sea (vv. 1-2), to be nourished by a spiritual food and drink from the Rock that was Christ (vv. 3-4). Reading the account of the Exodus through Christian eyes,

Paul claims that Israel had been supplied by God with a privileged participation in the benefits of Christ.[26] Despite this privilege, Israel fell. Thus, warns Paul: "Let anyone who thinks that he stands take heed lest he fall" (v. 12).

Having already insinuated baptismal and eucharistic instruction into his argument, Paul returns to the question of the pagan rituals and eating within those contexts. Although he seems to be wandering from one point to another, Paul is in fact arguing the same case throughout: the threat "the strong" pose to the community as a whole when they *rightly* insist that "an idol has no real existence" (8:4). The claim of "the strong" that the idol has no existence (see 8:4) is a valid slogan; Paul nevertheless insists that the Corinthians are to "shun the worship of idols" (10:14). After his presentation of himself as a positive model (chapter 9) and the experience of Israel as a warning (10:1-13), he is again appealing to "the strong," so that they might adopt a genuinely Christian attitude toward the sensitivities of "the weak."

Paul conducts his argument by first establishing some essential common ground between himself and "the strong." He raises two rhetorical questions, beginning with the expression "is it not …" (v. 16). Such a question (formed by the Greek: *ouki … estin;*) expects a positive answer.[27] He takes it for granted that the Corinthians will assent to the truth that the cup and the bread that they share in the Eucharist are to be identified with Christ:

> The cup of blessing that we bless, is it not a common union (Greek: *koinōnia*) in the blood of Christ? The bread that we break, is it not a common union (*koinōnia*) in the body of Christ? (10:16 AT)

The Revised Standard Version (RSV) translates *koinōnia* as "participation," but this does not catch the power of the original Greek. It would perhaps be better to translate it as "communion," which would indicate the depth and mutuality of the sharing involved, but that could lead to confusion. Christians have developed the practice, over the centuries, of speaking of "communion" as the practice of receiving the species at the liturgical celebration of the Eucharist. Thus I have used the clumsy but clear expression "common union." Paul shows immediately (v. 17) that he wants to indicate more than the union that happens between Christ and the believer implied by our traditional sacramental use of the term "communion."

Having established that the wine and the bread create a union, Paul argues that the union takes place at two levels: "Because there is one bread, we who are many are one body, for we all partake of the same loaf" (v. 17). It is not only that the person sharing the cup and the broken bread establishes a union with Christ. A further union is established through the "partaking" (Greek: *metechein*) of the *same loaf*: the union between all the members of the celebrating community.[28]

> Through sharing in the body and blood of Christ, believers are united with him and with each other. The physical gesture of eating and drinking at the Christian sacred meal has the effect of bringing into being a new Body which is the physical presence of Christ in the world (see 6:15; 8:12; 12:12-27). All are united with Christ through faith and baptism (Gal 3:26-28). The physical gesture of eating and drinking adds a new dimension. Since all share in the one drink which is Christ, and in the one bread which is Christ, Christ (to put it very crudely) becomes a possession which all hold in common, and are thereby forged into unity.[29]

Paul is not primarily concerned with teaching the Corinthian community about the meaning of their celebrations of the Eucharist. Such celebrations, and their significance, are taken for granted as he uses common eucharistic traditions as part of his broader argument and plea for union in the community, that the "strong" might care for the "weak." Yet he provides, in passing, a glimpse of a common understanding of the eucharistic meal shared by Paul and the Christians at Corinth. The Eucharist is food for "the body." This means that the celebration of the Eucharist maintains and strengthens the union between the believers and Christ, and that they become, together, the community (a body) that belongs to him.[30]

Clearly, Paul and "the strong" have points of agreement in their understanding of the Eucharist. Paul can base his broader argument upon mere allusions to shared knowledge and belief. Thus vv. 16-17 states a belief that was common to all at Corinth. On the basis of their shared Tradition, Paul can call his early Christian community to task. Recalling the practice of sharing the food offered as sacrifice in Israel, he reminds "the strong" of the common union (*koinōnia*) that the people offering the sacrifice had with the altar (v. 18). So it is with any food offered, even to the imaginary and worthless pagan idols (vv. 19-20). This enables Paul to make his central point: the act of taking part in a cultic meal established a close connection between the guests themselves and the power to which the victims had been offered (v. 21).[31]

> Paul clarifies for the Corinthians what *koinōnia*, participation in the body and blood of Christ, means from their own familiar experience of their pagan past and their pagan environment. He does not do this to say something new to them, but plainly to convince and win them over by something long familiar.[32]

In objective terms, "the strong" are theoretically correct. Paul has no intention of claiming that sacrificed food or pagan idols have any value (v. 19), although he does associate them with demons (vv. 20-21). However, as they have agreed with Paul concerning their eucharistic celebrations (vv. 16-17), and as they know from Israel's tradition of sacrificing at the altar (v. 18), ritual gestures have both a vertical and a horizontal implication. Paul insists that Christians who shared in the meals celebrated in pagan temples, in conjunction with the pagan sacrifices, were joining in more than a cheap meal! It was not only the food that was consumed. The horizontal "common union" that was generated by the shared table must also be considered. They joined themselves with pagans who believed that idols had a real existence, and in this way associate with the "vertical." Thus, the naïve Christians, in their supposed strength and knowledge, became "partners with demons" (v. 20), generating a "horizontal" breach with their brethren.

In vv. 21-22 Paul returns to the central importance of the "common union" that was created between Christ and the believer, and the community of believers who shared at the eucharistic table. To share in the cup and the table of the demons, no matter what "the strong" may have thought they were doing subjectively, was a public rupture between themselves and the rest of the community. Thus it could easily destroy the objective union created at the Table of the Lord, sharing his cup and his bread. "The strong" are thus told that it is impossible to participate at both the pagan tables and the Table of the Lord. As has already been shown in the experience of Israel (vv. 1-13), one must not understand the Christian sacraments of Baptism and Eucharist as securing the believer from all possible danger of contamination.

Paul closes his reflection by a sharp reminder of the ultimate authority of the Lord: "Shall we provoke the Lord to jealousy? Are we stronger than he?" (v. 21). In this way he looks back to his warning descriptions of what happened to an arrogant Israel that prided itself in its privileges: "With most of them God was not pleased" (v. 5. See vv. 1-13).[33] To threaten the common union established by the Lord between himself and his community, and within the community itself, by an arrogant exercising of one's privileged understanding and knowledge is unacceptable, and dangerous.

Paul calls upon a basic belief that he shared with his Corinthian converts. No matter what their variations on how they thought the Christian life should be lived,[34] Paul was able to remind them that at the Table of the Lord they established a union with Christ and a union among themselves.[35] "In it we receive the body of Christ and, by receiving it, are and show ourselves to be the body of Christ."[36] Sharing other meals, thinking themselves superior to any contamination from such nonsense as idols, demons, and sacrificed foods, the Corinthians broke the union with fellow Christians, essential for the life of "the body."

Paul uses the Corinthian community's celebration of the Eucharist to prove his point. He is not instructing his community on the place and significance of its eucharistic celebrations. He takes that instruction for granted. They know it well, and he is calling upon that knowledge in support of his argument. On the basis of the Corinthians' understanding of what happens at the eucharistic table, he is able to instruct them on the need to avoid their ritual associations with pagans. The basis of their understanding is their double *koinōnia*: their common union with Christ, and their common union with one another. As we will see, an echo of the case made in 10:14-22 is heard in 11:17-34.[37] Paul will recall their familiar celebration of the Eucharist because this *koinōnia* was seriously threatened.

1 CORINTHIANS 11:17-34

If the Corinthian believers were theoretically in agreement that the cup of blessing that they blessed and the bread that they broke established a *koinōnia* between the Lord and themselves and a *koinōnia* that was the community (10:14-22), the actual celebration of the Lord's table should have been marked by the "common union" at the level of the shared life of the Corinthian Christians. It appears that such was not the case (11:17-34).

Paul's discussion of the Corinthians' problematic participation in the Lord's Supper is approached in the following fashion. He first attacks the nature of their abuse of the eucharistic table in 11:17-22. This is followed by the Pauline version of the eucharistic words (vv. 23-25), with an additional exhortation that comes from his own pen (v. 26). Having reminded the community of Jesus' meal with his disciples, Paul then moves to his more theological conclusions and pastoral recommendations (vv. 27-34).[38] Within the overall argument of 1 Corinthians, chapters 8-14 are dedicated to the protection and affirmation of the importance of the "weaker" members of the community. What Paul has to say about the *koinōnia* created at the table in 10:16-17 serves as an immediate preparation for 11:17-34. Only when these literary contexts have been considered can we analyze the harsh words of vv. 27-28, often cited without reference to the original Pauline teaching.

The Greek expression translated "whoever, therefore, eats" (Greek: *hōste hos an esthiēi*) of v. 27 demands that the passage be interpreted in the light of what Paul has just written.[39] What was the "unworthy manner" mentioned in v. 27? Why must a man "examine himself" (v. 28)? The wider context of the passage under consideration provides an obvious response to these questions. It is found in Paul's attack on the Corinthian abuses in vv. 17-22 that are part of the wider problem of serious division in the community, especially their lack of care for "the weak." Paul tackles these abuses throughout 1 Corinthians 8-14, and 1 Corinthians 11:17-22 are part of this overall Pauline rhetorical strategy. Here he expresses his displeasure over the divisions between "those who have" and "those who have not" that seem to have developed since Paul had been with the community: "I hear that there are divisions among you" (v. 18). These divisions are described as follows:

> In eating, each one goes ahead with his own meal, and one is
> hungry and another is drunk. What! Do you not have houses to eat

and drink in? Or do you despise the Church of God and humiliate those who have nothing? What shall I say to you? Shall I commend you in this? No I shall not. (vv. 21-22)

The Lord's Supper was supposed to be a common meal, as has already been made clear in 10:14-22: the one body shared the one bread.[40] But Paul has heard that this has become impossible at Corinth because such divisions between the wealthy and the humble had arisen that no one was concerned about the other.[41] Paul indicates that there are some people who simply do not have enough to eat (v. 22: "the weak"), while there are others who own their own private homes where they could enjoy their wealth without creating divisions at the Table of the Lord (vv. 22, 34: "the strong").[42] It would be better for the wealthy Corinthians to do such lavish eating in their own houses, rather than pretend a unity that their behavior belies. Their behavior, in addition to humiliating the "have nots," shows that they hold true community in contempt.[43] This is the "unworthy manner" of participating in the Eucharist chastised by Paul in the much-abused passage in v. 27, and the reason for the request that a person should "examine himself" expressed in v. 28. The situation has been well summarized by C. Kingsley Barrett:

> The rich man's actions are not controlled by love; they therefore amount to contempt not only of the poor, but also of God, who has called into his Church not many wise, not many mighty, not many noble born (1:26). God has accepted the poor man, as he has accepted the man who is weak in faith and conscience (8:9-13; 10:29f.; Rom 14:1, 3f., 10, 13, 15:1, 7); the stronger (whether in human resources or in faith) must accept him too. It is by failure here that the Corinthians profane the sacramental aspect of the supper—not by liturgical error, or by undervaluing it, but by prefixing it to an unbrotherly act.[44]

Although Paul may be seen as primarily insisting on good order at the eucharistic meals, his complaints have a more profound motivation. As always with Paul, he turns to the saving death of Jesus Christ to ground his demands for Christian behavior. As the disunity is being created at the Table of the Lord, he recalls Jesus' own meal with his disciples. Paul is not inventing his brief narrative of vv. 23-25. It has come to him from earliest Christian Tradition. He is reminding the Corinthians of something that they had already learnt from him, and that he himself had received (v. 23a),[45]—the tradition of the eucharistic words of Jesus passed down to him.[46] As Paul reports them in 1 Corinthians (11:23-26), they are highlighted by the command, repeated over both the bread and the wine, to perform the action of breaking the bread and sharing the cup "in remembrance of me" (vv. 24 and 25).[47] While this twice repeated command most likely had its origins in the earliest liturgies, it is not only a liturgical instruction.

It is not enough to explain *where the words came from*. That question is a valid approach to an ancient text, as it asks important *historical* questions. It is what is called a *diachronic* approach to texts. However, there is a more important question: *what is their significance in the particular context in which they are now found?* This approach asks more theological and pastoral questions of a text, always locating those questions within a credible historical setting. It is called a *synchronic* approach to texts.[48] Synchronically, Paul is challenging his divided community to take seriously the words of Jesus: "You do this in memory of me." These words are not *only* a reminiscence of the liturgical practices of the earliest Church, or words inserted very early to ensure the ongoing celebration of the Lord's Supper. What must the Corinthian community do in remembrance of Jesus' broken body and shed blood? Paul's two-fold use of this liturgical formula is an important challenge to the Corinthians to shed their petty divisions based on a distinction between those who have more and others who have less. These words are a summons to a deeper appreciation of their being caught up in the mystery of the obedient self-giving death of Jesus Christ for them (v. 24).[49] In celebrating Eucharist the Corinthians are caught up into the rhythm of that death "for others." The Lord's Table calls them to a deeper appreciation of the eucharistic nature of the Christian life.[50]

To celebrate Eucharist is to commit oneself to a discipleship that "remembers" Jesus, not only in the breaking of the ritual bread and sharing the ritual cup, but also in "imitation" of Jesus, in the ongoing breaking of one's own body and spilling of one's own blood "in remembrance" of Jesus.[51] As Peter Henrici has rightly argued:

> When Jesus thus enjoins on his disciples the task of doing "this" in his remembrance, all his activity is meant—not only his symbolic

gesture at the Last Supper (which can and should be ritually repeated) but also his whole sacrificial attitude of delivering himself up to mankind in obedience to the Father.[52]

For this reason, Paul adds: "You proclaim the Lord's death until he comes" (v. 26).[53] The Lord's death is proclaimed in the world in the broken body and the spilt blood of a Church of disciples who live the Eucharist that they celebrate, until he comes again.[54] Paul is instructing his divided Corinthian community: "You break your bodies and spill your blood, and thus remember me."[55] While remembering involves gratitude, it is above all an acceptance of the responsibility to prolong the saving mission of Christ.[56]

> Thanks to this clarification made through the liturgy, the whole Christian life becomes an act of worship and proclamation: it "proclaims the death of the Lord until he comes again"—that is, it makes clear the meaning and the source of the eschatological tension that gives shape to the Christian life (cf. 1 Cor 7 and the letters to the Thessalonians).[57]

Looking back across Paul's intervention in 1 Corinthians 11:17-34, we can see that he first calls for unity in vv. 17-22. However, the call to unity is not a call to unity for unity's sake; it is much more. It involves a summons motivated by the need for the Corinthian believers "to remember," to practice at the level of life what they proclaim at the level of ritual (vv. 23-26). "'To remember' in the New Testament, signified almost always to recall something or to think about it in such a way that it is expressed in speech or is formative for attitude and action."[58] It is from this immediate context that one encounters the troublesome vv. 27-28. Paul's severe words in vv. 27-28 follow immediately upon his recalling to the memory of the Corinthian community the "rhythm" of the self-giving life of Jesus, through the words that the Corinthians pronounce in their celebrations of the Eucharist (vv. 23-26). He questions them and corrects them. The issue remains that of division in the community. To continue in their present practice would be to eat the bread and drink the cup "unworthily" (v. 27). Thus they must examine themselves carefully on these issues before approaching the eucharistic meal (v. 28). This reading of 1 Corinthians 11:27-28 *within the context* of 11:17-34 warns us against its traditional use as a Pauline imperative giving the subsequent Church authority to insist upon his words as a warning "full of terror" (DS 1646) against *all* who fail, *in any way*, and thus to distance the broken from the eucharistic table.[59]

In v. 29, Paul further instructs the Corinthians: "Anyone who eats and drinks without discerning the body eats and drinks judgment upon himself." This condemnation also needs to be carefully analyzed. There is a division over the interpretation of the expression "the body" in these words from Paul. A traditional Catholic interpretation has seen it as not discerning the eucharistic presence,[60] while the favored Protestant interpretation has been to see it as a reference to "the body of Christ," the community as "Church."[61] Most likely both interpretations are involved. "Not to discern the body" is to fail to recognize the Lord's presence in the Eucharist in the sense of the Lord who died for us (see v. 24: "This is my body which is for you [Greek: *huper humōn*]"). But it is not enough to see that the word "body" refers to the presence of Jesus in the Sacrament. In the light of what Paul had already said to the Corinthians about "the body" in 10:16-17, the context forces us to pay attention to the fact that Paul is particularly concerned that the Corinthians remember that the body of Jesus was given unto death, in obedience to the Father, in love for them—for all of them who form the one body that is the Church[62] Thus, a further meaning to "the body" must be discerned. If the Corinthians ignore the context of the whole community in their eucharistic meals, they are failing to discern "the body" of the community itself. They would be proclaiming the presence of the Lord in a way that ran counter to that very "rhythm" of the offering of Christ that they claimed to be "remembering" in their celebration (vv. 24-26).[63]

The Christian is called to repeat the self-gift of Christ in the "memory" celebrated both in cult and in life. Not to celebrate Eucharist in this way is to "eat and drink judgment" upon oneself (v. 29). By not recognizing the sacrificed "body" of Jesus in the Eucharist, one offends against the "body" that is the Church, called to repeat that sacrifice in its own life.[64] As in 10:14-22, Paul is using the community's understanding and practice of the Eucharist to correct their actual practice, asking them to recall the Tradition the Corinthians had received from him—and its implications! (v. 23).

"This counsel meant specifically for the Corinthian Christians who are being summoned to reckon with the selflessness of Jesus at the Last Supper and to cope with their questionable conduct."[65] To threaten the common union established by the Lord between himself and his community, and within the community itself, by an arrogant exercising of one's privileges and "strength," is unacceptable, and dangerous (vv. 30-31).[66]

> Paul touches on one of the deepest of all mysteries, if indeed it be true that the paradox of human existence is to be found in the fact that human beings are at once individual persons and essentially social beings. Believers in Jesus become more fully themselves and more closely associated with their brothers and sisters, the more intimately united they are with their Savior.[67]

CONCLUSION

Our study of the Pauline references to the celebration of the Eucharist within the community at Corinth has attempted to place Paul's understanding of those celebrations as a challenge to a divided community to recall that "Because there is one bread, we who are many are one body, for we all partake of the same loaf" (1 Cor 10:17). A critical and synchronic analysis of the context of the Pauline teaching on the Eucharist that surrounds 1 Corinthians 11:27-28 shows that this passage was originally written to accuse the Corinthian Christians of their sinfulness in so celebrating their eucharistic meals that some were excluded. Paul is passing on an ancient Tradition concerning the presence of the broken at the Table of the Lord.

> It is eating unfittingly when the Supper of the Lord is treated as one's "own supper." Then one becomes "guilty" inasmuch as the man who celebrates unfittingly sets himself alongside those who kill the Lord instead of proclaiming his death.[68]

This behavior contradicted what was an "agreed position," spelt out in 10:16-17. Thus there was a "lie" in the lives of the faithful: they were not proclaiming with their lives what they were celebrating in cult. There was a "contradiction between an early Christian congregation's quarrels and its understanding of itself as an eschatological community of love."[69] This could not be allowed in a genuine Christian community, and thus Paul is severe in his intervention.

The Corinthians could not claim to be "the body of the Lord" (the Church) as long as they did not "discern the body" (equally Church) in those lesser creatures, especially the poor and abandoned, whom they were excluding from the eucharistic table.[70] Although we are here dealing with a different "literary form" than the narrative texts that we will consider in the chapters that follow, we need to trace whether or not this Tradition, articulated by Paul in 54 CE, can be sensed in the Four Gospels. For Paul the message is clear: the eucharistic table is not only for the privileged, and any attempt to make it so must be exposed and corrected. The "lack of discerning" (see v. 29) that Paul would not allow in the Corinthian community should similarly not be allowed in any Christian community. As we have seen, his words to the Corinthians on this issue are stern: "What shall I say to you? Shall I commend you in this? No I will not" (11:22). Paul's words should warn us lest we, in our arrogance, merit the same accusations as we develop and defend practices that are aimed at excluding, rather than including, all who look to the eucharistic table in hope and faith as the place where they can meet the Lord, crucified for them (see 11:24).

The Church is called to recognize that it finds its very reason for existence in the needs of all who look to the Lord's Table for oneness with him, and for oneness in the community itself. Only then will it meet the Pauline requirements for a truly Christian Eucharist.[71] Circumstances and legislation that canonize division and exclusion need to come under scrutiny. They may merit for us the charge that Paul leveled at the Christian community in Corinth: "When you meet together it is not the Lord's supper that you eat" (1 Cor 11:20).

Paul tells the story of the night when Jesus was betrayed to remind the Corinthians that Jesus did not accept the suffering—which was his destiny—in some passive way. It was not something that was "for himself."[72] Fully aware that he had been called to a radical loyalty to both God and to his fellow human beings, the experience of Calvary was embraced to produce fruits that would save the world (see Phil 2:5-11). So must it also be for those who are caught up in the "rhythm" of Eucharist, a rhythm that touches both a eucharistic celebration and a eucharistic life. Disciples of Jesus are summoned to lives marked by a deep awareness that we are united to Jesus, to God, and to the rest of humankind. Like Jesus, we too live eucharistic lives that both recall the saving events that took place in the life and death of Jesus, and indicate that we are prepared to be victims, breaking our bodies and spilling our blood for others. In this way we will recall the Lord's death until he comes again (see 11:26). The eucharistic liturgy is the source and the summit of a eucharistic life given without limit (see *Sacrosanctum Concilium* 10). Such was the quality of the life of Jesus: it must mark the lives of all his disciples, as they live henceforth by and in him.

It is within this context that one can come more fully to appreciate what it means to celebrate the Eucharist:

> The eucharistic liturgy seems to complicate my life, since instead of simply devoting myself to my daily tasks I must set aside a little time for this occupation that seems useless but is in fact indispensable if I wish to bear witness to my Christian faith. The truth of this statement becomes inescapably clear once I look upon the Eucharist not as a "means" of obtaining graces but as an exercise of my Christian language. If I am to exist fully, I must express myself in this way.[73]

The Eucharist is not a prayer wheel that we are able to spin every day, and a little more solemnly on Sundays. It is the "language" of my life. It expresses more than anything else my being caught up into the saving mystery of the self-giving of Jesus in obedience and love unto death.

NOTES

1   See Philippe H. Menoud, "The Acts of the Apostles and the Eucharist," in *Jesus Christ and the Faith: A Collection of Studies by Philippe H. Menoud*, Pittsburgh Theological Monograph Series 18 (Pittsburgh: Pickwick Press, 1978), 84-106.

2   On these issues, see any good introduction to the New Testament. For example, the classical Werner G. Kümmel, *Introduction to the New Testament* (London: SCM Press, 1975), 269-79, or the more recent Raymond E.

Brown, *An Introduction to the New Testament*, The Anchor Bible Reference Library (New York: Doubleday, 1997), 511-26. See especially Raymond F. Collins, *First Corinthians*, Sacra Pagina 7 (Collegeville, MN: The Liturgical Press, 1999), 16-29; Fitzmyer, *First Corinthians*, 21-53. For a rich setting of Paul's ministry in Corinth, see Jerome Murphy-O'Connor, *St. Paul's Corinth: Texts and Archeology*, Good News Studies 6 (Wilmington, DE: Michael Glazier, 1983). On house churches and the Eucharist, and temple, banquets, and the body, see pp. 153-67, and Fitzmyer, *First Corinthians*, 428-29. Also helpful is Robert Banks, *Paul's Idea of Community: The Early House Churches in Their Historical Setting* (Exeter: Paternoster Press, 1979).

3   I make this statement, aware that some question it. See above, p. 38 note 45. On Paul's account in 1 Corinthians 11:22-25, and its relationship to Jesus' Last Supper, see Fitzmyer, *First Corinthians*, 430, 436-44.

4   For a helpful attempt to trace the history of the development of the traditions from the event of Jesus down to the narratives as we find them in the New Testament, see Léon-Dufour, *Sharing the Eucharistic Bread*, 157-79.

5   The written documents of the New Testament are only part of the reflection of the early Church. The living tradition of the earliest Church was largely oral. What appears in the written documents of the New Testament is like that part of an iceberg that emerges from the water. There is much more that remains unwritten (unseen). This is also the case with Paul. We are able to see some aspects of the Pauline understanding of the Eucharist because he had to address abuses in Corinth. This Pauline intervention may not give us a complete picture of the earliest Church's eucharistic thought and practice.

6   For an outstanding exercise in Paul's use of the memory of the earliest Church in establishing the significance of Jesus' self-gift in death, see Dale C. Allison Jr., *Constructing Jesus: Memory, Imagination, and History* (Grand Rapids: Baker Academic, 2010), 392-433.

7   The expression "literary context" indicates all that comes before and after the passage in question, within the overall structure and message of 1 Corinthians as a literary document. The expression "historical context" points to the situation in the life of the early Christians in Corinth that led Paul to "remember" their eucharistic celebrations and the link with the death of Jesus, as he had taught them (see vv. 23-26).

8   I apologize for the use of exclusive "man" language. It is retained out of respect for the RSV translation, and the original Greek (*dokimazetō de anthrōpos*). Rendering it generic (e.g. "one") or inclusive (e.g. "man or

woman") generates a very clumsy text. Occasionally throughout this study my respect for the RSV, and its loyalty to the original Greek, maintains its sometimes exclusive language.

9   Augustine, *In Johannis Evangelium Tractatus CXXIV*, LXII.1-6 (CCSL XXXVI, 483-85). The thought of the Catholic Church was well synthesized at the Council of Trent.

10   The abbreviation DS will be foreign to many readers. As you will find in the list of abbreviations located at the front of this book, it refers to a fundamental reference work used by theologians. First edited by Henry Denzinger, later editions came from Adolf Schönmetzer. It is an invaluable collection of all the major doctrinal and moral teachings of the Catholic Church, set within their origins (e.g., Council of Florence, Council of Trent, Vatican I, etc.), across its long history. The numbers given after the sigla DS are located in the margins.

11   It is interesting to consult the best of these manuals. See, for example, I. A. de Aldama, F. A. P. Solá Severino Gonzales, and J. F. Sagüés, *Sacrae Theologiae Summa*, Biblioteca de Auctores Cristianos II/73 (Madrid: La Editorial Catolica, 1953), 280-81. The author of this section (I. A. de Aldama) is modest in his claims, and is well aware of difficulties created by reading the passage within the overall context. However, the traditional argument is made. A similar care is shown by Henry Davis, *Moral and Pastoral Theology*, Heythrop Series 11, 4 vols. (London: Sheed and Ward, 1959), 3:101-102. After indicating the usual norms on the need for holiness in approaching the Eucharist, the author concludes: "The obligation of confessing conscious unforgiven mortal sin before celebrating Mass or receiving Holy Communion is probably an obligation of Ecclesiastical law" (p. 101). In a note, Davis refers explicitly to 1 Corinthians 11:28, concluding that it "does not clearly prove the existence of a divine precept" (p. 101 note 1).

12   See above, pp. 18-25.

13   Among many, see the helpful study of Wendell L. Willis, *Idol Meat in Corinth: The Pauline Argument in 1 Corinthians 8 and 10*, SBL Dissertation Series 68 (Chico, CA: Scholars Press, 1985), and especially John Fotopoulos, *Food Offered to Idols in Roman Corinth: A Social-Rhetorical Reconsideration of 1 Corinthians 8:1-11:1*, WUNT 2.151 (Tübingen: Mohr Siebeck, 2003). Fotopoulos provides an excellent survey of the scholarship, and the religious and cultural settings of Roman Corinth that impacted upon the Corinthian Christians, on pp. 1-48 (research), and 49-178 (religious and cultural settings).

14   There is evidence that Paul's authority in Corinth was tenuous. See James

Constantine Hanges, *Paul, Founder of Churches: A Study in Light of Evidence for the Role of "Founder-Figures" in the Hellenistic-Roman Period*, WUNT 292 (Tübingen: Mohr Siebeck, 2012), 378-433, especially pp. 391-400; Benjamin A. Edsall, *Paul's Witness to Formative Early Christian Instruction*, WUNT 2.365 (Tübingen: Mohr Siebeck, 2014), 98-121, 170-75. He nevertheless regularly intervenes into the Corinthian situation, evidenced by the back and forth discussions in 1 Corinthians, and the references to a number of different interventions in 2 Corinthians (see the summary in Edsall, *Paul's Witness*, 59).

15   On this, see Brendan J. Byrne, *Reckoning with Romans: A Contemporary Reading of Paul's Gospel*, Good News Studies 18 (Wilmington: Michael Glazier, 1986), 20-25; Moloney, *Reading the New Testament in the Church*, 93-106.

16   See Barth, *Rediscovering the Lord's Supper*, 65. This theme occurs, in different ways, across the Pauline letters. See, for example, Romans 15:1-3: "We who are strong ought to bear with the failings of the weak, and not to please ourselves; let each of us please his neighbor for his good, to edify him. For Christ did not please himself; but as it is written: 'The reproaches of those who reproached thee fell on me.'" Rome was not Corinth, and the problems were no doubt very different. But Paul's care for the weak is constant. See Brendan Byrne, *Romans*, Sacra Pagina 6 (Collegeville, MN: The Liturgical Press, 1996), 423-25; Frank J. Matera, *Romans*, Paideia Commentaries on the New Testament (Grand Rapids: Baker Academic, 2010), 320-22. Matera rightly interprets: "When the weak and the strong praise God as a community united in faith, then God and Jesus Christ will be praised" (p. 322). See also pp. 325-26.

17   On the socio-rhetorical importance of Paul's use of himself as an *exemplum*, see Fotopoulos, *Food Offered to Idols*, 223-27: "positive example of forsaking apostolic liberty for the advantage of the weak" (p. 223). This "example" moves easily into the negative example from Israel's history in 10:1-13 (see pp. 227-33).

18   For a very helpful study of this crucial passage, see Brendan Byrne, *Paul and the Christian Woman* (Homebush: St Paul Publications, 1988), 1-14.

19   Paul's discussion of the roles of women in the assemblies has generated a great deal of debate. Some have even suggested that 1 Corinthians 11:2-16 is so out of character that it must be a later insertion. That proposal is widely rejected. For fine discussions of this difficult passage, see Byrne, *Paul and the Christian Woman*, 31-58; Pheme Perkins, *First Corinthians*, Paideia Commentaries on the New Testament (Grand Rapids: Baker Academic, 2012), 132-41. See also the

exhaustive treatments of Fitzmyer, *First Corinthians*, 404-25, and Collins, *First Corinthians*, 393-424. Collins aptly entitles this section of his commentary, "Let Men be Men and Women be Women."

20 Especially Walter Schmithals, *Gnosticism in Corinth: An Investigation of the Letters to the Corinthians* (Nashville/New York: Abingdon Press, 1971). For a good survey, see C. Kingsley Barrett, *The Second Epistle to the Corinthians*, Black's New Testament Commentaries (London: A. & C. Black, 1973), 36-50.

21 For a presentation of the divided community, see Jerome Murphy-O'Connor, "Eucharist and Community in First Corinthians," *Worship* 50 (1976), 370-72 and 51 (1977), 64-69.

22 Care is called for here. Paul does not advocate a "free for all" admission to the table. The expulsion from the community of the man involved in an incestuous relationship in 1 Corinthians 5:1-6 indicates this fact. However, as is well known, the expulsion is made in hope of a later readmission (see vv. 5-6).

23 Scholars have argued that 10:1-22 do not belong to this context. For a survey, and a defense of the logic of Paul's argument, see Günther Bornkamm, "Lord's Supper and Church in Paul," *Early Christian Experience* (London: SCM Press, 1969), 123-25, 152-54. See also Willis, *Idol Meat in Corinth*, 268-75. Most contemporary scholars argue strongly for the unity of Paul's argument across this section of 1 Corinthians; see Richard A. Horsley, *1 Corinthians*, Abingdon New Testament Commentaries (Nashville: Abingdon Press, 1998), 134-42; Perkins, *First Corinthians*, 121-31; Anders Eriksson, *Tradition as Rhetorical Proof: Pauline Argumentation in 1 Corinthians*, Coniectanea Biblica New Testament Series 29 (Stockholm: Almqvist & Wiksell International, 1998), 135-73; Fotopoulos, *Food Offered to Idols*, 208-50 (see his presentation of the rhetorical units constituting 8:1-11:1, pp. 200-206); and Edsall, *Paul's Witness*, 74-88.

24 For the importance of Paul's pointing to himself as a model of Christ—to render that challenge real and historical—see Jerome Murphy-O'Connor, *Becoming Human Together: The Pastoral Anthropology of St Paul*, Good New Studies 2 (Wilmington: Michael Glazier, 1982), 141-53.

25 The RSV unhelpfully translates the Greek as "supernatural" food and drink.

26 On this, see Barrett, *The First Epistle to the Corinthians*, 218-29; Perkins, *First Corinthians*, 121-25.

27 BDF, 220 (para. 427): "Both *ou* and *mē* are still used in questions as in

classical Greek ...; often *ouki* when an affirmative answer is expected, *mē* ... when a negative one is expected."

28   For a precise study of the meaning of *koinōnia* here, see Léon-Dufour, *Sharing the Eucharistic Bread*, 209-11; Jerome Murphy-O'Connor, "Eucharist and Community in First Corinthians," *Worship* 51 (1977), 58-59; Fotopoulos, *Food Offered to Idols*, 233-35. For a more wide-ranging study of the background to the term, see Willis, *Idol Meat in Corinth*, 167-81. On its use in vv. 16-17, see 200-12. The term *metechein* is used by Paul as equivalent to *koinōnein*. On this, see Willis, ibid., 196-97.

29   Jerome Murphy-O'Connor, *1 Corinthians*, New Testament Message 10 (Wilmington: Michael Glazier, 1979), 97. See also Léon-Dufour, *Sharing the Eucharistic Bread*, 211-13.

30   See, among many, Horsley, *1 Corinthians*, 140-41. Barth, *Rediscovering the Lord's Supper*, 33-42, argues strongly against this case. The key to his argument lies in his claim that v. 17a should be read as a Christological declaration: "There is one bread (Jesus Christ)." His argument is somewhat forced, and distorts the flow of Paul's argument in 10:14-22.

31   Another essential aspect of the Pauline gospel is at stake here: monotheism. See Edsall, *Paul's Witness*, 103: Paul "characterizes his interlocutors as strict monotheists—in some ways even more strict than Paul himself turns out to be (10:19-22)." See also Fotopoulos, *Food Offered to Idols*, 235, 249.

32   Bornkamm, "Lord's Supper and Church in Paul," 127.

33   On the importance of vv. 1-13 for Paul's overall argument, see Willis, *Idol Meat in Corinth*, 123-63; Fotopoulos, *Food Offered to Idols*, 208-23.

34   As 1 Corinthians indicates, Paul is not always content with these "variations." See 1 Corinthians 5:1-6:20; 11:1-15:58 for indications of a "Pauline-sanctioned" community.

35   It is useful to notice that Paul uses this same "reminding" technique on two other occasions in 1 Corinthians. In 11:23 he recalls what they had learnt from him about the Eucharist, and in 15:1-3a what they had learnt from him about the resurrection. On both of these occasions Paul also indicates that what they had learnt from him was an earlier Tradition he had received.

36   Bornkamm, "Lord's Supper and Church in Paul," 144. See also Gerd Theissen, "Social Integration and Sacramental Activity: An Analysis of 1 Cor 11:17-34," in *The Social Setting of Pauline Christianity: Essays on Corinth* (Philadelphia: Fortress, 1982), 165-66; Murphy-O'Connor, *St. Paul's Corinth*, 153-61.

37   On this, see Frank J. Matera, *God's Saving Grace: A Pauline Theology* (Grand Rapids: Eerdmans, 2012), 134-42.

38   On this internal logic of 11:17-34, see Fitzmyer, *First Corinthians*, 426.

39   Luc Dequeker and Willem Zuidema, "The Eucharist and St Paul: 1 Cor. 11.17-34," *Concilium* 4 (1968), 28.

40   Bornkamm, "Lord's Supper and Church in Paul," 134-38, argues that the Pauline text indicates the practice of a common meal that preceded the sacramental action. Paul is attacking the abuse of that prior meal. See the discussion in Collins, *First Corinthians*, 430-31. Among others, Theissen, "Social Integration and Sacramental Activity," 151-53, claims that it is now impossible to determine the organization of the meal itself. The crucial elements were the breaking of bread and the giving of a cup in the name of the Lord.

41   The exact nature of the division is debated. Were the wealthier people not sharing with the less privileged, or not waiting for them? The discussion hinges upon the meaning of the Greek verb *prolambanei* ("takes before others have theirs" or "going ahead with eating"?) in v. 21. The idea of "waiting" is supported by the imperative "wait for one another" (*allêlous ekdechesthe*) in v. 33. Whichever meaning one takes, the basic social point is the same: the poor were disadvantaged. For the discussion, see Barrett, *The First Epistle to the Corinthians*, 262 and 276.

42   Theissen, "Social Integration and Sacramental Activity," 150-51. See also Hans Conzelmann, *1 Corinthians: A Commentary on the First Epistle to the Corinthians*, trans. James W. Leitch, Hermeneia (Philadelphia: Fortress, 1975), 195 note 26; Bornkamm, "Lord's Supper and Church in Paul," 126, and especially the extensive survey of Barry Smith, "The Problem with the Observance of the Lord's Supper in the Corinthian Church," *Bulletin of Biblical Research* 20 (2010), 517-44.

43   See Murphy-O'Connor, *1 Corinthians*, 110-11.

44   Barrett, *The First Epistle to the Corinthians*, 263-64. For an interesting study of the social and theological background to these difficulties, see Theissen, "Social Integration and Sacramental Activity," 145-74. See also Murphy-O'Connor, "Eucharist and Community in First Corinthians," 64-69; Collins, *First Corinthians*, 416-21.

45   Paul uses this ironic approach to his communities on several occasions. By repeating to them formulae that they already know and use, he is asking them to practice what they preach, to put their lives where their words

are. As well as 1 Corinthians 11:23-26, the same approach is particularly powerful in his recalling a hymn on Jesus' emptying himself unto death to the self-oriented Philippian community (Phil 2:5-11). See Moloney, *Reading the New Testament in the Church*, 102-106.

46 For an excellent detailed discussion of the history and meaning of the Pauline version of the institution narrative, see Fitzmyer, *First Corinthians*, 436-44.

47 The Lukan version of the eucharistic words has the same command (see Luke 22:19). On this, see Léon-Dufour, *Sharing the Eucharistic Bread*, 102-16. See the useful comparison of the various versions of Jesus' words over the bread and the cup in Perkins, *First Corinthians*, 143-44.

48 See Francis J. Moloney, "Synchronic Interpretation," in *The Oxford Encyclopedia of Biblical Interpretation*, ed. Steven McKenzie, 2 vols. (Oxford/New York: Oxford University Press, 2013), 2:345-54.

49 This is particularly powerful if v. 24 is to be read as "my body, broken for you." In defense of this reading, see Jacques Duplacy, "A propos d'un lieu variant de 1 Co 11,24: 'Voici mon corps (-, rompu, donné etc.) pour vous'," in *Le Corps et le corps du Christ dans la Première Epître aux Corinthiens*, Congress de l'ACFEB, Tarbes, 1981, Lectio Divina 114 (Paris: Cerf, 1983), 27-46; Collins, *First Corinthians*, 432.

50 Léon-Dufour, *Sharing the Eucharistic Bread*, 113, puts it well: "Here we have once again the three dimensions of memory: (1) by means of the present cultic action (2) we go back to the Jesus who at a point in history manifested and made real the presence of God the deliverer, and (3) who gives an everlasting salvation. ... He is here, and I did not realize it! He is here, and so I open myself to the multitude of human beings." See also Collins, *First Corinthians*, 427-30.

51 For more detail on this perspective, see Hans Kosmala, "Das tut zu meinem Gedächtnis," *Novum Testamentum* 4 (1960), 81-94; Peter Henrici, "'Do this in remembrance of me': The sacrifice of Christ and the sacrifice of the faithful," *Communio: International Catholic Review* 12 (1985), 146-57; Fitzmyer, *First Corinthians*, 440-41. See the comprehensive study by Fritz Chenderlin, *"Do This as My Memorial,"* Analecta Biblica 99 (Rome: Biblical Institute Press, 1982).

52 Henrici, "'Do this in remembrance of me'," 148-49. For a similar position from a dogmatic theologian, see Karl Rahner, *The Practice of Faith: A Handbook of Contemporary Spirituality*, ed. Karl Lehmann and Albert Raffelt (New York: Crossroad, 1984), 175-79. See, for example, p. 175: "We

can only receive the grace of Eucharist insofar as we personally also realize the sacrifice contained in it."

53   Against Barth, *Rediscovering the Lord's Supper*, 42-44, I am reading v. 26, along with all commentators, as a Pauline comment on vv. 23-25, not as part of his eucharistic tradition. This does not mean, however, that the elements that form the comment were not, in themselves "traditional." The fact that they appear in Luke 22:19 is a good indication that they were part of the tradition. See, on this, Conzelmann, *1 Corinthians*, 201-202; Barrett, *The First Epistle to the Corinthians*, 270; Collins, *First Corinthians*, 425-31; Eriksson, *Traditions as Rhetorical Proof*, 187-89; Edsall, *Paul's Witness*, 86.

54   For further consideration of this argument, with bibliography, see John D. Laurance, "The Eucharist as the Imitation of Christ," *Theological Studies* 47 (1986), 286-96. Especially useful is the survey of contemporary discussions on 291-94. See Bornkamm, "Lord's Supper and Church in Paul," 140-41. Eriksson, *Traditions as Rhetorical Proof*, 188: "What Paul says in 11:26 is that believers celebrating the Lord's Supper proclaim the Lord's death in its eschatological significance." See also Beverley Gaventa, "'You Proclaim the Lord's Death': 1 Corinthians 11:26 and Paul's Understanding of Worship," *Review and Expositor* 80 (1983), 377-87.

55   I am not arguing that v. 26 is *only* about the eucharistic lifestyle of all who celebrate Eucharist. It is *also* that. See Léon-Dufour, *Sharing the Eucharistic Bread*, 220-27. See also Kodell, *The Eucharist in the New Testament*, 80: "Scholars have become aware that both ideas may be contained in the call to remember: the Eucharist as a reminder to God and as a reminder to the followers of Jesus. God is reminded of his covenant promises in Jesus so that he will fulfill them, and the disciples are reminded of Jesus' self-gift in life and death so that they may imitate his example." See also Jeremias, *The Eucharistic Words of Jesus*, 237-55, and the fine theological reflections upon 11:2-14:40, supporting the positions taken above, in Perkins, *First Corinthians*, 166-70.

56   See Murphy-O'Connor, "Eucharist and Community in First Corinthians," 60-62.

57   Henrici, "'Do this in remembrance of me'," 155. See also Laurance, "The Eucharist as imitation of Christ," 289: "Not only do truly Christian actions contain Christ in his saving events but ... they do so because those same events somehow include in themselves the reality of all Christian living in this world." See the reflections of Martelet, *The Risen Christ and the Eucharistic World*, 170-73.

58   Nils A. Dahl, "Anamnesis: Memory and Commemoration in Early Christianity," in *Jesus in the Memory of the Early Church* (Minneapolis: Augsburg, 1976), 13. See also pp. 21-24 on eucharistic memory, concluding: "Early Christianity was not only faith and worship, but also a way of life" (24).

59   As Fitzmyer, *First Corinthians*, 426, puts it: "[T]here can be no real celebration of the Lord's Supper as long as their liturgical assemblies are marred by unworthy conduct that is divisive and factious and not marked by the same concern 'for others' that Jesus manifested at the Last Supper." Contemporary writers and official documents continue this uncritical use of 1 Corinthians 11:27-28, without any reference to its literary and theological context. See, for example, Everett A. Diederich, "Reflections on Post-Conciliar Shifts in Eucharistic Faith and Practice," *Communio: International Catholic Review* 12 (1985), 234. See also "Propositions on the Doctrine of Christian Marriage," in *International Theological Commission: Texts and Documents 1969-1985*, ed. Michael Sharkey (San Francisco: Ignatius Press, 1989), 174.

60   See, for example, Antonio Piolanti, *The Holy Eucharist* (New York: Desclée, 1961), 45-46; Pierre Benoit, "The Accounts of the Institution and What They Imply," in *The Eucharist in the New Testament: A Symposium*, ed. Jean Delorme et al., trans. E. M. Stewart (London: Geoffrey Chapman, 1964), 93. A contemporary Catholic scholar, Murphy-O'Connor, *1 Corin- thians*, 114, comments as follows: "It is sometimes said that what Paul demands here is that participants distinguish the Eucharist from common food, but this does not fit the context, and betrays a preoccupation with the doctrine of the real presence characteristic of a much later era."

61   See the discussion of Barrett, *The First Epistle to the Corinthians*, 273-75. See also, Bornkamm, "Lord's Supper and Church in Paul," 148-52.

62   Against Theissen, "Social Integration and Sacramental Reality," 148-49. Theissen argues that the words over the bread have a "practical meaning": "This bread is here for all of you." The self-giving death of the historical Jesus is in Paul's mind, not the universal availability of the bread. The latter is a consequence of the former. See Kodell, *The Eucharist in the New Testament*, 78-81.

63   See Fitzmyer, *First Corinthians*, 446-47. Rahner has appreciated this in his use of 1 Corinthians 11:29. See Rahner, *The Practice of Faith*, 178: "The meaning of 1 Corinthians 11:29 will always remain true: by sins against the love of neighbor we eat and drink judgment for ourselves in the Lord's Supper."

64   For these reflections, I am in debt to a personal communication from Brendan Byrne, SJ. See also Dequeker and Zuidema, "The Eucharist and St Paul," 29-30; and Charles Perrot, "Lecture de 1 Co 11:17-34," in *Le Corps et le Corps du Christ dans la Première Epître aux Corinthiens*, 96: "Among the Corinthians, it is not 'the real presence' of their Lord which is difficult for them, but the Cross … and this theme sounds throughout the whole of the letter."

65   Fitzmyer, *First Corinthians*, 446.

66   1 Corinthians 11:30 speaks of the weak, the sick, and the dead in the community, and links this phenomenon to their poor use of the Lord's Table. This difficult verse indicates that the destructive powers of the old age, sickness, and death are still active. But it also means that they are sent to them from the Lord to execute his judgment. See Collins, *First Corinthians*, 436-37. On the whole of vv. 30-34, see Bornkamm, "Lord's Supper and Church in Paul," 150. While sickness and death obviously point to the fact that we all die and face God's final judgment, they also have an educative value *already during our lives*, warning us now that we may not be blessed at the end of our lives. On this see Fitzmyer, *First Corinthians*, 448.

67   Léon-Dufour, *Sharing the Eucharistic Bread*, 229.

68   Conzelmann, *1 Corinthians*, 201; Collins, *First Corinthians*, 435-41. See also William F. Orr and James A. Walther, *1 Corinthians*, The Anchor Bible 32 (New York: Doubleday, 1976), 274: "Judgment comes because they do not discriminate the divine nature of this fellowship and are guilty of splitting it apart and mistreating its humbler members."

69   Theissen, "Social Integration and Sacramental Activity," 168.

70   Barth, *Rediscovering the Lord's Supper*, 68: "It is … absurd to prevent from sitting at the table any person who is invited by Christ and desires to follow Christ's call. These very suspect or condemnable persons may be messengers of Christ."

71   See also the remarks of Martelet, *The Risen Christ and the Eucharistic World*, 37-39.

72   For a recent important study of this, see Allison, *Constructing Jesus*, 387-433.

73   Léon-Dufour, *Sharing the Eucharistic Bread*, 288. See the whole of pp. 283-89, upon which these last few paragraphs depend.

CHAPTER THREE

THE GOSPEL OF MARK

The Four Gospels begin a new literary form. In his own fashion, each Evangelist uses events from the life, teaching, death, and resurrection of Jesus to communicate a message about what God has done for us in and through Jesus Christ.[1] Above all, they are inspired proclamations of profound Christian truths. Most likely, none of the Evangelists was an eyewitness to the life of Jesus (see Luke 1:1-4). They reached back into the memory of the Church, to the early Christian Tradition about Jesus, to gather and order many reports about the life and ministry of Jesus, and placed them side by side to generate the four longer stories that we now know as the Gospels of Mark, Matthew, Luke, and John. Mark is especially important in this respect. He was the first to produce a Gospel (about 70 CE), and both Matthew and Luke used that story as their major source as they composed their own accounts of the life, teaching, death, and resurrection of Jesus. Despite the dependence of Matthew and Luke upon Mark's account, each Evangelist tells his own version of the story of Jesus. In doing so the four Evangelists made a significant contribution to the emerging Church, articulating the earliest Tradition in their narratives (see *Dei Verbum* 12).[2]

The Gospels eventually became part of the written (i.e. "scriptural") revelation of God and God's design that impacts upon all subsequent Christian belief and practice, and eventually part of the Christian Canon. We must not look to them as textbooks that provide us with abstract discussions about Jesus and the Eucharist, or any other issue that may interest us.[3] Each of them contains important witness to Jesus' miraculous provision of loaves and fishes, and his meal with his disciples the night before he died.[4] By means of these narratives, the Gospels play an important role in representing the significance of the earliest Church's eucharistic thought and practice. The teaching of each of the Gospel stories can be found through careful, respectful, and faith-filled interpretation of these narratives, the authors' use of symbols and metaphors, the development of characters in the story, the deliberate ordering of the material of the story itself, the passing of time and the speed of the telling, and other features that are characteristics of "story."[5]

Our search to discover what the authors of the Gospels wanted to say about the Eucharist must pay close attention to the fabric of each approach to telling the story of Jesus of Nazareth.[6] In literary terms, we need to discover the point of view of each story. "Point of view" has been defined as "the way the story gets told—the mode or perspective established by an author by means of which the reader is presented with the characters, action, setting and events which constitute the narrative in a work of fiction."[7] Tracing Mark's consistent "point of view" enables the interpreter to detect what the experience of Eucharist meant for the author, the disciples, and the readers of the story of Jesus as Mark tells it.[8] There is every indication in the Gospel of Mark that the Christians addressed by the author— the original audience for this Gospel, members of an early Christian community—were suffering confusion and some failure in their understanding of what God had done in Jesus, and what was required of them as Jesus' disciples. The Gospel of Mark summons them to a closer "following" of Jesus, a more committed Christian life, and it comforts them in their difficulties and failures.[9]

THE DISCIPLES

Among the many features of a good narrative there are two crucial elements that must work together to generate a unified story:

　　a) The characters or players in the drama.[10]
　　b) The plot within which they act out their part.[11]

The Gospel of Mark is famous for its portrait of the disciples of Jesus.[12] Apart from Jesus—the leading character in the plot—the disciples are the main protagonists in this Gospel. They are called in Jesus' first public act (Mark 1:16-20), and they accompany him in his Galilean ministry (1:16-8:30). Across the second half of the Gospel they are in continual interaction with him, showing increasing fear, and inability to understand or accept what he is asking of them until, as he is arrested in the Garden of Gethsemane, they abandon him (8:31-14:50). A literary critic, writing in general of protagonists in a narrative, has unwittingly described Mark's disciples well. They are:

> … the vehicles by which all the most interesting questions are raised; they evoke our beliefs, sympathies, revulsions; they incarnate the moral vision of the world inherent in the total novel. In a sense they are what the novel exists for; it exists to reveal them.[13]

Jesus' disciples, according to Mark's Gospel, share privileged access to Jesus' person and mission. They respond immediately to the "call" to follow Jesus (1:16-20; 2:13-14; 3:13-19). They witness the wonders that he does, and they also receive private instruction from him (4:11, 34; 7:17; 10:10). "The Twelve" are called to "be with him," so that they might participate in the spread of God's reign by preaching and having authority to cast out demons (3:13-15). They are formally sent out on that mission by Jesus himself (6:7-12). If we only had this side of the story it would be clear that Mark wished to use the disciples as paradigms for those privileged to be called to the Christian life. We, Mark's twenty-first century audience, would be happy to associate ourselves with this success story. There could be a sympathetic association between the "disciples of Jesus" who play a leading role in the Gospel of Mark and the "disciples of Jesus" who are reading, hearing, or witnessing a performance of the narrative of the Gospel.

Such is not the case. As quoted above, William Harvey wrote of the possibility that characters in a narrative can create a "revulsion" in the reader. What is surprising about the disciples in the Gospel of Mark is that as the story of Jesus progresses, the failure of the disciples increases. Indeed, the disciples consistently fail in the Gospel of Mark. They fail to understand his parables (4:13; see also 7:18) and his miracles (4:40-41). On returning from their mission they are anxious to tell Jesus all the things that they had said and done (6:30). They are unable to understand Jesus' walking on the seas, just as they have not understood the miracle of the loaves, because their hearts are hardened (6:51-52). After the second miracle of the loaves, they again fail to understand, and Jesus accuses them of having hardened hearts, of being blind and deaf (8:17-21). They want to set up an exclusive discipleship, hostile to others who do not see things their way (9:38-41; 10:13-16). Across the central section of the Gospel, as Jesus' movement toward death and Jerusalem becomes explicit (8:22-10:52), Jesus speaks three times of his oncoming passion, and each time the disciples either fail or refuse to understand (8:32; 9:32-34; 10:35-45).[14] While this may not produce "revulsion" in the reader, the disciples are certainly not the heroes of the narrative, in the normal sense of the word "hero." A Christian audience that earlier in the narrative may have been attracted by the response of the disciples and been prepared to join them in their following of Jesus, on arrival at Mark 10:45, has become increasingly aware of their fragility.

The failure of the disciples comes to a head in the passion story. Judas, "one of the Twelve," betrays Jesus (14:10-11), Peter denies him (14:66-72), and his most intimate followers—Peter, James, and John—sleep through his hour of agonizing prayer (14:32-42). Their final exit from the story is found in 14:50: "And they all forsook him and fled." This is the last appearance of the disciples in the Gospel of Mark and their flight immediately receives comment in the brief parabolic narrative that Mark reports. There was also a young man "following." He too, at the threat of danger, fled, leaving the only covering that he had on his body—a linen cloth—in the hands of his assailants. Like the disciples who have just fled, he is naked in his nothingness.[15] There are no male disciples at the cross of Jesus in Mark's Gospel, only women who had followed him from Galilee look on from afar (15:40-41). Nor, surprisingly, are the male disciples found in his brief resurrection story (16:1-8).[16] There are, however, hints of an eventual restoration to their place "following" Jesus. The flight of the disciples is marked by the parallel flight of a young man, naked in his nothingness, but at the empty tomb the women find "a young man, sitting on the right side, dressed in a white robe" (16:5). The similarities between the parable of the naked young man associated with the fleeing disciples in 14:41-52, and the presence of the young man whose clothing is described at the empty tomb at 16:5, are too close to be irrelevant. The reader senses restoration.[17] The women followers from Galilee are commissioned: "Go tell his disciples and Peter that he is going before you to Galilee; there you will see him, as he told you" (v. 7). Their silence (v. 8) pushes the story of failure, which can only be overcome by the never-failing presence of God, into the final verse of the Gospel. The readers of the Gospel are challenged to recognize their own failure, but to proclaim the Gospel: Jesus will meet the failing disciples, as he has told them in the Gospel.[18]

Has Mark used Jesus' disciples as characters to arouse "belief, sympathy or revulsion" (Harvey)? Scholars have interpreted this evidence in the Gospel in a variety of ways. Many claim that, for Mark, the disciples offer no paradigm for the Markan Church or for the Church of any age, as they fail and thus create only "revulsion." As one of these scholars has put it:

> I conclude that Mark is assiduously involved in a vendetta against the disciples. He paints them as obtuse, obdurate, recalcitrant men who at first are unperceptive of Jesus' messiahship, then oppose its style and character, and finally totally reject it. As a coup de grace, Mark closes his Gospel without rehabilitating the disciples.[19]

This interpretation throws into relief the failure, but underplays and misunderstands the importance of the positive side of the disciples' story. What is the reader to make of the earlier part of the narrative? Even as late as 10:32 the disciples, despite all their fear and failure, are still called "those who followed" (Greek: *hoi de akolouthountes*). The two sides of the disciples' response to Jesus must be held in tension, as there is a need to take into account both the positive and the negative in the story of the disciples; it is the story of all disciples.[20] For Mark, it is especially the story of his own community—a community of (failing?) disciples. The Gospel of Mark reveals disciples for what they are. The failure of the disciples is a message about the overpowering need for dependence upon Jesus and trust in God's saving power through him. Discipleship is a mixture of privilege and egoism, of success and failure. The Gospel of Mark presents this experience very forcefully, and such an understanding of discipleship doubtless results from the experience of discipleship in an early Christian community. This Gospel story, therefore, addresses the problem of the ambiguity of all who seek to live as Christian disciples through the portrait of Jesus' first disciples.

THEY DID NOT UNDERSTAND
ABOUT THE LOAVES

It is against the background of the broader canvas of the presentation of disciples throughout Mark's story of Jesus that we should approach the accounts of Jesus' multiplication of the loaves and fishes. There are obvious eucharistic hints in both of Mark's accounts of the multiplication of the bread and the feeding of the multitudes (Mark 6:31-44; 8:1-9). Before turning to a close analysis of these passages, we need to establish their literary context, and trace their position and role within the "plot" of Mark's narrative structure. In our search for helpful teaching from the Gospel of Mark on the early Church's understanding of the Eucharist, it is important to appreciate how the storyteller has used the narratives of the multiplication of the loaves and fishes within his overall plot. As has often been said: text without context is pretext. The location of the two miracle stories, Mark 6:31-44 and 8:1-9, in such close literary proximity, is already a hint to the interpreter that they are to be understood in the light of one another, linked by the elements of the Markan story that surround them.

Meyer H. Abrams describes "plot" in this way: "The plot in a dramatic or narrative work is the structure of its actions, as these are ordered and rendered toward achieving particular emotional and artistic effects."[21] Our interpretation of Mark 6:31-44 and 8:1-9 devotes attention to the many hints of their deeper meaning provided by the wider context of the first half of the Gospel of Mark. All commentators agree that Peter's confession of Jesus as "the Christ" (8:27-30) forms the central piece of Mark's literary structure.[22] For the purposes of our interpretation of the two miracle stories that appear in 6:31-44 and 8:1-9, "the structure of the actions" (Abrams) of the first half of the Gospel—Mark 1:1-8:30—calls for brief comment. It clearly moves toward a confession of Jesus as the Christ in 8:29. The second half (8:31-16:8), culminating in the death and resurrection of Jesus, will explain what it means to confess Jesus as "the Christ." He will be the suffering Son of Man and, only as such, the Son of God. Mark 1:1-8:30 unravels the mystery of Jesus as the Messiah, culminating in Peter's confession in 8:29, while 8:31-16:8 plots an even deeper (and darker) mystery: the mystery of the Son of Man and Son of God, culminating in a cross and an empty tomb.[23]

The narrator begins with a prologue to the life and teaching of Jesus (1:1-13). The reader is thus informed that Jesus of Nazareth is "the Christ, the Son of God" (vv.1,11), witnessed to by God himself (vv. 2-3), full of and directed by the Spirit (vv. 10, 12). In the desert, ministered to by the angels and "with the wild beasts," he is also a sign of a renewal of God's original created order.[24] A powerful summary follows as Mark reports Jesus' bursting onto the scene and preaching the Gospel (1:14-15). This summary statement of Jesus' activities is followed by the call of the first disciples (1:16-20). As the public ministry of Jesus opens, he overcomes the evil of sickness and devil possession (1:21-45), but finds unresolved conflict in the official representatives of Israel (2:1-3:6). This part of the Gospel concludes in 3:6: "The Pharisees went out and immediately held counsel with the Herodians against him, how to destroy him."

A further summary of Jesus' ministry is again found at the opening of the next section (3:7-12), and this is also followed by discipleship material. This time, in the calling and commissioning of "the Twelve," Jesus forms a "new family"—"to be with him" and to share in his life and mission (3:13-19a). The narrator then tells of the inability of both Jesus' physical "family" and his cultural and religious "family" to understand and accept him (3:19b-35). Through a series of parables (4:1-34) and miracles (4:35-5:43) Jesus instructs his new family, preaching the Kingdom, and demonstrating the power of its presence. To them is made known the mystery of the Kingdom of God (see 4:11). On return to "his own country" (6:1), his people ask the right questions about the origin of his wisdom and power: "Where did this man get all this?" But they give the wrong answer: "Is this not the carpenter, the son of Mary?" (see 6:2-3). The reader knows that Jesus is "of God" (see 1:1,11) and that his presence inaugurates the presence of the Kingdom "of God" (see 1:15).[25] But the characters in the story, Jesus' townsfolk, claim that he is "of Mary." Jesus is amazed at their unbelief (6:6a). By this stage in the unfolding narrative, a "new family" has been created—"Whoever does the will of God is my brother and sister and mother" (3:35)—and instructed (4:1-6:6a).

Having met opposition from Israel, and then from "his own," Jesus turns decisively to his disciples. This section of the narrative again begins with a summary of Jesus' activity (6:6b) and further discipleship material, as he sends out his disciples "two by two" into the mission (6:7-13). The following narrative, solemnly concluded with another decision about Jesus—Peter's confession, "You are the Christ" (8:29)—is highlighted by the two feeding miracles (6:31-44; 8:1-9). While 1:14-3:6 featured Jesus and his encounter with Israel, and 3:7-6:6a the encounter between Jesus and "his own," the focus of the narrator's attention in 6:6b-8:30 is on the "new family" of the disciples that had been established through vocation (1:16-20) and commissioning (3:13-19).[26]

First recognized by Robert H. Lightfoot, and now almost universally accepted (with variations) by most commentators, the two feeding miracles of 6:31-44 and 8:1-9 determine the structure and shape the message of Mark 6:6b-8:30, a section of the narrative particularly interested in the "new family" of Jesus.[27] Analysis of the apparent repetition of almost identical miracles must begin by seeing that each of them is followed by a boat trip, during which Mark indicates that the disciples fail to understand (6:45-52; 8:16-21).

Immediately after the first feeding, Jesus comes to them on the water (6:45-52). Despite all they have experienced, the disciples fail to grasp the meaning of Jesus' manifestation of himself.

> And he got into the boat with them and the wind ceased. And they were utterly astounded, for they did not understand about the loaves, but their hearts were hardened. (6:52)

After the second feeding story, the disciples again set out across the lake. This time Jesus is with them in the boat. He speaks to them about "the leaven" of the Pharisees (8:15), but the disciples presume he is making reference to the "one loaf" that they have on board (8:14), as they had forgotten to bring bread with them. Jesus speaks strongly to them, recalling both the feeding miracles:

> Jesus said to them, "Why do you discuss the fact that you have no bread? Do you not yet perceive or understand? Are your hearts hardened? Having eyes do you not see, and having ears do you not hear? And do you not remember? When I broke the five loaves for the five thousand, how many baskets full of broken pieces did you take up?" They said to him, "Twelve." "And the seven for the four thousand, how many baskets full of fragments did you collect?" And they said to him, "Seven." And he said to them, "Do you not yet understand?" (8:17-21)

It is against this background of the disciples' lack of understanding that we must interpret Mark's telling of the feeding stories of 6:31-44 and 8:1-9.

Many elements in these stories have close contacts with the later ritual celebration of the Eucharist.[28] The actions of Jesus in both stories—"taking" the loaves, "looking up to heaven," "giving thanks," "breaking bread," and "giving" it to the disciples (see 6:41 and 8:6)—are obvious links with the ritual celebration of Eucharist in the Markan community. The Greek word used for "fragments" (*klasmata*) is an important eucharistic term in later texts.[29]

These accounts reflect the belief of the first readers of this story, the Markan community. They were aware of the nourishment that the encounter with the eucharistic Lord provided. Yet, the author insists, the Lord himself does not make the distribution. Importantly for the Christian community, that is a task that has been given by the Lord to the disciples themselves. In the first miracle, seeing the lonely place and the lateness of the hour, the disciples ask Jesus to send the multitude away to the surrounding villages to buy themselves something to eat. Jesus replies: "You give them something to eat" (6:37). After taking, blessing, and breaking the loaves, Jesus "gave them to the disciples to set before the people" (v. 41). The second miracle is inspired by Jesus' compassion for the crowd, which has "come a very long way" (8:3). There is no command to the disciples to feed the people, but they are given the task. Again we read that Jesus "gave them [the broken loaves] to his disciples to set before the people; and they set them before the crowd" (v. 6).

The feeding of the multitudes is a task that the disciples must perform. This partly explains why these two miracle stories are found at this stage of Mark's plot. The author is concerned here to present Jesus' missioning of his disciples. One needs to look both backward and forward into the surrounding narrative context to understand properly the author's point of view in telling the bread miracles. The first miracle story (6:31-44) follows Jesus' sending out the Twelve on mission (6:7-13), and a lengthy description of the death of John the Baptist (6:14-29), which hints that such will be the destiny of all who are prepared to take the risk of following Jesus down his way.[30] After this interlude, the disciples return from the mission, full of their own importance and success (6:30). The feeding story that follows (6:31-44) is set within Jewish territory, but the question of the mission of the disciples has already been seriously raised in all the material that immediately preceded it (vv. 7-30).

The theme of mission again emerges powerfully between the first and the second feeding accounts (7:1-30). The passage opens with a polemical encounter between Jesus and Israel (7:1-23). The point at issue is "eating." The verb "to eat" (Greek: *esthiein*) and the word for "bread" (Greek: *artos*) highlight the conflict (see 7:2, 3, 4, 5). While Israel judges "eating" by "what is outside" (vv. 15 and 18), the real causes of sinfulness are to be found elsewhere. The vices listed in vv. 21-22 "come from within" (v. 23). Some of these are to be expected, as they come from the Decalogue, but there are further vices that separate people: envy, slander, pride, and foolishness. While Israel uses external criteria for assessing ritual cleanliness, Jesus points out that lasting divisions are created by much more profound defects. Writing to his own community, is Mark warning the people against their own tendencies to be divided by envy, slander, pride, and foolishness? It is not only the breach of Torah (evil thoughts, fornication, theft, murder, adultery, coveting, wickedness, deceit, and licentiousness) that defiles, but also the internal strife created by envy, slander, pride, and foolishness that tears community apart.[31]

Having made this point, Jesus sets out for a journey that will locate him in Gentile territory, until he returns to the Jewish world of Dalmanutha in 8:10. So that the audience will make no mistake about Jesus' presence in a Gentile world, the narrator stresses the geography of Jesus' movements: "And from there he arose and went away to the region of Tyre and Sidon" (7:24), and "Then he returned from the region of Tyre and went through Sidon to the Sea of Galilee through the region of the Decapolis" (v. 31). On this journey through Gentile lands and peoples, Jesus cures a Syrophoenician woman's daughter and thus reverses the established order of those at table and those seeking the crumbs that fall (7:27).[32] The arrogance of a people that attempts to instruct Jesus on table-fellowship (7:1-8) is thrown into disarray by the response of a woman who frankly confesses her nothingness. She receives Jesus' gift of life for her daughter because she recognizes the radical nature of her need and nothingness.[33]

Still in a Gentile land, he cures a deaf mute and the accompanying Gentile crowd acclaim Jesus in terms that recall the prophet Isaiah's description of the Messiah (7:37; see Isaiah 35:5-6).

The second feeding (8:1-9) is set in Gentile territory. Within an overall context of mission, Jesus himself feeds both Jews and Greeks.[34] What of the disciples in these feeding miracles? In both accounts they want to send the crowds away (6:35-36; 8:4). Jesus will not allow this. He thus commands them, "You give them something to eat" (6:37), and he involves them in the actual feeding (6:41, 8:6). As throughout the Gospel, the disciples are called to a privileged participation in the mission of the Lord. In this case, it is a call to feed both the Jews (6:37) and the Gentiles (8:6). The Church is for both Jew and Gentile, nourished by the disciples of Jesus, but the disciples do not understand. Indeed, they should have recalled that some of his earlier meals with them had overturned the barriers set up by the religious authorities to exclude some people from table-fellowship (see 2:15-17, 18-22). As Léon-Dufour has commented: "Those surprising meals had symbolised in a transparent way the universality of his message: the reign of God that is at hand is available to every human being."[35] But the disciples "did not understand about the loaves" (6:52).

Mark has set the two accounts of Jesus' sending his disciples to feed both Jewish and Gentile multitudes at the heart of his story of the mission of the disciples.[36] The disciples do not understand about the loaves and they are unwilling to perform their missionary task. They would prefer the people to look after themselves. Behind this narrative lie hidden the difficulties of the early Christian community over the mission to the Gentiles, no more profoundly felt than when it gathered for Eucharist. This section of Mark's Gospel reflects the pain that was keenly felt as many struggled both for and against the opening of the community's eucharistic table to both Jewish Christians and Gentile Christians. The problem of "table-fellowship" in the early Church was understandably widespread, and it is reflected in other parts of the New Testament (see especially Acts 10-11 and Gal 2:11-21).

The question of an "exclusive" concept of presence at the eucharistic table stands behind these two feeding miracles, placed strategically within the context of 6:6b-8:30, where the theme of the universal mission of Jesus and of the Christian community has also emerged. Mark has told his version of the two miracles of feeding the multitudes to teach the members of his community that they are to share in the universal mission of Jesus, cost what it may (see 6:14-29: the death of John the Baptist). At the heart of that mission was eucharistic table-fellowship: one bread for many different people, even though the disciples in the story would have liked to send them away, or exclude them from the table. Jesus, taking from the poverty and insufficiency of the disciple's mere few loaves and fishes (6:41 and 8:6), feeds the multitudes on both the Jewish and the Gentile side of the lake.

As the disciples in Jesus' story merited the stern words of Jesus (8:17-21) because they failed to understand the meaning of the loaves, the disciples of the Markan community—the audience to whom this story is proclaimed—are warned that they should be careful not to repeat such hardness of heart, the blindness of an *exclusive* understanding of the Lord's table.

JESUS' LAST MEAL WITH HIS DISCIPLES

Jesus insists that disciples must continue his universal mission by feeding both Jews (6:31-44) and Gentiles (8:1-10). A new Tradition, rooted in the life, teaching, death, and resurrection of Jesus of Nazareth, has come into existence. Our attention can now turn to the most explicit eucharistic text in this Gospel: the Markan version of the last meal that Jesus shared with these same disciples. Mark's telling of the story of the meal, celebrated with his disciples on the night before he died (14:17-31), is full of surprises.[37]

Along with the use of characters, acting out their roles within a plot, contemporary narrative criticism is also pointing out the importance of seeing the "rhetoric" of the narrative itself. While characters are the actors, and the plot is the placing of one event after another to create an impression and lead toward a conclusion, the rhetoric of a narrative is made up of the stylistic features that the author deliberately employs as he unfolds his plot.[38] Rhoads, Dewey, and Michie define these stylistic features as the literary devices used by the narrator to hold the audience's attention from one episode to another.[39] It is not enough to ask what a narrative is telling an audience; one must also ask why the story is shaped in a particular fashion. A careful reader, and especially one who hears it read or watches it performed, is not only interested in what is said, but also in how it is said. The literary shape of a story also determines its message.[40]

One of the features of Markan style is the tendency to "frame" stories. Often the narrator will single out an important narrative and splice another story into two parts, using these two elements to begin and end the central narrative. This means that the narrator opens a certain narrative with the description of an action, only to interrupt it by introducing another, quite different, action. The interrupted narrative is resumed once the central piece has come to its conclusion. An example of this is the frame of Jairus' summoning Jesus to come to his daughter (5:21-24) and the actual raising of Jairus' daughter (vv. 35-43) around the cure of the woman with the flow of blood (vv. 25-34). *Both* women are "dead" to Israel. One is in a continual state of ritual impurity because of her flow of blood, and the other is a corpse. But *both* women are restored to wholeness and the possibility of holiness through the taboo-breaking touch of Jesus.[41] Another well-known example is the frame of Jesus' cursing of the fig tree (11:12-14) and the sight of the withered tree (vv. 20-21) around the story of Jesus' ending all business and cultic practices in the Temple in Jerusalem (vv. 15-19): The fig tree and the Temple have *both* missed the opportune time (see v. 13: *kairos*) of the presence of the Kingdom. The list could go on (see also 3:20-35; 6:7-30; 14:1-11, 54-72), as it is a structure dear to Mark.[42] Sections of Mark's Gospel that are framed in this way must be interpreted as a whole. The narrative that forms the frame serves as a guide to the interpretation of the narrative within the frame, and vice-versa. Mark 14:17-31 is a good example of this element of Markan style. The narrator has told the central story of Jesus' final meal with his disciples (14:22-25) within the frame of two narratives that predict Judas' betrayal of him (vv. 17-21), Peter's denials, and their abandoning him in flight (vv. 26-31).[43]

Before analyzing the section of the Gospel contained within the unit of 14:17-31, we need to see whether there are further indications of Mark's plotting of his narrative. The framed passage that interests us (14:17-31) forms part of a wider literary pattern. Mark 14:1-72, the account of Jesus' last evening with his disciples, his prayer, his arrest, and the Jewish trial, proceeds by means of alternating scenes that report activities of either Jesus or the disciples. Mark has deliberately situated accounts that tell of what was happening to Jesus between other narratives that tell of the failure of one or all of the disciples. This is a contrived literary pattern, shifting the focus of the audience from the disciples (marked [A] in the structure which follows) to Jesus (marked [B]) and back to the disciples again (returning to [A]). This deliberately contrived pattern can be seen in the following division of the passage:[44]

A]—14:1-2: Plot (failure).

    B]—vv. 3-9: Anointing of Jesus.

A]—vv. 10-11: Judas (disciples' failure).

    B]—vv. 12-16: Jesus' instructions to the disciples for the preparation of the Supper.

A]—vv. 17-21: Prediction of Judas' betrayal (disciples' failure).

    B]—vv. 22-25: The Supper shared by Jesus and the twelve.

A]—vv. 26-31: Prediction of the denial of Peter and the failure of all the disciples (disciples' failure).

    B]—vv. 32-42: The experience of Jesus and his disciples at Gethsemane.

A]—vv. 43-62: Arrest (disciples' failure).

    B]—vv. 53-65: The Jewish trial of Jesus.

A]—vv. 66-72: Peter's denial (disciples' failure).

Although vv. 1-2 do not mention disciples, the need of the chief priests to arrest Jesus "by stealth" is closely linked with vv. 10-11. There Judas looks for an opportunity to betray Jesus to the chief priests. A close relationship exists between the discussions of the chief priests in vv. 1-2 and the decision of one of the disciples in vv. 10-11.

Once aware of this overall literary structure, it is evident that we are not only dealing with a typical Markan frame in vv. 17-31, but also a longer literary unit that has at its center the encounter between Jesus, who is going to his death, and the disciples, who—in many ways—are causing that death through their ignorance and failure. There are eleven scenes in Mark 14:1-71, and the account of Jesus' final meal with his disciples before going to his death is the sixth of them. It thus lies at the heart of the account of Jesus' last night with his disciples. The story of the disciples seems to descend into deeper and more tragic failure as the Gospel progresses. The opening section of the story of Jesus' passion—juxtaposing the light of Jesus and the darkness of failure and betrayal—draws this feature of his narrative into sharp relief.

The meal account appears in the plot as the centerpiece of 14:1-72. This overall structure indicates that the narrative is deeply concerned with the contrast between Jesus' gift of himself unto death and the failure of his disciples. Mark is not only interested in telling a story of the passion of Jesus; he is equally concerned to tell of the failing disciples. Central to the whole of the Markan presentation of the disciples is, as we have seen, their steady movement away from Jesus toward flight and failure. This failure will reach its depths in 14:50: "And they all forsook him and fled." It is matched at the very end of the Gospel by the failure of the women, who had remained with Jesus through his crucifixion and burial (see 15:40-41, 47): "And they went out and fled from the tomb; for trembling and astonishment had come upon them; and they said nothing to any one, for they were afraid" (16:8).

Equally central to the Markan story of disciples, however, is the never-failing presence of Jesus to his ever-failing disciples. This is especially evident in Jesus' instruction of his struggling disciples on their way to Jerusalem in 8:22-10:52.[45] Mark 14 tells of the continued and final failure of the disciples. But this account of darkness, weakness, and flight is thrown into relief by the light of the loving obedience of Jesus who prays to his Father: "Abba, Father, all things are possible to thee; remove this cup from me; yet not what I will, but what thou wilt" (14:36). Aware of this overall message, we can now turn to consider the central piece (14:17-31) of the whole account (14:1-72) in more detail.[46]

In the first section of the passage, the beginning of the frame (14:17-21), Mark paints in details that indicate that Judas, who will betray Jesus, belongs to the inner circle of his friends. Jesus "came with the twelve," a group that was especially appointed in 3:14 "to be with him" in a unique way (v. 17). The setting for Jesus' prediction of his betrayal is the meal table, a place sacred among friends.[47]

The tragedy is heightened by the idea that it is someone who shares table-fellowship who will betray Jesus. This theme takes us back to the role of the disciples in the feeding miracles of 6:31-44 and 8:1-9. There we saw that they wanted to "exclude" others from the Table of the Lord. Now one of them is about to break what they thought was their own exclusive table-fellowship. Jesus deepens this theme further as he comments that the betrayer will be "one who is eating with me" (v. 18). In response to the puzzled queries of his disciples (v. 19), the sense of a broken intimacy is intensified by the words of Jesus that link Judas with the group of "the Twelve" commissioned "to be with him" (3:14): "It is one of the twelve, one who is dipping bread into the dish with me" (14:20). Jesus is to be betrayed by a person who has shared the most intimate of experiences with him.[48]

A similar attention to the closeness that exists between Jesus and his future betrayers is found in the other section of the frame devoted to the rest of the disciples (14:26-31). There Jesus predicts that they "will all fall away" (v. 27). He uses the image of the shepherd and his sheep (v. 27), but his predictions lead to profound expressions of love and devotion. Peter swears an unfailing loyalty, better than all the others who may fall away (v. 29), and even claims that he is prepared to lay down his life out of loyalty and love for his master (v. 31). It is important to notice the narrator's brief concluding remark to this passage. Peter is not alone in swearing his loyalty and love. Mark adds: "And they all said the same" (v. 31). There can be no mistaking Mark's desire to communicate to his readers a sense of foreboding, as these men from Jesus' most intimate circle will prove to be the very ones who deny, betray, and abandon him. Themes that began to emerge around the disciples in their failure to "understand about the loaves, but their hearts were hardened" (6:52) have come to a head.

Shedding light across the entire passage of 14:1-72, at its center is the Markan version of Jesus' last meal with disciples who have not understood about the loaves, whose hearts are hardened, and who will betray and abandon him (14:22-26). The theme of table-fellowship with failing disciples opens the passage: "And as they were eating, he took bread, and blessed, and broke it, and gave it *to them* and said, 'Take …'" (v. 22). This theme is continued in the sharing of the cup, where the same recipients are again specified: "And he took the cup, and when he had given thanks he gave it *to them*, and they all drank of it" (v. 23). There is a bond between Jesus and the disciples that Jesus does not abandon: all eat the bread broken (v.22), all drink of the cup (v. 23), and all sing a hymn together (v. 26). Although neither Mark nor Matthew have the words "for you" in their reporting of Jesus' words over the bread broken (as do Luke [22:19] and Paul [1 Cor 11:24]) or the cup shared (as does Paul [1 Cor 11:25]), there is an intimate dialogue set up between Jesus and the disciples around the table. He commands them: "Take" (14:22), and they do.[49]

But there is more to the passage than the signs of a bond between the people around the table. The words over the bread and the cup point to the Cross: a body given in death and blood poured out as the result of a body broken (vv. 22 and 24). They point to something beyond the day of crucifixion. The blood is to be a covenant, "poured out for many" (v. 24), and Jesus comments that he will not "drink again of the fruit of the vine *until* that day when I drink it new in the Kingdom of God" (v. 25). The word "until" (Greek: *heôs*) has a temporal function within the sentence that forces the reader to look beyond the events of the crucifixion. The blood poured out for many and the drinking of it again in the Kingdom look well beyond Good Friday. Jesus' words, in the midst of predictions of betrayal, flight, and denial, ring out a message of trust and hope.

The Markan community celebrated Eucharist. This is evident from the eucharistic formulae about eating the bread and drinking from the cup found in Mark 6:41-42; 8:7-8; 14:22-25. Expressions that reflect a ritual have been read back into the story of Jesus' meals beside the lake, and with his disciples on the night before he died: to take (6:41; 8:6; 14:22-23), to give thanks (Greek: *eucharistein*: 8:6; 14:23), to break (6:41, 8:6; 14:22), to give (6:41; 8:7; 14:23), to bless (6:41; 8:7; 14:22), to eat (6:42; 8:8; 14:22), and broken pieces (Greek: *ta klasmata*: 6:43, 8:8). The account of Jesus' last meal with his disciples is cast in such a way that it has become the first of many subsequent meals "in the Kingdom." The members of the Christian community who were the first readers of the Gospel of Mark were instructed that they are the recipients of a Tradition that began with the life, teaching, death, and resurrection of Jesus, and was to be repeated and safeguarded in their own eucharistic celebrations.

Similarly, Jesus' reference to the establishment of the "Kingdom of God" in 14:25 looks to another important Markan theme that has been growing in importance as Jesus moves toward his death. In the closing section of the public ministry, in bitter polemic with the authorities of Israel, Jesus makes his first reference to the "new temple" founded on the rejected cornerstone (see 12:10-11). The theme becomes more important through the Jewish trial (14:58) and in the abuse that the passers-by hurled at the crucified Jesus (15:29-30). In his death, the old temple is destroyed, the holy of holies is opened through the tearing apart of the dividing veil and made available to the entire world (15:37-38).[50]

This "new temple," founded upon the rejected corner-stone (see 12:10), is the Markan community itself, called to mission, and called to a sharing of its table, where Jesus was present, no matter how seriously the community may have failed to respond to that presence. As we have already seen in our study of the two miracles of the multiplication of the bread, this sharing of the presence of the Lord must take place in mission. The disciples must feed both Jew and Gentile at the Table of the Lord. This presence was recalled, in the midst of the disciples' failure, as they shared in the broken bread and the cup in their eucharistic celebrations. What Mark argues does not detract from the significance of Jesus' words and actions with the bread and the cup. But Mark had no need to instruct disciples on that issue. His easy use of eucharistic language and symbols indicates that his audience needed no further "teaching." The celebration of Eucharist was already part of their lives, and they were aware of what the words and actions signified. Mark is using that to indicate how what they celebrate should impact upon their lives as disciples.

A body is given and blood poured out to set up a new covenant reaching beyond the Cross into the definitive establishment of the Kingdom. A covenant with whom? The readers of this passage— both the original Markan community and all subsequent Christian communities, Jew and Gentile—are aware that the body broken and the blood poured out have set up a new covenant. Almost two thousand years of Christian history tells the readers and hearers of the Gospel of Mark today that they form part of a covenanted Kingdom, thanks to the original presence of Jesus to failing disciples, the first recipients of the bread and the cup. The fundamental significance of the scene is not the transformation of bread and wine, or even in the meaning assigned to the bread and the cup, but in the establishment of a community that is united to Jesus in a special way. The action over the elements is subordinate to this purpose.[51] Through the gift that the Master symbolically makes of himself, the group of twelve enters now (and will remain after the departure of Jesus) into a close contact with their host: they will be inseparable from him who is leaving them.[52]

Mark has given us an account of Jesus' gift of himself unto death to establish a new and lasting Kingdom with the very people who frame the narrative of the meal: a betrayer, a denier, and people who will abandon him. The meal that Jesus shared was not a meal for "the worthy" (14:22-25). *It was a meal for those people who were closest to Jesus but who, faced with the challenge to love him even unto death, betrayed, denied, and abandoned their Lord* (14:17-21, 26-31).

CONCLUSION

As the members of the Markan Church reflected upon their own experience, they knew all too well that the Lord had given himself, and that he continued to give himself to disciples who failed. For this reason, when they came to tell the story of the beginnings of Jesus' presence to them in a meal, they told it in this striking way: a gift of self in love to those who have failed him most. Jesus loves his failing disciples with a love that is in no way matched by the love that they bear him. The disciples also knew that the task of taking the Table of the Lord into the mission was not a simple one. They had to cross barriers never crossed before. They were summoned to share the Table of the Lord with both Jew and Gentile, but this found them wanting. Here old prejudices came to the surface. The traditions they had received and respected from the religion and ritual practice of Israel, were being severely challenged by a Tradition that had its roots in the life, teaching, death, and resurrection of Jesus of Nazareth. They were challenged in their moments of hesitation by the words of Jesus: "You give them something to eat" (6:36).

> The evangelist has linked Eucharistic texts with some of the most painful pastoral questions of his church: mission and reconciliation. Both involved deep divisions that may have erupted at the Eucharistic celebration; both involved painful alienations which could only be

healed and ultimately reconciled in the table-fellowship of Eucharist. There Jew and Gentile could share one bread; there too, a sadder-but-wiser church could repent of its failures and once again take up the bond of discipleship. The source of hope in both instances was not to be found in the fragile disciples themselves but in the compassion and strength of the Risen Christ.[53]

Mark's theology of the Eucharist is closely related to his theology of discipleship, that is, to his understanding of the Christian community. The story of failure that is so critical to the portrait of the disciples of Jesus in the Gospel of Mark may have some of its roots in historical memory of the failure of the original disciples, especially Judas and Peter. However, the elevation of this theme to one of the major elements in the plot of the Gospel indicates that, whatever its origins, it is a major part of the Mark's "point of view." He addresses a Christian community marked by its own experience of failure. The Markan theme of the failure of the disciples is not primarily a message on how to be a good disciple of Jesus. It is a message about the crucial need in the Church for radical dependence upon the person of Jesus. Disciples may never succeed in the response to the call to lose themselves in following the way of Jesus (see 8:34-9:1). A journey, which involves turning the values of the world upside-down, often produces fear and failure (see, for example, 10:32, 14:50, and 16:7-8). Nevertheless, the vocation to live through the mystery of failure, depending only upon the greater mystery of the love and power of God shown to us in Jesus, stands at the heart of the message of the Gospel of Mark. It is also at the heart of the Markan understanding of the eucharistic presence of Jesus to his Church.[54]

What must not be underestimated, however, is that Mark's understanding of the Eucharist in this way came from the earliest Christian Tradition. We have seen clear traces of this same Tradition in 1 Corinthians 10-11, written some sixteen years before Mark. The dependence of Matthew and Luke upon Mark is part of the reason why they continue to use this early Christian Tradition. But each Synoptic Evangelist uses the same Tradition in a slightly different fashion. And John will develop it further.

1   For an extended analysis of the new literary form that was created by Mark, and followed by the other Evangelists, see Collins, *Mark*, 19-43.

2   The Gospel of John has no literary dependence upon the earlier Gospels. He does not use Mark in the same way as Matthew and Luke use Mark. However, he was aware of the earlier accounts, as we can see in a number of passages in the Fourth Gospel (especially John 6:1-72). On this, see D. Moody Smith, *John Among the Gospels*, 2nd ed. (Columbia: University of South Carolina Press, 2001). For some further reflections on this question, see below, p. 191 note 2.

3   For a contemporary presentation of each of the Gospels, Francis J. Moloney, *The Living Voice of the Gospel: The Gospels Today*, 2nd ed. (Melbourne: John Garratt, 2006), and, more recently, the briefer presentation in Moloney, *Reading the New Testament in the Church*, 113-39.

4   Those who question that the account of a Last Supper began with Jesus, regularly claim that the Gospel of John shows no awareness of that tradition. I will indicate evidence in that Gospel that he was well aware of it, but that he used it differently.

5   Out of respect for the tradition, I will regularly refer to the authors of the Gospels of Mark, Matthew, Luke, and John as "Mark," "Matthew," "Luke," and "John" without wishing to indicate anything concerning their historical identity, or even their gender. I will use male pronouns to refer to them. These names were associated with the Gospels in the second century. One of the reasons for giving each story its own author at that time was to ensure the individuality of each of them. There was a tendency in the second century to construct one story from the four, which endangered the uniqueness of Matthew, Mark, Luke, and John. See Martin Hengel, "The Titles of the Gospels and the Gospel of Mark," in *Studies in the Gospel of Mark* (Philadelphia: Fortress, 1985), 64-84.

6   Another way to approach Mark's point of view is to trace his own contributions to the traditions that came to him. This can be a speculative task, but a work dedicated to this issue has shown considerable Markan creativity in the passages we are considering. See E. J. Pryke, *Redactional Style in the Markan Gospel: A Study of Syntax and Vocabulary as Guides to Redaction in Mark*, SNTS Monograph Series 33 (Cambridge: Cambridge University Press, 1978), 159-60, 162, 171-72.

7   Meyer H. Abrams, *A Glossary of Literary Terms*, 5th ed. (New York: Holt, Reinhart and Winston, 1985), 144.

8   Narrative critical theory correctly distinguishes between a *historical author* ("Mark"), an author whose point of view is expressed by means of the narrative, generally called *the implied author*, and a *narrator*, the voice actually heard in the narrative. For the sake of simplicity (and because it is widely acknowledged that in the first-century Christian Gospels the voice of the author, the implied author, and the narrator can be considered to be the same), I will collapse the three literary features into the name of the author of the respective Gospel. In this case, I will use "Mark." For detailed studies of this theory see Stephen D. Moore, *Literary Criticism and the Gospels: The Theoretical Challenge* (New Haven: Yale University Press, 1989); Francis J. Moloney, "Narrative Criticism of the Gospels," *Pacifica* 4 (1991), 181-201; Robert M. Fowler, *Let the Reader Understand: Reader-Response Criticism and the Gospel of Mark* (Minneapolis: Fortress, 1991).

9   For a more developed treatment of this see Francis J. Moloney, *Mark: Storyteller, Interpreter, Evangelist* (Peabody, MA: Hendrickson Publications, 2004), 159-81. I have been helped in the reflections that follow, especially regarding the eucharistic background to Mark 6:31-44 and 8:1-9, by Donald Senior, "The Eucharist in Mark: Mission, Reconciliation, Hope," *Biblical Theology Bulletin* 12 (1982), 67-72.

10   On the characters in the Gospel of Mark see David Rhoads, Joanna Dewey, and Donald Michie, *Mark as Story: An Introduction to the Narrative of a Gospel*, 2nd ed. (Philadelphia: Fortress, 1999), 98-136; Elizabeth S. Malbon, *In the Company of Jesus: Characters in Mark's Gospel* (Louisville: Westminster John Knox, 2000); idem, "Characters in Mark's Story: Changing Perspectives on the Narrative Process," in *Mark as Story: Retrospect and Prospect*, ed. Kelly R. Iverson and Christopher W. Skinner, Resources for Biblical Studies 65 (Atlanta: SBL, 2011), 45-69; Christopher W. Skinner and Matthew Ryan Hauge, eds., *Character Studies in the Gospel of Mark*, Library of New Testament Studies 483 (London: Bloomsbury/ T. & T. Clark, 2014).

11   See, on the plot of the Gospel of Mark: Rhoads, Dewey, and Michie, *Mark as Story*, 73-97; Moloney, *Mark: Storyteller, Interpreter, Evangelist*, 47-58; R. Alan Culpepper, *Mark*, Smith & Helwys Bible Commentary (Macon, GA: Smith & Helwys, 2007), 18-25.

12   For a fine critical survey of this theme in the Gospel of Mark, including an assessment of current scholarship, see C. Clifton Black, *The Disciples According to Mark: Markan Redaction in Current Debate*, Journal for the Study of the New Testament Supplement Series 27; 2nd ed. (Grand Rapids: Eerdmans, 2012).

13   William J. Harvey, *Character and the Novel* (London: Chatto & Windus, 1965), 56.

14   On this section of the Gospel, see Moloney, *The Gospel of Mark*, 171-214. See the outstanding commentaries of Craig A. Evans, *Mark 8:27-16:20*, Word Biblical Commentary 34B (Nashville: Thomas Nelson, 2001), 3-135; Joel Marcus, *Mark*, The Anchor Yale Bible 27-27A, 2 vols. (New York/New Haven: Doubleday/Yale University Press, 2000-2009), 2:590-766.

15   See Moloney, *The Gospel of Mark*, 299-300; Harry Fleddermann, "The Flight of a Naked Young Man (Mark 14:51-52)," *The Catholic Biblical Quarterly* 41 (1979), 412-18; Culpepper, *Mark*, 511-13; Marcus, *Mark*, 2:999-1000.

16   Mark 16:9-20, found in many Bibles, was added to the Gospel. As the note to the passage in the widely-used *The New Jerusalem Bible* (London: Darton, Longman & Todd, 1985), 1685, explains: "The longer ending of Mk., vv. 9-20 is included in the canonically accepted body of inspired scripture, although some important MSS omit it, and it does not seem to be by Mark. It is in a different style, and is little more than a summary of the appearances of the risen Christ, with other material, all of which could be derived from various NT writings." The original Gospel ended at 16:8. On this, see Norman Perrin, *The Resurrection Narratives: A New Approach* (London: SCM Press, 1977), 20-22. For more detail, see Moloney, *The Gospel of Mark*, 340-41, 355-62; Collins, *Mark*, 803-18.

17   See Moloney, *The Gospel of Mark*, 342-54. See also Neil Q. Hamilton, "Resurrection, Tradition and the Composition of Mark," *Journal of Biblical Literature* 84 (1965), 415-21; Culpepper, *Mark*, 585-86.

18   See Moloney, *The Gospel of Mark*, 350-54; Thomas E. Boomershine and Gilbert L. Bartholomew, "The Narrative Technique of Mark 16:8," *Journal of Biblical Literature* 100 (1981), 213-23; Thomas E. Boomershine, "Mark 16:8 and the Apostolic Commission," *Journal of Biblical Literature* 100 (1981), 225-39. See also J. Lee Magness, *Sense and Absence: Structure and Suspension in the Ending of Mark's Gospel*, Semeia Studies (Atlanta: Scholars Press, 1986); Evans, *Mark 8:27-16:20*, 539-40.

19   Theodore J. Weeden, *Mark—Traditions in Conflict* (Philadelphia: Fortress, 1976), 50-51.

20   See Robert C. Tannehill, "The Disciples in Mark: The Function of a Narrative Role," *Journal of Religion* 57 (1977), 386-405; Moloney, *Mark: Storyteller, Interpreter, Evangelist*, 185-99.

21 Abrams, *A Glossary*, 127.

22 For an outstanding recent study of this question, see Gregg S. Morrison, *The Turning Point in the Gospel of Mark: A Study in Markan Christology* (Eugene, OR: Pickwick Publications, 2014).

23 For more detail, see Moloney, *The Gospel of Mark*, 16-22; Marcus, *Mark*, 1:62-64.

24 For this perspective, see Francis J. Moloney, *Beginning the Good News: A Narrative Approach*, Biblical Studies 1 (Homebush: St Paul Publications, 1992), 43-71. See also Marcus, *Mark*, 1:137-40, 168-71.

25 The manuscript evidence for the presence of the expression "Son of God" in Mark 1:1 has long been discussed, and scholars are divided on the issue. For a recent strong defense of its originality, and a fine survey of the discussion, see Tommy Wasserman, "The 'Son of God' was in the Beginning (Mark 1:1)," *The Journal of Theological Studies* 62 (2011), 20-50.

26 On this three-fold division of Mark 1:14-8:30, among many, see Moloney, *The Gospel of Mark*, 18-19. See especially Marcus, *Mark*, 2:589-92.

27 First highlighted by Robert H. Lightfoot, *History and Interpretation in the Gospels* (London: Hodder & Stoughton, 1935), 113-17, Mark 6:6b-8:30 is dominated by a literary structure determined by the two bread miracles. For its development and application to the interpretation of this section of the Gospel, see Moloney, *The Gospel of Mark*, 116-17.

28 On the eucharistic elements in the tradition, see Robert M. Fowler, *Loaves and Fishes: The Function of the Feeding Stories in the Gospel of Mark*, SBL Dissertation Series 54 (Chico: Scholars Press, 1981), 132-47. See also Sanae Masuda, "The Good News of the Miracle of the Bread: The Tradition and its Markan Redaction," *New Testament Studies* 28 (1982), 201-203; Moloney, *The Gospel of Mark*, 130-32, 154-55.

29 For a detailed study of the process that led from a feeding miracle in the life of Jesus to the Markan eucharistic refashioning of that story, see Jean-Marie van Cangh, *La Multiplication des Pains et l'Eucharistie*, Lectio Divina 86 (Paris: Editions du Cerf, 1975), 67-109.

30 See Francis J. Moloney, "Mark 6:6b-30: Mission, the Baptist, and Failure," *The Catholic Biblical Quarterly* 63 (2001), 663-79.

31 See Moloney, *The Gospel of Mark*, 143-44.

32 Philip Esler, *Community and Gospel in Luke–Acts: The Social and Political Motivations of Lucan Theology*, SNTS Monograph Series 57 (Cambridge:

Cambridge University Press, 1987), 89-91, analyses Mark 7:1-30 and its understanding of food laws and table fellowship. He concludes: "We are surely meant to see this image as a justification for the eucharistic fellowship of Jews and Gentiles in the Christian community."

33   See Moloney, *The Gospel of Mark*, 144-48.

34   On the significance of the Jewish and Gentile feedings, see van Cangh, *La Multiplication des Pains*, 111-31, and, more briefly, Moloney, *The Gospel of Mark*, 154-56.

35   Léon-Dufour, *Sharing the Eucharistic Bread*, 185; Marcus, *Mark*, 2:410, 420-21. For Crossan, *The Historical Jesus*, 332-53, Jesus celebrated "meals without boundaries," and this is one of the main features of what he terms the "brokerless kingdom."

36   See Brendan Byrne, *A Costly Freedom: A Theological Reading of Mark's Gospel* (Collegeville: The Liturgical Press, 2008), 121-33.

37   Not all would see the section 14:17-31 as a unit. Some scholars separate vv. 26-31 from the Supper, because of the "and they went out" in v. 26. See, for example, Vincent Taylor, *The Gospel According to St. Mark* (London: Macmillan, 1966), 548. Others separate vv. 27-31, linking v. 26 to vv. 22-25, as they see in the singing of the hymn (v. 26) a reference to the use of the second half of the Hallel Psalms as the conclusion to table-fellowship. See, for example, William L. Lane, *Commentary on the Gospel of Mark*, The New International Commentary on the New Testament (Grand Rapids: Eerdmans, 1974), 509-10. The overall "plot" of 14:1-72 demands my division.

38   For an outline of the rhetoric of the Gospel of Mark, see Rhoads, Dewey, and Michie, *Mark as Story*, 39-62. See also, H. C. Kee, *Community of the New Age: Studies in Mark's Gospel* (London: SCM Press, 1977), 50-76.

39   See Rhoads, Dewey, and Michie, *Mark as Story*, 46-47.

40   Given the low levels of literacy in antiquity, recent interpretation has been focusing increasingly on the oral performance of the Gospel stories as their initial form of communication. See the helpful study by Kelly R. Iverson, "Performance Criticism," in *The Oxford Encyclopedia of Biblical Interpretation*, 2 vols. (New York/Oxford: Oxford University Press, 2013), 2:97-105. See the helpful essay of David Rhoads, "Performance Criticism: An Emerging Methodology in Second Temple Studies," *Biblical Theology Bulletin* 36 (2006), 118-33, 164-84; and Joanna Dewey, "The Survival of Mark's Gospel: A Good Story?" *Journal of Biblical Literature* 123 (2004), 495-507.

For an influential study that sets the Gospel of Mark within performance expectations in antiquity, see Whitney T. Shiner, *Proclaiming the Gospel: First Century Performance of Mark* (Harrisburg, PA: Trinity Press International, 2003). However, important questions are posed by Larry W. Hurtado, "Oral Fixation and New Testament Studies? 'Orality', 'Performance' and Reading Texts in Early Christianity," *New Testament Studies* 60 (2014), 321-40.

41   See Moloney, *The Gospel of Mark*, 106-11.

42   On Mark 11:12-25, see Moloney, *The Gospel of Mark*, 221-28. On the Markan "framing" practice (technically called "intercalation"), see Rhoads, Dewey, and Michie, *Mark as Story*, 51-52; Kee, *Community of the New Age*, 54-56; Thomas Shepherd, "The Narrative Function of Markan Intercalation," *New Testament Studies* 41 (1995), 522-40. John R. Donahue, *Are You the Christ? The Trial Narrative in the Gospel of Mark*, SBL Dissertation Series 10 (Missoula: Scholars Press, 1973), 57-63, uses intercalation for his reading of the Markan trial accounts. It is often presupposed that Mark was too naïve an author to have used such techniques. Donahue's response to this point of view is: "The present work moves in opposition to the above views by studying what Mark actually did, not what he could or could not have done" (p. 3).

43   See, for this structure, Rudolf Pesch, *Das Markusevangelium*, Herders theologischer Kommentar zum NT II/1-2 (Herder: Freiburg, 1977), 2:345-46. Klemens Stock, *Boten aus dem Mit-Ihm-Sein: Das Verhältnis zwischen Jesus und den Zwölf nach Markus*, Analecta Biblica 70 (Rome: Biblical Institute Press, 1975), a close study of the relationship between Jesus and the Twelve, comments: "One must see in 14:17-31 a consciously constructed unit" (p. 167). See also the reflections of Culpepper, *Mark*, 528-31.

44   See Moloney, *The Gospel of Mark*, 276-79. Léon-Dufour, *Sharing the Eucharistic Bread*, 187-88, identifies this pattern as the "juxtaposition of light and darkness," but he only takes it as far as v. 31. Some commentators create a narrative break after 14:52, as 14:53-72 tell of the Jewish trial, and 15:1-20 report the Roman trial. This classification of 14:53-15:20 as "Jesus on Trial" (see, for example, Byrne, *A Costly Freedom*, 230-38) misses the dramatic interventions of Peter's denial (14:66-72), and the ironic royal proclamation of 15:1-5 (Pilate) and 15:16-20 (the soldiers). Léon-Dufour's "juxtaposition of light and darkness" is lost.

45   See Norman Perrin, "The Christology of Mark: A Study in Methodology," *Journal of Religion* 51 (1971), 173-87; Moloney, *The Gospel of Mark*, 171-214. This understanding is now widely accepted. See, for example, Marcus, *Mark*, 2:590-766.

46   See especially Donald Senior, *The Passion of Jesus in the Gospel of Mark*, The Passion Series 2 (Wilmington: Michael Glazier, 1984), 47-67.

47   On the importance of meals in the biblical tradition see Léon-Dufour, *Sharing the Eucharistic Bread*, 35-38.

48   See, on this passage, Vernon K. Robbins, "Last Meal: Preparation, Betrayal, and Absence," in *The Passion in Mark: Studies on Mark 14-16*, ed. Werner Kelber (Philadelphia: Fortress Press, 1976), 29-34. Robbins' study (following the interpretation of Theodore Weeden) understands the disciples as negative characters. The disciples have it completely wrong, and thus the author uses them as a foil to present a point of view that "corrects" their errors, presumably present in the Markan community. For a critical survey and rejection of this scholarship, see Jack D. Kingsbury, *The Christology of Mark's Gospel* (Philadelphia: Fortress Press, 1983), 25-45; Marcus, *Mark*, 1:75-79.

49   Léon-Dufour, *Sharing the Eucharistic Bread*, 60-62, 117-18, 130-32, 195-96, rightly insists on this "dialogic" character of the Markan/Matthean account.

50   See Donald H. Juel, *Messiah and Temple: The Trial of Jesus in the Gospel of Mark*, SBL Dissertation Series 31 (Missoula: Scholars Press, 1977), and the more recent and wide-ranging study of Timothy C. Gray, *The Temple in the Gospel of Mark: A Study of Its Narrative Role* (Grand Rapids: Baker Academic, 2010).

51   What is said here in no way detracts from the significance of Jesus' words and actions with the bread and the cup. But Mark had no need to instruct disciples on that issue.

52   Léon-Dufour, *Sharing the Eucharistic Bread*, 196.

53   Senior, "The Eucharist in Mark," 71.

54   See Moloney, *Mark: Storyteller, Interpreter, Evangelist*, 191-97.

CHAPTER FOUR

THE GOSPEL OF MATTHEW

Matthew tells a story of Jesus that often depends very heavily on his use of the earlier Gospel of Mark that appeared about 70 CE. A familiarity with the Gospel of Matthew, however, indicates that it was written for a very different audience, probably late in the 80's of the first century. Matthew addressed a largely Jewish-Christian community that was crossing the threshold of an emerging post-War Jewish tradition to form another Tradition in the mission to the Gentiles. Although the question of the Gentiles was part of Mark's concerns, for Matthew it is more central and he handles it differently. His community was in a very different time and place. Most likely, it appeared in a situation where Jews and Christians rubbed shoulders, and the members of Matthew's Christian community, painfully, began to see that they could no longer remain within the confines of the strictly Jewish world. Although we cannot be certain, there is widespread agreement that this Jewish-Christian community produced its Gospel in Antioch, where there is evidence for the proximity of a large Jewish community and an emerging Christian community.[1] It was painful for these early Christians because Christianity began as a Jewish religious movement. The structures and practices of Judaism provided the basis for earliest Christianity.

After the destruction of Jerusalem, its Temple, and consequently the cult associated with the Temple in 70 CE, Israel had to reconstitute itself. Before the Jewish War there had been Sadducees, Pharisees, Essenes, Zealots, and no doubt other ways of being a follower of the Law of Moses, but the great survivors of the war were the Pharisees.[2] A way of life centered upon the Synagogue and attempting to make God relevant to every aspect of life through the Law and its application, was the basis of the Judaism that rose from the chaos of so much destruction. The Gospel of Matthew came into existence within this historical and religious setting. It was the result of the Christian experience and reflection of a community that had begun its life in close association with traditional Israel. Tension and confusion were growing between Matthew's community and "the Synagogue across the street."[3] Ultimately, the Christian belief of the members of the community of Matthew, that Jesus was the Christ, forced them to distance themselves from their former religious world, which they loved so much, and invited them to move into the Gentile mission (see, for example, Matt 10:1-42 and especially 28:16-20).

This was not an easy passage. Many members of the community wondered, worried, and perhaps resisted abandoning the old and tried ways of approaching God that they had inherited from Israel's time-honored religion. The Gospel of Matthew has a point of view that helps an early Christian community to "cross the bridge" from post-70 Israel into a community that bases its faith and hope in Jesus of Nazareth as the Christ, the Son of God (see Matt 16:16).[4] This also necessarily meant involvement in the Gentile mission (28:16-20). However, unlike other early Christian documents, including the Gospel of Mark, both the author and the readers of the Gospel of Matthew looked back to their roots within the history of Israel as God's chosen people with love and respect. A tension between the mission to "the lost sheep of Israel" (10:6; 15:24) and "all nations" (28:19) is present throughout the Gospel.

Nowhere is this tension more keenly felt than in Jesus' words at the beginning of the Sermon on the Mount:

> "For truly I say to you, *till* [Greek: *heōs an*] *heaven and earth pass away*, not an iota, not a dot, will pass from the law *until* [Greek: *heōs an*] *all is accomplished*. Whoever then relaxes one of the least of these commandments and teaches others to do the same, will be called least in the kingdom of heaven; but whoever does them and teaches them shall be called great in the kingdom of heaven." (5:18-19; italics added)

At the beginning of his ministry, Jesus commits himself seriously to the fulfillment of the Law of Israel. Such a point of view is perfectly at home within a community intent upon living the Law of Israel. However, at the end of the Gospel a very different point of view emerges.

The risen Lord sends the disciples out to all nations, universalizing a mission once reserved to the lost children of Israel, baptizing new converts, usurping the unique initiation rite of circumcision, and teaching them to observe all the things he had taught them, replacing the teaching of Torah with the word of Jesus (28:16-20). Does this remarkable conclusion to the Gospel of Matthew not conflict with Jesus' teaching reported earlier in the same Gospel (5:18-19)?

The answer to this important question depends upon an understanding of Jesus' indications that there would be a time in the future when the restriction of the mission to a perfect living of the Law would no longer bind his disciples. The Law would have to be lived in its perfection "*till* (*heōs an*) heaven and earth pass away ... *until* (*heōs an*) all is accomplished" (5:18). When might that time be? Scholars regularly take this future time, when the minutiae of the Law could be abandoned, as pointing to the final end of all time, but this interpretation creates serious difficulties.[5] At the very end of the Gospel the strict observance of the Law seems to have been laid aside, as the person and mission of Jesus become the criterion for what the early Christian community must do as it faces the task of the Gentile mission (see 28:16-20).

The end of the Gospel does not seem to match the body of the Gospel, which reports the ministry of Jesus and his disciples sent out during his ministry "to the lost sheep of the house of Israel" (10:6; 15:24). There are only two occasions during his ministry when Jesus turns to the Gentiles, but even these moments point to the crucial nature of his mission for Israel. The two occasions on which Jesus ministers to Gentiles are reported in two miracles: Jesus' response to the request of the Gentile centurion (8:5-13), and his response to the pleas of the Canaanite woman (15:21-28). Both of these miracles are presented as exceptions to his rule. To the centurion Jesus laments the little faith of Israel, and speaks of the future universal assembly at the table of Abraham (8:10-11), and he responds to the woman: "I was sent only to the lost sheep of the house of Israel" (15:24). There is a clear intention on the part of the author to limit the activities of the Jesus of the Gospel story to "the lost sheep of Israel."[6] The same limitation is found in Jesus' instructions to the disciples in his missionary discourse to them: "Go nowhere among the Gentiles, and enter no town of the Samaritans, but go rather to the lost sheep of the house of Israel" (10:5-6). It can be justifiably claimed that, even given the two exceptions of miracles performed for Gentiles, the public life of Jesus and the mission of his accompanying disciples are dominated by a limitation to Israel.

Matthew's descriptions of the death and resurrection of Jesus tell of spectacular and dramatic events. The events that accompany Jesus' death and resurrection are recorded in this fashion only in Matthew's paschal story. Their description depends heavily upon traditional Jewish apocalyptic (end-time) imagery. Adding these images to surround Jesus' death and resurrection suggests that Jesus' passion and resurrection mark the "turning point of the ages." As Jesus dies, the Temple veil is torn from top to bottom, there is an earthquake, rocks split, and the saints rise from their now open tombs (27:51-54). His resurrection is marked by a further earthquake, an angel who moves the stone, lightning and snow-white clothing (28:2-3).[7] Scenes that, according to traditional Jewish apocalyptic, should have marked the end of human history (see, for example, Ezek 37:12; Zech 14:4-5; Dan 7:9; 10:6-9; 1 Enoch 71:1-2; 2 Enoch 1:3-7) have been drawn back into history to describe the death and resurrection of Jesus.[8]

By using these graphic and other-worldly descriptions, taken from Israel's traditional imagery to describe the end of all time, Matthew informs the audience that there is an "end-time" quality and function in these culminating moments of Jesus' story. At the death and resurrection of Jesus, heaven and earth pass away (see 5:18). The problem caused by the apparent contradiction between Jesus' teaching at the beginning of his ministry in 5:18-19 and his teaching as the risen Lord in 28:16-20 is resolved. The perfect observance of the Law has marked the life and mission on Jesus and his disciples. But in the paschal events of Jesus' death and resurrection, the time has come when they "pass away" (see 5:17). The audience understands that, at one level, the events of the death and resurrection of Jesus are the time when all due observance of the Law and the Prophets has been accomplished (see 5:17). The stage is set for a new mission: "make disciples of all nations" (see 28:16-20). It is, therefore, the task of the Christian community to accept the commission of the risen Jesus. To cling to the ways of the Law and the Prophets, the centerpiece of the post-70 Jewish leadership's reconstruction of their Jewish life and practice, meant to betray God's new design for them as the "true Israel," through the story of the life and teaching, the death and the resurrection of Jesus.[9]

The Gospel of Matthew was written to convince an early Jewish-Christian community of these truths. The author looked to several sources for information and inspiration. As we have seen, his main source was the Gospel of Mark.[10] The author follows the order of events as they succeed one another in Mark's Gospel, using almost all of the story of Jesus as Mark recorded it. The author also uses material that cannot be found in Mark, but which Matthew seems to share with Luke, and there is material that can only be found in Matthew. But the Gospel of Matthew cannot and must not be reduced to a loose amalgamation of identifiable sources. From our analysis thus far, it can already be sensed that the author has used whatever "sources" for the life and teaching of Jesus were available to him from earliest Christian tradition to tell the story in his own way.[11] The Gospel of Matthew (as also the Gospels of Mark, Luke, and John) has a unique understanding (a "point of view") of the new Tradition about the relationships between God and humankind, established in and through the life and teaching, death and resurrection of Jesus of Nazareth. The Gospel of Matthew must be judged and interpreted in its own right, however much we may be helped to trace his point of view by comparing what he writes with Mark, his major source. The Matthean story of Jesus addresses a particular Christian community in the early Church, as it journeys away from the old securities that post-war Judaism was re-establishing, into their own understanding of God's design. A part of that design was the Gentile mission (see 28:16-20).

DISCIPLES WHO FAIL

We have seen that a major theme of the Markan story of Jesus was the never-failing presence of Jesus to his disciples. This theme was highlighted in the Markan account of Jesus' final meal with them—told in Mark 14:17-31—within a context of the light and darkness of the presence of Jesus and the failing disciples in 14:1-72. For the Markan story, the theme of sinfulness and failure is important. It forms part of a wider theology that makes sense of a failing discipleship and no doubt reflects an early Christian Church struggling with its own experience of failure. The story of Jesus as it is retold in the Gospel of Matthew does not repeat Mark's message. Although present, there is a change of direction in Matthew's use of the theme.[12]

In the Gospel of Mark the disciples will not and cannot understand the teaching and the person of Jesus, or the cost of discipleship. For Matthew they do "understand." For Matthew the disciples do not fail totally. Indeed, they often appear to grasp very clearly who Jesus is and what he is demanding of them. They fail, rather, in *their inability to put into action what they have come to understand.* The disciples are a major presence in Matthew's version of the two miracles of the multiplication of the loaves and the fish (14:13-21; 15:32-38). Both Mark and Matthew reproduce discussions between Jesus and the disciples in boat trips that immediately follow the miracles (Mark 6:45-52; 8:14-21; Matt 14:22-33; 16:1-12). The Gospel of Mark points out the failure of the disciples on both occasions.[13] The Matthean parallel reinterprets this misunderstanding. Matthew does not report the disciples' misunderstanding. Instead, a term appears that is found on the lips of Jesus several times in the Gospel of Matthew: he speaks of the disciples as "you of little faith" (Greek: *oligopistoi*; see also 6:30; 8:26; 14:31; 16:8).

After the first feeding miracle, as Jesus comes to his frightened disciples across the sea, the reaction of the disciples is recorded as follows in Mark and Matthew:

Mark 6:51b-52	*Matthew 14:33*
And they were utterly astounded *for they did not understand* about the loaves, but their hearts were hardened.	And those in the boat *worshipped him* saying, "Truly you are the Son of God."

Mark makes it clear that, as well as the fear of the disciples, there was no understanding. But Matthew leads into this final response to Jesus' appearance across the waters by developing the fearfulness of the disciples. "They were terrified, saying, 'It is a ghost!' And they cried out in fear" (Matt 14:26). Yet, surprisingly, despite their terror and fear they understood exactly who it was who had come to them across the waters. He is the Son of God, and they respond accordingly with an act of worship.

After the second feeding miracle, again in a boat as they cross the lake, the reaction of the disciples is recorded as follows in the Gospels of Mark and Matthew:

Mark 8:14-21	Matthew 16:6-12
"Take heed, beware of the leaven of the Pharisees and the leaven of Herod."	"Take heed and beware of the leaven of the Pharisees and the Sadducees."
And they discussed it with one another, saying,	And they discussed it among themselves saying,
"We have no bread."	"We brought no bread."
And being aware of it, Jesus said to them,	But Jesus, being aware of this said,
	"O you of little faith,
"Why do you discuss the fact that you have no bread?	why do you discuss among yourselves the fact that you have no bread?
Do you not yet perceive or understand?	Do you not yet perceive?
Are your hearts hardened? Having eyes do you not see, and having ears do you not hear?	
And do you not remember? [Jesus recalls the two miracles and their aftermath.]	Do you not remember … [Jesus recalls the two miracles and their aftermath.]
And he said to them,	
"Do you not yet understand?"	*Then they understood* that he did not tell them to beware of the leaven of bread, but of the teaching of the Pharisees and the Sadducees.

The contrast between the Markan theme of the disciples' lack of understanding (see Mark 8:21) and the Matthean presentation of the same disciples as *understanding* (see Matt 16:12) but *of little faith* (see 16:8) is clear. In these parallel passages the difference in the reaction of the disciples in their encounter with Jesus in the boat is explicit. In Mark the narrator has Jesus ask the disciples: "Do you not yet understand" (Mark 8:21), while in Matthew the narrator makes the comment: "Then they understood" (Matt 16:12). The two versions of the exchange between Jesus and his disciples that follow the accounts of the bread miracles in Mark and Matthew respectively highlight the differing points of view found in the Gospel of Mark and the Gospel of Matthew. The disciples in Mark simply do not understand. This is not so with the Matthean disciples. They understand (see 16:12), but they have little faith (16:8).

Failure among disciples can also be dramatic in the Gospel of Matthew. Matthew highlights, on the one hand, the uniqueness of the person and the authority of Simon Peter (see 14:28-31; 16:16b-19; 17:24-27), but on the other, Peter's repeated hesitation and failure (see 14:30-31; 16:21-23; 26:31-35, 69-75).[14] Not only Simon Peter hesitates and fails. On the final page of the story, as the disciples gather on a mountain in Galilee, responding to the command of the angels at the empty tomb (see 28:10) in the presence of their risen Lord, who sends them out on a mission to the entire world, Matthew reports: "And when they saw him they worshipped him; but some doubted" (28:17). The response of Simon Peter and all the disciples in the story of the Gospel of Matthew reflects the real-life experience of the Christian community receiving Matthew's story—hesitating and doubting before the task of the Gentile mission.[15]

But Matthew, strongly aware of the "little faith" of the disciples, confidently communicates a message of Jesus as the Emmanuel, God-with-us. The Gospel opens with a prophecy: "Behold a virgin shall conceive and bear a son, and his name shall be called Emmanuel (which means God with us)" (1:23). Despite the little faith and the hesitation of the disciples' response to Jesus, Matthew closes his Gospel with a promise from the risen Christ indicating that this presence will go on: "And lo, I am with you always, to the close of the age" (28:20). The theme of the "little faith" of the disciples across Matthew's Gospel establishes that weakness and failure were a problem, despite the promises of the Scriptures (1:23) and the final words of Jesus (28:20). In the Gospel of Matthew the message of the Risen Christ is communicated to the disciples by women who have discovered the empty tomb, and had an encounter with the risen Lord (28:1-10). They do not flee in silence and fear. The disciples have a solemn final encounter with the risen Lord, and are given a mission (vv. 16-20). But even Matthew indicates that this encounter generates two responses: some believe, while others still doubt (28:17). However fragile the disciples' faith in the presence of the risen Lord might be, Matthew insists upon the presence of the Emmanuel, God in the midst of his people until the close of the age: "I am with you always, to the close of the age" (28:20).[16]

As Mark addressed a community suffering from fear and flight in the midst of failure to live up to the challenge of belief in a crucified and risen Son of God, Matthew spoke to an audience with its own experience of failure. They *know* that Jesus is the risen Lord among them till the end of the ages, but they are *people of little faith* and still doubt. Although different, the two Evangelists paint a narrative portrait of disciples that continues to speak eloquently to disciples of all times, believing but still doubting.[17]

ISRAEL AND THE DISCIPLES AT THE BREAD MIRACLES

A hesitation to leave the tried ways of the Pharisees and the Sadducees is an important theme for the Gospel of Matthew (see 23:1-39). The story reflects the context of a difficult Synagogue-Christian relationship. Some of Matthew's Christian community—perhaps troubled by their departure from the established traditions of Israel— were sorely tempted to return to the secure ways within the Judaism they knew and loved. Thus Matthew refashions a number of the stories that had come to him from the Gospel of Mark. This is especially true when we trace Matthew's perspective as he retells the section of the Gospel of Mark that contained the accounts of two bread miracles (Matt 13:53-16:23; see Mark 6:31-8:10).

The bread miracles in Matthew's Gospel are strategically located. After a confident proclamation of the coming of the Messiah (1:1-4:16), which acts as a Prologue to the entire Gospel, Jesus begins his ministry of preaching, teaching, and healing in Israel (4:17-11:1). The encounters between Jesus and the leaders of Israel steadily develop into a crisis (11:2-16:12). Despite this hostility Jesus sets out to face his opponents in Jerusalem (16:13-20:34). There he will undergo death and resurrection (21:1-28:15) and "on the mountain" commission his disciples (28:16-20).[18]

At the heart of 11:2-16:12, Jesus' so-called parable discourse (13:1-52) sets up an opposition between those who know the secrets of the Kingdom of heaven, and those who do not. For the latter group, even what they have will be taken away from them (see v. 12). Jesus closes this discourse with a comment: "Therefore, every scribe who has been trained for the kingdom of heaven is like a householder who brings out of his treasure what is new and what is old" (13:52). He leaves the place of the parables (13:53. See also 7:28; 11:1) and the crisis between Jesus and Israel intensifies from 13:53-16:12. With the confession and the blessing of Simon Peter in 16:13-20, a new series of episodes begins, unified by the theme of Jesus' journey to Jerusalem. The die is cast as crisis increases in 11:2-16:12. It is within that "moment" of the narrative, and in the light of the overall rhetoric of that moment, that the accounts of the two bread must be interpreted. Stories may be analyzed and different "moments" in the flow of the narrative identified. But these "moments" are not separated from one another by impenetrable brick walls, firmly closing out one stage of the story from another. The crisis of 11:2-16:12 will play itself out as Jesus journeys to Jerusalem (16:13-20:34), goes through death and resurrection in that place (21:1-28:15), and the risen Jesus commissions his disciples (20:16-20). The two bread miracles have a message that resonates across the latter half of the Gospel.

Keeping this important principle in mind, the events that lead into and out of the two bread miracles in Matthew unfold as follows:[19]

13:53-14:12: The rejection of Jesus and the Precursor

13:53-58: Unbelief leads to Jesus' rejection of the people of "his own country."

14:1-12: The slaying of John the Baptist, who introduced the fulfillment of all righteousness (see 3:15), an anticipation of the episode that brings the fulfillment to completion (see 5:17-18): the slaying of Jesus.

14:13-21: The first bread miracle
14:22-15:20: Israel and Peter fail
14:22-33: Jesus comes to frightened disciples on the stormy sea. Peter shows his "little faith."

15:1-14: Jesus attacks the traditions of Israel.

15:15-20: An ignorant Peter asks for an explanation of this attack.

15:21-31: Jesus turns to the Gentiles
15:21-28: Curing of the Canaanite woman.

15:29-31: Curing of many "along the sea of Galilee," leading to the glorification of the God of Israel.

15:32-39: The second bread miracle
16:1-23: Israel, Peter, and the disciples fail
16:1-4: The Pharisees ask for a sign.

16:5-12: Jesus and the disciples "of little faith" discuss the leaven as they cross the lake.

16:13-23: Peter confesses that Jesus is the Christ, the Son of God and he is blessed. Jesus sets out for Jerusalem, but the same Peter refuses to accept Jesus as Son of Man and he is cursed as Satan.

Matthew surrounds his account of the two miraculous feedings with a context marked by a bitter attack from Jesus upon "his own country," official synagogue-centered Judaism, and some severe criticism of Peter and the disciples.[20] In the midst of this rejection and misunderstanding, Jesus turns to the Gentiles, and God is glorified among them. The first miracle, the feeding of a Jewish multitude (14:13-21), is introduced after Jesus' rejection "of his own country" because of their little faith and the Herodian slaying of John the Baptist (14:1-12). Anger and rejection are in the air as the bread miracle (vv. 14-21) leads to an encounter between Jesus, his frightened disciples, and a failing Peter (vv. 22-33). Jesus then attacks Israel, but Matthew alone explains the brief "parable" of Jesus concerning that which enters the mouth and that which comes out of the mouth (15:11). He responds to the disciple's concern over his treatment of the Pharisees: "Every plant which my Father has not planted will be rooted up. Let them alone, they are blind guides. And if a blind man leads a blind man, both will fall into a pit" (15:13-14).

However, to Peter, who asked for the explanation (v. 15), he also speaks strongly: "Are you still without understanding?" (v. 16). The audience has been prepared for Peter's failure. Prior to Jesus' invective against Israel and its leaders, he has reported Peter's littleness of faith when summoned by Jesus to come to him across the stormy waters (14:28-31). Harsh though Jesus' attack upon Israel may have been, Matthew has no illusions about Jesus' own disciples and their leader, Simon Peter. Israel, whom Jesus has fed in the first of the bread miracles (14:13-21), may have lost its way in rejecting Jesus. The Christian community, under the leadership of Peter, also has its moments of "little faith" (see 14:31).

Leaving, for a moment, the two cures reported in 15:21-31, the immediate aftermath of the second bread miracle (15:32-39) is marked by events that stress the understanding yet little faith of the disciples in general and of Peter in particular. In 16:5-12 the disciples are shown to understand Jesus' reference to the teaching of the Pharisees and the Sadducees (16:12), but they are still people of little faith (v. 8). The narrator then reports Peter's understanding that Jesus is the Christ, the Son of God (16:16). For this he receives a blessing (vv. 17-19). However, as Jesus sets out for Jerusalem, Peter fails when asked to follow a suffering Son of Man (16:22) and for this he is cursed as Satan (v. 23). Matthew alone has used terms that refer to Peter as a rock, but in contrasting ways. In 16:18 he is "the rock" (Greek: *petra*) upon which the Church is built, while in 16:23 he is "the rock of stumbling" (Greek: *skandalon*). The same foundational figure is capable of being contrasting "rocks": the rock upon which the community is built, and the rock upon the path of Jesus, travelling toward his destiny in Jerusalem, over which he might stumble. The ambiguity of the disciples is especially obvious in their leader.[21]

These carefully written and strategically placed accounts of the failure of both Israel and the disciples—the literary setting for the two bread miracles (14:13-21 and 15:32-39)—marks the close of Jesus' Galilean ministry. Matthew deliberately sets the two miracle stories within contexts of Jesus' increasing criticism of traditional Israel

(5:1-20; 16:1-4), and failure on the part of all the disciples and of Peter, the chief disciple (14:22-33; 15:15; 16:5-12; 21-23).[22] In 16:13-23, Jesus turns away from Galilee: "From that time Jesus began to show his disciples that he must go to Jerusalem and suffer many things from the elders and the chief priests and scribes, and be killed, and on the third day be raised" (v. 21).

The Matthean accounts of the two miracles indicate, as in Mark, that they are written in terms that recall the celebration of the Eucharist. Jesus "took ... looked up to heaven ... blessed ... broke and gave the loaves" (14:19; 15:36). Jesus' miracles of feeding with bread would have recalled the Matthean community's own celebrations of his presence to them, nourishing them at the eucharistic table. However, the context of the first bread miracle (14:13-21) makes it clear that the multitude was Jewish (as in Mark 6:31-44), but the recipients of the broken bread in the second miracle (15:32-39) are more difficult to identify.

Matthew does not devote the care of Mark in indicating that Jesus, through his disciples, nourishes a Jewish crowd in the first miracle and Gentiles in the second. In the first miracle (14:13-21), all reference to the Jewish crowd as "a sheep without a shepherd" (Mark 6:34. See Num 27:17; Ezek 34:5) and the sitting down in companies of hundreds and fifties (see Exod 18:21-25; Num 31:14; Deut 1:15) is omitted. In the second miracle (15:32-39) there is no hint of the Gentile origin of the second crowd. Mark's indication, "Some of them have come a long way" (Mark 8:3), does not appear.[23]

While scholars debate this question, perhaps Matthew is more subtle in presenting Jesus as providing nourishment for the Gentiles than is generally recognized.[24] Matthew does all he can to avoid conflicting understandings of what God has done for traditional Israel and what he continues to do for the "true Israel." The second bread miracle is immediately preceded by the episodes of the curing the Canaanite woman (15:21-28) and the curing of many people "along the Sea of Galilee" (vv. 29-31). The Gentile theme is clearly introduced through Jesus' rare interaction with a Gentile in the Gospel of Matthew in the curing of the Canaanite woman (15:21-28). But Matthew's interest in the Gentile theme can also be found in the briefly reported but spectacular miracle "along the Sea of Galilee

... on the mountain" (v. 29) in 15:29-31. Matthew is reworking an episode found in the Gospel of Mark.

At this stage of Jesus' ministry, Mark 7:31-37 reports the cure of a deaf mute in the Decapolis, a Gentile land. Corresponding to that miracle, Matthew 15:29-31 tells, somewhat clumsily, of Jesus on a mountain "along the sea of Galilee" (v. 29). He cures all who are maimed, lame, blind, and dumb (v. 30; see Isaiah 35:5-6). The cures lead the unidentified crowd to respond: "They glorified the God of Israel" (Matt 15:31). Matthew's miracle, administered by Jesus on the top of a mountain, yet "along the sea of Galilee," forms a link between two other important "mountain scenes" in this Gospel: 5:1-7:28 (the Sermon on the Mount) and 28:16-20 (the final commission of the risen Jesus to his disciples). As we saw in the more general reflections on the background to the Gospel of Matthew, at the beginning of Jesus' public life, in the Sermon on the Mount he taught that "till heaven and earth pass away, not an iota, not a dot will pass from the law until all is accomplished" (5:18). At the end of Jesus' ministry, as heaven and earth have passed away through the events of his death and resurrection he sends out his disciples to "make disciples of all nations" (28:19).

In 15:29-31, at the close of his Galilean ministry, immediately following upon his curing of the daughter of the Gentile Canaanite woman, Jesus opens the way to that final mission to the Gentiles. As the prologue to the Gospel closed (Matt 4:15-16), Matthew set the agenda for Gentiles as he told his audience that Jesus' presence in Galilee was the fulfillment of Isaiah 9:1-2:

> The land of Zebulun and the land of Naphthali,
> towards the sea across the Jordan,
> *Galilee of the Gentiles*—
> the people who sat in darkness
> have seen a great light,
> for those who sat in the region
> and the shadow of death light has dawned.

An initial promise of such a fulfillment of Isaiah 9:1-2 is found in Jesus' miraculous activity on the mountain, "along the sea of Galilee" (15:29-31). The two passages that immediately precede the second miracle of the multiplication of the bread in Matthew focus their attention upon a Gentile audience: the cure of a Canaanite woman (15:21-28) and the curing of the multitude with many diseases (vv. 29-31). The promise of Jesus' presence to the Gentiles is now being partially fulfilled. It is a Gentile crowd that expresses its wonder by glorifying "the God of Israel" (15:31).[25]

> Perhaps Matthew means to suggest that the crowds are made up of Gentiles. He would then be following up the story of the Canaanite woman's daughter, with the apparent hesitation of Jesus to use his healing powers for the benefit of a Gentile, with this account of multiple healings of Gentiles, and the conversion of Gentile multitudes to the God of Israel. Once the barrier of racial privilege is broken at one point, the mission of Jesus no longer is restricted to Israel; among the Gentiles he heals the disabled—gives hearing to the deaf, speech to the dumb, and sight to the blind; and in the next episode he will feed the Gentiles with the bread of life as he has previously fed the thousands of Israel.[26]

The scene is thus set for the second bread miracle (vv. 32-39). The multitude Jesus feeds is the crowd that has just glorified the God of Israel, "along the Sea of Galilee." The feeding of the immense crowd and the gathering of the seven baskets of remnants show that the ministry to the Gentiles is not closed.[27] From 16:13-23 the journey to Jerusalem will begin, leading to the passing away of both heaven and earth, and the final commission to "all nations" (28:16-20). The promise of Jesus' earlier contacts with the Gentile world is now part of the mission of the Church.

All are called to glorify the one God and Father of Jesus. The traditional leaders of Israel (see 15:1-14), the people from Jesus' own country (see 13:53-58), Herod and his entourage (see 14:1-12), and Peter and the disciples (see 14:22-33; 15:15-20; 16:5-12, 13-24) have all failed to do so in anything like the response of the Gentiles in 15:31. Yet, in the midst of so much failure Jesus feeds both Israel (14:13-21) and the Gentiles (15:32-39). Indeed, the Gentiles come to glorify the God of Israel, as God is made known through the person and teaching of Jesus (15:31). Despite the failure of the leaders of Israel and the foundation group of the true Israel (Peter and the disciples), the mission to the Gentiles is pursued. Matthew has certainly softened the sharp distinctions between a Jewish and a Gentile meal in Mark 6:31-44 and 8:1-9, but he heightens the failure of both traditional Israel under the leadership of the blind Pharisees, and the new people of God—fearful and doubting disciples under the leadership of the fearful and doubting Peter. Nevertheless, associating the disciples with his task (14:16-19; 15:36), Jesus nourishes an Israel that fails (14:13-21) and a Gentile people that has glorified the God of Israel (15:31, 32-39).

The disciples collaborate in distributing the bread in both miracles, but Jesus makes the distribution possible by giving the elements of the meal to them (14:19; 15:36). Matthew makes a further subtle point. In reporting Jesus giving the bread to his disciples in the first miracle (14:19), the narrator uses a tense of the Greek verb "to give" indicating an action that has taken place in the past. This action of "giving" is now closed. The aorist tense (Greek: *edōken*) is used, indicating a period of time in the past that has come to its conclusion.[28] The use of the aorist to speak of the disciple's gift to a wholly Jewish community indicates for the reader that the community can no longer continue as a Jewish community. That era lies behind the experiences of Matthew and his community. In the second miracle the tense of the verb "to give" is changed; a verb in the imperfect tense is used (Greek: *edidou*). This Greek tense indicates something that began in the past, and remains in the past but is still taking place.[29]

It is an action begun in the story of Jesus and the original disciples as he nourished Israel. It is an action that has now come to an end (14:19). But Jesus repeats that gift to a Gentile multitude, in that feeding of "all nations" (see 28:19). That feeding continues well beyond that reported historical moment from the past. The audience's attention is focused upon the place of the Eucharist in the ongoing life of the Christian community. There is a call to unity unique to the Gospel of Matthew's treatment of the bread miracles. Israel, the Church, and the Gentile world—no matter how sinful or how little their faith may be—are called to nourish others and be nourished by the same Lord.[30]

Here one senses the reason for the different "point of view" of the Matthean story, when compared with its Markan source. The Markan narrator speaks boldly of the radical break that must come between the newness of Christianity and the now obsolete ways of old. The Jesus of the Gospel of Mark can proclaim: "No one puts new wine into old wineskins; if he does the wine will burst the skins, the wine is lost and so are the skins; but new wine is for fresh skins" (Mark 2:22). The Matthean Jesus teaches quite differently:

> "Neither is new wine put into old wineskins; if it is, the skins burst, and the wine is spilled, and the skins are destroyed; but new wine is put into fresh wineskins, and so both are preserved." (Matt 9:17)

The same point is made when, in an almost autobiographical note, Jesus explains the task of the Christian scribe: "Every scribe who has been trained in the kingdom of heaven is like a householder who brings out of his treasure what is new and what is old" (13:52).[31]

The subtlety of Matthew's use of the two bread miracles indicates that confusion over the separation between Jew and Gentile was intense and complex. An originally Jewish community, most likely located in cosmopolitan Antioch, the Christian community had begun to receive Gentiles into their midst. The Gospel that emerged from this community attempted to draw both Jew and Gentile, despite the sinfulness and the "little faith" of the Christian community itself, into the one People of God around the one Table of the Lord. Matthew had no desire to alienate Israel, in which his community had been born, or the Gentile mission, into which the community was now being sent. Jesus calls both Jew and Gentile into the one People of God. Both Jew and Gentile are on a mission to "all the nations." Jesus, who will be with them till the end of all time (see 28:20), nourishes them all at the eucharistic table.

THE LAST SUPPER

Matthew's account of a meal celebrated on the day before Jesus died (Matt 26:3-75) looks back to the carefully arranged literary structure of Mark 14:1-71: the failure of the disciples alternates with the experience of Jesus.[32] After a final passion prediction (26:1-2) that is only found in the Gospel of Matthew, the text unfolds as follows:

A]—26:3-5: Plot (*failure*).

    B]—vv. 6-13: *Jesus* is anointed.

A]—vv. 14-16: Judas (*disciple's failure*).

    B]—vv. 17-19: *Jesus'* instructions for the preparation of Passover.

A]—vv. 20-25: Prophecy of the betrayal of Judas (*disciple's failure*).

B]—vv. 26-30: The Supper shared by *Jesus* and the disciples.

A]—vv. 31-35: Prediction of the denial of Peter and the failure of all the disciples (*disciples' failure*).

B]—vv. 36-46: *Jesus'* experience of Gethsemane.

A]—vv. 47-56: Arrest of Jesus and the flight of the disciples (*disciples' failure*).

B]—vv. 57-68: The Jewish trial of *Jesus*.

A]—vv. 69-75: The denials of Peter (*disciple's failure*).

Matthew's presentation of the disciples across the Gospel story as a whole tends to soften the intensity of Mark's critique of their unbelief, fear, and flight. As we have seen, he does not highlight their unfaith, but their inability to understand. They understand, but they suffer from doubt and "little faith."[33] When it comes to the passion narrative (Matt 26:1-28:15), we find "the damning description of their betrayal, desertion and denial."[34] Thus, in reporting Jesus' final meal with his disciples, Matthew has no hesitation in taking up and repeating the central literary pattern of a prophecy of betrayal, a shared meal, and a prophecy of denial and flight (see Matt 26:20-35; Mark 14:17-31).[35] The bread is broken and the wine shared as a gift of Jesus' own body and blood (26:26-29) within the setting of disciples who fail (26:20-25 [Judas], 30-35 [Peter and all the other disciples]).

The text is almost identical to Mark 14:17-31,[36] with some slight but important variations that intensify the portrait of the failing disciples. In the narrative before the meal (Matt 26:21-25), Matthew heightens the drama of Judas' betrayal. Mark's Gospel has a general indication that "one of you" (Mark 14:18), "one of the twelve" would betray Jesus (14:20). This indication is followed by the lament over "that man by whom the Son of Man is betrayed" (14:21). Judas is never named, nor does he enter the story actively. Matthew refashions his source to stress Judas' personal failure. Jesus first indicates generally "one of you will betray me" (Matt 26:21). He then shifts away from a more general reference to one of the Twelve "who is dipping bread in the same dish with me" (Mark 14:20), to state, with specific reference to an action already completed before the eyes of all: "He who dipped his hand in the dish with me" (Matt 26:23). After the lament over the betrayer, Judas actively enters the story: "Judas, who betrayed him, said, 'Is it I, Master?' He said to him, 'You have said so'" (Matt 26:25). In Matthew's Gospel, little is left to the imagination. One of the Twelve, whose name was Judas, is the betrayer. A scene is set in which a clearly indicated and named disciple, one of the Twelve, has shared a sacred meal with Jesus. After this setting—heightening and personalizing the theme of betrayal—the story of the supper is told in a way *almost* identical to Mark 14:22-26.

There is one important feature of Matthew's version of the meal that calls for close attention. Only in the Gospel of Matthew does the reader find an addition to Jesus' words over the cup: "for the forgiveness of sins" (Matt 26:28). There is widespread agreement among scholars that Matthew has made explicit what was implicit in the other traditions: the covenant presupposes the forgiveness of sins. All other words over the cup make reference to the covenant (see Mark 14:24; Luke 22:20; 1 Cor 11:25), but only Matthew has words on the lips of Jesus that speak of a covenant "for the forgiveness of sins." These words recall Jeremiah 31:34 and Isaiah 53:10-12.[37] No doubt Matthew, with his well-known concern to relate the actions of Jesus with the promises of the Old Testament, recalls the prophets' promise of a covenant for the forgiveness of sins. But is that all that can be gleaned from his insertion of these words on the forgiveness of sins? Matthew's heightened interest in the sinfulness of the people sharing the bread broken and the cup poured also plays a role in the interpretation of this addition. Matthew has repeated the Markan account of the setting and the details of the meal, but the concentration upon the person of Judas is heightened, just as the audience's awareness of the failure of all the disciples will also be increased in the passage that follows (vv. 30-35).

The explicit reference to the blood of the covenant poured out for many *for the forgiveness of sins* (v. 28) reflects *both* Matthew's community's own liturgical practice *and* the author's message that "by sharing the one bread and drinking the one cup, the disciples share in the saving effects of Jesus' atoning sacrifice."[38] Which disciples will share in the saving effects of Jesus' atoning sacrifice? Jesus breaks his body and pours out his blood for the disciples mentioned both before and after the account of the meal itself. The forgiveness that is offered is certainly linked to the promise of the new covenant, but it is also linked to the sinfulness of the betrayers and deniers who are sharing the meal with Jesus.[39] Ulrich Luz eloquently interprets Matthew's vision of Christian life:

> In the celebration of the Lord's Supper the church shares in the saving power of the death of Jesus. ... We can see here that the words of interpretation on the breaking of bread and the cup are not merely parables that explain; they are a word of promise that permits the churches in the ritual of eating and drinking to share in the saving power of Jesus' death. The passages in Matthew that summon to the forgiveness of sins (18:21-22, 23-35; cf. 6:12) receive their depths from the Lord's Supper. *To forgive others their guilt is to participate in the mission of Jesus and to reflect the gift received from him.*[40]

Matthew again slightly retouches the passage that deals with the future denials of Peter and the flight of all the disciples (26:31-35). As with the prediction of Judas' denials (26:20-25), Matthew retouches his Markan source to make the disciples' failure more specific. In Mark, Peter claims he would never fail Jesus, "even though they all fall away" (Mark 14:29). Matthew has Peter indicate *why* they might fall away: "Though they all fall away *because of you*" (Matt 26:33). Mark associates the rest of the disciples with Peter's profession of loyalty in general terms—"And they all said the same" (Mark 14:31)—but Matthew makes specific reference to *all the disciples*: "And so said all the disciples" (Matt 26:35).

Matthew reports the final meal shared by Jesus and his disciples for his own community, in his own way. There was a need to associate failing disciples with Jesus. At the eucharistic table, the members of Matthew's community recalled, in their sinfulness, that their founding disciples also failed. Indeed, Matthew's slight but significant reinterpretation of his Markan source focuses its attention even more closely upon the fact that it was, above all, the disciples who failed. It is to the failing disciples that Jesus commands: "Take, eat" (26:26) and "Drink of it, all of you" (26:27).

> In the passion narrative of Mark, disciples show themselves unreliable, cowardly, betraying and denying their master. Matthew's account accentuates this. In narrative form the story-teller is describing what is found on Jesus' lips in the Fourth Gospel:

"Without me you can do nothing" (John 15.5). Up to the passion the disciples are with Jesus, or minister with his authority (10.10); in the passion they desert him, and their authority, understanding and courage desert them. Yet it is to such fallible disciples that Jesus addresses the final commission of the Gospel, and promises to be with them "till the end of the age" (28.20b).[41]

CONCLUSION

The Gospel of Matthew addresses disciples who are failing. But their failure is not one of unfaith, ignorance, fear, and flight, as in Mark's Gospel. In some ways it is worse! They understand well enough, but they fall short of the total commitment required by Matthew's understanding of true Christian faith. There is still doubt and hesitation when it comes to leaving behind the secure traditions of the Pharisees and the Sadducees, and setting out into the Gentile mission, teaching what Jesus has taught them (see 28:19). Like Mark—upon whose story he depends for his narrative of Jesus' death and resurrection— Matthew presents the Eucharist as the saving presence of Jesus Christ's unconditional self-gift for all, for the forgiveness of sins, empowering a broken people. Through his slight rewriting of the account he found in the Gospel of Mark, Matthew's story of Jesus' presence to the broken at the eucharistic table is more complex. Appearing slightly later than Mark, and in a different setting, Matthew addresses a more complex situation. His Gospel addresses a community where both Jew and Gentile gather at the eucharistic table. Jews and Gentiles are called to recognize that the broken body and the spilt blood of Jesus—"remembered" at the eucharistic table—is for them, for the forgiveness of their sins (26:28).[42]

A new Tradition has begun in the person, teaching, death, and resurrection of Jesus. An essential part of that Tradition was mission to the Gentiles. But this is not the only difficulty the community had to face. In faithfully handing down this new Tradition, Matthew was also concerned to preserve God's gift of the tradition of Israel: the Law and the Prophets. His Gospel insists that the Christian way is a perfection of the ways of God in and through Israel (see 5:17-18; 28:16-20). The community of Jesus is the new Israel, but a total rejection of the past was unacceptable. Both Jew and Gentile, the "old" and the "new," were gathered and nourished at the Table of the Lord. The Church, personified in the disciples and in Peter, came to the same table to be nourished in its brokenness. Across the Gospel story, both Israel and the foundational characters of the Christian community fail. In reporting the Last Supper, Matthew stresses the failure of a disciple called Judas and that of the rest of the disciples along with Peter. But he insists that the blood of the covenant is poured out "for the forgiveness of sins" (26:28). Both the Israel, in which this early Christian community had its birth, and the Gentile mission that now occupies the attention of the disciples in their "little faith" (28:16-20), are nourished at the same Table of the Lord.[43]

NOTES

1   In support of Antioch as the location for the birth of the Gospel of Matthew, and a study of the significance of the city and its Christian community in earliest Christianity, see Raymond E. Brown and John P. Meier, *Antioch and Rome: New Testament Cradles of Catholic Christianity* (New York: Paulist Press, 1983), 12-86. This section was written by Meier.

2   For the general background, see Moloney, *Reading the New Testament in the Church*, 22-44. Among many studies of this period, a balanced survey of this stage in Israel's religious and political history can be found in David M. Rhoads, *Israel in Revolution 6-74 C.E: A Political History Based on the Writings of Josephus* (Philadelphia: Fortress, 1976).

3   This expression comes from Krister Stendahl, *The School of St. Matthew*, 2nd ed. (Philadelphia: Fortress, 1968), xi. Unlike many scholars, I do not think that the main thrust of the Gospel is a "polemic" between Matthew's community and the Synagogue. The separation from the Synagogue, however, created a crisis of identity, and confusion among Matthew's new Christians. A parallel crisis was also experienced by post-war Judaism, now without its Holy City, Temple, cult, priesthood, etc. Israel was also seeking its post-war identity. See William D. Davies, *The Setting of the Sermon on the Mount* (Cambridge: Cambridge University Press, 1966), 256-72; Jacob Neusner, *Ancient Israel after the Catastrophe: The Religious World View of the Mishnah* (Charlottsville: University Press of Virginia, 1983).

4   For a presentation of the overall structure and theology of the Gospel of Matthew, see Moloney, *The Living Voice of the Gospel*, 93-126.

5   David C. Sim, *The Gospel of Matthew and Christian Judaism*, Studies in the New Testament and Its World (Edinburgh: T. & T. Clark, 1998), 252-55, resolves this dilemma by claiming that the Matthean Christians were totally committed to the minutiae of Jewish Law and practice, including circumcision. Less sure, but still suggesting that the practices of Israel were to be continued in the post-resurrection period, are the outstanding commentators, W. D. Davies and Dale C. Allison, *A Critical and Exegetical Commentary on the Gospel of Matthew*, International Critical Commentary, 3 vols. (Edinburgh: T. & T. Clark, 1988-1997), 3:685, and Ulrich Luz, *Matthew*, trans. James E. Crowe, Hermeneia, 3 vols (Minneapolis: Fortress, 2001-2007), 3:631-32.

6   Note that both miracles worked for Gentiles are not to heal the ills of the person making the request. The Centurion and the Canaanite woman plead on behalf of others. This may also be a subtle hint, for the audience, of the need to reach beyond one's own needs into the Gentile mission. See Donald Senior, *Matthew*, Abingdon New Testament Commentaries (Nashville; Abingdon Press, 1998), 97-99, 180-83; Craig S. Keener, *A Commentary on the Gospel of Matthew* (Grand Rapids: Eerdmans, 1999), 268-70, 417-18; Donald Hagner, *Matthew*, Word Biblical Commentary 33-33A, 2 vols. (Dallas: Word, 1993-1995), 1:205-206, 2:443; Luz, *Matthew*, 2:11-12, 341-42.

7   Donald Senior, *The Passion of Jesus in the Gospel of Matthew*, The Passion Series 1 (Wilmington: Michael Glazier, 1985), 157: "These details, most of them typical of Jewish descriptions of the endtime, give Matthew's account an electric charge and reinforce the impression that from the moment of Jesus' obedient death a new and decisive age of salvation has begun." See also Davies and Allison, *Matthew*, 3:628-36, 664-66; Luz, *Matthew*, 3:562-69.

8   For a detailed argument of this interpretation, see John P. Meier, *Law and History in Matthew's Gospel*, Analecta Biblica 71 (Rome: Biblical Institute Press, 1976), 25-40. See also Dale C. Allison, *The End of the Ages Has Come: An Early Interpretation of the Passion and Resurrection of Jesus* (Philadelphia: Fortress, 1985), 40-50.

9   This sentence calls for explanation, which can only be summarily provided here. Matthew is convinced that the movement "across the road" from Synagogue to Christian community was part of God's eternal design, now made possible in and through Jesus Christ. God has not "changed his mind" about his chosen people. Matthew regards the Christian people as "the true Israel." The Synagogue has lost its way, highlighted by its destruction of Jesus. Matthew's regular claim that what happens in Jesus "fulfils" the Scriptures is but one of the ways he shows this (see 1:22-23;

2:5-6, 14-15, 17-18, 23; 3:3, 14). Jesus "fulfils all righteousness." Francis J. Moloney, "Matthew 5:17-18 and the Matthean Use of *dikaiosunē*," in *Unity and Diversity in the Gospels and Paul*, eds. Christopher W. Skinner and Kelly R. Iverson, Early Christianity and Its Literature 7 (Atlanta: SBL, 2012), 33-54.

10   On these questions, see above, p. 12 note 6.

11   A careful examination of Matthew's characters, plot, and rhetoric indicates a different thrust from the Markan narrative structure. On this see Jack D. Kingsbury, *Matthew as Story* (Philadelphia: Fortress Press, 1986). See also Moloney, *The Living Voice of the Gospel*, 107-19.

12   This is regularly pointed out by commentators. For a good survey, see B. Rod Doyle, "Matthew's Intention as Discerned by his Structure," *Revue Biblique* 95 (1988), 39-41.

13   See above, pp. 78-79.

14   On the presentation of Simon Peter in Matthew's Gospel, see Raymond E. Brown, Karl P. Donfried, and John Reumann, eds., *Peter in the New Testament: A Collaborative Assessment by Protestant and Roman Catholic Scholars* (Minneapolis/New York: Augsburg/Paulist, 1973), 75-107. See also the significant recent studies of Martin Hengel, *Saint Peter: The Underestimated Apostle*, trans. Thomas H. Trapp (Grand Rapids: Eerdmans, 2010), and Markus Bockmuel, *Simon Peter in Scripture and Memory* (Grand Rapids: Baker Academic, 2012).

15   For a comprehensive study, see Ulrich Luz, "The Disciples in the Gospel According to Matthew," in Graham Stanton, ed., *The Interpretation of Matthew*, Issues in Religion and Theology 3 (London: SPCK, 1983), 98-128.

16   On this, see Xavier Léon-Dufour, "Présence du Seigneur Ressuscité (Mt 28:16-20)," in *A Cause de l'Evangile: Etudes sur les Synoptiques les Actes offertes: au Père Jacques Dupont, O.S.B: à l'occasion de son 70e anniversaire*, Lectio Divina 123 (Paris: Editions du Cerf, 1985), 195-209. See especially pp. 204-9.

17   For a precise study of the Matthean community, "seeing" yet "doubting," see Eugene A. Laverdiere and William G. Thompson, "New Testament Communities in Transition," *Theological Studies* 37 (1976), 571-82.

18   These so-called "moments" in the narrative are identified by what can be called "textual markers," showing that a new theme is emerging. For example, 1:1 begins the prologue to the story. In 4:17 Jesus formally begins

his proclamation of the advent of the Kingdom (see Mark 1:14-15). Jesus teaching in Galilee is terminated in 11:1, with a passage that looks back to 4:17. 11:2 opens a new section, as Matthew introduces John the Baptist, his question about Jesus, and his execution, which anticipates the execution of Jesus. As mentioned above, 16:13-23 begins the "journey" to Jerusalem with Peter's confession, and Jesus' self-revelation as the Son of Man who must suffer and die in Jerusalem. In 20:21 Jesus and the disciples approach Jerusalem and the Mount of Olives, while in 28:16 Jesus and the disciples assemble at "the mountain to which Jesus had directed them." The flow of the narrative described above, with some minor differences, has also been established (on somewhat different literary grounds) by Frank J. Matera, "The Plot of Matthew's Gospel," *The Catholic Biblical Quarterly* 49 (1987), 233-53. See also Brendan Byrne, *Lifting the Burden: Reading Matthew's Gospel in the Church Today* (Collegeville, MN: The Liturgical Press, 2004), 11-16.

19 I am not attempting any detailed internal structuring of this section of Matthew's Gospel. For a summary of attempts to do so see Jerome Murphy-O'Connor, "The Structure of Matthew XIV-XVII," *Revue Biblique* 82 (1975), 362-71. The bread miracles do not play a crucial role in Murphy-O'Connor's suggested structure. See also Charles H. Talbert, *Matthew*, Paideia Commentaries on the New Testament (Grand Rapids: Baker Academic, 2010), 179-81, for a similar survey. Talbert (pp. 179-200) interprets 13:54-16:20 in three cycles: 13:54-14:36, 15:1-39, and 16:1-20. The two bread miracles play key roles in the first and the second of these cycles.

20 See Kingsbury, *Matthew as Story*, 57-77.

21 Eduard Schweizer, "Matthew's Church," in *The Interpretation of Matthew*, 136: "Peter says and hears in an exemplary way for all disciples … This presents … what every disciple could experience: the courage of faith which at once turns to little faith when wind and wave assail it, and which remains ultimately dependent on the gracious help of its Lord."

22 While commentators see a close literary link between the two Markan bread miracles, this is not the case with Matthew. See, for example, Daniel Patte, *The Gospel According to Matthew: A Structural Commentary on Matthew's Faith* (Philadelphia: Fortress Press, 1987), 223: "Each of the two feeding stories contributes to the development of specific points and themes of the section of the Gospel to which they respectively belong." A majority rejects the suggestion that the Markan use of Jewish and Gentile audiences is in question. Some suggest that the second miracle is a Matthean rewriting

of the first, while others propose two independent but parallel sources were used. See, for example, Keener, *Matthew*, 418-19, who follows the suggestion of Craig Blomberg, *Matthew*, The New American Commentary 22 (Nashville: Broadman Press, 1992), 245, among others, that they imitate the double feeding miracles of Elijah and Elisha. John Nolland, *The Gospel of Matthew*, The New International Greek Testament Commentary (Grand Rapids: Eerdmans, 2005), 642-46, claims that it is the same crowd, and the same occasion (p. 642). Talbert, *Matthew*, 192, suggests that both are directed to Israel, but that the second asks whether the leftovers of the miracle are "a foreshadowing of his benefits to the gentiles (cf. 15:27)." For Senior, *Matthew*, 184, Matthew has his own point of view in the second telling of the miracle story, but it is "unclear" whether it is directed to Gentiles or not. Others accept that it represents a feeding of the Gentiles. See, for example, Joachim Jeremias, *Jesus' Promise to the Nations*, trans. Samuel H. Hooke, Studies in Biblical Theology 24 (London: SCM Press, 1967), 25-39; Frederick W. Beare, *The Gospel According to Matthew* (Oxford: Blackwell, 1981), 344-48; Hagner, *Matthew*, 2:448-52. In strong support of this view, with helpful indications of the narrative links between Matthew's bread stories, see the structure offered by Jean Radermakers, *Au fil de l'évangile selon saint Matthieu*, 2 vols. (Bruxelles: Institut d'Etudes Théologiques, 1974), 1:47-52.

23   It is widely recognized that, although Matthew is using Mark, he has deliberately refashioned the second miracle to bring it closer to the first. Matthew heightens the eucharistic allusions in both and he shows more interest in the disciples and their "little faith." On this, see van Cangh, *La Multiplication des Pains*, 143-48; Bas van Iersel, "Die wunderbare Speisung und das Abendmahl in der synoptischen Tradition (Mk VI 35-44 (par.), VIII 1-20 par.)," *Novum Testamentum* 7 (1964), 192-94; Nolland, *Matthew*, 642-46.

24   Matthew's purpose across this section of the Gospel has been well caught by David E. Garland, *Reading Matthew: A Literary and Theological Commentary* (Macon, GA: Smyth & Helwys, 2001), 161-67. This brief analysis of 15:1-16:12, which does not regard the second bread miracle as directed to Gentiles, is nevertheless entitled "Bread for All." Esler, *Community and Gospel in Luke–Acts*, 91-93, misses Matthew's subtle use of the broader context. He concludes that "his community was composed either exclusively of Jews or exclusively of Gentiles" (p. 92). This hardly accords with the evidence. See, for example, Meier, *Law and History*, 7-24. Whatever one makes of Meier's suggestion that Matthew was a Gentile convert to Judaism (pp. 14-21: not likely), he is correct when he writes of the community as "a Jewish-Christian church becoming increasingly Gentile" (p. 7).

25   See Jeremias, *Jesus' Promise*, 29 note 1; John C. Fenton, *Saint Matthew*, The Pelican New Testament Commentaries (Harmondsworth: Penguin Books, 1963), 257; Robert H. Gundry, *Matthew: A Commentary on His Literary and Theological Art* (Grand Rapids: Eerdmans, 1982), 319; David Hill, *The Gospel of Matthew*, New Century Bible (London: Oliphants, 1972), 255. This suggestion is roundly rejected by Hagner, *Matthew*, 2:446; Luz, *Matthew*, 2:344-45.

26   Beare, *Matthew*, 346. I am aware that I am siding with a minority view here. Some details that lead me to this view are: (1) The heavy focus upon Israel, the disciples, Peter, *and Gentiles* in the narratives that surround the miracle stories (on this, see Byrne, *Lifting the Burden*, 123-24); (2) The Matthean rewriting of Mark 7:31-37 in Matthew 15:29-31. *Both* are located in Gentile territory, and the Gentile use of Isaiah 35 to acclaim Jesus in Mark 7:37 is expanded by the Gentile glorification of the God of Israel in Matthew 15:31 (perhaps echoing Isaiah 29); (3) The elegant replacement of "some of them have come a long way" (Mark 8:3) with "lest they faint on the way" (Matt 15:32); (4) Despite his careful repetition of the earlier account, Matthew does not change the critical number that points to a Gentile world: "seven" (vv. 36, 37); (5) Matthew's retention of Mark's use of distinctive Jewish and Gentile words for "baskets" (Greek: *kophinos* and *spuris*) in 14:20 and 15:37, repeated in 16:9-10 (see Mark 6:43 and 8:8, repeated in 8:19-20). See the discussion of this in Moloney, *The Gospel of Mark*, 155. Richard T. France, *The Gospel of Matthew*, The New International Commentary on the New Testament (Grand Rapids: Eerdmans, 2007), 603, explains the two words for the baskets as "a merely stylistic variation," adding that the baskets of 16:38 might be bigger. Why, if the numbers present and the fragments collected are less? If, as the commentators consistently claim, the Jewish-Gentile inclusion has been *carefully* eliminated (see, for example, Davies and Allison, *Matthew*, 2:558), why do these details remain? Matthew is too careful to leave these details in place if his purpose was to change the Markan use of the bread miracles as feeding both Jew and Gentile. On what evidence does Luz, *Matthew*, 2:344, claim that Jesus returns to the Jewish side of the lake? There is not the slightest indication of this in the text. On the contrary, moving on from the district of Tyre and Sidon (15:21), passing along by the Galilee of the Gentiles (15:29), Jesus fulfils Isaiah 9:1-2. He is on the Gentile side of the lake.

27   For an excellent study of Matthew 15:29-31, see Terence L. Donaldson, *Jesus on the Mountain: A Study in Matthean Theology*, Journal for the Study of the New Testament Supplement Series 8 (Sheffield: JSOT Press, 1985), 122-35. Like most, Donaldson differs from my interpretation by concluding that

Gentiles are excluded from the miracle and the meal of 15:29-39, and thus the tension between Jesus' mission to "the lost sheep of the house of Israel" and "all nations" is only partially resolved (see pp. 131-35). See the response from Hagner, *Matthew*, 2:445, and my previous note.

28   BDF, 166-67.

29   See BDF, 166-67, 169. This change of tenses in Matthew's use of the verb "to give" is never raised by the commentators (see, for example, Davies and Allison, *Matthew*, 2:491, 573; Luz, *Matthew*, 2:314, 345). Without further ado, Luz comments: "He repeats those words from the first feeding" (p. 345). This is not true as the change in tense makes a difference. This issue can be added to the details given above in note 26 that call for closer attention.

30   This is well caught by Radermakers, *Au fil de l'évangile de saint Matthieu*, 2:213: "The meal table is now accessible to everyone, even the Gentiles, as long as they recognize in faith that the salvation which has been given to them comes through the people of Israel and is perfected in Jesus. The children of Israel, in their own turn, grasping the messianic significance of the cures which Jesus works, can come to the Eucharistic table, that of the desert (14:13, 15) given to the twelve tribes. But it is also open to the whole of history, symbolised by the number 'seven,' which gathers all peoples to nourish them, through the intervention of the disciples, with bread which prevents their failing on the way." Garland, *Reading Matthew*, 161-67, catches this well in his section, "bread for all."

31   The Matthean Jesus does not abandon or abolish "the old," for which he has great respect. See Reinhard Neudecker, *Moses Interpreted by the Pharisees and Jesus: Matthew's Antitheses in the Light of Early Rabbinic Literature*, Subsidia Biblica 44 (Rome: Gregorian and Biblical Press, 2012), who shows Matthew's coherence with Rabbinic discussions. As always in works of this nature, the dating of the Rabbinic material can be problematic.

32   The dependence of Matthew upon Mark for the passion narrative is "hardly controversial." Luz, *Matthew*, 3:301 sums up the consensus: "The Markan passion and Easter narrative is the only written source for Matthew 26-28 as a whole." I am offering a macro-structure of the overall narrative. In smaller detail (especially in vv. 36-46) there is a further interplay between Jesus' openness to God and the disciples' failure. See Theissen and Merz, *The Historical Jesus*, 416-17, for the peculiarities of Matthew's words of institution. The overall succession of events, as given here, is also identified by Hagner, *Matthew*, 2:751. He does not make the contrast between the darkness of failure and the light of Jesus' self-revelation.

33 The one occasion in Matthew where the failure of the disciples is shifted elsewhere is in Matthew's rewriting of the request of the sons of Zebedee, James and John, for positions on his right and left when he comes to his glory (Mark 10:35-40). Matthew eases the arrogance of the two disciples by having their mother make the request (Matt 20:20-21). For the rest, although in different ways, they match Mark's disciples in their inability to follow Jesus unconditionally. Like the Markan disciples, at the arrest of Jesus they forsake Jesus and flee (26:56).

34 Doyle, "Matthew's Intention as Discerned by his Structure," 47. See also Luz, "The Disciples," in *The Interpretation of Matthew*, 99-104.

35 See Kingsbury, *Matthew as Story*, 86-87.

36 Commenting on Matthew's version of the supper, and its relationship to Mark's Gospel, Robbins, "Last Meal," 22, comments that "the verbal agreement indicates direct copying." For a detailed study of Matthew's dependence upon Mark, see Donald Senior, *The Passion Narrative According to Matthew: A Redactional Study*, Bibliotheca Ephemeridum Theologicarum Lovaniensium XXXIX (Louvain: Leuven University Press, 1975), 66-99.

37 See, for example, Léon-Dufour, *Sharing the Eucharistic Bread*, 148; Hill, *The Gospel of Matthew*, 339; Eduard Schweizer, *The Good News according to Matthew* (London, SPCK, 1976), 491; John P. Meier, *Matthew*, New Testament Message 3 (Wilmington, DE: Michael Glazier, 1980), 319-20; Hagner, *Matthew*, 2:773; Davies and Allison, *Matthew*, 3:474-75.

38 Meier, *Matthew*, 320. See also Byrne, *Lifting the Burden*, 204-6.

39 The obviously important historical study of what the words and actions of Jesus at the meal meant historically (diachronically) should not lead us to lose sight of what they mean in their present Gospel context (synchronically).

40 Luz, *Matthew*, 3:381-82. Emphasis mine. Ulrich Luz's commentary upon Jesus' death and resurrection, accompanied by a moving analysis of the art (including many reproductions from different eras in the history of art), Christian theological traditions, music, community practices, and devotions that find their roots there in *Matthew*, 3:297-644, is superlative. It is unparalleled in the contemporary literature. It deserves to be extracted from the three-volume Hermeneia commentary and published as a stand-alone volume.

41 Doyle, "Matthew's Intention as Discerned by his Structure," 47. See pp. 51-53 on the importance of the theme of "being-with" for Matthew's Church (i.e. "disciples").

42   See Keener, *Gospel of Matthew*, 626-27. He concludes: "Disciples who experience redemption freely by God's kindness must not forget the great cost of that redemption."

43   See Luz, *Matthew*, 3:383-85.

CHAPTER FIVE

THE GOSPEL OF LUKE

The Gospel of Luke is a remarkable voice from the earliest decades of the Christian Tradition.[1] Many of the great "stories from the New Testament" come to us from this Gospel: the Good Samaritan (Luke 10:25-37), Martha and Mary (10:38-42), the Prodigal Son (15:11-32), Dives and Lazarus (16:19-31), the Pharisee and the Tax Collector (18:9-14), Zacchaeus in his tree (19:1-10), and the journey to Emmaus (24:13-35). When we celebrate Christmas, we largely recall the Lukan story of the annunciation, birth, and infancy of Jesus, closely associated with the annunciation, birth, and infancy of John the Baptist.[2] It is full of wonders as an old priest loses and then regains his speech, and angels sing praise to God from on high. There is the joy of a virgin mother, the meeting of two expectant mothers, aware that their fruitfulness is a gift of God, and shepherds from the fields, summoned to the side of a newly born King of Israel (1:1-2:52). The darker shades of Matthew 1-2 hardly appear. The Wise Men from the East are the only Matthean characters to appear in our Christmas pageantry.[3]

As these few examples demonstrate, memorable stories abound in the Gospel of Luke; the lasting impressions those stories have made upon centuries of Christian tradition show the ability of the author to create impressive narratives.[4] We must not underestimate the skills of the authors of the Gospels of Mark and Matthew; as we have seen, both have composed literary works of great power. Nevertheless, the Gospel of Luke outclasses them with a succession of unforgettable and original stories, found only in this Gospel. Respect for Luke's story-telling ability can be traced in its widespread use in both the literary and pictorial traditions of Western culture.[5]

Scholars look behind the Gospel of Mark to identify the traditions he received.[6] As we have seen in our study of Matthew's use of Mark's eucharistic tradition, the Gospel of Matthew used Mark and other sources (e.g. "Q," and material unique to Matthew) to develop his own point of view. Although Luke also uses Mark and "Q," the task of identifying the remaining sources for the third Gospel is not so simple. Scholars debate whether such traditional parts of the story of Jesus as his death and resurrection have been told by Luke on the basis of Mark, or whether the narrator is telling quite a different story.[7] Nowadays, most are happy to accept that, generally speaking, the Gospel of Luke has Mark, Q, and unique Lukan traditions as sources, but that he used them very creatively.[8]

The passages in the Gospel of Luke that are overtly or covertly eucharistic display these creative characteristics. As well as the single account of the feeding of the multitude (Luke 9:10-17), and that of the Last Supper (22:14-38), the third Gospel added the dramatic events of the journey to Emmaus on Easter Day (24:13-35) to the Gospel traditions that speak of Jesus' presence to his disciples through the Eucharist. The final encounter between Jesus and all the disciples in Jerusalem (24:36-52) also contains hints of Eucharist. Our study to this point has uncovered a certain consistency—despite major differences in the points of view being articulated—regarding the Jesus' self-giving presence to the frail and to sinners across 1 Corinthians and the Gospels of Mark and Matthew. This chapter traces Luke's special rendering of these traditions, and their further use in material unique to the Lukan Gospel. It is helpful to test whether the author of the third Gospel remains faithful to the early Church's Tradition concerning the presence of Jesus to his disciples (the Church) in the Eucharist.

THE MULTIPLICATION OF THE LOAVES

Mark and Matthew both report two miracles in which Jesus fed the multitudes. The Gospel of Luke has only one (Luke 9:10-17).[9] In both Mark and Matthew, Jesus associates the disciples closely with himself in the nourishing of the crowds through the distribution of bread (see Mark 6:37, 41; 8:6; Matt 14:16, 19; 15:36). Both accounts are written to recall the community's celebration of the Eucharist, especially in the description of the gestures of Jesus with the bread: taking, raising his eyes, blessing, breaking, and giving. We have reflected upon the Markan and Matthean accounts within their wider literary context, linking the two miracles of the bread with their wider "story," devoting attention to what happens before and after the actual accounts of the bread miracles. Mark and Matthew use the bread stories to address divisions and potential sinfulness in their respective Churches. By looking back upon the failures from the story of Jesus, the Evangelists are able to address the problems of division and a temptation to exclude others in an early Christian community, especially when it came to sharing the eucharistic table. The theme of the presence of the eucharistic Jesus to his fragile disciples is never used to chide or discourage. On the contrary, it is used to exhort and encourage failing disciples, both in the "then" of the story of Jesus, and in the "now" of the early Christian communities addressed by Mark and Matthew. These inspired texts from Scripture have continued to do so across the centuries.

The Lukan version of this event makes a very different point. To start with, Luke locates the bread miracle at a stage in his account where he has eliminated a long sequence from the Markan story. The events of Mark 6:44-8:26 report Jesus' hostile encounter with the leaders of Israel about what makes a person clean or unclean (7:1-23). In two journeys across the sea he warns his failing disciples about the dangers of their hardness of heart and their blindness (6:45-52; 8:14-21). Scholars generally refer to this feature of the Gospel of Luke as "the great omission." As we have seen, within that section, Mark (repeated by Matthew [Matt 14:22-16:12]), heightens the contrast and conflict between Jesus and Israel. Jesus moves from Israel into the Gentile world, challenging hesitant disciples to do the same. In contrast to our study of the two bread stories in Mark and Matthew, it is the so-called Lukan "great omission" that provides the wider context for the bread miracle.

Luke's two volumes were written in and for a Gentile world. One of the several issues that concerned these early Gentile Christians was the question of their origins within the Christian movement.[10] Subsequently, an important theme in both the Gospel of Luke and the Acts of the Apostles is the founding significance of the Apostles. Far flung from the "beginnings" of the Christian movement, these Christians needed to be shown how they belonged to those beginnings, and that they had every reason to be confident about the message that had been handed on to them (see 1:1-4).[11] One of Luke's methods for doing this is his close association of the disciples with Jesus throughout his ministry. Across Luke–Acts disciples are deliberately presented as repeating the experiences of Jesus in their own Christian lives.[12] These disciples were the "apostles" eventually responsible for bringing the person and teaching of Jesus Christ to all the nations (see Luke 24:46-47; Acts 1:8). Although the term "apostle" had already been used in its Christian sense by Paul (see, for example, Rom 1:1; 11:13; 1 Cor 1:1; 15:9; Gal 1:1, 17, 19), it is hardly found in the Gospels of Mark and Matthew.[13] But it is very important for the Gospel of Luke and the Acts of the Apostles. The noun—from the Greek verb *apostellein,* meaning "to send out"—is applied to the Twelve Apostles, the original missionaries who form the foundation of the post-Easter Church (see Luke 6:13). They were the link between the Church of the time of Luke and the time of Jesus himself (see, for example, Luke 24:44-49; Acts 1:15-26).[14]

Luke 9:1-50 closes the first section of the Gospel and opens the second, as Jesus turns toward Jerusalem (v. 51). It is dominated by narratives that prepare for the crucial future role of the "apostles." At this turning point in the Lukan narrative, Luke focuses upon them as they receive important instruction concerning the person of Jesus and their own destiny, before they set out with Jesus on the road to Jerusalem (see 9:51: "When the days drew near for him to be taken up, he set his face to go to Jerusalem," and the association of the disciples with Jesus' journey in vv. 52-56).[15]

This turning point in the story opens with the Twelve being instructed by Jesus for their mission. They are then sent out (Luke 9:1-6; see also Mark 6:6b-13). While they are away, the perplexity of Herod over the person of Jesus, told in such lurid detail in Mark (Mark 6:14-29), is reduced to a minimum (Luke 9:7-9).[16] Luke focuses the audience's attention on Herod's question about the person of Jesus. Herod asks: "Who is this about whom I hear such things?" (v. 9). The apostles return and the bread miracle follows (vv. 10-17).[17] Luke's juxtaposition of Herod's question against Jesus' miracle serves partly to respond to Herod's question: he is a worker of great signs, able to nourish the multitudes; but there is more.

As in the Gospels of Mark and Matthew, Luke associated the disciples with the nourishing of the multitudes (9:13, 16). However, there is an important difference in some of the details. In both Mark and Matthew they are called "the disciples" (Mark 6:35; Matt 14:15), but in Luke 9:12 they are called "the twelve." The episode at Emmaus is foreshadowed as the eucharistic moment takes place "as the day began to wear away" (v. 12. See 24:29).[18] "The twelve" ask Jesus to send the people away (v. 12), but he commands them: "You give them something to eat" (v. 13). Jesus takes from the poverty of their five loaves and two fish, looks up to heaven, blesses, breaks, "and gave them to the disciples to set before the crowd" (v. 16). After the feeding, with its obvious eucharistic overtones (v. 16: take, look up to heaven, blessed, broke, gave, to set before the crowd), twelve baskets remain.[19] As Joseph A. Fitzmyer has commented, "The 'twelve' baskets obviously has a symbolic reference to the 'Twelve' in v. 12; they each bring back a basketful and now have enough to feed still others."[20] Luke's vision of founding apostles, and their association with Jesus in this ministry of nourishing the people, is very important for his re-telling of the traditional story of the feeding of the multitudes. The association of "the twelve" in the story of Jesus "then" speaks to a Church looking back to trace its roots in the life of Jesus to make sense of its "now."[21] "Jesus, the divine shepherd, feeds the true Israel of his followers by the hand of their leaders, his ministers."[22]

Further answers to Herod's question are next provided by Peter's confession that Jesus is "the Christ of God" (v. 20), complemented by the voice from heaven announcing that Jesus, who converses with two other figures from Israel's sacred past who have ascended to heaven, Moses and Elijah, is "my Son, my Chosen" (v. 35). Some of the apostles—Peter, James, and John—witness this (vv. 28, 32-33). Driving out the demon, which was *beyond the authority of the disciples*, leads to dismay and "all were astonished at the majesty of God" (vv. 37-43).[23] This series of revelations, responding to the question posed by Herod in v. 9 comes to a conclusion when Jesus solemnly announces to the disciples: "Let these words sink into your ears; for the Son of Man is to be delivered into the hands of men" (v. 44).

Titles of honor and indications of the ultimate authority of Jesus do not tell the entire story. There is always a clear indication that such honor and authority come only through the experience of the Cross. It is not enough to "marvel at everything" (v. 43b). This crucial moment of preparation of the disciples, before they set out with Jesus for Jerusalem, instructs them that they are following Jesus to suffering and death in Jerusalem. This awareness is demanded from them by the words of Jesus that only Luke reports: "Let these words sink into your ears" (v. 44). There is a deliberate association of the disciples with Jesus throughout the gradual revelation of Jesus' person, dignity … and destiny. As well as being the recipients of this revelation, threaded through the entire narrative one finds explicit instructions to the disciples (see vv. 1-6, 23-27, 46-50). Climaxing the first half of the Gospel and opening the second, the narrator announces: "When the days drew near for him to be received up, he set his face to go to Jerusalem. And he sent messengers ahead of him" (v. 51). The future founding apostles of the Churches have now been instructed on their task, and they have been shown who it is they are following. They set out for Jerusalem together with Jesus (see vv. 52-56).

This overview of Luke 9:1-50 shows that the themes that were developed around the Markan and Matthean accounts of the bread miracles are not found in the Gospel of Luke. The absence of Mark 6:44-8:27//Matthew 14:22-16:12 (the so-called "great omission"), indicates to an audience familiar with the stories of the other Synoptic Gospels that Luke wants to say something different in his use of the tradition of the miracle of the loaves and fish.[24] Luke's closing section of the Galilean ministry (9:1-50) is highlighted by the instruction of the future twelve apostles.[25] But there are three further significant meals in this Gospel: the meal shared by Jesus and the apostles on the day of the Unleavened Bread (22:7, 14-38), a meal that Jesus shares at Emmaus with two of his disciples (24:13-35), and a final meal with "the eleven" who have remained in Jerusalem (24:36-49). The story of these meals will be told to show that apostles and disciples—who had been given privileged access to a deeper understanding of who Jesus was and what he was about to do in 9:1-50—did not always live up to the instructions they received in those days before they set out for Jerusalem (vv. 51-56). Despite the uniqueness of the Lukan version of the Last Supper—the account of the journey to Emmaus, and back to Jerusalem, and the final instruction of the disciples, before Jesus' ascension—the Tradition of the eucharistic presence of Jesus to fragile disciples returns.[26]

THE LAST SUPPER

The Gospel of Luke contains an account of the disciples' last meal with Jesus (22:14-38) that is strikingly different from that of Mark 14:17-31 and Matthew 26:14-35. It is accepted that Luke was probably not depending upon the Gospel of Mark for this part of the story, but worked creatively with other sources.[27] Thus, rather than a tracing a use of possible sources, contemporary scholarship focuses upon this narrative as a special example of Luke's literary skills. Two themes in particular seem to be intertwined in this account. Throughout the Gospel of Luke there is a notable interest in food and meals.[28] This theme comes to a climax in the final meal celebrated with the twelve before Jesus dies (22:14-38), and in the meal that the risen Lord shares with those same apostles, less Judas (24:36-49). A further unique feature of the Lukan Last Supper is its setting within a long "final discourse" that Jesus delivers to his disciples.[29]

LUKAN MEALS

The supper recorded in 22:14-38 brings to a climax a long series of suppers through the Gospel. These suppers are consistently marked by Jesus' questioning the status quo: he shares the table with sinners, and he radically questions the Pharisees on the numerous occasions where he is reported to have been invited to dine with them.[30]

Jesus shared a meal with Levi, the sinful tax collector. More than that, there were other sinners at the table who had been gathered by Levi to share fellowship with Jesus (5:27-32). Invited as "a prophet" (see 7:39) to share the table with another important religious figure, Simon the Pharisee, Jesus shows that his love cannot be contained within the limitations of conventional religion. He allows and even encourages the intimacy of a woman well-known for her sins (7:37). Her love has drawn her to the table and to Jesus' forgiveness (7:36-50). Again at table with the Pharisees, he challenges them to recognize their lack of true justice (11:37-54). He uses a further meal with the Pharisees to heal the disadvantaged man with dropsy on a Sabbath, to question the way the Pharisees "religiously" organized their meals, and to urge them to follow his example: "When you give a feast, invite the poor, the maimed, the lame, the blind, and you will be blessed because they cannot repay you" (14:14. See 14: 1-24).

The challenge that Jesus issues through the sharing of meals and his questioning of the status quo within the context of these meals is important for a proper understanding of the Lukan "point of view." As with all four Gospels, Luke tells of Jesus' words and actions in the "then" of what is technically called the "narrated time," that is, the Gospel's reporting of the life and times of Jesus, to question the "now" of current Christian practice. Commenting on Luke's parable of the great supper (14:16-24), John R. Donahue concludes:

> Within Christian communities, some of the most violent debates continue to rage over inclusiveness, often centered on the celebration of the Lord's Supper. Yet when Luke's Jesus told a parable about eating bread in the kingdom of God, he shattered his hearer's expectations of who would be the proper table companions. Can his parabolic word continue to challenge our expectations?[31]

The final eloquent witness to this important Lukan theme is found in 19:1-10. In an episode that both looks back across the rest of the Gospel for its meaning, and points forward to the final days of Jesus' presence, Jesus' encounter and meal with Zacchaeus is a fitting climax to his journey toward the city of Jerusalem. This is the city from which Jesus would be "taken up" (see 9:31, 51), and equally the place from which the disciples would be sent out to the ends of the earth (see Acts 1:8). As Jesus approaches Jerusalem he catches sight of Zacchaeus. Despite the murmuring opposition of the people standing by, Jesus publicly announces that he will stay and dine with Zacchaeus, a chief tax collector, a notorious sinner. In his own turn, Zacchaeus commits himself to the way of Jesus by promising to give half his possessions to the poor. Christology and discipleship blend in a reciprocal gift of self to the broken ones.[32]

Jerome Neyrey has commented on the function of Jesus' shared meals within the Lukan narrative strategy:

> Jesus' inclusive table fellowship mirrors the inclusive character of the Lukan Church: Gentiles, prostitutes, tax collectors, sinners, as well as the blind, lame, maimed and the poor are welcome at his table and in his covenant.[33]

This Gospel permits no illusions about the composition of the Church of Jesus Christ. It is not made up of "perfect people." On the contrary, it is made up of people who have become Christians because they have been the recipients of the apostles' witnessing to the person and message of Jesus (see 24:45-48). The risen Christ commissions his apostles:

> Thus it is written that the Christ should suffer and on the third day rise from the dead, and that repentance and forgiveness of sins should be preached in his name to all nations, beginning from Jerusalem. You are witnesses of these things. And behold I send the promise of my Father upon you; but stay in the city until you are clothed with power from on high. (24:46-49. See also Acts 1:8)

It is from this background of meals shared with sinners that we can best understand 22:14: "And when the hour came, he sat at table and the apostles with him."[34] Despite the importance for the overall argument of Luke–Acts that the apostles must play an essential and foundational role on the other side of the death and resurrection of Jesus, they too share this final meal with their Master as sinners and broken people. They are the last of a long group of broken and sinful people who have shared meals with Jesus during his life and ministry.

Luke understands "the broken" gathering at the Table of the Lord more broadly and more boldly than Mark and Matthew. It is not a question of Gentile and Jew sharing a table founded upon disciples who had failed Jesus. From the heart of a largely Gentile Church, Luke's Jesus-story has little interest in those questions. The third Gospel goes to some lengths to show that there are many ways in which one can be considered an "outsider." Indeed, for Luke, they are specially blessed (see 6:20-23). There are those who are guilty of sin, like the prostitute and the tax-collector, and there are Pharisees who suffer from their self-righteousness. There are disciples who fail Jesus through the weakness of their faith, and there are members of the twelve who deny him (Peter) and who betray him (Judas). Finally there are the Gentiles, the materially poor, and the physically maimed people from the highways and the byways who are all welcomed at the table of Jesus.[35]

Within this broad canvas of broken people who are offered the possibility of a real salvation through sharing meals with Jesus, the apostles will be able to give eloquent witness to repentance and forgiveness of sins to all the nations (24:47). Their own lives as followers and apostles of Jesus result from such an experience. They experience the repentance and forgiveness to which they eventually bear witness.[36] As Philip Esler has shown, Jesus' practice of sharing meals with outcasts will be continued by the apostles themselves in the second volume of these two "books" addressed to Theophilus (see Luke 1:3-4; Acts 1:1), the Acts of the Apostles. While the theme of Jesus' acceptance and forgiveness of the broken highlights his table in the Gospel, the early Church's acceptance of the Gentiles marks the tables shared by the apostles in the Acts of the Apostles. Commenting on the conversion of Cornelius in Acts 10:1-11:18, Esler comments: "What matters to Luke is the legitimation of complete fellowship between Jew and Gentile in the Christian community, not just the admission of the Gentiles to those communities."[37] Apostles who have experienced forgiveness and admission to the Table of the Lord are able to preach and practice such a mission to other "outsiders."

THE LAST MEAL

The theme of Jesus' presence to the broken and the sinful throughout the Gospel—which stands as the basis of what the apostles will witness to the ends of the earth—reaches its high point at the Last Supper. "This final meal on the feast of Passover crowns the meals, both everyday and festive, which he has taken with his disciples and with sinners during his earthly life."[38] The theme of meals celebrated by Jesus is continued into the Last Meal. We have already seen that Mark used a pattern of alternating the actions of Jesus and the failure of the disciples in Mark 14:1-71, and that this literary pattern was repeated in Matthew 26:3-75.[39] Those carefully arranged narratives told the story of the last moments of Jesus' unfailing presence to his failing disciples. Luke may have been aware of this pattern, as he also appears to use a similar alternating pattern in the construction of Luke 22:14-38.

In the Lukan account of the Last Supper there is an alternation, on the one hand, between Jesus' teaching about the establishment of the Kingdom through his death and resurrection and the apostles' involvement in it, and on the other hand, explicit indications of the future betrayal and denial of these same apostles. The passage can be presented as follows:

A]—22:14-18: The sharing of the first cup, and the promise of the fulfillment of the Kingdom.

B]—vv. 19-23: The account of the meal and the prediction of the betrayal of Judas.[40]

A]—vv. 24-30: The part that the disciples will play in the Kingdom.

B]—vv. 31-34: The prayer of Jesus for Peter, but the prophecy that he will yet deny Jesus.

A]—vv. 35-38: The difficulties that will confront the disciples in their future mission.[41]

The alternation of themes is present and this enables Luke to continue the tradition contrasting Jesus' gracious self-gift with those to whom he offers it: his disciples, made up of a betrayer, a denier, and others who are unable to understand. This contrast is present also in Mark and Matthew.

There are, however, many differences between the Markan and the Lukan schemes. We find another literary form lies behind Luke 22:14-38. It is also a discourse during which Jesus addresses his final words to his disciples. But Luke 22:14-38 is *not only* a farewell discourse.[42] In Mark 14:1-71, we found the blending of direct speech and narrative, but the Lukan development of the theme of the failure of the apostles is all-pervading. It is not only found in those passages dedicated specifically to it (vv. 19-23, 31-34).

Here one senses the skill of the story-teller. The sinners are strongly present. We read in v. 21: "the hand of him who betrays me is with me on the table." This ominous note sets the tone. The obtuseness and brokenness of the apostles in general are indicated through the report of a dispute (v. 24). Peter's betrayal is predicted (v. 34). It is reported that the apostles will need "strengthening" (v. 32), implying that they are weak and frail. They seem, moreover, to misunderstand Jesus' missionary instructions in vv. 35-38. While Jesus hints of the trials, imprisonments, persecutions, and death that await the apostolic mission, and which indeed take place in the Acts of the Apostles, they take his symbol of a "sword" literally. This leads to Jesus' comment to close all such discussion: "Enough!" (v. 38).[43] Thomas W. Manson has described this final reaction of Jesus to his failing disciples as "the utterance of a broken heart."[44]

Jesus' table includes Judas, his betrayer, Peter, who denied him, and the squabbling and obtuse apostles. Jesus eats with people who fail, even at the Last Supper. Although handled with more subtlety than Mark or Matthew, the presence of Jesus to his disciples at the Last Supper is even more markedly a presence to the broken. This theme, which has highlighted so many of the meal scenes throughout the Gospel, has been drawn to a fitting conclusion in 22:14-38. The disciples will be worthy candidates for the future mission, witnessing to repentance and the forgiveness of sins to all the nations (24:47).[45]

The motley group that shares the Table of the Lord, and which indicates how this table should be administered in the Church, has been well described by Markus Barth:

> Whoever sits at table with Jesus must also accept the other guests in Christ's company. Jesus is never without his elect, including especially the outcast. No one can have Jesus for oneself alone; Jesus is met with a strange entourage—the publicans and the sinners, the poor and the bums from the hedges and byways, a notorious woman whom Jesus permitted to touch his feet, the prodigal sons and such treacherous and cowardly disciples as Judas and Peter and the other disciples who partook of Jesus' last meal (none of whom loved him enough to arrange his funeral). Whoever considers those table companions of Jesus too bad, too base, too little, too far removed from salvation to be met at Jesus' side does not see, accept, and believe Jesus as he really is. Whoever feels too good and too noble to be found in that company cannot sit at the Lord's table. Only when the bums just mentioned have been received and waited upon is Jesus received, and only then does Jesus accept the service rendered to him.[46]

A MEAL THAT IS ALSO A FAREWELL DISCOURSE

The other important feature of Luke 22:14-38 noticed by recent scholarship is the presence of a literary form described as a "farewell speech." We have already seen that the structured presentation of the text differs from the Markan use of a similar pattern of alternating themes. This is due, largely, to the fact that the Lukan report of the Last Supper is *not only* a narrative about a shared meal, *but also* a final discourse. The deliberate use of this widely recognized literary form indicates that while early Christian Tradition of the Last Supper is being recalled, a unique literary form is utilized.[47] But this literary form does not override the essential message of Jesus' presence to his disciples revealed across all the New Testament accounts of the final meal. The form of a final testament, associated with the Tradition of Jesus' unfailing presence to his fragile disciples, produces a narrative that is testamentary in literary form, but it is not *only* a final testament.[48]

In Mark 14:1-71, the account of Jesus' words and actions with the bread and wine at the final meal formed the centerpiece of the passage (14:17-31). This not the case in the Gospel of Luke. It forms part of the second section of the structure (22:19-23), dedicated to the prophecy of the betrayal of Judas. Luke 22:14-38 is not primarily about Jesus' eucharistic words. It is about the last testimony that Jesus left his disciples, within the context of a meal, as he parted from them. As Paul Minear has commented, "In this story the center of gravity lies not in the words of institution but, as at earlier tables, in the four key dialogues between Jesus and the disciples."[49]

The practice of placing a "farewell speech" on the lips of a great man as he goes to his death is a reasonably common practice in many religious writings from the first three centuries of the Christian era.[50] It is particularly widespread in the biblical literature.[51] In the Old Testament we find farewell speeches in Genesis 47-50 (Jacob), in Joshua 23-24 (Joshua), and in Deuteronomy 31-34 (Moses). In fact, the whole of the Book of Deuteronomy can be regarded as Moses' farewell speech. In the New Testament, Paul gives a farewell speech at Miletus (Acts 20:17-35), and Peter is portrayed as giving a farewell speech (2 Peter 1:12-15). Jesus delivers a form of a farewell speech in Luke 22:14-38 and in John 14:1-16:33. There is considerable interest on the part of New Testament scholars in a series of Jewish testamentary texts where this technique is used, especially *The Testaments of the Twelve Patriarchs*, which has its origins in the second century BCE, modeled on Jacob's last words in Genesis 49.[52]

The main features of a farewell speech find correspondence in Luke 22:14-38. The Lukan report of Jesus' last meal with his disciples, as well as being a development of the tradition of Jesus' final meal with his disciples, can also be seen as a good example of the final discourse genre.[53] There are four elements fundamental to this form:

1. Prediction of death. The speech is understood by the patriarch, who is about to depart, as his "farewell" to his disciples. Thus there is some indication or prediction of his oncoming death in all of the testaments. In some cases, the death is unexpected (*Testament of Levi* 1:2; *Testament of Naphtali* 1:2-4; *Testament of Asher* 1:2). This prediction serves as the occasion for the speech. In the *Lukan Last Supper discourse*, this is found in 22:15, "I have earnestly desired to eat this passover with you before I suffer," and in 22:22, "For the Son of Man goes as it has been determined." Earlier references to the future suffering, death, and resurrection of the Son of Man (9:22, 44; 18:31-33) leave no doubt in the audience's mind that a departure through death is imminent.

2. Predictions of future attacks upon the dying leader's disciples. This feature of the farewell speech is also basic to its structure. One of the motivations for the speech is to forewarn disciples that they are in imminent danger. Most of the testaments portray this imminent danger as a sign of the end time. In the Lukan Last Supper discourse this feature is found in 22:31-34: "I have prayed for you that your faith may not fail; and when you have turned again, strengthen your brethren … I tell you, Peter, the cock will not crow this day, until you three times deny that you know me." It is also present in 22:36: "Now let him who has a purse take it, and likewise a bag. And let him who has no sword sell his mantle and buy one." Here, as elsewhere, we find the blending of the tradition concerning the denials of Peter, and its use as a warning in the testament.

3. An exhortation to ideal behavior. The testaments devote a lot of attention to the difficulties to be endured in the future. They are to be met with a behavior that will both protect the members of the group from danger and help them overcome their difficulties. In the *Lukan Last Supper discourse*, there is again the intrusion of the uniquely Lukan use of his meal theme, where failing disciples are the object of his exhortation. The meal Tradition and the testamentary form blend. The instruction to ideal behavior of the "farewell discourse" is found within the context of disciples who squabble (22:24).[54] The exhortation then follows in vv. 25-26:

"The kings of the Gentiles exercise lordship over them; and those in authority over them are called benefactors. But not so with you; rather let the greatest among you become as the youngest, and the leader as one who serves." (See the whole of vv. 24-27.)

4. A final commission. Instructions are given to the disciples of the departing patriarch concerning their reconstitution after his departure. In the *Lukan Last Supper discourse* the blending of the traditional theme of Jesus' presence to the broken at the meal table again intrudes, as it is within the context of a future denial that Peter is commissioned (vv. 33-34). Nevertheless, even though the commission is delivered to failing disciples, it still stands. The apostles are to continue what he has left with them, even after his departure. This is found in Luke 22:31-32:

"Simon, Simon, behold Satan demanded to have you that he might sift you like wheat, but I have prayed for you that your faith may not fail; and when you have turned again, strengthen your brethren."[55]

The Lukan use of the theme of the meal has served to show that Jesus shared his Last Supper with broken disciples, while the use of the literary form of a farewell discourse establishes them as his legitimate successors. Both themes are important for Luke. His skilful narrative has enabled the blending of the traditional meal theme and the literary pattern of a farewell speech.[56] By intermingling both, Luke has been able to continue the tradition found in Mark and Matthew: the presence of Jesus to the broken and sinful disciples. But he has also been able to reinforce an important Tradition within the Gentile settling of the Lukan Church: the disciples and apostles are the legitimate successors of Jesus of Nazareth.

The disciples are instructed and commissioned in the midst of failure (see especially vv. 31-38). Luke has produced a singular example of the farewell discourse form. Jesus' disciples, despite the brokenness of their table fellowship with the Lord, are also the apostles, the ones who will continue his presence "to all nations" (24:47; Acts 1:8).[57] A departing Jesus commissions failing disciples in a farewell discourse delivered at the last of a long series of meals that Jesus has shared with broken people. The message is clear:

Jesus will not distance himself from them because they fail him. The keynote of his ministry, and especially his table fellowship has been "He was reckoned with transgressors" (Is 53:12; Lk 22:37), both by his own desire and the will of his persecutors (see 23:32). And he will continue to share his life with sinners in the kingdom meals of the time of the Church.[58]

THE JOURNEY TO EMMAUS— AND THE RETURN TO JERUSALEM

The Gospels of Mark and Matthew both promise the reconstitution of a disbanded and failed group of disciples "on the other side" of Jesus' death and resurrection. They do this within the context of the Last Supper: "I shall not drink again of the fruit of the vine, until that day when I drink it new in the kingdom of God" (Mark 14:25; Matt 26:29). Neither Mark nor Matthew reports a scene after the resurrection where this promise is fulfilled. It was not needed as the prophecy points to the actual celebration of the Eucharist as it was practiced in both the Markan and the Matthean communities.

In the Gospel of Luke, Jesus makes such a prediction on two occasions (Luke 22:16 and 18). Luke, however, goes further than either Mark or Matthew by reporting two occasions when the risen Jesus shares a meal with his disciples. The first of these meal scenes is recorded in Luke 24:13-35: the journey to Emmaus. All the episodes of the resurrection account are linked by an insistence that everything took place on the one day. The account opens with the naming of a given day: "On the first day of the week" (24:1). The reader is next told, "That very same day two of them were going to a village named Emmaus" (v. 13). Toward the end of their journey, Jesus' fellow-travelers say: "Stay with us for it is towards evening and the day is now far spent" (v. 29). After the breaking of the bread, "They rose that same hour and returned to Jerusalem." They make their report, but "as they were saying this, Jesus himself stood among them" (v. 36). This is the final presence of Jesus to his disciples in the Gospel (see v. 51, where he leaves them).

The whole of Luke's Gospel has been directed toward this "day." As Jesus began his journey toward Jerusalem in 9:51, the narrator commented, "When the days drew near for him to be received up, he set his face to go to Jerusalem." That "journey" comes to its close in Jerusalem through "the things that have happened there" (24:18).

On this resurrection "day" we sense that we are at the end of a long journey. In fact, one of the most important themes of the Gospel of Luke and its companion work, the Acts of the Apostles, is the theme of a journey.[59] Throughout the Gospel, a journey leads to Jerusalem, where the paschal events take place (see especially 9:51). At the beginning of Acts, the early Church is still in Jerusalem. The Spirit is given there, and it is from there that a second journey begins, reaching out to the ends of the earth.[60] The center-point of Luke–Acts is the city of Jerusalem. The journey of Jesus leads him there. In Jerusalem the Paschal events take place, and he ascends to his Father from that city. Jerusalem is the end of the journey of Jesus; the journey of the apostles begins there. They are commissioned to go out to all the nations, but they are to "stay in the city" to await the gift of the Spirit (24:49). There they are given the Spirit (Acts 2:1-13), there they first become "church," one in heart and soul, celebrating the Lord's presence in their meals (2:42-47). However, it is from Jerusalem that they eventually set out, witnesses "in Judea and Samaria and to the ends of the earth" (Acts 1:8; see also 20:7-11; 27:33-36).[61] The city of Jerusalem acts as a fulcrum, around which God's salvation history swivels.[62]

As Jerusalem is the center of God's history, the opening remarks of the journey to Emmaus signal the wrong choice made by two disciples.[63] "That very day"—in the midst of the paschal events—two disciples were going to Emmaus, "about sixty stadia away from Jerusalem" (24:13). They are walking *away from Jerusalem* (Greek: *apo Ierousalēm*), the central point of God's story. In doing so they are turning away from the very place in which God will reveal himself in his Son, who has journeyed from Nazareth (Luke 1-2) to Jerusalem, the place from which he will be made known to the ends of the earth (Acts 1:8; 28:16-31).[64] Unlike Mark and Matthew, Luke never tells his readers that the disciples abandoned Jesus. They were even present at the cross, looking on from a distance (see 23:49), and women who had been with him from his time in Galilee (8:1-3) have followed him to his tomb (23:55-56) and announced the Easter message. But these two disciples have broken that pattern. They walk away from the place and the day of the Paschal events. This aspect of the journey to Emmaus is central to Luke's resurrection story.

This impression is further reinforced once the reader/listener notices the details of the account itself. The paschal events are in the forefront of their minds and the subject of their conversation as they walk away (v. 14), and as the risen Jesus joins them and "went with them" (v. 15). The use of the personal name "Jesus," followed by "himself" (Greek: *kai autos Iēsous*), makes it clear to the reader (but not to the disciples) that the fellow-traveler is certainly Jesus.[65] He has reached out to sinners with pardon—and even offered salvation—on the cross (23:34, 39-43). Now, as the Risen One, he "walks with" these two disciples who are abandoning God's saving story. God is also behind this encounter. Luke does not say that they were unable to recognize Jesus, but that "their eyes were kept from recognizing him" (v. 16). There is a mysterious "other" directing the presence of Jesus with disciples, indicated by the use of the divine passive voice of the verb (Greek: *ekratounto*).[66] God is not mentioned as the subject of the action, but despite the absence of the name, God is responsible. However much they may be abandoning God's story, God is not abandoning them.[67] Jesus opens the conversation by asking them what they were discussing with one another as they walked. They continue to walk away from Jerusalem as they discuss the events that took place there. But at Jesus' question, they stop (v. 16).

A hint of something new has entered the story, but it does not last, as one of them, named Cleopas, responds to Jesus' question.[68] He wonders how Jesus could even ask such a question. Surely, every visitor to Jerusalem would know "the things that have happened there in these days" (v. 18). This is incredible irony, as Cleopas asks Jesus—indeed a visitor to Jerusalem who had journeyed from Galilee to the city—to bring to a climax part of God's saving design. This journey has been under way since 9:51, when Jesus set his face for Jerusalem, "as the days drew near for him to be received up." Cleopas asks the very "visitor," to whom these events happened, why he does not know about them.[69] Jesus, who has been at the center of the events, is also the measure of their significance. But the two disciples know only of the "events," not their ultimate significance. Indeed, "their eyes were kept from recognizing him" (v. 16).

A catechetical–liturgical process begins in v. 19, where, in response to Jesus' further query about the events, they show the extent of their knowledge of "what has happened" in Jerusalem. Crucial to their response to Jesus is their explanation of their expectations of Jesus: "We had hoped that he was the one to redeem Israel" (v. 21). They have not understood the significance of the life, teaching, death, and resurrection of Jesus. They are yet to discover that the resurrection of Jesus is the resurrection of the Messiah, but "the Messiah *of God*" (see 9:20), not the Messiah of their expectations. Jesus' way of responding to the Father has not fulfilled their hopes for the one who would redeem Israel. But they do know of *the facts* of his life, teaching, death, and resurrection:[70]

- They know of his life, teaching, and miraculous ministry: Jesus of Nazareth, a prophet mighty in word and deed (v. 19).
- They know of his death: "Our chief priests and rulers delivered him up to be condemned to death, and crucified him" (v. 20).
- They know of the events at the tomb: "it is now the third day" (v. 21), women have been at the tomb early in the morning, but "they did not find his body" (v. 23).
- They have even heard the Easter proclamation: there has been a vision of angels who said: "He is alive!" (v. 23).
- If, perhaps the witness of the women was not enough, "some of those who were with us" have been to the tomb, and found it empty. "But him they did not see" (v. 24).

The two disciples on the way to Emmaus know everything ... but him they did not see (vv. 15-17). They have not remembered the words of Jesus (see 24:7-8, 44), and thus do not understand the *significance* of these *events*, and they continue their walk away from Jerusalem.[71]

The audience encounters the practices of the Lukan Church through the subsequent liturgy of the word. Jesus chides them for their foolishness, and opens the word for them, explaining that it was necessary that the Christ should suffer many things to enter his glory (vv. 25-26). He "interpreted to them in all the scriptures the things concerning himself" (v. 27). Jesus journeys with these disciples who have abandoned God's journey, and on the way a "liturgy of the Word" takes place. He calls to their memory the necessity for the Christ to suffer in order to enter into his glory (v. 26). They should have recalled this, as the women at the tomb should have recalled it (see vv. 6-7).

Not only did Jesus teach these truths (see 9:22, 44; 18:31-33), but it was the true meaning of "all the Scriptures," beginning with Moses and the prophets, whose promises Jesus fulfils (v. 27).

The narrative has now reached a turning point. Initiative must come from the erring disciples. Has the word of Jesus made any impact upon them? The Greek of v. 28 reads: "He pretended (Greek: *prosepoiēsato*) to be going further."[72] Jesus has unfolded God's plan through the explanation of the Scriptures. The disciples must now take some initiative in response to Jesus' biblical catechesis.[73] They do so generously: "Stay with us for it is toward evening, and the day is now far spent" (v. 29). As the evening of the Easter "day" draws in, the littleness of faith that led them to leave Jerusalem and the eleven is being overcome by the presence of the risen Lord (v. 15) and the instruction of his word, asking them to remember (vv. 25-27). A process of repentance and forgiveness is under way, generated by the action of Jesus who walks with his fragile disciples.

At the meal the disciples recognize him in the breaking of the bread (vv. 30-31). Jesus has set out to follow and to journey with these failing disciples, as they walked away from God's designs for his Messiah (see v. 26). Yet he has accompanied them and opened the word of God to them. Finally, he is recognized in the breaking of the bread.[74] The memory of the many meals that Jesus has shared with them—and especially the meal he shared on the night before he died (22:14-38)—opens their eyes and anticipates the many meals that will be celebrated in the future.[75] Touched by Jesus' word and presence in their failure, the immediate reaction of the failed disciples is to turn back on their journey: "And they rose that same hour and returned to Jerusalem" (v. 33).[76] The journey "away from Jerusalem" (v. 13: Greek: *apo Ierousalēm*) has been reversed as they turn back "to Jerusalem" (v. 33: Greek: *eis Ierousalēm*). Once they arrive back to the place they should never have abandoned and to the eleven apostles upon whom the community is founded, before they can even utter a word about their experience, they find that Easter faith is already alive. They are told: "The Lord has risen indeed and has appeared to Simon" (v. 34). Easter faith has been born in Jerusalem.

The use of the name "Simon" calls for attention. As the Gospel opens, the audience comes to know of a man called "Simon" (4:38).

Within the context of a miraculous catch of fish he is called to be a disciple of Jesus and Jesus introduces a new name for him "Peter" (see 5:8). The audience is reminded of this transformation in the Lukan list of the twelve apostles: "Simon, whom he named Peter" (6:14). From that point on, throughout the Gospel, he is called "Peter" (see 8:45, 51; 9:20, 28, 32-33; 12:41; 18:28). At the Last Supper, where the mingling of the themes of Jesus' sharing his table with the broken and the commissioning of his future apostles is found, he is still "Peter" (22:8, 34, 54, 55, 58, 60-61). Only in foretelling his future denials does Jesus emphatically revert to the name he had before he became a disciple: "Simon, Simon, behold, Satan demanded to have you that he might sift you like wheat" (22:31). The return to "Peter" at the end of Jesus' words is, in itself, a sign that all is not lost (v. 34). Yet, it is to the failed Simon that the risen Lord has appeared, to restore him to his apostolic role (24:34). The name "Simon," without any link with the apostolic name "Peter," appears only before this man's call to be a follower of Jesus (4:18) and at the end of the Emmaus story, when two failing disciples are restored to God's saving story that is taking place in Jerusalem. There another sinner, Simon, has also been blessed by the presence of the risen Lord (23:34).[77]

The failed disciples have returned to another disciple who had failed his Lord. This return home, however, has happened because the risen Lord reached out to them in their brokenness, and made himself known to them in the breaking of the bread:

> Here … we find Jesus eating with outcasts, but this time the outcasts are two of his own disciples who have abandoned their journey of faith, fled Jerusalem, and embarked on their own journey. Jesus crosses the boundaries of disloyalty and breaks the bread of reconciliation with these disciples. Strengthened by the risen Jesus, Cleopas and his companion hasten back to Jerusalem and rejoin the journey of discipleship.[78]

Two disciples with inadequate faith had decided to walk "away from Jerusalem" (v. 13), and the Easter proclamation announced the presence of the risen Lord to the fragile Simon: "The Lord has risen indeed, and has appeared to Simon" (v. 34). This unforgettable story, the subject of imaginative art, poetry, and dramatic representation across the centuries, retains the powerful message that lies at the heart of Luke's Gospel: despite all human sin and frailty, the kingdom of God has been definitively established through the death and resurrection of Jesus. It is rendered present to fragile disciples in the celebration of the Eucharist.

THE RISEN JESUS INSTRUCTS AND COMMISSIONS HIS DISCIPLES

The return of the two disciples from Emmaus to Jerusalem leads into Jesus' final appearance to the apostles. Jesus "stood among them" as they were discussing the events of Simon and the travelers to Emmaus. The traditional Easter greeting of Jesus' peace generates only fear, as they think they are seeing a ghost (vv. 36-37). Consistent with all the Gospels, the appearance of the risen Jesus produces doubt and fear (see Mark 16:8; Matt 28:17; John 20:1-2, 11-17, 24-29). Neither the vision of his hands and feet, nor his request that they touch him, can convince them that he is not a ghost (vv. 39-40). Their fear does not turn into faith, but unfaith and amazement, mixed with joy (v. 41ab).[79] There is only one way to resolve this unfaith and amazement: to again celebrate a meal, thus continuing the long tradition of the many meals celebrated with the apostles during his life and ministry (vv. 41c-43),[80] and to remind them of his word and the fulfillment of the Scriptures (vv. 44-46). Although commentators almost universally argue that "the scene is intended to stress the identity and the physical reality of the risen Christ who has appeared to his disciples,"[81] more is involved. Jesus is with the apostles from this point on, until he leaves them in the ascension in v. 51. The meal-table is the place where he gives them his final instructions, based upon Scripture (v. 46), and commissions them to go to "all nations" (v. 47). He leads them to Bethany, blesses them, and is taken up into heaven (vv. 50-51). Only now do the apostles demonstrate their faith. They worship him (v. 52). All fear, doubt and amazement have disappeared. Read as a single narrative unit, there are close parallels between the experience of the Emmaus disciples and the experience of the eleven apostles.

Emmaus	*Jerusalem*
Talking to each other (v. 14)	Talking to each other (v. 35)
Jesus appears (v. 15)	Jesus appears (v. 36)
He is not recognized (v. 16)	He is not recognized (v. 37)
Jesus asks a rhetorical question (vv. 25-26)	Jesus asks a rhetorical question (vv. 38-40)
Instruction based on Scripture (v. 27)	Instruction based on Scripture (v. 44)
Revealing actions with bread (vv. 30-31)	Revealing actions with bread and fish (vv. 41-42)
Jesus disappears (v. 31)	Jesus disappears (v. 51)
The apostles return to Jerusalem (v. 33)	The apostles return to Jerusalem (v. 52)

The parallels between 24:13-35 and 36-52 suggest that the post-resurrection meals at Emmaus and Jerusalem are carefully constructed to bring to a climax the many meals across the Gospel.[82] Fulfilling Jesus' promise at the meal before his death, his sharing table with his disciples (vv. 13-35) and apostles (vv. 36-49) announces that the kingdom of God has come (see 22:14-23).[83] The use of fish in vv. 42-43 indicates that Jesus is physically present among them, but it also reminds the reader of an earlier episode. A link has been created across the Gospel between the final commission to the eleven in 24:36-39 and his initial formation of that same group in 9:10-17, where Jesus had earlier given them bread and fish (9:16).

Jesus drew the disciples who had lost their way at Emmaus back to Jerusalem through a eucharistic table. At another table he commissions his apostles to witness repentance and the forgiveness of sins to all the nations (vv. 44-49). Jesus' suffering and death have interrupted fellowship at table. It has been re-established by his resurrection, as he promised in 22:16, 18. The apostles have experienced failure, in the person of Peter. But Peter's denials have led him, in sorrow, to repentance (22:54-62). The disciples have experienced failure in the journey of Cleopas and his companion *away from Jerusalem*. But their disappointment with the way God has acted through his Christ, who had to suffer to come to glory, has been overcome by Jesus' journeying with them, and opening the Scriptures. They experienced the presence of the risen Lord at the table, leading them to repentance and forgiveness of sins (24:13-35).

As this is the case, a double dynamic is at work in Jesus' commission to the apostles, and both elements will drive their future mission. All that Jesus has said is the fulfillment of God's design, mapped out in the Law of Moses, the prophets, and the psalms. The suffering, crucified, and risen Christ has fulfilled God's design (vv. 44-46). Thus, in the first place, on the basis of their having witnessed the fulfillment of God's design in and through the words and deeds of Jesus, they are to preach repentance and forgiveness of sins to all nations (v. 47). Further, as has been made obvious in the two meal encounters in vv. 13-35 and vv. 36-43, it is *their own experience of repentance and forgiveness of sins* that is the basis upon which the apostles are commissioned to witness to all the nations (v. 47).[84] They have witnessed the fulfillment of God's design in the words and deeds of Jesus. Luke's story tells of disciples and apostles who have experienced repentance and the forgiveness of sins in their own journeys with the Christ. Even in the presence of the risen Lord they are afraid, doubt, and are amazed (vv. 36-43). The risen Jesus tells them to wait in the city of Jerusalem. There the power from on high will be given to them, and from Jerusalem they will set out to preach repentance and the forgiveness of sins in the name of Jesus (vv. 47-49). As followers of Jesus who have themselves sinned, they are eminently qualified to do so![85]

CONCLUSION

Like the Gospels of Mark and Matthew, the Gospel of Luke sets the eucharistic presence of the Lord in the midst of many of the followers of Jesus who could be described as "broken": sinners, unfaithful disciples, failing apostles, the physically impure, the marginalized, and Gentiles. The account of the feeding of the multitudes with bread (9:10-17), although eucharistic, does not repeat the questions the Markan and Matthean Gospels put to their communities of disciples who were not sufficiently open to the ways of the Lord. It is used for the formation of future missionaries, the twelve apostles who will feed all the nations. However, the widespread use of "table settings" across the Gospel—to provide the contexts for Jesus' radical questioning of the status quo—paves the way for the meals that conclude the Lukan story of Jesus. Both in the Last Supper and at the table at Emmaus, failed and sinful disciples are touched by the presence of the Lord. At the Last Supper (22:14-38) the overall background of Jesus' many meals with sinners is used to indicate that even here he is prepared to call to himself the broken people. Into this background the Lukan author has inserted the tradition of a farewell discourse. The blending of these two features—the meals of Jesus and the farewell discourse—produces its own difficulties. Jesus' instructions for the future are given to a group of squabbling disciples (vv. 24-30) and he commissions Peter, who will deny him (vv. 31-34). This leads to an impure form of the "farewell discourse" tradition, but nothing is lost for the audience. Through this blending of the two features the reader discovers that, sinners though they may be, the people at the table will eventually become the apostles and thus living witnesses to repentance and the forgiveness of sins (24:47). What is important is that these apostles "witness" to something they have experienced.

On the eventful "day" of the resurrection, sinful disciples, discouraged by the strange ways of God who decreed that the Messiah must suffer many things (see 9:22; 22:22; 24:26, 46), walk away from Jerusalem. Through the liturgy of the journey to Emmaus, disciples are called back to the way of the Lord, symbolically centered upon the city that is, in fact, the central point where God leads Jesus back to himself and sends the apostles to all the nations. Jesus sets out after his failing disciples, and calls them back to himself through the breaking of the bread (24:13-35). Throughout the Gospel, at the Last Supper, and finally at Emmaus, Jesus shares his table with the broken.[86]

This reading of the eucharistic texts across the Gospel of Luke, when set within the narrative framework of the story of Luke–Acts, reinforces the results of our reading of the Gospels of Mark and Matthew. The unique re-telling of the last meal (22:14-38), the addition of the Emmaus journey (24:13-35), and a final encounter with the apostles (24:36-49), combined with the traditional resurrection stories of an empty tomb, appearances, and a commission,[87] suggests that the Lukan tradition has taken the early Church's understanding of the Eucharist as Jesus' presence to the broken to even greater depths.

NOTES

1   This affirmation is true on formal grounds alone. Rightly regarded as one of the so-called Synoptic Gospels, sharing with Matthew a literary dependence upon Mark and "Q," and following the Markan plot of ministry in Galilee, journey to Jerusalem, ministry in Jerusalem, and death and resurrection in Jerusalem, Luke's Gospel simply "goes its own way" on many occasions. It also contains episodes from the life of Jesus, and teachings of Jesus, that are not found elsewhere in the New Testament. On this question, see the fine synthesis of Bovon, *Luke*, 1:6-8, and the more detailed study of Christopher F. Evans, *Saint Luke*, New Testament Commentaries (London: SCM Press, 1990), 15-29. A very user-friendly survey can be found in Mark Allan Powell, *Introducing the New Testament: A Historical, Literary, and Theological Survey* (Grand Rapids: Baker Academic, 2009), 147-57.

2   See Augustin George, *Études sur l'Oeuvre de Luc*, Sources Bibliques (Paris: Gabalda, 1978), 43-65, for a study of the literary and theological significance of the parallel presentation of Jesus and John the Baptist in the Gospel of Luke.

3   For the narrative coherence and quality of Luke 1-2, see Mark Coleridge, *The Birth of the Lukan Narrative: Narrative as Christology in Luke 1-2*, Journal for the Study of the New Testament Supplement Series 88 (Sheffield: JSOT Press, 1993).

4   See the classical contribution of Henry J. Cadbury, *The Making of Luke–Acts* (London: SPCK, 1927), and the more recent studies, Charles H. Talbert, *Reading Luke: A Literary and Theological Commentary on the Third Gospel* (New York: Crossroad, 1982), and Robert C. Tannehill, *The Narrative Unity of Luke–Acts: A Literary Interpretation*, Foundations and Facets: New Testament, 2 vols. (Philadelphia: Fortress Press, 1986).

5   Among many, Rembrandt and Caravaggio have left unforgettable pictorial interpretations. For an example of the literary tradition, see David L. Jeffrey and I. Howard Marshall, "Emmaus," in *A Dictionary of Biblical Tradition in English Literature*, ed. David L. Jeffrey (Grand Rapids: Eerdmans, 1992), 236-37.

6   Redactional-critical work on the Gospel of Mark attempts to trace the traditions that Mark used, and then recover his theological perspectives by seeing how he shaped them. It is widely accepted, for example, that a pre-Markan passion narrative can be identified. For different perspectives, see Marion Soards, "The Question of a PreMarcan Passion Narrative," in Raymond E. Brown, *The Death of the Messiah: A Commentary on the Passion*

Narratives in the Four Gospels, Anchor Bible Reference Library, 2 vols. (New York: Doubleday, 1993), 2:1492-524 (Appendix IX), and Collins, *Mark*, 621-26, 819. A feature of Collins' commentary is the assiduous search for pre-Markan traditions.

7   This led to the development of a theory of an independent proto-Lukan tradition by Burnett H. Streeter, *The Four Gospels: A Study of Origins* (London: Macmillan, 1924), 233-70. It has been largely abandoned. For a very good survey of the theory see Vincent Taylor, *The Passion Narrative of St Luke: A Critical and Historical Investigation*, ed. Owen E. Evans, SNTS Monograph Series 19 (Cambridge: Cambridge University Press, 1972), 3-38. Taylor adopts the theory in his analysis of the Lukan passion narrative.

8   For a study of the Lukan passion and resurrection narratives, in which only the discovery of an empty tomb by women (Luke 24:1-12) is shared with the other Synoptic Gospels, see Francis J. Moloney, *The Resurrection of the Messiah: A Narrative Commentary on the Resurrection Accounts* (New York/Mahwah, NJ: Paulist Press, 2013), 69-99. Only Luke tells of the walk to Emmaus (vv. 13-35), the appearance and commissioning of the disciples that repeats many of the themes of the Emmaus account (vv. 36-49), and the departure of Jesus by ascension (vv. 50-53).

9   Luke uses Mark 6:30-44 creatively. For a comparison, see Joseph A. Fitzmyer, *The Gospel According to Luke*, The Anchor Bible 28-28A, 2 vols. (New York: Doubleday, 1981), 1:762-63; Gerhard Schneider, *Das Evangelium nach Lukas*, Ökumenischer Taschenbuchkommentar zum Neuen Testament 3/1-2, 2 vols (Gütersloh/München: Gerd Mohn/Echter, 1977), 1:205; Bovon, *Luke*, 1:352-55.

10   Among many, see Brown, *An Introduction to the New Testament*, 269-74; Carroll, *Luke*, 5-6; Moloney, *The Living Voice of the Gospel*, 165-201, and especially Robert Maddox, *The Purpose of Luke–Acts*, Studies of the New Testament and Its World (Edinburgh: T. & T. Clark, 1982).

11   In the "dedication" of the work to Theophilus, Luke makes it clear that he (a third-generation Christian; see vv. 1-3) writes to maintain the trust and confidence of his audience in the work of God that took place in Jesus and that is continued through his apostles. This is made especially clear by Luke's use of the Greek word *asphaleia* in v. 4, translated as "truth" by the RSV, but the expression contains a meaning of "trustworthiness" and "certainty." See Coleridge, *The Birth of the Lukan Narrative*, 232-34. Coleridge translates v. 4: "that you may know the well-foundedness of what you have been taught" (p. 233). See also Heinz Schürmann, *Das Lukasevangelium*, Herders

theologischer Kommentar zum Neuen Testament (Freiburg: Herder, 1969), 1-17; Loveday Alexander, *The Preface to Luke's Gospel: Literary Convention and Social Context in Luke 1.1-14 and Acts 1.1*, SNTS Monograph Series 78 (Cambridge: Cambridge University Press, 1993), 102-42.

12   On this, see Robert F. O'Toole, *The Unity of Luke's Theology: An Analysis of Luke–Acts* (Good News Studies 9; Wilmington, DE: Michael Glazier, 1984), 62-94.

13   The expression is found in Mark 6:30, where it does not have a technical meaning. It looks back to Jesus' action of "sending them out" in v. 7. It is more formal in Matthew 10:2, but that is the only place where it is found in Matthew. Some early manuscripts add "whom he named apostles" to the calling of the twelve in Mark 3:14, but this is clearly secondary. On the Markan texts, see Moloney, *The Gospel of Mark*, 77 note 11; 128-29.

14   For a survey of the complex discussion over the development of the concept and language of an "apostle" in the early Church, see Dietrich Müller and Colin Brown, "Apostle" in *The New International Dictionary of New Testament Theology*, ed. Colin Brown, 3 vols. (Exeter: Paternoster Press, 1975), 1:128-37. See especially the special note on the use of "apostle" in Luke–Acts on pp. 135-36 (Colin Brown). See also Hans Dieter Betz, "Apostle," in *The Anchor Bible Dictionary*, ed. David Noel Freedman, 6 vols. (New York: Doubleday, 1992), 1:309-11.

15   Carroll, *Luke*, 209-20, summarizes 9:18-27 (revelation of Jesus as the suffering Son of Man) and 9:28-36 (the transfiguration) as parts 1 and 2 of the "decisive disclosure of Jesus' identity."

16   Mark 6:14-29 is extravagant in its telling of the circumstances that led to the execution of John the Baptist. See Moloney, *The Gospel of Mark*, 125-28. Matthew 14:1-12 is more reserved, editing Mark quite heavily. Luke omits it completely. For Luke, the witness of the Baptist precedes Jesus (see Luke 16:16). And thus he can focus upon the Christological importance of Herod's puzzlement.

17   It is here that the "great omission" of Mark 6:44-8:27 occurs.

18   See Schneider, *Lukas*, 1:206. For further links with the Emmaus story of 24:13-35, see Robert C. Tannehill, *Luke*, Abingdon New Testament Commentaries (Nashville: Abingdon Press, 1996), 156-57.

19   Schneider, *Lukas*, 1:206-207.

20   Fitzmyer, *Luke*, 1:769; Tannehill, *Luke*, 154-55. Bovon, *Luke*, 1:358, also comments: "The twelve carrying baskets would then stand for the twelve

apostles and Israel." Mark also uses the symbol of "the Twelve" significantly, with reference to Israel and the founding twelve tribes (see, for example, Mark 3:13-14; 6:7; 9:35; 10:35-41; 14:10, 17). But only Luke uses the expression in the bread miracle.

21   On the importance of the role of the twelve in the miracle, as preparation for their journey to Jerusalem with Jesus, see Carroll, *Luke*, 206-209; Brendan Byrne, *The Hospitality of God: A Reading of Luke's Gospel* (Collegeville: The Liturgical Press, 2000), 85. See also van Cangh, *La Multiplication des Pains*, 148-55; van Iersel, "Die wunderbare Speisung," 148-55. On the narrative links between the Lukan account of the bread miracle and the rest of the Gospel, see Tannehill, *Narrative Unity*, 1:216-19.

22   Evans, *Saint Luke*, 401. Luke T. Johnson, *The Gospel of Luke*, Sacra Pagina 3 (Collegeville, MI: The Liturgical Press, 1991), 144-61, analyses 9:1-50 as follows: "Preparing a leadership for the people" (vv. 1-17), "Recognizing Jesus" (vv. 18-36), and "Flawed followers" (vv. 37-50).

23   Carroll, *Luke*, 222, suggests that the episode is used "to give the disciples a wake-up call."

24   Such familiarity would not have been part of the experience of the original Lukan audience, but it is available to later generations as a guide toward an appreciation of the uniqueness of the Lukan account.

25   As Bovon, *Luke*, 1:360, states: "The mediating role of the Twelve anticipates their later, post-Easter responsibilities of office, although Christ understands this office not in the sense of ruling over others, but of service to himself and thereby to the individuals who belong to him." See also Schürmann, *Das Lukasevangelium*, 514-15. This outstanding commentary was left unfinished at 9:50. Professor Schürmann passed away in 1999.

26   For Johnson, *Luke*, 157-61, this theme is already introduced into the narrative in 9:37-50, so it is not later in the story that the audience meets it for the first time.

27   For a detailed analysis, see Fitzmyer, *Luke*, 2:1385-406. See also, more briefly, the recent commentaries of Bovon, *Luke*, 1:6-8; 3:153-56; Carroll, *Luke*, 424-25; and the summary of the peculiarities of the Lukan text in Theissen and Merz, *The Historical Jesus*, 417.

28   See the study of Robert J. Karris, *Luke: Artist and Theologian: Luke's Passion Account as Literature* (New York: Paulist Press, 1985), 47-78. See also Jerome Neyrey, *The Passion According to Luke: A Redaction Study of Luke's Soteriology* (New York: Paulist Press, 1985), 8-11; Barth, *Rediscovering the Lord's Supper*, 71-74.

29   See especially Léon-Dufour, *Sharing the Eucharistic Bread*, 85-95, 230-47; Neyrey, *The Passion According to Luke*, 5-48. Bovon, *Luke*, 153 note 2, accepts that the Lukan text belongs to the literary genre of a testament, but rightly insists that it "is not only a farewell speech." What follows will have occasion to show that this is the case.

30   For a detailed study of the significance of sharing one's table in Jewish thought and practice, see Esler, *Community and Gospel in Luke–Acts*, 71-86.

31   John R. Donahue, *The Gospel in Parable* (Philadelphia: Fortress Press, 1988), 146.

32   For appreciations of the Zacchaeus story that indicate its strategic role within the Lukan narrative, see Schneider, *Lukas*, 376-78; Jean-Noël Aletti, *L'art de raconter Jésus Christ* (Paris: Seuil, 1989), 17-38. See also Tannehill, *The Narrative Unity*, 1:122-25; Bovon, *Luke*, 590-602.

33   Neyrey, *The Passion According to Luke*, 10. See the excellent synthesis of Kodell, *The Eucharist in the New Testament*, 106-13. See also Josephine Massyngbaerde Ford, *Bonded with the Immortal: A Pastoral Introduction to the New Testament* (Wilmington: Michael Glazier, 1987), 280-89. Karris, *Luke: Artist and Theologian*, 70, whimsically comments: "Jesus got himself crucified because of the way he ate."

34   Only the Gospel of Luke adds "and the apostles with him." Compare Mark 14:17: "He came with the twelve," and Matt 26:20: "He sat at table with the twelve disciples."

35   For a thorough survey of scholarly discussion of the Lukan Church, see François Bovon, *Luke the Theologian*, trans. Ken McKinney, 2nd ed. (Waco, TX: Baylor University Press, 2006), 329-463. For some studies of Luke's special interest in the marginalized, see Halvor Moxnes, *The Economy of the Kingdom: Social Conflict and Economic Relations in Luke's Gospel*, Overtures to Biblical Theology (Philadelphia: Fortress, 1988); Tannehill, *The Narrative Unity*, 1:103-39; Evans, *Saint Luke*, 99-104; Luke T. Johnson, *Prophetic Jesus, Prophetic Church: The Challenge of Luke–Acts to Contemporary Christians* (Grand Rapids: Eerdmans, 2011). See also the excursus on poverty and wealth in Carroll, *Luke*, 374-77.

36   See Francis J. Moloney, "Luke 24: To be Witnesses of the Forgiveness and Compassion of Jesus," in *Apostolic Passion "Give me Souls"*, ed. Rafael Vicent and Corrado Pastore (Bangalore: Kristu Jyoti Publications, 2010), 183-95.

37   Esler, *Community and Gospel in Luke–Acts*, p. 96. His excellent study of

the sharing of the table in Acts is found on pp. 93-109. He has not considered the theme in the Gospel.

38   Léon-Dufour, *Sharing the Eucharistic Bread*, 233.

39   See above, pp. 83-85; pp. 115-16.

40   There is difficulty with the original text here, as some ancient manuscripts omit the second word over the cup (22:19b-20). In defense of the longer reading, see Jeremias, *The Eucharistic Words of Jesus*, 139-59. For a briefer survey, also in defense of the longer text, see Fitzmyer, *Luke*, 2:1387-89. Even if one were to accept the shorter reading, my structure would hold. More recently, Bovon, *Luke*, 3:154-56, who represents a majority position, defends the longer reading, while Evans, *Saint Luke*, 788-89, and Carroll, *Luke*, 433-37, reject it. For a good summary of the evidence, concluding that vv. 19b-20 should be retained, see Metzger, *A Textual Commentary*, 148-50.

41   See, for example, Carroll, *Luke*, 433-34.

42   See Bovon, *Luke*, 3:152 note 3.

43   For an excellent commentary upon Luke 22:35-38, which I have followed, see Neyrey, *The Passion According to Luke*, 37-43. Along the same lines, see Fitzmyer, *Luke*, 2:1428-31.

44   Thomas W. Manson, *The Sayings of Jesus* (London: SCM Press, 1971), 341. See also Paul S. Minear, "A Note on Luke 22:36," *Novum Testamentum* 7 (1964-65), 128-34; Byrne, *Hospitality*, 174.

45   See Léon-Dufour, *Sharing the Eucharistic Bread*, 234.

46   Barth, *Rediscovering the Lord's Supper*, 73. See also Kodell, *The Eucharist in the New Testament*, 105: "The Last Supper is the final meal in a series during Jesus' ministry. There he teaches his disciples how they are to act after he is gone by his interpretation of the bread and wine, by his last instructions, and by sharing table fellowship with his betrayer." For similar sentiments, see Talbert, *Reading Luke*, 206-11.

47   A number of commentators, recognizing this, comment upon 22:14-20 as a Christian adaptation of the Jewish Passover tradition, and then see vv. 21-38 as "instruction," or even a farewell discourse. See, for example, Schneider, *Lukas*, 443-56; Evans, *Saint Luke*, 779-82, 791-92; Johnson, *Luke*, 336-50. Johnson is especially helpful on the "farewell discourse" genre on pp. 347-49.

48   See Tannehill, *Literary Unity*, 263: "Whether or not 22:14-38 technically belongs to a recognized genre which can be called 'farewell discourse' or

'farewell address,' Jesus' words are uttered in the light of his impending death and with awareness of the new situation which the apostles are entering, as appears in the command to 'do this for my memory,' the effort to prepare the apostles for their new role as leaders in 22:24-27, and a gift of a share in Jesus' royal power in 22:28-30." See his fine commentary on 22:14-38 on pp. 263-70.

49 Paul S. Minear, "Some Glimpses of Luke's Sacramental Theology," *Worship* 44 (1970), 326. I am following majority scholarly tradition, accepting that vv. 19b-20 are original. See above, note 40.

50 For the background, see Charles H. Dodd, *The Interpretation of the Fourth Gospel* (Cambridge: Cambridge University Press, 1953), 420-23; Francis J. Moloney, *Glory not Dishonor: Reading John 13-21* (Minneapolis: Fortress, 1998), 4-7.

51 For what follows I am depending on the work of Neyrey, *The Passion According to Luke*, 6-8. Although scholars have long been aware of the literary form of a farewell speech, the uncovering of a large number of "testaments" at Qumran—especially significant parts of *The Testaments of the Twelve Patriarchs*—has led to increased interest from Christian scholars. Originally pre-Christian, the present text of these testaments has numerous Christian interpolations, but they at least offer evidence of the early Christian use of a Hebrew scriptural tradition. See Robert A. Kugler, "Testaments," in *Encyclopedia of the Dead Sea Scrolls*, ed. Lawrence H. Schiffman and James C. VanderKam, 2 vols. (Oxford/New York: Oxford University Press, 2000), 2:933-36, and idem, "Twelve Patriarchs, Testaments of The," in *Encyclopedia of the Dead Sea Scrolls*, 2:952-53.

52 For an introduction and an annotated critical text of this document (prepared by Howard C. Kee), see James H. Charlesworth, ed., *The Old Testament Pseudepigrapha*, 2 vols. (London: Darton, Longman & Todd, 1983), 1:775-828.

53 Here I am following Neyrey, *The Passion According to Luke*, 7. See also Léon-Dufour, *Sharing the Eucharistic Bread*, 245-46; Johnson, *Luke*, 336-50. For a strong argument in defense of this position, see William S. Kurz, "Luke 22:14-38 and Greco-Roman and Biblical Farewell Addresses," *Journal of Biblical Literature* 104 (1985), 251-68.

54 In the testaments there are frequent references to the future failings of the patriarchs' sons, generally associated with the end time. See, for example, *Testament of Levi* 10:1-5; 14-16; *Testament of Isaachar* 6:1-4; *Testament of Dan* 5:7-8; *Testament of Naphtali* 4:1-5. On one occasion only there is a

reference to present sinfulness, but the patriarch's exhortation quickly moves into a discussion of the evils of the end time. See *Testament of Judah* 23:1.

55 Neyrey, *The Passion According to Luke*, 31-37, offers an excellent study of these verses. He shows convincingly that Jesus' words are a "commissioning" of Peter. He even suggests "that this verse (32b) contains a solemn commissioning of Peter comparable to Mt 16:17-19 and Jn 21:15-17" (p. 34). The theme of failure on the part of the commissioned future leader is also an important result of Luke's "blending" of his meal theme with the "farewell discourse." See, on this, Léon-Dufour, *Sharing the Eucharistic Bread*, 241-42; Tannehill, *Narrative Unity*, 1:263-68.

56 This blending of the themes of failure and commissioning for a future brings its difficulties. The patriarch never gives his instructions to the sort of squabbling disciples found in Luke 22:24-27. Although the testaments do speak of a future sinfulness (see above, note 53), the "commissioning" never takes place within the context of a prophecy of future denial of the patriarch. See, on this, Léon-Dufour, *Sharing the Eucharistic Bread*, 236-39 and 243-45. He notes that "certain departures from the testamentary genre are significant" (243-44). They arise largely from the Lukan blending of the meal theme with the testamentary genre.

57 Here we find another marked difference between the *Testaments of the Twelve Patriarchs* and Luke 22:14-38. Many of the patriarchs speak at length of their sinful past, especially their sexual dalliances and their mistreatment of Joseph. See, for example, *Testament of Reuben* 1:6-10; 2:11-15; *Testament of Simon* 2:6-13; *Testament of Gad* 2:1-5. Obviously, there is no place for this theme in the Gospel of Luke, nor in a report of the events that took place on the night before Jesus died. Tannehill, *Narrative Unity*, 1:268, nevertheless writes: "The lawlessness of the apostles in the passion story fulfils scripture, and so it, too, has a place within God's purpose, which is able to make use of human failure and rejection."

58 Kodell, *The Eucharist in the New Testament*, 117.

59 On this theme through the Gospel of Luke, see Moloney, *The Living Voice of the Gospel*, 166-93. It should be noticed, however, that this physical movement, which marks the journey of Jesus to Jerusalem (Gospel), and the parallel journey of the disciples to the ends of the earth (Acts), is only part of the journey theme. There is also a steady—and perhaps even more important—"journey" of increasing intensity of teaching and understanding (matched by misunderstanding) as the story unfolds (see pp. 190-93). See also Stephen D. Moore, "Luke's Economy of Knowledge," in *Society of*

Biblical Literature Seminar Papers 1989, ed. David J. Lull (Atlanta: Scholars Press, 1989), 38-56.

60   For a brief account of the "journey" in the Acts of the Apostles, see Moloney, *Reading the New Testament*, 140-54.

61   On the eucharistic texts in Acts, see Menoud, "The Acts of the Apostles and the Eucharist," 84-106. Menoud argues that 16:34 is also concerned with "the table of the Lord" (see pp. 89-90).

62   For detail, see Richard J. Dillon, *From Eye-Witnesses to Ministers of the Word*, Analecta Biblica 82 (Rome: Biblical Institute Press, 1978), 89-91.

63   For what follows, on Luke 24:13-49, see also Moloney, *The Resurrection of the Messiah*, 81-89.

64   See also Stuart Moran, *A Friendly Guide to the Gospel of Luke* (Melbourne: Garratt Publishing, 2013), 45-47. Remarkably, major commentators do not see the importance of the Luke's indication that the two disciples were walking "away from Jerusalem" (Greek: *apo Ierousalēm*). See, for example, I. Howard Marshall, *The Gospel of Luke: A Commentary on the Greek Text*, New International Greek Testament Commentary (Grand Rapids: Eerdmans, 1978), 892-93 (a lengthy discussion of the location of Emmaus); Eduard Schweizer, *The Good News According to Luke*, trans. David E. Green (London: SPCK, 1984), 370. Johnson, *Luke*, 393 and Fitzmyer, *Luke*, 2:1562, suggest that Emmaus is mentioned because it is "in the vicinity of Jerusalem" (Fitzmyer), and thus there is no journey away from Jerusalem. Similarly, see Dillon, *From Eye-Witnesses*, 85-86. They see the importance of Jerusalem, but suggest that Emmaus is so close that they do not leave the city.

65   See Johnson, *Luke*, 393. This is the last time in the direct narrative that the name appears.

66   The so-called "divine passive" is a way of indicating the action of God without mentioning the name, widely used in biblical literature, respecting the Jewish tradition never to name God.

67   Tannehill, *Luke*, 352, rightly points out that the disciples are not without guilt in their inability to recognize Jesus: "This concealment reflects their unreadiness to deal with Jesus' death. This is a culpable failure that must be overcome." See also idem, *Narrative Unity*, 1:227.

68   See Moran, *A Friendly Guide*, 45. For speculations about the identity of Cleopas and the other disciple, see Evans, *St Luke*, 906-7.

69   See Byrne, *Hospitality*, 187. This is missed by many who regard Jesus as "another traveler," like the disciples (see, for example, Schweizer, *Luke*, 372).

70   Their knowledge of the "brute facts" of the resurrection story is widely recognized. For a suggestive analysis of what this means for Lukan thought, see Dillon, *From Eye-Witnesses*, 55-56, 110-11; Johnson, *Luke*, 393-94.

71   For an excellent study of the inherent, but misunderstood, Lukan Christology involved in the disciples' words to Jesus, see Dillon, *From Eye-Witnesses*, 111-45.

72   See BDAG, 884, s.v. *prospoieō*: "make/act as though, pretend."

73   This shift in the initiative is more than "a narrative device meant to bring loveliness and humanity to the story" (Johnson, *Luke*, 396), although it also does that.

74   For a fully documented discussion of the eucharistic character of 24:30, see Jacques Dupont, "The Meal at Emmaus," in J. Delorme, et al., *The Eucharist in the New Testament*, 115-21. See also Marshall, *Luke*, 898, and especially Dillon, *From Eye-Witnesses,* 149-55. Dillon has further pointed out that in both Luke and Acts "breaking of the bread" is associated with instruction concerning Jesus' person and mission.

75   See Byrne, *Hospitality*, 190: "In the exposition of the word and in the eucharistic celebration (Word and Sacrament) he will be present to them throughout the remainder of the 'day,' the day of the Church, whose preaching in his name and in his Spirit will extend the 'day' of salvation (cf. 4:16-20) to the end of time." See also Johnson, *Luke*, 396, 399.

76   The fact that they "return to Jerusalem" in v. 33 further enhances the importance of their traveling "away from Jerusalem" in v. 13. Many scholars have seen the theological importance of this "return." For detail of this scholarship, see Dillon, *From Eye-Witnesses*, 92-94. Dillon finds himself in difficulty here. He has not appreciated the importance of the going "away from Jerusalem" in v. 13, and thus can only be "tentatively affirmative" (p. 93) of these suggestions.

77   Most scholars see this return to "Simon" as an indication of the traditional nature of 24:34, reflecting Easter confessions that are much older than Luke's Gospel (see 1 Cor 15:4). See, for example, Fitzmyer, *Luke*, 2:1569: "a stereotyped formula for appearances." See also Marshall, *Luke*, 899-900. I am suggesting that there is a more subtle Lukan point at stake. For a similar suggestion, see Dillon, *From Eye-Witnesses*, 100 note 88. See also Tannehill, *Narrative Unity*, 1:292-93.

78   Robert J. Karris, "God's Boundary-Breaking Mercy," *The Bible Today* 24 (1986), 27-28. For a good study of the defects of the disciples in the Gospel

of Luke, especially as they emerge over the passion narrative, see Tannehill, *Narrative Unity*, 1:153-74.

79   The presence of "joy" in what is otherwise described as lack of faith is puzzling. Johnson, *Luke*, 402, helpfully suggests that v. 41 indicates a purely emotional experience that is too powerful for true belief, and a restatement of the basic Lukan truth that resurrection faith requires the interpretative word (see vv. 44-46). See also Tannehill, *Luke*, 359-60. Marshall, *Luke*, 902, suggests: "It was too good to be true."

80   The importance of the table-fellowship in this passage has been shown by Demetrius R. Dumm, "Luke 24:44-49 and Hospitality," in *Sin, Salvation and the Spirit: Commemorating the Fiftieth Year of the Liturgical Press*, ed. Daniel Durkin (Collegeville: The Liturgical Press, 1979), 230-39. See also Tannehill, *Luke*, 357-58.

81   Fitzmyer, *Luke*, 2:1575. See also Talbert, *Reading Luke*, 238-39. For some helpful reflections on the need for this point of view in the Lukan community, see E. Earle Ellis, *The Gospel of Luke*, New Century Bible (London: Oliphants, 1974), 274-76.

82   See Tannehill, *Narrative Unity*, 1:289-93.

83   See Senior, *The Passion of Jesus in Luke*, 56-58.

84   On this, see Dillon, *From Eye-Witnesses*, 197-203. See also idem, "Easter Revelation and Mission Program in Luke 24:46-48," in *Sin, Salvation and the Spirit*, 240-70. For the ongoing importance of this commission in Acts, see Johnson, *Luke*, 402-3.

85   On the Easter appearances as a restoration of failed discipleship, see Tannehill, *Narrative Unity*, 1:277-301. As he writes: "What was closed can be reopened" (p. 299). It must be, as the apostles are the main protagonists in the Acts of the Apostles. See also Moloney, "Luke 24: To be Witnesses," 183-95; George, *Études sue l'Oeuvre de Luc*, 387-94.

86   There is a growing sensitivity among scholars of Luke's special interest in the "lost ones." This has always been noticed as central to the three parables in Luke 15, but the theme is now seen as all-pervasive. See especially, Donahue, *The Gospel in Parable*, 126-93. With particular reference to the way in which the Emmaus story embodies a theme that runs through the entire Gospel, see Dillon, *From Eye-Witnesses*, 240-49. Interestingly (for our purposes), Dillon entitles this section of his study: "Guest and Host of the Unworthy." See also O'Toole, *The Unity of Luke's Theology*, 109-48; Karris, *Luke: Artist and Theologian*, 23-78; and the studies cited above in note 35.

87   For a study of the constitutive elements of resurrection stories, see Charles H. Dodd, "The Appearances of the Risen Christ: An Essay in Form-Criticism of the Gospels," in *More New Testament Studies* (Manchester: University Press, 1968), 102-33. See also, Raymond E. Brown, *The Virginal Conception and Bodily Resurrection of Jesus* (London: Geoffrey Chapman, 1973) 96-125.

CHAPTER SIX

THE FOURTH GOSPEL

Each of the so-called Synoptic Gospels—Mark, Matthew, and Luke—expresses a unique "point of view." When we turn to the Fourth Gospel we find ourselves in a different world.[1] The overall story hardly ever fits the scheme of the Synoptic Gospels, and John's understanding of the life, preaching, death, and resurrection of Jesus is unique.[2] The Fourth Gospel is dominated by the conviction that God gave the gift of his Son to the world that he loves so much, that the world might have life (see John 3:16-17).[3] In the light of the consistent Tradition found in Paul, Mark, Matthew, and Luke, our investigation must test whether John indicates that this "gift" manifests itself in the world and in the Church through the eucharistic presence of Jesus to the broken.

Contemporary interpretations of the Fourth Gospel take a variety of positions on the presence or absence of sacramental teaching in this Gospel. Some scholars have argued for an understanding of many of the events from the life of Jesus as deeply impregnated with a sacramental understanding of God's action in Jesus. Where there is the possibility of sacramental teaching, John implies such teaching.[4] Others have claimed that John has no interest in the idea of sacraments, and may well be anti-sacramental.[5] We cannot survey this scholarship within the pages of this study.[6] There is no overtly sacramental teaching in the Johannine story. But many contemporary scholars find hints of eucharistic teaching throughout this subtle Gospel.[7] The miracle of the marriage feast at Cana (John 2:1-11) can be interpreted symbolically to see the wine that Jesus provides as eucharistic. The Johannine version of the miracle of the multiplication of the bread (6:1-15), like the Synoptic stories, reflects a eucharistic background. The people "recline" for a meal (vv. 10-11),

Jesus "takes," "gives thanks" (Greek: *eucharistēsas*), and distributes both the bread and the fish to the reclining crowd (v. 11). Fragments remain, and are collected (vv. 12-13). But the "sign" of the bread is misunderstood (vv. 14-15). As often with the Johannine miracles, the misunderstanding of the sign leads into the discourse on the bread from heaven (vv. 25-59).[8] A symbolic reading of the Gospel has also been applied to Jesus' gift of himself at the footwashing (see especially 13:15) as "analogous in content within the context of the narrative of the supper."[9] The allegory on the vine (15:1-5) is sometimes seen as eucharistic in its repeated use of the theme of "abiding."[10]

This brief list (by no means exhaustive) of "hints" from the Fourth Gospel indicates that considerable industry has been devoted to uncovering John's sacramental instruction. Some of it is fanciful.[11] John *never* dedicates an explicit and overt passage to Jesus' eucharistic meal with his disciples.

EUCHARISTIC HINTS IN JOHN 6:1-15, 6:51-58, AND 19:34

Among several suggested passages that have a eucharistic background, three stand out: 6:1-15, 6:51c-58, and 19:34.[12] The first of these, the Johannine version of the miracle of the loaves and fish, contains many uniquely Johannine themes. For example, consistent with John 5:1-10:42, which deals with the celebration of the feasts of the Jews, John locates the miracle at the time of Passover (see 6:4). He also wishes to associate Jesus' gift of the bread with the Mosaic gift of the manna, and thus the theme of "the mountain," recalling Sinai, appears in v. 3.[13] The report of the miracle itself has much in common with the Synoptic accounts, especially Mark 6:31-44, Matthew 14:23-31, and Luke 9:10-17.[14]

In a way common to John's understanding of Jesus as all-knowing, Jesus raises the problem of feeding the multitude to test his disciples, although already knowing what he will do (vv. 5-6). The disciples indicate they have very little to offer, five barley loaves and two fish (vv. 7-9). From that point on, Jesus is in command of the situation (vv. 10-13). He has the five thousand recline for a meal. He then "took" (Greek: *elaben*) the loaves, gave thanks (Greek: *eucharistēsas*), and distributed them among the people. He does the same with the fish. Jesus himself distributes the bread and fish, unlike the Synoptic Gospels, where he engages the disciples with the distribution. The fragments are gathered (v. 13). The meal remains open as the fragments (Greek: *ta klasmata*), an expression used in the early Church to refer to the eucharistic species, are now available in the twelve baskets. The report of the miracle, as in the Synoptics, is heavily laden with language that recalls the celebration of the Lord's Supper: take, give thanks, distribute, gather, and fragments.[15] These are expressions that are found in the earliest records of the Christian Eucharist.[16] As with the Synoptic Gospels, John's use of these familiar expressions indicate that his community celebrated Eucharist. The audience is aware that the bread miracle points toward Jesus' eucharistic feeding of the multitudes. But for John this symbolic gift to the people that remains open generates misunderstanding. Recalling the promise that a prophet like Moses would return in the days of the Messiah, the people identify him as "the prophet," and wish to force him to become their king. Jesus leaves the scene (vv. 14-15).[17]

The hint of the Eucharist in 6:1-15 disappears, as Jesus reveals himself to his disciples crossing the stormy sea as "I AM HE" (vv. 16-22; see v. 20). The crowd that he had fed by the side of the lake is not present for this encounter. Only the disciples in the boat have received this further revelation of Jesus as the presence of the divine.[18] The two miracles (vv. 1-15 and vv. 16-22) generate a long discourse to the crowd that had been fed, and had followed Jesus and the disciples to Capernaum (vv. 22-24). Although the theme of "bread from heaven" dominates the discourse (vv. 25-59), Jesus is not speaking to the crowd and the disciples about the Eucharist. For the uninitiated, this can come as a surprise; but John is using the Jewish tradition that the gift of the manna "from heaven" had ceased when Israel entered the Promised Land (see Exod 16:35; Joshua 5:10-12). Nevertheless, the Lord continued to nourish his people. He replaced the manna with another "bread from heaven": the Law given by Moses. Across the discourse (vv. 25-59) Jesus insists that the crowds will not be satisfied with the bread given by Moses and the fathers of Israel (see vv. 27-30). That bread is no longer available, and the Patriarchs are dead. Jesus alone can give the true bread from heaven: he will make God known to them. Only he can do this, as he is the Son of God. Belief in Jesus, the Son of God, will produce eternal life. Only the Son knows God, comes from him, and thus makes him known (vv. 31-50).[19] The Law was given through Moses; the fullness of the gift of the truth took place in and through Jesus Christ (see 1:17 AT).[20]

This teaching can only generate difficulties for the post-Easter Johannine community, believers who "believe without seeing" (see 20:29). If they receive life from believing in the revelation of Jesus as the Son of God (see vv. 29, 35, 40, 47), where do they encounter this revelation of God? Jesus closes the discourse by providing an answer to that question for the original audience that received this Gospel, and for believers of all time. In vv. 51-58, Jesus speaks of eating the flesh of the Son of Man and drinking his blood (vv. 53-54). In the explicit eucharistic terminology of vv. 51-58, the members of the first-century Johannine community hear that they are to decide for or against God's revelation in his Son at their celebration of the Eucharist[21] There they encounter the revelation of God in and through his Son, as they eat the flesh and drink the blood of the Son of Man. It is in the broken body and the spilt blood of the eucharistic celebration that they shall "look on him whom they have pierced" (19:37).[22]

The same issue facing the post-Easter Johannine audience—living the "absence of the physical Jesus"—is behind the account of the blood and water flowing from the pierced side of the crucified Jesus after his death in 19:34. Johannine thought is dominated by a theology of the Cross as Jesus' supreme achievement. There Jesus is lifted up and exalted (see 3:13-15; 8:28; 12:23, 32-33), glorifying the Father (7:37-39; 12:28; 13:31-32 etc.).[23] But John's presentation of the crucified Jesus as the revelation of God who so loved the world that he handed over his only Son (see 3:16) raises a further question, similar to the discourse of 6:25-50. Where can the Johannine community, "who have not seen and yet believe" (20:29), find and experience this revelation of a God of love upon the Cross? Where do they "gaze upon him" (19:37)? The answer is found in the John's account of the blood and water flowing from the side of the pierced Jesus in 19:34. What is especially important for an understanding of the report of the flow of blood and water in v. 34 is the following rare direct intervention of John into the narrative. He insists with some passion that what they are being told is true. They are hearing it from a witness, and he is telling them of the flow of blood and water from the crucified Jesus: "that you also may believe" (19:35).[24]

The message of Jesus' discourse in 6:25-59 would lead the members of a Johannine audience seeking an experience within their life as a believing community to ask where the revelation of God in his Son can be found. In a similar manner the account of the revelation of God's glory on the Cross generates a parallel need in the community— where can a later believing community experience this revelation? In 19:34 (as in 6:51-58) John responds to the needs of an early Christian community by telling its members that they will find the presence of the pierced one in their eucharistic celebrations.[25]

The above brief sketch of these eucharistic passages of the Fourth Gospel—6:1-15, 6:51-58, and 19:34—provides evidence that John and his community celebrated the Eucharist. Such celebrations are taken for granted by John as he points his community to the revelation of God in the broken body and the spilt blood of the crucified Jesus. What is equally evident is that John uses his understanding of the role of the Eucharist in the life of the community to develop a theological and pastoral approach not identified in the other New Testament passages we have considered. In this Gospel there is an understanding of Eucharist as "presence," as throughout the other Gospels, but the author of this Gospel adapts that theology to address the needs of a community sensing its distance from the saving events of the life and death of Jesus (see 20:29). John does not develop narratives that explicitly tell of Baptism and Eucharist. He takes those celebrations for granted. His audience is immediately aware that these fundamental Christian experiences are behind his hints. "It is in the Sacraments of Baptism and Eucharist that the Johannine Church can find the presence of the absent one."[26]

This message was addressed to a community wondering, at the end of the first century, where and how they might encounter the Christ, the Son of God, believe in him, and thus have life in his name (see 20:30-31). John was offering a significant response to a troubled community.[27] The theme of "presence" is evident, as in our other New Testament witnesses. But there is a further common element across all New Testament eucharistic texts: each of them look back to the loving self-gift of Jesus in crucifixion for their meaning. Both

6:51-58 and 19:34 make sense only in the light of the Cross. But the understanding of the Eucharist as Jesus' presence to the broken that can be traced in 1 Corinthians, Mark, Matthew, and Luke is not found in those passages in the Fourth Gospel (6:1-15, 6:51-58; 19:34). Nevertheless, all New Testament witnesses look to the community's celebration of the Eucharist as the saving presence of the crucified one for its meaning.

There is a further passage in the Fourth Gospel, sometimes suggested as "sacramental," that deserves special attention: the narrative of the footwashing and the gift of the morsel in John 13:1-38.[28] After the solemn announcement that Jesus, knowing his hour had come to return to the Father, is about to show his remarkable love for his own "unto the end" (13:1), a footwashing and a meal are reported. The footwashing has baptismal hints (see especially 13:6-11),[29] and Christian tradition has associated the events reported in 13:1-38 with the Eucharist, in the light of the overt eucharistic focus found in the accounts of the Last Supper in all three Synoptic Gospels. For many Christian traditions, John 13:1-15—the passage on the "example" that Jesus gives to his own in washing their feet—is used as the Gospel reading for the celebration of Holy Thursday, the liturgical commemoration of the Last Supper.

But, significantly, in the Fourth Gospel there is no account that parallels the setting and the ritual at the table reported in the Synoptic Gospels. The closest Johannine parallel to this ritual is found in a quite different setting, a discourse beside the lake of Tiberias (see 6:1). Here, we find words (but not actions) that recall Jesus' Last Supper. He tells his disciples and "the Jews": "The bread which I shall give is my flesh for the life of the world" (6:51).[30] John has used his report of Jesus' final meal with his disciples as the setting for his sharing a long "farewell discourse" with them (14:1-16:33), flanked with a narrative of the footwashing and the gift of the morsel (13:1-38), and a final prayer (17:1-26). Rejecting possible eucharistic allusions in the use of the image of the vine and the verb "to abide" in 15:1-11,[31] there is only one place in 13:1-17:26 where the eucharistic practice of the Johannine community might come into play: in the account of the footwashing and the gift of the morsel, with its associated discourses and events in 13:1-38. The possibility of eucharistic elements in the

Johannine account of Jesus' final night with his disciples in 13:1-38 deserves careful attention.

THE PROBLEM OF THE LAST DISCOURSE

John 13:1-38 forms part of a larger literary unity, a so-called last discourse (13:1-17:26) which is marked by a number of well-known literary tensions.[32] A scholar who has devoted great energy to the study of John 13-17, Fernando Segovia, wrote in 1982: "Nowadays hardly any exegete would vigorously maintain that John 13:31-18:1 constitutes a literary unity as it stands."[33]

The tensions that scholars uncover in John 13:1-17:26 have led to the attempted recovery of various "strata," reflecting different historical moments in the Johannine community's experience and reflection, placed side by side to form the passage as a whole. Thus John 13:1-17:26 is the final collection of many traditions that have been remembered, told, and perhaps performed, in various times and situations throughout the life of the Johannine Church, prior to the final composition of the Gospel of John as it has come down to us in the Christian Canon of Sacred Scripture.[34] No doubt 13:1-17:26 had a long and complicated literary history, and we can trace some of that history, reflecting the history of the community itself, through careful analysis.[35] A reading of the discourse in its present shape indicates that, on the basis of literary form alone, 13:1-38 (a narrative) and 17:1-26 (a prayer) stand apart. John 14:1-16:33 can correctly be regarded as a discourse. However, it is also marked by strange contradictions and tensions, especially the words of Jesus in 14:31, which appear to lead nowhere. There is a repetition of themes in 14:1-31 in 16:4-33, with chapter 16 more elegantly restating chapter 14's themes of Jesus' departure, its motivation, and consequences.[36] The allegory of the vine with its theme of abiding, and the contrasting words of Jesus on the hatred and violence that are found in 15:1-16:3 are unique, and appear to some as having little logical link with the discourses in chapters 14 and 16.[37]

If 13:1-17:26 presents literary problems for the interpreter, severe tensions are also found within the narrative of John 13:1-38.[38] There appears to be a double interpretation of the footwashing scene. The first of these (vv. 6-11) speaks of the disciples having a part in the death of Jesus, with hints of baptismal practices. This theme disappears in v. 12. A more exhortative passage follows in vv. 12-20, written to encourage the imitation of Jesus. Because it is judged as "moralistic" in tone, it is often read as a later addition to what was originally a theological reflection on Jesus' gift of himself to his disciples in love, and an invitation that the disciples join him in the loving gift of themselves.[39] It is widely accepted that vv. 31-38 should be separated from the more narrative accounts of the footwashing and the gift of the morsel of vv. 1-30. It appears clumsy to link Judas' ominous departure from the upper room into the darkness (v. 30) with Jesus' exultant proclamation: "Now is the Son of Man glorified and in him God is glorified; if God is glorified in him, God will glorify him in himself, and glorify him at once" (vv. 31-32).[40] The proclamation of the glorification of the Son of Man is judged to be the beginning of the discourse proper.[41] Some scholars understand vv. 31-38 as the original introduction to 13:31-14:31, the more primitive form of the discourse,[42] while others see it as a solemn introductory summary to the entire discourse in its final form.[43]

Stories of events that took place on the evening before Jesus' arrest, trial, and execution; several discourses on Jesus' departure, the future mission, sufferings, and obligations of his disciples; and a prayer of departure—all had their independent history in the story-telling of the Johannine community. This process of telling and re-telling the Johannine tradition would have been repeated many times until the canonical Gospel of John finally emerged in the shape that has come down through the Christian centuries. Because of this process, the end-product, even though it sometimes has untidy seams, is thoroughly "Johannine" in all its parts.[44] But an author consciously took these various strata from the recorded memory of his community and deliberately laid them side by side to form 13:1-17:26 as we now have it. However obvious the seams might be to the eye of the literary and historical critic, once the various parts of John 13:1-17:26 were put together, the reader is challenged to make something of the narrative as it stands. The reader strives, "even if unconsciously, to fit everything together in a consistent pattern."[45] If almost one-third of the Gospel story is dedicated to 13:1-17:26, then it must have been of particular importance to the author, whatever its sources and its history within the development of the Johannine community and its Gospel story.

An author attempts to communicate with a reader in and through the narrative. That such communication continues to take place is shown by the text's ongoing readership in the Church. Segovia, who in 1982 was pessimistic about the literary unity of the passage, in 1991 expressed the need "to address the character of 13:31-16:33 as an artistic and strategic whole with a highly unified and coherent literary structure and development, unified and coherent strategic concerns and aims, and a distinctive rhetorical situation."[46]

THE LITERARY DESIGN OF JOHN 13:1-38

After the reflections of both the narrator (12:37-43) and Jesus (12:44-50) that conclude the Johannine account of the public ministry, 13:1 points the narrative in a new direction. Jesus is alone with his disciples in the upper room. It is "the most significant transition in the Gospel, introducing not only the scene of the footwashing but the entire second half of the Gospel."[47] But where does the unit end? Are we to consider only 13:1-30, or did the author intend that vv. 31-38 be read as part of the story of the footwashing and the gift of the morsel?[48] The material in vv. 31-38 is not pure discourse. There is also the report of an encounter between Simon Peter and Jesus in vv. 36-38 where the future denials of Simon Peter are foretold. This passage closely matches the similar prophecies, earlier in the narrative, that told of the future betrayal of Judas (vv. 10b-11, 21-22) and picks up Peter's earlier misunderstanding of Jesus' gesture in the footwashing (see vv. 6-10a). There are other literary indications that bind the words of Jesus to Peter in vv. 36-38 with his earlier words about Judas in vv. 10b-11, especially Jesus' promise that what Peter cannot know and understand now will become clear later (v. 7; vv. 36-37. See also v. 19).

A feature of John 13:1-38 is the regular appearance of a typically Johannine expression: "Amen, amen I say to you" (see vv. 16, 20, 21, 38). This expression is found *only* in the Fourth Gospel, where it appears 24 times.[49] It appears in 13:1-38 more times (four uses) than in any other chapter of the Gospel, and it appears only three times in the rest of the last discourse (14:12; 16:20, 23).[50] The second reference to the betrayal of Judas (v. 21) opens with this Johannine expression, while the prophecy of the denials of Peter closes with it (v. 38). The use of the Johannine expression "amen, amen I say to you," at the beginning and the end of the prophecies of betrayal and denial reported in vv. 21-38 may keep vv. 31-38 more closely associated with 13:1-30 than with the rest of the discourse in chapters 14-17. The themes of the failure of Judas and Peter play no further role in the discourse proper. It does not reappear until the passion narrative, where it returns as a major element in the drama (18:1-11, 15-18, 25-27).[51]

The Johannine use of the double "amen" serves as an important indication of the overall structure of this part of the narrative. John has deliberately positioned double "amen" sayings in vv. 17, 20, 21, and 38 to create the following carefully structured plot:

1. **Verses 1-17:** The footwashing is dramatically reported, and a number of discussions surround the narrative. This section features John's comments (see vv. 1-5), dialogue between Jesus and Peter (vv. 6-10a), and Jesus' words on Judas (vv. 10b-11), in the midst of the failure and ignorance of the disciples. *The section concludes with the double "amen" in vv. 16-17.*

2. **Verses 18-20:** Jesus speaks to his disciples, and his words form the literary center of the passage. *The section concludes with the double "amen" in v. 20.*

3. **Verses 21-38:** In a narrative that matches vv. 1-17, John tells of Jesus' gift of the morsel, and a number of discussions surround the narrative. The context of betrayal and denial intensify (vv. 21-30, 36-38). *The section opens and closes with a double "amen" in v. 21 and in v. 38.*

In the first major section of vv. 1-38, the double "amen" appears in v. 16, opening two statements from Jesus, one about the relationship between servant and master (v. 16) and another about knowing and doing (v. 17). These statements of vv. 16-17 look back to the remarks from John's introduction in vv. 1-5 where the themes of (a) Jesus and "his own," (b) Jesus' "knowing," and (c) Jesus' "doing" are spelt out: "When Jesus *knew* that his hour had come ... having loved *his own* who were in the world, he loved them to the end (v. 1). ... Jesus *knowing* that the Father had given all things into his hands ... *rose* from the supper, *laid aside* his garments, and *girded himself* with a towel" (vv. 3-4).

Jesus' "knowing" that his hour had come, and that the Father had given all things into his hands, led to an active "doing": he loves his disciples *to the end* (Greek: *eis telos*), and as a sign of this, he washes their feet: knowledge flows into action.[52] John 13 opens with a message to the audience that the "knowing" and "doing' of Jesus touches the life of the disciples, whom he loves unconditionally ("to the end"). The narrative reporting Jesus' washing the feet of his disciples, and calling them "to have part with him," follows. At the close of the section, after the solemn introduction of the double "amen," Jesus tells the disciples that, in their relationship to him as his servants and sent ones (v. 16), they are called to repeat what "the master" has done. Blessed are they if, knowing these things, they do them (v. 17). He has given them an "example" (v. 15).

The verb "to know" reappears in v. 18: "I know whom I have chosen." But another theme emerges that was not found in vv. 1-17. It is not only Jesus' knowledge that is stressed, but also the fact that he has "chosen" his disciples. Not only has he chosen them, but they are to become his "sent ones": "He who receives any one whom I send receives me" (v. 20). The "chosen ones" are further described as "any one whom I send." The closely linked themes of being chosen and being sent mark the beginning and the end of vv. 18-20. The themes of choosing and sending, surrounding Jesus' hope that the disciples will eventually come to believe who he is in v. 19 ("you will believe that I AM HE"), form a unit, rounded off by the double "amen" in v. 20.

The double "amen" opens and closes vv. 21-38. The section is also framed with Jesus' prophecies concerning the failure of members of his innermost circle of friends, the disciples with whom he is sharing his table: Judas (vv. 21-30) and Peter (vv. 36-38). Intertwined through the passage dealing with the betrayal of Judas is the theme of the gift of the morsel. On receiving the morsel, Judas leaves the upper room, and the passion is set in motion. This is the significance of the introduction to Jesus' words of exultation in v. 31a: "When he had gone out …". The action of Judas is crucial to John's understanding of the glorification of Jesus through the Cross. One should not force a break in the narrative between Judas' exit into the night in v. 30 and the words of Jesus in vv. 31-32. John makes clear reference to Judas in v. 31a (literally: "When, *therefore*, he had gone out" [AT]; Greek: *hote oun exêlthen*) because he wants his audience to *link* the two. There is a logical and causal link between the departure of Judas into the dark (vv. 30-31a) and the glorification of Jesus through the Cross (vv. 31b-32).

THE GIFT OF THE MORSEL:
A EUCHARISTIC INTERPRETATION

The final section of the narrative, vv. 21-38, focuses upon Jesus' gift of the morsel to Judas and its aftermath, within the context of misunderstanding, prophecies of betrayal, and denials, accompanied by Jesus' command to love as he has loved (vv. 34-35). An overview of John's use of the theme of Baptism in vv. 1-17—a passage that has many parallel features with vv. 21-38—guides an understanding of the implications, for our study, of Jesus' gift of the morsel to Judas. Attention must also be devoted to the central statement of vv. 18-20, which provides a key to the significance of the actions that precede and follow, and the subsequent parallel to vv. 1-17 that deals with the gift of the morsel in vv. 21-38.[53]

THE FOOTWASHING AND ITS AFTERMATH (VV. 1-17):
A SKETCH

Crucial for the interpretation of John 13:1-38 are John's introductory words in 13:1. Jesus is aware that the hour of his return to the Father is imminent. However, the "end" of his life among his disciples is at hand: "having loved his own who were in the world, he loved them to the end (Greek: *eis telos*)." The expression "to the end" has a double meaning. It refers, obviously, to a chronological end. For John this means Jesus' death, resurrection, and return to the Father. But the quality of Jesus' love for his own is also indicated by the expression. He not only loved them until the time of his departure through death, resurrection, and ascension, he also loved them in a way unimaginable by human standards. He loved them "consummately."[54]

The first narrative section, regarding Jesus' washing of the disciples' feet and giving the morsel to Judas, begins with a declaration of love and ends with the typically Johannine double "amen" (vv. 16-17). It unfolds in three parts, identified by the events and the major players in those events:

1. **Verses 1-5:** The narrator announces that Jesus "knows" that the hour of his departure to the Father has come. What is about to be told will demonstrate the consummate perfection of Jesus' love for his own (v. 1). These words are immediately followed by an indication that the devil had already decided in his heart that Judas would betray Jesus (v. 2). Too often the translators report that "the devil had already put it into the heart of Judas" (RSV). This does not correctly render the Greek,[55] and disturbs the narrative. It is not until in v. 27, after Judas takes the morsel, that Satan enters him. "Knowing" these things does not deter Jesus from moving into action. He prepares himself and washes the disciples' feet (vv. 3-5). As we have mentioned, Jesus' *love* and *knowledge* flow into *action*.

2. **Verses 6-11:** Peter objects to Jesus' washing his feet, and Jesus dialogues with him (vv. 6-10b). Here the link between the footwashing and the practice of Baptism emerges. Peter can "have no part" with Jesus unless he is prepared to be washed by Jesus (v. 8). Through the footwashing, the disciple "has part" in the saving effects of Jesus' death and resurrection.[56] This leads to Jesus' first statement on Judas' future betrayal (vv. 10c-11).

3. **Verses 12-17:** Jesus instructs the disciples on the significance of what he has done for them, and asks that they do the same, following his example (vv. 12-15). Widely regarded as a later "moralizing" interpretation of the footwashing, it is nothing of the kind. The pattern of teacher and lord kneeling in self-gift for his own must continue as a mark of the followers of Jesus. He has given them an example they are to repeat in their lives of service, no matter what their future roles might be. The choice of the Greek word for "example" (v. 15. Greek: *hypodeigma*) continues the theme of self-gift in love, even to death. The Greek expression, found only in John 13:15 in the entire New Testament, appears in some well-known Jewish texts that speak of exemplary death (LXX 2 Macc 6:28; 4 Macc 17:22-23; Sir 44:16). "Jesus' death ... as it is here interpreted through the footwashing, is the norm of life and conduct for the believing community."[57] The double "amen" closes the section that has asked that disciples be servants of their master, blessed by a knowledge that flows into action (vv. 16-17).

As the section opened, Jesus' love and knowledge flowed into action in vv. 1-5. In a beautifully balanced sentence, it closes with his words to disciples: "If you *know* these things, blessed are you if you *do* them" (v. 17).[58] As Jesus has demonstrated love in action in the footwashing, he has given them an example: they are to demonstrate love in action by following his example (v. 15), unto death—to the end (*eis telos*).

THE CENTRAL STATEMENT (VV. 18-20)

The stunning centerpiece of 13:1-38 is found in vv. 18-20.[59] Between vv. 1-17 and vv. 21-38 the rationale for both the footwashing and the gift of the morsel is spelt out. Despite its brevity, the passage is articulated by means of three distinct affirmations:

1. **Verse 18:** Jesus has *chosen* fragile disciples, one of whom will betray him.
2. **Verse 19:** Why he has done this: "that you may believe that I AM HE."
3. **Verse 20:** Solemnly—introducing his words with the double "amen"—Jesus *sends out* these disciples, that both Jesus and the one who sent him may be received.

In v. 18 and v. 20 Jesus speaks of his relationship with the disciples. He knows whom he has chosen, and he is aware that one of them will strike out against him. He recalls Psalm 41:10, stating that one of them, who shares the table and eats his bread (Greek: *ho trōgōn mou ton arton*), has lifted his heel against him (v. 18). The betrayer, who has lurked throughout this narrative (see vv. 2, 10c-11), is again mentioned in v. 18. Despite the failures and the betrayals, however, *Jesus has chosen these disciples*. In v. 20 he points out that he has not only chosen them (v. 18), but he will send them out (v. 20). Closing this central section with a further double "amen," Jesus assures them that he sends them out so that they can make Jesus known, just as Jesus has made the Father known. Anyone who receives his sent ones, therefore, will also receive the Father. *Jesus will send out these disciples to make known both the Father and the Son*. For this remarkable mission, Jesus has chosen and sent out ignorant, fragile disciples, even one who will betray him.

The question "why" must be asked. To choose and send out those who fail, betray, and deny makes no sense. The response to that question is provided in v. 19, the central statement of 13:1-38: "I tell you this now, before it takes place, that *when it does take place you may believe that I AM HE*" (Greek: *hina pisteusēte hotan genētai **hoti egō eimi***). In Jesus' act of footwashing—symbolizing his consummate love-unto-death for disciples who fail to understand and who will betray him—the God and Father of Jesus is revealed.[60] It will shortly be matched by the gift of the morsel that also tells of self-gift unto death for disciples who do not understand him, who betray him, and deny him (vv. 21-38). As yet, the unconditional self-gift of Jesus on the Cross for his fragile disciples has not taken place, but it is anticipated in the loving gestures of the footwashing and the gift of the morsel. The reader/hearer *of the story* is well aware that what is anticipated by these gestures will take place on the Cross, but the disciples *in the story* do not. They continue in their ignorance, their false promises, and their misunderstanding.

The post-Easter Johannine community is told that Jesus has chosen disciples, and sent them out as bearers of his presence and the presence of the Father who sent him (vv. 18, 20). He is telling his disciples all these things now, before the event of the Cross, so that when that consummate revelation of love takes place, then they might believe that he is the presence of the divine among them (v. 19: that I AM HE). If the earlier statements about the counter-cultural nature of Jesus' actions in his example to the disciples are surprising (vv. 12-15), his revelation of why he is giving himself unconditionally in love to disciples, chosen and sent out by him, who not only do not love him in the same way, but who will deny him, betray him, and misunderstand him, transcends all possible human explanation. This is what it means to love *to the end* (v. 1; Greek: *eis telos*), consummately, in a way that the world can never comprehend. The love of Jesus for his own *to the end* is the revelation of the incomprehensible love of God. In these gestures of loving self-gift, anticipating the Cross, Jesus makes known the love of God. They demonstrate Jesus' love in action to stunned readers and hearers *of the story*, who are themselves fragile disciples of Jesus.[61]

Matching the structure of vv. 1-17, the closing section of 13:1-38 also has three parts:

1. **Verses 21-25:** The narrator indicates Jesus' profound emotional condition. Opening with a double "amen," Jesus again forecasts the future betrayal of Judas. The Beloved Disciple, at the request of Simon Peter, asks who this might be.
2. **Verses 26-30:** Jesus indicates that he will give the morsel to his betrayer. A brief dialogue between Jesus and Judas follows the gift of the morsel. No one at the table understood what was happening as Judas goes out into the darkness of the night.
3. **Verses 31-38:** As Judas departs, the Passion begins. Jesus announces that the moment of the glorification of the Son of Man and the revelation of the glory of God is "now." He issues a new commandment: that they love one another as he has loved them. Peter continues to misunderstand Jesus and his destiny, and Jesus, closing this section with a final double "amen," foretells his threefold denial before cock-crow.

In v. 21, Jesus' words open with the double "amen." He raises the question of the betrayer, and begins a dialogue with his own that will lead to the revelation of the identity of the betrayer at the table (v. 26. See v. 18). There is also a parallel between v. 1, where the narrator reported Jesus' knowledge and love, and v. 21a, where another emotional experience is mentioned: Jesus is troubled in spirit. A link with the Cross was established in v. 1 through words that spoke of Jesus' love for his own *to the end*. The Cross is again close at hand in the words "troubled in spirit."[62] Jesus' indicates that one of the disciples, present at the table (see vv. 12, 18), will betray him (v. 21b). These words set off a reaction among the disciples around the table, who are not moving in the world of Jesus. They are "uncertain (Greek: *aporoumenoi*) of whom he spoke" (v. 22).[63] Ignorance, confusion, and misunderstanding continue (see vv. 6, 7, 9, 12-13).

The Beloved Disciple appears for the first time in the story.[64] He is lying at table, "close to the breast of Jesus," (v. 23) a position of affectionate closeness.[65] Despite his position of honor, he is included in the perplexity of v. 22. Peter, subordinated to the Beloved Disciple, asks, "Tell us who it is of whom he speaks" (v. 24). This special disciple, like all the other disciples at the table, is ignorant of the full meaning of Jesus' words. His question shows ignorance, and triggers the words and actions that follow: "Lord, who is it?" (v. 25).

The one who is to betray him will be part of an intimate human gesture: at table, dipping the morsel and sharing it (v. 26a). Jesus' actions fulfill his words: "So when he had dipped the morsel, *he took it* and gave it to Judas, the Son of Simon Iscariot" (v. 26b). Because most early interpreters of John 13 could not accept the possibility that the morsel given to Judas might be regarded as eucharistic, the textual tradition is very disturbed here. The above translation of v. 26b accepts the Greek words "he took it" (*lambanei kai*) as original.[66] We will return to the significance of this detail below. It is only after the reception of the morsel that Satan enters into Judas (v. 27a). In v. 2 the reader was told that the devil had decided that Judas was to betray Jesus, but in v. 27a Satan enters into Judas. He is now part of a satanic program, diametrically opposed to the program of God revealed in Jesus. Yet, in an exquisite final gesture of love, Jesus shares the dipped morsel with his future betrayer (v. 26). Does the most evil disciple in the story (see 6:70-71; 12:4-6; 13:2) share a morsel that points to the Eucharist (13:26)?[67] Does the unbelievable continue to occur as Jesus' unconditional love (v. 1: *to the end*) is revealed in his actions?

Because Jesus' consummate love for his failing disciples (v. 1) is not recognized as the key to the interpretation of John 13, almost all scholars and all preachers shy clear of a eucharistic interpretation, suggested by the questions raised in the previous paragraph.[68] Those who have seen the passage as eucharistic use 1 Corinthians 11:29 to claim that Satan enters the sinful Judas because he takes the eucharistic morsel without discerning.[69] This interpretation has no place within the Johannine story of Jesus' unbelievable love for his disciples.[70]

Looking back to vv. 18-20—the centerpiece of 13:1-38—as Jesus addressed his disciples in v. 18, he told them that the events about to happen would fulfill Psalm 41:10b: "One who eats my bread has lifted his heel against me." The LXX translation of the first part of the Psalm ("One who eats my bread") uses the regular Greek verb for human eating (*esthiō*); but in 13:18, John uses the verb "to munch, to grind with the teeth" (*trōgō*).[71] John has deliberately replaced the verb in the Greek of the LXX with a more vigorous and physical word.[72]

The only other use of the verb *trōgō* in the Gospel of John is found in the eucharistic passage of 6:51-58, where it appears *four times* (6:54, 56, 57, 58). Framed between uses of the usual verb for human eating (*phagō*: see 6:51, 52, 53, and 58), the more physical verb appears in 6:51-58, the most explicit eucharistic passage in the Gospel.[73] In 13:18, John refashions the LXX version of an Old Testament passage, linking the gift of the morsel to Judas with Christian traditions that surrounded the Last Supper (see also Mark 14:18 and Luke 22:21, where Ps 41:10 also provides background). These eucharistic hints would not have been missed by John's original audience.

But there is more. Above I included "and he took" in my translation of v. 26, but these words are not found in some early manuscripts.[74] They recall Jesus' deliberate action of "taking" bread in the bread miracles of all four Gospels (Mark 6:41; 8:6; Matt 14:19; 15:36; Luke 9:16; John 6:11), reflecting the eucharistic thought and practice of the early Church. The same expression is found in the Synoptic and Pauline reports of the Last Supper (Mark 14:22; Matt 26:26; Luke 22:19; 1 Cor 11:23).[75] Given the eucharistic hints involved in the verb used by John in 13:18 and in 6:51-58, the originality of the words indicating that Jesus *took* the morsel before giving it to Judas must be maintained.[76] The future eucharistic celebration of Jesus' presence in the community Eucharist is a sub-theme to the meal and the gift of the morsel (vv. 21-38), just as a future Baptism ritual is a sub-theme to the footwashing (vv. 1-17). Jesus gives the morsel to the most despised character in the Gospel's narrative. The audience and all subsequent Christian readers of the Gospel have been horrified by this suggestion. But Jesus' never-failing love for *such* disciples, a love that reaches out even to the archetype of the evil disciple, reveals the unique God and Father of Jesus Christ who loves the world unconditionally (see 3:16-17; 13:18-20).

A brief "aside" on the reception history of this passage is in order at this stage. For centuries, Christians—reading John 13:1-38 as if it were an exact report of what actually took place on that night—have been horrified by the suggestion that Jesus might have shared the eucharistic morsel with Judas. This horror influences the exegetical decisions of even the most critical interpreters. Given the variety of eucharistic traditions that we have examined (at least Mark/

Matthew; Luke/Paul; John), and the central liturgical significance of the "memorial" of this meal across the centuries, it is impossible to establish from the data of the New Testament *what actually took place* at the meal that night. As in the early Church and subsequent centuries, many contemporary Christians continue to be shocked by an interpretation that suggests a eucharistic background to Jesus' gift of the morsel to Judas in John 13:26. We must detach ourselves from our impressions of *what actually happened* on that night, to recognize that John has given us a superlative narrative to communicate the overwhelming enormity of God's love, manifested in and through Jesus. A blow-by-blow reconstruction of what Jesus may or may not have done on that night is beyond our historical knowledge. We do not have enough data, and what we do have (in Paul and the Four Gospels) cannot be forged into a unified, historically verifiable account.

Largely unrecognized, however, is the fact that the same possibility is found in the Synoptic accounts of the Last Supper. Judas has already associated himself with the plot to kill Jesus (Mark 14:10-11; Matt 26:14-16; Luke 22:3-6), but he is present at the last meal (Mark 14:17-21; Matt 26:20-25; Luke 22: 14, 21-23). Never is the reader told that he departed. Indeed, Luke has Jesus state: "the hand of him who betrays me is with me on the table" (Luke 22:21).

Returning to our reading of vv. 21-38, the audience has been told several times that Jesus *knows* Judas' intentions (vv. 2, 10c-11, 18, 21-26). Satan's designs for Judas now unfold: Satan entered into Judas (v. 27a). Jesus sends Judas on his way, recommending that he do his task as quickly as possible (v. 27b). There are no subtle allegories behind these words of Jesus; they are dramatic words that lead to vv. 28-29, indicating the universal ignorance of the disciples. Not one of the people at the table understood. The "no one" (Greek: *oudeis*) includes the Beloved Disciple (v. 28). How it is possible that *no one* understands, after the clarity of the question and the response to the question in word and deed in vv. 25-26?

Ignorance and confusion reign, and the best *some of the disciples* can do is guess that Jesus is telling Judas, the guardian of the money box, to make some purchases for the feast, or give something to the poor (v. 29). After receiving the morsel, Judas immediately went out, and it was night (v. 30a). Now controlled by Satan, Judas walks away from the light of the world (see 1:4, 7; 8:12; 9:5), into the night and the darkness of those who reject Jesus and who plan to kill him (see 1:5; 3:2; 8:12; 9:4; 11:10; 12:35, 46). At the beginning of Jesus' ministry, Nicodemus, one of "the Jews," moved from the night toward Jesus (3:2). That journey is still in progress (see 7:50-51; 19:38-42).[77] Now, as Jesus' life comes to an end, one of "his own" moves away from the light into the night (13:30a).

Judas' action leads to a "shout of triumph" from Jesus.[78] The author links Jesus' proclamation in vv. 31-32 with the departure of Judas.[79] The audience is already aware that Jesus will be "lifted up" to make God known (see 3:13-14; 8:28), to draw everyone to himself (12:32-33). As this is the case, Judas' departure into the darkness to betray Jesus unto death (31a), leads *logically* to Jesus' statement of vv. 31b-32. Themes foreshadowed across the Gospel gather. The "hour" has come (see 12:23, 27, 31; 13:1); now is the time for the glorification of the Son of Man and for God to be glorified (11:4; 12:23, 28). On the Cross, Jesus begins his "hour" of glorification; but his death will reveal the "the glory of God." The term "glory" (Greek: *doxa*), once used to describe the visible manifestation of God at Sinai, has been consistently applied in the Gospel to refer to the works of Jesus (see 2:11; 5:44; 7:18; 11:4, 40; 12:41, 43). In these works God has been manifest, and the Cross will be the time and place where that manifestation reaches its perfection, its goal, its end (*telos*).[80]

Because Judas has been taken over by Satan after receiving the morsel, in a radical rejection of the love of God revealed in and through Jesus' gift of the morsel (v. 31a), Jesus will be "lifted up." Jesus can thus proclaim that *now* the Son of Man will be glorified, and the glory of God will be seen in the glorification of Jesus through the Cross (vv. 31b-32b). The glorification of Jesus and the revelation of the glory of God, so intimately associated with the crucifixion, will take place *now* (v. 32c).[81] Judas' exit sets in motion the events promised by Jesus in vv. 18-20 as the time and the place when the disciples, chosen and sent by Jesus, might come to believe that Jesus is the revelation of God (v. 19: "that when it does take place you may believe that *I AM HE*").

Jesus turns to his disciples and addresses them with a term of endearment, "little children" (v. 33. Greek: *teknia*), reinforcing the presentation of Jesus' unconditional love for his failing disciples. But he looks back to words spoken to "the Jews" in an angry encounter with them recorded in 7:33.[82] Jesus recalls that moment in the past, marked by conflict and danger, and tells his disciples that they will seek him, but not find him because, as he told "the Jews": "Where I am going you cannot come" (v. 33. See 7:34). The audience finds in one verse (v. 33), a term of endearment, a statement from Jesus that a time is close at hand when he will no longer be with his disciples, and a potential association of the disciples with "the Jews." As "the Jews" would not and could not understand who Jesus was and where he was going in his return to the Father, so it is also with Jesus' ignorant and failing disciples. Yet they remain his disciples, his "little children," lost, yet loved, in their misunderstanding, failure, and ignorance (v. 33).

To these "little children," he gives a new commandment (vv. 34-35). Earlier Jesus gave the disciples an example (v. 15a). Both the example and the new commandment are closely associated with Jesus' demand that his disciples follow him into loving self-gift unto death, symbolized by the footwashing and the morsel. It was also implied by the command to follow Jesus' example that the disciples must do to one another *as Jesus had done for them* (v. 15b). It becomes more explicit in the new commandment that they love one another, *even as Jesus has loved them* (v. 34b). The link between the example and the commandment is clear.[83] Disciples of Jesus will be identified as such because they love one another as Jesus has loved them (v. 35). In the time of Jesus' absence (see v. 33) they are to repeat the love of Jesus, to render present the unconditional love that marked the lifestyle of Jesus (vv. 34-35).[84]

In v. 7a, Jesus told Peter: "What I am doing you do not know *now*." In proof of Jesus' statement, Peter now asks what is meant by the proximate absence of Jesus, caused by his going to a place where they cannot come (v. 36a). Jesus repeats the words he said to all the disciples in v. 33: he is going to a place where Peter cannot follow "*now*." Jesus tells Peter that even though he cannot follow him "*now*" (v. 36b), that he shall follow "*afterwards*" (v. 36c; see v. 7b). A narrative tension exists between the "*now*" of the story, as failing and misunderstanding disciples are the center of the action (vv. 7a,

36b), and the time of an "*afterwards*" when this situation will be transformed (vv. 7b, 36c. See 2:22; 12:16; 21:18-19).[85]

But Peter claims there is no tension. Earlier he attempted to dictate terms to Jesus about *whether* he should have his feet washed (vv. 6-8), and then about *how* he should be washed (v. 9); now he asks Jesus a question indicating there is no journey he is not prepared to make with Jesus (v. 37). Peter is thinking of human journeys into some dangerous place and time; Jesus is speaking of his return to the Father. Peter and Jesus are working on two different levels and the audience recognizes that they are at cross-purposes. Peter claims he is prepared to lay down his life for Jesus, as the Good Shepherd had earlier said that he would lay down his life for his sheep (see 10:11, 15, 17). This is exactly what Jesus asks of his disciples in the gift of his example (v. 15) and the gift of the new commandment (vv. 34-35). But such love flows from a radical following of Jesus, and never from an imposition of one's own world-view upon God's design.

Jesus prophesies that Peter will be thwarted by his own ignorance. He will fail, as he will deny Jesus three times before the cock crows (v. 38). The setting of the meal ends, bathed in the light of Jesus' incredible demonstration of his unconditional love for "his own" *to the end* (v. 1), made even more brilliant by the surrounding darkness of the forthcoming betrayal of Jesus by Judas (see vv. 2, 10-11, 18, 21-30, 31a), the ignorance of Peter and all the disciples (vv. 6-9, 28-29, 36-37), and the future denials of Peter (v. 38).

CONCLUSION

John 13:1-38 tells of the ignorance, betrayal, and denial of Jesus by the disciples with whom he shares his table. But Jesus commits himself to these same disciples, "his own ... little children," loving them consummately until death (13:1), washing their feet (vv. 4-11), and sharing a morsel of bread, even with his betrayer (vv. 21-30). The center of the narrative (vv. 18-20) is crucial for the overall message of 13:1-38. Jesus knows whom he has chosen. These disciples, whose feet he has washed (vv. 1-17), and Judas who has received the morsel (vv. 21-38), will turn against him (see v. 18). These are the ones he has chosen. The cruel reality of their turning against him (vv. 2-3, 10-11, 21-30, 36-38), lifting their heel against their host (v. 18b), alters nothing. In fact, he will send them forth as his representatives and as the representatives of his Father (vv. 18a, 20). It is in the acceptance of these failed, yet loved, disciples that one will receive both Jesus and the Father (v 20).

In Jesus' choosing and sending ignorant and failing disciples— dramatically portrayed in the abject failure of both Judas and Peter— Jesus' uniqueness and oneness with God can be seen. His love for his failing disciples is, above all, the final proof of his claim to be the one who makes God known (v. 19: I AM HE). Jesus does not reveal the love of God through any acclaim gained by a human success story, but by loving, unto death, those intimate friends and associates who have betrayed and denied him. This is the message that the Johannine Jesus leaves his disciples, as they gather at his table on the night before he died. Only after the events of the near future, when these things "take place," may the disciples come to know and believe that Jesus can claim *I AM HE*. They will have been loved "to the end" (13:1) by one whom they have betrayed and denied. This is a remarkable understanding of God, of Jesus, and of his self-giving love for his disciples. God's love, transcending and challenging all human criteria and human experience, is revealed. Equally surprising is that, despite their ignorance, failure, betrayals, and denials, the disciples are to imitate Jesus, loving one another as he loved them, so that the world might recognize them as disciples of Jesus Christ (vv. 15, 20, 34-35). "As the tragedy of human blindness is worked out so is the eminence of divine love."[86] Both the disciples in the story and the audience require more instruction before the events of "the hour" can be transformed from the failures of "now" into the knowledge (v. 6) and the following that take place "afterward."

The eucharistic elements in John 13 are not the main features of the chapter. However, the story of the gift of the eucharistic morsel is central to the overall and larger message of the Johannine Jesus, who summoned the Church to a new quality of love (13:13-17, 34-35). He was able to do this because he gave himself in love to disciples who did not love him in anything like the same way. Indeed, he even gave himself to Judas! Xavier Léon-Dufour has perceptively indicated that the eucharistic traditions of the earliest Church have been transmitted in two forms: the cultic form and the testamentary form.[87] In his analysis of the Johannine material, he writes of chapters 13-16 as avoiding the cultic form, containing an important eucharistic witness in the testamentary form: "The love Christians have for one another is the real symbol of Christ's presence in this world."[88] I am suggesting that this same message, based in the prior and extraordinary revelation of the love of God in Jesus (13:18-20), can be traced through an analysis of the structure and theology of 13:1-38, where Jesus' gift of the morsel still has hints of the Johannine community's eucharistic cult.

John continues the tradition that associated the Eucharist with a bread miracle (6:1-15, 51-58), and adds another eucharistic hint to link the revelation of Jesus' self-giving love on the Cross (19:34-35). These passages reflect the eucharistic practice of the post-Easter Johannine community. A community that no longer has a physical experience of the presence of Jesus in their midst is instructed that he can be found in the broken body and the spilt blood of their eucharistic celebrations. The author of this story of Jesus would not have been able to tell it in this way unless an early Christian community celebrated the Eucharist. John takes eucharistic tradition and practice for granted. Despite the difference of pastoral and theological applications that are apparent across the books of the New Testament, one element remains firm: the Eucharist is centered on Jesus' loving self-gift on the Cross.

However, in a spectacular fashion, the Fourth Gospel repeats and deepens what we have already discovered in Paul's First Letter to the Corinthians, and the Gospels of Mark, Matthew, and Luke: the Eucharist celebrates and proclaims the presence of Jesus to the broken. We are dealing with a eucharistic Tradition that associates the celebration of the Eucharist as the presence of Jesus to the broken: disciples who fail and who are sinful. As Sandra Schneiders has written: "Jesus' action was subversive of the sinful structures in which not only Peter [and Judas], but all of us, have a vested interest."[89]

1   The Fourth Gospel is the product of a long Christian and literary history. It is the result of great originality in marrying traditional narratives and other sources with a unique Johannine contribution. The final document, which would have appeared about 100 CE, is arguably the most subtle theological work in the New Testament. See Raymond E. Brown, *An Introduction to the Gospel of John*, ed. Francis J. Moloney, Anchor Reference Library (New York: Doubleday, 2010).

2   Among many, see Francis J. Moloney, "Johannine Theology," in *The New Jerome Biblical Commentary*, ed. Raymond E. Brown, Joseph A. Fitzmyer, and Roland E. Murphy (Englewood Cliffs: Prentice-Hall, 1989), 1417-26. There is no literary dependency of John upon the Synoptic Gospels. On this, see Smith, *John Among the Gospels*. John knows the Synoptic Gospels (particularly Mark and Luke), but does not use them as, for example, Matthew uses Mark. There are places in the Gospel of John (especially 6:1-72 and the passion narrative) where a creative use of earlier tradition (Mark and Luke respectively) is obvious. On this, see Michael Labahn and Manfred Lang, "Johannes und die Synoptiker. Positionen und Impulse seit 1990," in *Kontexte des Johannesevangeliums: Das vierte Evangelium in religions- und traditionsgeschichtlicher Perspektive*, ed. Jörg Frey and Udo Schnelle, WUNT 175 (Tübingen: Mohr Siebeck, 2004), 443-514; Jean Zumstein, *L'Évangile selon Jean*, Commentaire du Nouveau Testament IVa-b, 2 vols. (Geneva: Labor et Fides, 2007-2013), 1:30-32. Zumstein, throughout his commentary, applies a theory of *relecture* and *réécriture* of earlier traditions. On this process, see the explanation of Brown, *An Introduction*, 290-92 (these pages are the work of the editor).

3   See Moloney, *Love in the Gospel of John*, 37-69.

4   Especially important has been the work of Oscar Cullmann, *Early Christian Worship*, Studies in Biblical Theology 10 (London: SCM Press, 1953), 37-116. See also Sandra M. Schneiders, "Symbolism and the Sacramental Principle in the Fourth Gospel," in *Segni E Sacramenti Nel Vangelo Di Giovanni*, ed. Pius-Ramon Tragan, Studia Anselmiana 67 (Rome: Editrice Anselmiana, 1977), 221-35.

5   The classical statement of this position is found in Hugo Odeberg, *The Fourth Gospel: Interpreted in Relation to Contemporaneous Religious Currents in Palestine and the Hellenistic-Oriental World* (Uppsala: Almqvist, 1929). On John 6, see pp. 235-69.

6   Excellent surveys can be found in the older but still valuable work of

William F. Howard and C. Kingsley Barrett, *The Fourth Gospel in Recent Criticism* (London: Epworth Press, 1955), 195-212, and the surveys of Raymond E. Brown, "The Johannine Sacramentary," in *New Testament Essays* (London: Geoffrey Chapman, 1967), 51-76; idem, "The Eucharist and Baptism in John," in *New Testament Essays*, 77-95; Robert Kysar, *The Fourth Evangelist and His Gospel: An Examination of Contemporary Scholarship* (Minneapolis: Augsburg, 1975), 249-62. Jan Heilmann, *Wein und Blut: Das Ende der Eucharistie im Johannesevangelium und dessen Konsequenzen*, Beiträge zur Wissenschaft vom Alten und Neuen Testament 204 (Stuttgart: Kohlhammer, 2014), 1-8, offers an overview, but largely of German scholarship. He refers to the recently published David C. Bienert, *Abendmahl im johanneischen Kreis: Eine exegetische-hermeneutische Studie zur Mahltheologie des Johannesevangeliums*, Beihefte zur Zeitschrift für die neutestamentliche Wissenshaft 202 (Berlin: de Gruyter, 2014) for a complete survey. This recent book was not available at the time of writing.

7   See, most recently, Heilmann, *Wein und Blut*, who has argued at length that there are certainly indications of Johannine "meals," but questions scholarly association of these indications with Eucharist.

8   See Eduard Lohse, "Miracles in the Fourth Gospel," in *What About the New Testament? Essays in Honour of Christopher Evans*, ed. Morna Hooker and Colin Hickling (London: SCM Press, 1975), 64-75. See also Xavier Léon-Dufour, "Les miracles de Jésus selon Jean," in *Les Miracles de Jésus selon le Nouveau Testament*, ed. Xavier Léon-Dufour (Paris: Seuil, 1977), 269-86.

9   Sandra M. Schneiders, "The Footwashing (John 13:1-20): An Experiment in Hermeneutics," *The Catholic Biblical Quarterly* 43 (1981), 81 note 22.

10   Kodell, *The Eucharist in the New Testament*, 118-20, 126-29. For a criticism of the over-use of the Fourth Gospel in this sense, see Léon-Dufour, *Sharing the Eucharistic Bread*, 272-75. However, this must be read in terms of pp. 261-67, where Léon-Dufour develops his own "symbolic reading" of John. See also idem, "Towards a Symbolic Reading of the Fourth Gospel," *New Testament Studies* 27 (1980-81), 439-56. For Léon-Dufour the divine lurks behind the presence of Jesus across the entire narrative. As such, the expression "sacramental" can be used to describe all the words and actions of Jesus as "of God." They are the thinly veiled human revelation of the divine.

11   See the assessment of the many suggestions made over the years in Brown, "The Johannine Sacramentary," 75-76. Brown (in 1967) classifies a number of possible "hints" as "acceptable" that I would regard as "rejected," to use his language. I have no doubt that the later Raymond Brown and I

would have parallel assessments. However, he readily accepts 6:1-15, 51-58, and 19:34 as "acceptable."

12   See Francis J. Moloney, "When is John Talking about Sacraments?" *Australian Biblical Review* 30 (1982), 10-33. Documentation and discussion of the various scholarly positions can be found in this article. Schneiders, "The Footwashing," 81 note 22, creates a useful distinction between material that is "equivalent in content" and "analogous in function." I would claim that 6:1-15, 6:51-58, and 19:34 are "equivalent in content," and in this sense "eucharistic."

13   See Zumstein, *Saint Jean*, 1:209.

14   For a detailed comparison, see Michael Labahn, *Offenbarung im Zeichen und Werke*, WUNT 2.117 (Tübingen: Mohr Siebeck, 2000), 165-76.

15   The use of the expressions "he took" (Greek: *elaben*) and "when he has given thanks" (Greek: *kai eucharistēsas*) together is found elsewhere in the New Testament only in Paul's version of Jesus' words at the Last Supper in 1 Corinthians 11:23b-24.

16   See Francis J. Moloney, *The Gospel of John*, Sacra Pagina 4 (Collegeville, MI: The Liturgical Press, 1998), 196-201, and the literature cited there. See also, among many, Cullmann, *Early Christian Worship*, 93-102; Edwyn C. Hoskyns, *The Fourth Gospel*, ed. Francis N. Davey (London: Faber & Faber, 1947), 289-90; Udo Schnelle, *Das Evangelium nach Johannes*, Theologischer Handkommentar zum Neuen Testament 4 (Leipzig: Evangelische Verlagsanstalt, 1998), 116-27; Andrew T. Lincoln, *The Gospel According to Saint John*, Black's New Testament Commentaries (London/New York: Continuum, 2005), 212-13; Frederick B. Bruner, *The Gospel of John: A Commentary* (Grand Rapids: Eerdmans, 2012), 363-64.

17   See Moloney, *John*, 198-201. A Jewish document that appeared about the same time as the Gospel of John expresses this hope: "And it shall come to pass at that self-same time that the treasury of manna shall again descend from on high, and they will eat of it in those years, because these are they who have come to the consummation of time" (2 Baruch 29:8).

18   The limitation of revelation of Jesus as I AM HE in vv. 16-22 to the disciples in the boat is a significant narrative strategy for John that cannot be pursued here. At the end of the discourse, these same disciples find that Jesus' word is "too hard," and they leave him (vv. 60-66).

19   See Moloney, *John*, 201-20. On the Law as "the bread from heaven," see Peder Borgen, *Bread from Heaven: An Exegetical Study of the Concept of the*

Manna in the Gospel of John and the Writings of Philo, Supplements to Novum Testamentum 10 (Leiden: E. J. Brill, 1965), 147-92.

20   For this interpretation and translation of John 1:17, see Moloney, *John*, 40-41, 46.

21   The call to decision is indicated with Jesus' words, "unless (Greek: *ean mē*) you eat the flesh of the Son of Man and drink his blood, you have no life in you." This aspect of vv. 51-58 is magnificently developed by Heilmann, *Wein und Blut*, 189-209, 231-38. In the midst of misunderstanding and separation (see vv. 60-72), the disciples are called to believe across the entirety of vv. 25-58. Eating and drinking are metaphors to communicate that message.

22   I have argued this case at length in Francis J. Moloney, "John 6 and the Celebration of the Eucharist," *The Downside Review* 93 (1975), 243-51; idem, "The Function of Prolepsis in the Interpretation of John 6," in *The Interpretation of John 6*, ed. R. Alan Culpepper, Biblical Interpretation Series 22 (Leiden: Brill, 1997), 129-48; and idem, *The Johannine Son of Man*, 2nd ed. (Eugene: Wipf & Stock, 2007), 87-107. Raymond E. Brown, *The Gospel According to John*, Anchor Bible 29-29A, 2 vols. (Garden City: Doubleday, 1966-70), 1:287, rightly claims that "the backbone of vss. 51-58 is made up of material from the Johannine narrative of the institution of the Eucharist." See also idem, "The Eucharist and Baptism in John," 77-92; Barnabas Lindars, *The Gospel of John*, New Century Bible (London: Oliphants, 1972), 236, 239-45, 267-70; Brendan Byrne, *Life Abounding: A Reading of John's Gospel* (Collegeville, MI: The Liturgical Press, 2014), 108-25. For a contemporary rejection of this interpretation, see Craig S. Keener, *The Gospel of John: A Commentary*, 2 vols. (Peabody, MA: Hendrickson, 2003), 1:689-91. The literary and theological links with Eucharist are rejected by Heilmann, *Wein und Blut*, 155-73. I have serious difficulties with his weakening of the Johannine use of *sarx* ("flesh": vv. 51c, 52, 53, 55, 56), his lack of a decision about the interplay between *phagein* and *trōgein* as verbs for eating (vv. 51, 52, 53, 54, 56, 57, 58), the link with the use of *trōgein* in 13:18 (see below), and the theological/pastoral issue mentioned above: the presence of the absent one, among other issues. But the study is a very healthy balance to the over-sacramentalizing of the passage (see previous note). He states his agenda on p. 298, and it deserves attention: "The text of John's Gospel was a ritual resource for those who received it; ritual did not shape the text" (my paraphrase of the German: "Der Text des JohEv war *in seiner Rezeption ritualprägend*, nicht die Rituale waren textprägend." Stress in original.).

23   On this theology of the Cross as the revelation of God's love, see Moloney, *Love in the Gospel of John*, 135-60.

24   A weakness of the case made by Heilmann, *Wein und Blut*, 281-89, rejecting any eucharistic background to 19:34, is his almost total neglect of 19:35. Why does John intervene so forcefully at this stage to speak to a later generation, those who believe but who have not seen?

25   E. Malatesta, "Blood and Water from the Pierced Side of Christ," in *Segni e Sacramenti nel Vangelo di Giovanni*, ed. Pius-Ramon Tragan, Studia Anselmiana 66 (Rome: Editrice Anselmiana, 1977), 164-81; Cullmann, *Early Christian Worship*, 114-16; Hoskyns, *Fourth Gospel*, 532-36; Moloney, *John*, 505-6, 509-19; Schnelle, *Johannes*, 292-94; Bruner, *John*, 1125; Zumstein, *Saint Jean*, 2:258-59; Sebastian A. Carnazzo, *Seeing Blood and Water: A Narrative-Critical Study of John 19:34* (Eugene, OR: Pickwick Publications, 2012). See especially Brooke F. Westcott, *The Gospel According to John* (London: John Murray, 1908), 279: "Thus we are brought by this sign of 'blood and water' to the ideas which underlie the two Sacraments and which are brought home to faith in and through them; and the teaching of the third [see John 3:3-5] and sixth chapter is placed at once in connection with the Passion." Many commentators do not see Baptism and Eucharist here, but rightly link the passage to 7:37-39, and the life-giving effect associated with Jesus' death and the gift of the Spirit. See, for example, Byrne, *Life Abounding*, 322-33; Keener, *John*, 2:1151-54; Heilmann, *Wein und Blut*, 286-91. Keener provides a good survey of the many interpretations of this enigmatic passage, as does Bruner, *John*, 1127-31.

26   Moloney, "When is John Talking about Sacraments?" 25.

27   Just what these "troubles" were is at the heart of a great deal of contemporary Johannine research. See, for important initial suggestions, Raymond E. Brown, *The Community of the Beloved Disciple: The Life, Loves and Hates of an Individual Church in New Testament Times* (London: Geoffrey Chapman, 1979). For the ongoing discussion, see R. Alan Culpepper and Paul N. Anderson, eds., *Communities in Dispute: Current Scholarship on the Johannine Epistles*, Early Christianity and Its Literature 13 (Atlanta: SBL Press, 2014), especially the studies by R. Alan Culpepper, "Setting the Stage: Context for the Conversation" (pp. 3-15), Urban C. von Wahlde, "Raymond Brown's View of the Crisis of 1 John: In the Light of Some Peculiar Features of the Johannine Gospel" (pp. 19-45), Paul N. Anderson, "The Community that Raymond Brown Left Behind: Reflections on the Johannine Dialectical Situation" (pp. 47-93), and R. Alan Culpepper, "The Relationship Between the Gospel and 1 John" (pp. 95-118). See also Toan Do, *Rethinking the*

Death of Jesus: An Exegetical and Theological Study of Hilasmos *and* Agapē *in 1 John 2:1-2 and 4:7-10*, Contributions to Biblical Exegesis and Theology 73 (Leuven: Peeters, 2014), 3-26, on the uniqueness of the author and the theology of 1 John.

28   For a good discussion of the possible sacramental interpretation of John 13, see Rudolf Schnackenburg, *The Gospel According to St John*, trans. Kevin Smith, Cecily Hastings, et al., Herder's Theological Commentary on the New Testament IV/1-3, 3 vols. (London/New York: Burns & Oates/ Crossroad, 1968-1982), 3:39-47.

29   See, among many, Barnabas Lindars, *The Gospel of John*, New Century Bible (London: Oliphants, 1972), 451-52; C. Kingsley Barrett, *The Gospel According to St John*, 2nd ed. (London: SPCK, 1978), 441-42. The issue is well surveyed in Brown, *John*, 558-59.

30   It is widely accepted that this formula embodies part of the eucharistic words that would have been used at the celebrations of the Johannine community. On this, see Brown, *John*, 284-85; Jeremias, *The Eucharistic Words of Jesus*, 117-18.

31   See especially Heilmann, *Wein und Blut*, 241-80.

32   See Brown, *John* 2:581-604. For a survey of contemporary attempts to resolve these difficulties, see Fernando F. Segovia, *Love Relationships in the Johannine Tradition: Agapē/Agapan in I John and the Fourth Gospel*, SBL Dissertation Series 58 (Chico, CA: Scholars Press, 1982), 81-97; idem, *The Farewell of the Word: The Johannine Call to Abide* (Minneapolis: Fortress Press, 1991), 1-58.

33   Segovia, *Love Relationships*, 82. A similar assessment of John 13 is provided by Schnackenburg, *St John*, 3:7: "Without literary criticism, it is not possible to understand the text of 13:1-30 in its present form."

34   This approach has been expertly and sensitively used in the major commentaries of Schnackenburg and Brown. It is the basis of Segovia's earlier work. See also John Painter, "The Farewell Discourses and the History of Johannine Christianity," *New Testament Studies* 27 (1980-81), 525-43.

35   See, for example, the helpful study of Fernando F. Segovia, "John 15:18-16:4a: A First Addition to the Original Farewell Discourse," *The Catholic Biblical Quarterly* 45 (1983), 210-30.

36   See the chart listing these repetitions in Brown, *John*, 2:588-91.

37   I accept that we can trace elements of a prehistory that had an independent narrative (13:1-38), and a tradition of Jesus' final prayer (17:1-26). The

discourse itself has its oldest form in 14:1-33, but this discourse has been told and retold, and eventually shaped into a later version, now found in 16:4-33. The discourse that deals with "abiding" (15:1-11), loving as Jesus loved (vv. 12-17), and being hated as Jesus was hated (15:18-16:3), had a separate Johannine history. But it is not enough to trace these *possible* formative elements, and claim to have uncovered the meaning of 13:1-17:26.

38   See, among many, Fernando Segovia, "John 13:1-20. The Footwashing in the Johannine Tradition," *Zeitschrift für die Neutestamentliche Wissenschaft* 73 (1982), 31-51; idem, *Love Relationships*, 121-25.

39   For a recent attempt to construct a source for vv. 1-20, see especially Christoph Niemand, *Die Fusswashungerzählung des Johannesevangeliums: Untersuchungen zu ihrer Entstehung und Überlieferung im Urchristentum* (Studia Anselmiana 114; Rome, Pontificio Ateneo S. Anselmo, 1993), 81-256. For a thorough survey of scholarly attempts to trace sources, see 24-49.

40   As we will see below, the association of Judas (v. 31a: "when he had gone out") with vv. 31b-32 is generally disregarded by even the most astute commentators.

41   Among many, see Segovia, *Love Relationships*, 136-79. X. Léon-Dufour, *Lecture de l'Évangile selon Jean*, 4 vols (Paris: Seuil, 1988-1996), 3:23-24, argues that 13:1-32 is a unit, and that the discourse begins with vv. 33-38. For a recent comprehensive survey, see Francis J. Moloney, "The Literary Unity of John 13,1-38," *Ephemerides Theologicae Lovanienses* 91 (2015), 33-36.

42   See, for example, Brown, *John*, 2:605-16.

43   See, for example, Barrett, *St John*, 449-53.

44   The Gospel as a whole has a unified style and language. See Barrett, *St John*, 5-15; M. Hengel, *Die johanneische Frage: Ein Lösungsversuch mit einem Beitrag zur Apokalypse von Jörg Frey*, WUNT 67 (Tübingen: J. C. B. Mohr [Paul Siebeck], 1993), 238-48. This is the result of continual re-working over the decades of the Johannine community's telling and re-telling of the story of Jesus. Eventually, the entire story (whatever its sources) adopts what is nowadays called an "idiolect," i.e., a form of linguistic expression unique to a given community and its situation.

45   Wolfgang Iser, *The Implied Reader: Patterns of Communication in Prose Fiction from Bunyan to Beckett* (Baltimore: Johns Hopkins University Press, 1978), 283. For my impression of what that "consistent pattern" might be, see Francis J. Moloney, "The Function of John 13-17 within the Johannine

Narrative," in *What is John? Volume II: Literary and Social Readings of the Fourth Gospel*, ed. Fernando F. Segovia, Symposium 7 (Atlanta: Scholars Press, 1998), 43-66.

46   Segovia, *Farewell*, 284. This "about-face" by Segovia is an indication of the increased interest in New Testament scholarship in *synchronic* readings, as well as the more historically oriented *diachronic* interpretations, once so dominant. See Moloney, "Synchronic Interpretation," 345-54. Many years ago, Dodd, *The Interpretation of the Fourth Gospel*, 290, made a comment that retains its relevance: "I shall assume that the present order is not fortuitous, but deliberately devised by somebody—even if he were only a scribe doing his best—and that the person in question (whether the author or another) had some design in mind, and was not necessarily irresponsible or unintelligent."

47   R. Alan Culpepper, "The Johannine *hypodeigma*: A Reading of John 13:1-38," *Semeia* 53 (1991), 135.

48   For an extensive study of this question, summarized in what follows, see Francis J. Moloney, "The Literary Unity of John 13,1-38," 33-53.

49   It is the double use of the "amen" that is unique to John. "Amen, I say to you" is found in the Synoptic Gospels, especially in Matthew (31 times). An excellent note on John's use of this expression can be found in John H. Bernard, *A Critical and Exegetical Commentary on the Gospel according to St John*, International Critical Commentary, 2 vols. (Edinburgh: T. & T. Clark, 1928), 1:66-67.

50   The double "amen" plays an important structural role wherever it appears in 13:1-17:26. See Y. Simoens, *La gloire d'aimer: Structures Stylistiques et interprétatives dans la Discours de la Cène (Jn 13-17)*, Analecta Biblica 90 (Rome: Biblical Institute Press, 1981), 115-29, 151-73. Simoens' work has greatly influenced my reading of John 13:1-17:26.

51   See also Culpepper, "The Johannine *hypodeigma*," 133-34.

52   The "knowledge" of Jesus dominates 13:1-38. See Culpepper, "The Johannine *hypodeigma*," 134-37.

53   For my recent and fully documented studies of 13:1-38, see Francis J. Moloney, *Love in the Gospel of John*, 99-117, and idem, "*Eis telos* (v. 1) as the Hermeneutical Key for the Interpretation of John 13:1-38," *Salesianum* 86 (2014), 27-46.

54   On this, see Moloney, *Love in the Gospel of John*, 105. I use the quaint English word "consummately," as it catches the link between the verb used

when Jesus dies and pours down the Spirit in 19:30. The RSV translated Jesus' final words in 19:30 as "It is finished." The verb used, however, is a form of the Greek noun *to telos* (13:1): *tetelestai* (19:30). The Latin Vulgate caught the link between 13:1 (Jesus' consummate love) and 19:30 with the expression *consummatum est* ("it is consummated"). Jesus himself explains this in 17:4: "I have brought to perfection the task that you gave me to do" (AT).

55   See Édouard Delebecque, *Évangile de Jean: Text traduit et annoté*, Cahiers de la Revue Biblique 23 (Paris: Gabalda, 1987), 183: "The Greek phrase demands this meaning." See also Barrett, *St John*, 439.

56   It may appear to some readers that the link with Baptism is hard to identify. It is made through the Greek expression *echein meros met'emou* ("to have part with me"). As Barrett, *St John*, 441, explains: "John has penetrated beneath the surface of baptism as an ecclesiastical rite, seen it in its relation to the Lord's death, into which converts were baptized (cf. Rom 6.3), and thus integrated it into the humble act of love in which the Lord's death was set forth before the passion." Barrett describes Peter as in danger of having "no share in the benefits of Jesus' passion, and no place among his people."

57   R. Alan Culpepper, "The Johannine *hypodeigma*," 144. See also Richard A. Burridge, *Imitating Jesus: An Inclusive Approach to New Testament Ethics* (Grand Rapids: Eerdmans, 2007), 343-45. For the possibility that the Johannine Christians practiced a rite of footwashing to recall the teaching of Jesus, see John C. Thomas, *Footwashing in John 13 and the Johannine Community*, Journal for the Study of the New Testament Supplement Series 61 (Sheffield: Sheffield Academic Press, 1991), 126-85; Keener, *John*, 2:902.

58   The English captures this balance, but the original Greek is very clear: *ei TAUTA **oidate*** (conditional)—*makarioi este* (beatitude)—*ean **poiēte** AUTA* (conditional). See Simoens, *La gloire d'aimer*, 84-85.

59   This passage (vv. 18-20) even forms the "material center" of 38 verses, with the center of the center being v. 19. See Zumstein, *Saint Jean*, 2:31-33.

60   The use of "I AM HE" in the Gospel of John, in an absolute sense (i.e., without any modification, as in "I am the light of the world" [9:5], "I am the way, and the truth, and the life" [14:6]), is another feature of this Gospel. Based in the revelation of the name of God to Moses as "I am who I am" in Exodus 3:14, the expression "I am he" was used throughout the Old Testament (Hebrew Bible: *ani hû*; Greek LXX; *egō eimi*) to refer to the revealing presence of God (see LXX Deut 32:39; Exod 41:4; 43:10-11, 25; 46:4; 48:12; Isaiah 43:10; 45:18). John takes this tradition further by having

Jesus boldly proclaim "I AM HE" (see 4:26; 6:20; 8:24, 28, 58; 18:5-8), and thus claim that he is the revealer of God *par excellence*. Among many, see the excursus of Brown, *John*, 1:533-38; Philip B. Harner, *The "I Am" of the Fourth Gospel: A Study in Johannine Usage and Thought*, Facet Books Biblical Series 26 (Philadelphia: Fortress, 1970); and Zumstein, *Saint Jean*, 226-28.

61 Zumstein, *Saint Jean*, 31-33, also makes a strong link with the post-Easter Church, but does not fully appreciate the Christological significance of vv. 18-20. He explains how Jesus' choice of Judas was not a mistake, but part of God's design, indicated by the fulfillment of Scripture in v. 18. This is true, but is not the major thrust of vv. 18-20, the centerpiece of 13:1-38.

62 These words echo Psalms 42-43, a Psalm associated in the tradition with the Passion (see also 11:33 and 12:27, where it is used to point to the Passion). See Johannes Beutler, "Psalm 42/43 im Johannesevangelium," *New Testament Studies* 25 (1978-79), 34-37; Charles H. Dodd, *Historical Tradition in the Fourth Gospel* (Cambridge: Cambridge University Press, 1965), 37-38, 69-71.

63 The Greek verb *aporeō* ("to be at a loss, to be uncertain or perplexed") only appears here in the Gospel of John. Its other rare appearances in the New Testament (Mark 6:20; Luke 24:4; Acts 25:20; 2 Cor 4:8; Gal 4:20) always refer to ignorance and perplexity. See BDAG, 119, s.v. *aporeō*. See also Schnelle, *Johannes*, 219; Zumstein, *Saint Jean*, 2:37.

64 At least, the first time with the description of "the Beloved Disciple." Some already see this anonymous disciple present in the unnamed disciple of 1:35-40. See, for example, James H. Charlesworth, *The Beloved Disciple: Whose Witness Validates the Gospel of John?* (Valley Forge, PN: Trinity Press International, 1995), 326-36. See the survey of Frans Neirynck, "The Anonymous Disciple in John 1," *Ephemerides Theologicae Lovanienses* 66 (1990), 5-37.

65 The Greek expression indicating this closeness to the breast of Jesus (*en tōi kolpōi tou Iēsou*) is very close to the expression used in 1:18 to speak of Jesus' turned in loving union with the Father (Greek: *eis ton kolpōn tou patros*) during his ministry. See Moloney, *John*, 40-41, 46-47.

66 The words "he took it (*lambanei kai*)" are found in all Gospel narratives of Jesus' gift of bread at a final meal with his disciples. Reasons for accepting this reading will be given below.

67 Almost all contemporary scholars reject this suggestion. For the earlier discussion, see Michel-Joseph Lagrange, *Évangile selon Saint Jean*, Etudes Bibliques (Paris: Gabalda, 1927), 362-63. Most modern scholars either

regard the use of the morsel as a method of eliminating Judas from the upper room (e.g. Schnackenburg, *St John*, 3:30), or an indication that Judas chooses Satan rather than Jesus (e.g. Brown, *John*, 2:578).

68   See, for example, Lincoln, *Saint John*, 379; Zumstein, *Saint Jean*, 2:38-39.

69   See, for example, Walter Bauer, *Das Johannesevangelium*, 3d ed., Handbuch zum Neuen Testament 6 (Tübingen: J. C. B. Mohr [Paul Siebeck], 1933), 175. See also Augustine, *In Johannis Evangelium Tractatus CXXIV*, LXII.1-6 (CCSL XXXVI, 483-85). Augustine interprets John 13:26-27 with the help of 1 Corinthians 11:27 and Luke 22. With his customary insight, however, he recognizes that Jesus gives the Eucharist to Judas: "*Quid erat autem panis traditori datus, nisi demonstratio cui gratiae fuisset ingratus* ('Why was the bread given to the traitor, but as a demonstration of the grace he had treated with ingratitude')." Judas is damned (on the evidence of 1 Corinthians 11:27 and Luke 22); but he has been graced by Jesus' gift.

70   As we have seen in Chapter Two, it is also a mistaken interpretation of 1 Corinthians 11:29.

71   BDAG, 396, s.v. *esthiō*; 1019, s.v. *trōgō*. As with heavily used verbs in many languages, the verb "to eat" appears in two forms: *esthiō* and *phagō*, *phagomai* (see 6:5, 23, 26, 31, 49, 50, 51, 52, 53).

72   There has been some discussion of whether the two verbs differ greatly in meaning in the late Greek of the New Testament. For the position taken above, see Ceslaus Spicq, "*Trōgein*: Est-il synonyme de *phagein* et de *esthiein* dans le Nouveau Testament?" *New Testament Studies* 26 (1979-80), 414-19.

73   In agreement with Spicq, I regard the fourfold use of *trōgō* in a setting where *phagō* is used eight times as deliberate, and not just a "use of verbal variety" (as is argued, among others, by Francis T. Gignac, "The Use of Verbal Variety in the Fourth Gospel," in *Transcending Boundaries: Contemporary Readings of the New Testament: Essays in Honor of Francis J. Moloney*, ed. Rekha M. Chennattu and Mary L. Coloe, Biblioteca di Scienze Religiose 187 [Rome: LAS, 2005], 195). This connection between v. 18 and the eucharistic passage in 6:51-58 is recognized by Zumstein, *Saint Jean*, 2:31-32, but he does not link it with the gift of the morsel to Judas, reported in v. 26.

74   See discussion of the evidence in Metzger, *A Textual Commentary*, 205.

75   As well as the commentaries, see van Iersel, "Die Wunderbare Speisung," 167-94.

76   As also in Bauer, *Johannesevangelium*, 174; Schnackenburg, *St John*, 3:30. It is easier to explain why it was eliminated (to avoid any hint of Judas and the Eucharist) than to explain why a scribe would insert it, if it was not there originally. Text critics advocate a principle that chooses the "more difficult text" (*lectio difficilior*) as the original. The inclusion of "and he took" is the *lectio difficilior* in v. 26.

77   On this passage see Schnelle, *Johannes*, 220. On its function for the story of Nicodemus in the Fourth Gospel see Francis J. Moloney, *Signs and Shadows: Reading John 5-12* (Minneapolis: Fortress, 1996), 90-93.

78   The expression comes from George H. C. Macgregor, *The Gospel of John*, Moffat New Testament Commentary (London: Hodder and Stoughton, 1928), 283.

79   As mentioned earlier, this is one of my many problems with the majority position that ends the narrative in John 13 with v. 30, and makes 13:31-14:31 the first discourse. For example, neither Schnackenburg (*St John*, 3:49-52), nor Brown (*John*, 2:606, 608-10) give one word to the exit of Judas in v. 31a. Notable exceptions are Peter Ellis, *The Genius of John: A Composition-Critical Commentary on the Fourth Gospel* (Collegeville, MI: The Liturgical Press, 1984), 216: "Judas' departure into the night to betray Jesus elicits the declaration that the hour has *now* indeed come," and Lincoln, *Saint John*, 386: "Judas's exit into the night confirms that Jesus' hour has come."

80   On the Johannine use of "glory" (Greek: *doxa*), see Moloney, *Love in the Gospel of John*, 51-54, 91-96, 122-33.

81   For a detailed study of 13:31-32, see Francis J. Moloney, *The Johannine Son of Man*, 2nd ed. (Eugene, OR: Wipf & Stock, 2007), 194-202.

82   Readers will notice that I place quotation marks around "the Jews." These characters in John's Gospel are not the people known to us as the Jews. They are people in the story who have made a decision against Jesus, his revelation of God, and subsequently, his followers. John Ashton, *Understanding the Fourth Gospel* (Oxford: Clarendon Press, 1991), 151, points out correctly that one must "recognise in these hot-tempered exchanges the type of family row in which the participants face one another across the room of a house which all have shared and all call home." See further, Francis J. Moloney, "'The Jews' in the Fourth Gospel: Another Perspective," in *The Gospel of John: Text and Context*, Biblical Interpretation Series 72 (Leiden/Boston: Brill, 2005), 20-44.

83   See Andreas Dettwiler, *Die Gegenwart des Erhöhten: Eine exegetische Studie zu den johanneischen Abschiedsreden (Joh 13:31-16:33) unter besonderer*

Berücksichtigung ihres Relecture-Characters, Forschungen zur Religion und Literatur des Alten und Neuen Testaments 169 (Göttingen: Vandenhoeck & Ruprecht, 1995), 74-79. It is seldom noticed by scholars who separate vv. 31-38 from vv. 1-30. Schnackenburg, *St John*, 3:12, 52-54, uses it as one element in his claim that vv. 34-35 are an editorial addition.

84   The theme of v. 17 returns: "If you know these things, blessed are you, if you do these things" (AT).

85   A close literary and theological link exists between this "later" following of Peter in 13:36, and Jesus' command to follow, associated with the death of Peter in 21:18-19.

86   Robert Kysar, *John*, Augsburg Commentary on the New Testament (Minneapolis, MI: Augsburg, 1986), 219.

87   Léon-Dufour, *Sharing the Eucharistic Bread*, 82-95.

88   Léon-Dufour, *Sharing the Eucharistic Bread*, 252. See pp. 249-52 for his remarks on John 13-16.

89   Schneiders, "The Footwashing," 91. She wrote only of the footwashing. The same applies to the gift of the morsel, and thus I have added the parenthetic reference to Judas.

CHAPTER SEVEN

DIVORCE, REMARRIAGE, AND THE EUCHARIST

The New Testament witness to the life, teaching, death, and resurrection of the person of Jesus of Nazareth has many faces. The analysis of the various authors' use of their experience and understanding of the Eucharist, traced through the pages of this book, is but one example of that fact. This is often difficult for contemporary Christians to grasp, as they have little familiarity with the development of early Christian literature and the formation of the Church's Sacred Scriptures.[1] The writings of the New Testament provide inspired foundational documents to Christian history. Before the documents that eventually became the New Testament began to appear, the Christian story was well under way. A list of writings that were accepted as the Sacred Scripture of the Christian Church took three centuries to be finalized.[2] Even though a product of early Christian experience, the New Testament communicates "what actually happened," and how the Spirit-directed Church reflected upon the significance of those events (*Dei Verbum* 12). Christianity looks back to the texts of the New Testament as an authoritative, inspired witness that opens our eyes to the "fact" of Jesus of Nazareth, and the presence of the Spirit leading the Church to an authoritative interpretation of the "significance" of the many subsequent implications that emerged from that event.

The New Testament witnesses to a Last Supper that Jesus shared with fragile disciples. It became the first of many suppers at which the crucified and risen Christ has been present to his Church over the centuries. All versions of the eucharistic words of Jesus found in the Synoptic Gospels are marked by the word "until" (Greek: *heōs*). Paul uses a parallel expression (Greek: *achri hou*) in his personal additional comment to the words of Jesus he reports:

"until (*heōs*) that day when I drink it new in the kingdom of God." (Mark 14:25)

"until (*heōs*) that day when I drink it new with you in my Father's kingdom." (Matt 26:29)

"until (*heōs*) the kingdom of God comes." (Luke 22:18)

"You proclaim the Lord's death until (*achri hou*) he comes." (1 Cor 11:26)

In the midst of betrayal, denial, and the terror of an oncoming death, all the accounts report Jesus' confident proclamation of his future presence to his disciples at a meal that will mark the reigning presence of God among them. Paul adds an essential indication that links the celebration of the ritual to the life and practice of later believing Christians, proclaiming the Lord's death until he comes. Eucharistic cult will nourish a eucharistic lifestyle, and thus render the crucified and risen Jesus as part of human history until his final return. For the faith of the Christian churches, the Last Supper was the first of many suppers that would endure in Christian ritual and Christian life until the end of time.[3]

JESUS AT TABLE WITH THE BROKEN

This study has attempted to uncover the message of each New Testament author who left explicit reflection on the meaning and celebration of the Eucharist. Paul and each Gospel account tell the story of an event that took place in the "then" of the life of Jesus in order to challenge the "now" of a particular community in the earliest Christian Church—and beyond. As the contemporary Church reads and proclaims these inspired texts from our Sacred Scripture, they continue to challenge our contemporary eucharistic faith and practice—"now."

Although their accounts differ, there is consistency in the reporting by Paul and the Gospel narratives of this meal. They all look to the saving effect of Jesus' death and resurrection for their meaning. Jesus transforms a traditional ritual meal by breaking bread and sharing wine as a promise of his loving-self gift in his broken body and his spilt blood.[4] This event, generally called the Last Supper, is regarded by most as the bedrock event upon which the celebration of the Eucharist— one of the central rituals of the Christian tradition—is founded.[5] As well as the intimate link with Jesus' passion, Paul and the authors of the Gospels have used their eucharistic teaching to communicate a further fundamental idea: the Eucharist is the presence of Jesus to the broken, the betrayers, the deniers, the frightened, the poor, and the marginalized, as well as the rich. The presence of this theme in the different use of a meal tradition in John's account of Jesus' final evening with his disciples in John 13:1-38 is a strong indication that it was central to the early Church's understanding of the Eucharist. The bread miracles of the Gospels of Mark (6:31-44; 8:1-10) and Matthew (14:13-21; 15:32-39) are also determined by this theme. It is *not* found in the bread miracles in Luke and John. These evangelists report only one bread miracle, and have another point of view to communicate at that stage of their story of Jesus.

Without doubt, Jesus shared his table with others. Are there any indications of the people with whom he shared his table? What was the reaction of his contemporaries to his practice of meal-fellowship? The evidence of the New Testament is consistent. We have already seen that some of the Lukan material deals with Jesus' sharing his table with sinners and outcasts, but the evidence for such table fellowship reaches wider than Luke's account. According to the Gospels, Jesus' contemporaries were staggered by his preparedness to share his own table with sinners (Mark 2:15; Luke 15:1-2), to deliberately visit the tables of tax collectors (Luke 19:5), and to allow a prostitute to attend to him at a table where he was an invited guest (Luke 7:36-38). In these situations, his table-fellowship was most unsuitable for a religious leader or a Rabbi. He was active in sharing his table with the irreligious. Some passages in the Gospels give direct reports of such meals (see Mark 2:16-17; Matt 11:19; Luke 15:1-2; 19:8), while others refer indirectly to Jesus' sharing of the table with sinners and irreligious people (Matt 20:1-16; 21:28-32; Luke 7:41-43).

We have reports of Jesus' sharing his own table and the table of others in this form of table-fellowship, and we also hear of the consternation and anger that this created among "the religious" (see

Mark 2:16; Matt 11:19; Luke 15:2; 19:7. See also Luke 15:25-32). As if this were not enough, the Gospels also report that the broken, the sinful, and "the unrighteous" were privileged and delighted to share such fellowship (Luke 19:9; Mark 2:19). Jesus' parables often return to this practice, speaking boldly of God's kingdom as a place where the accepted absolutes of religion, history, and culture will be overturned, where the outcasts and the sinners will be welcomed at the table (Luke 14:12-24, 15:11-32; Matt 8:11; 11:16-19).[6]

The Gospels, therefore, agree that Jesus shared his table with sinners and outcasts, with the broken, and that he spoke boldly of such sharing as a sign of the in-break of God's presence as king. It is unlikely that such narratives and parables were created *ex nihilo* to give a solid basis to the presence of some socially unacceptable people in the later Christian community. Jesus of Nazareth shared his table with the marginal and the rejected people of society. It was one of the unsettling authentic practices of Jesus' public life. It came to the story-tellers and the missionaries who formed the Gospel traditions from the memory of Jesus' own lifestyle. This conclusion is admitted by all who have investigated the life and practice of the historical Jesus.[7]

> His table-fellowship with 'tax-collectors and sinners' ... is not a proclamation in words at all, but an acted parable; it is the aspect of Jesus' ministry which must have been most meaningful to his followers and most offensive to his critics.[8]

The early Church founded its understanding of the Eucharist on the basis of the dangerous memory of Jesus' table-fellowship. As the early Church "remembered" its beginnings, it also accepted the dangerous memory of Jesus' sharing his table with the broken people of his society and culture. The Eucharist was no exception to this practice. As Jesus shared his table with the broken and the outcasts, early Christians were summoned to share their eucharistic table with the broken. Although a developing liturgy and theology of Eucharist can be traced in the New Testament record, they are founded upon the bedrock of the memory of Jesus' meals throughout his ministry. "[T]his festive meal prolongs and climaxes the frequent meals which Jesus and the Twelve have shared; much more than any previous meal it is filled with a sense of solemn expectation."[9] The earliest Christian communities did not understand their celebrations as a perfect Church welcoming a perfect community to its table.[10] Looking back to the experience of failure and sinfulness that had marked the historical beginnings of the Church, the New Testament authors spoke boldly of the love of Jesus, sharing his table, and his body and his blood with them and for them.

The earliest Church looked back to a Tradition of Jesus' sharing meals with the broken and the marginalized. They articulate this Tradition in their reflections upon the Eucharist in the accounts of the multiplication of the loaves and fish in Mark and Matthew. In the narrative presentations of Jesus' final meal with his disciples in the Gospels, and with Paul's description of Jesus' words and actions "the night before he died," this theme is continued. Our long investigation of Paul's encounter with his Corinthian community, and the Gospels of Mark, Matthew, Luke, and John has brought us to this point. We are now well situated to take a further step in our analysis of the New Testament. If Jesus' table includes the broken, then what does the New Testament have to say to those who suffer from broken relationships and marriages? The Synod on the Family is facing the critical question of divorce, remarriage, and participation in the eucharistic meal. Following the process of *ressourcement* so essential for any renewal of the Catholic Tradition, we must reflect upon what the New Testament tells us about marriage and divorce. Do current practices in some Christian Churches, especially in the Catholic Church, reflect the authentic Tradition that comes to us from our inspired beginnings?

DIVORCE AND REMARRIAGE IN THE NEW TESTAMENT

Jesus' teaching on divorce is a question of central importance to the Christian churches.[11] If the traditions surrounding the gift of the Eucharist feature an expression of love and compassion for the fragile that leaves us amazed, what of Jesus' teaching on divorce and remarriage? This question, moved by the desires of Pope Francis, and the agenda of the Synod of Bishops on the Family, is the motivation for this study. In order to attempt a correlation between the teaching of the New Testament on the Eucharist, and the teaching of the New Testament on marriage and divorce, further interpretative principles must be made clear.[12] Given the paucity of material in the Bible dealing with this question, it is not surprising that very little material in the New Testament is dedicated to Jesus' attitude to divorce and remarriage. But what is found in Paul, Mark, Matthew, and Luke is confronting to contemporary sensitivities, and calls for a brief but clear analysis as we bring this study to closure. An uncritical affirmation that Jesus prohibited divorce does not do justice to what is recalled in our inspired Scriptures, but the fact that he did so must be given its due importance.[13] But Jesus' prohibition of divorce and remarriage is not the only word on the issue found within the pages of the New Testament. A neglect of the subtleties expressed across the pastoral and theological (re-)interpretations of Paul, Mark, and Matthew, accepted by the Church as the inspired Word of God, would betray the teaching of the New Testament as a whole.

In terms of the texts, Jesus' teaching on divorce and remarriage appears in 1 Corinthians 7:10-11, Mark 10:1-12, Matthew 5:32, 19:1-12, and Luke 16:18. The material itself, however, comes from three sources:

1. Paul (1 Corinthians 7:10-11)
2. "Q" (Matthew 5:32 and Luke 16:18)
3. Mark (Mark 10:11-12, paralleled by Matthew 19:11-12).[14]

On the basis of these three sources the following reflection on the teaching of the New Testament on divorce and remarriage will articulate itself in four stages:

1. Can we claim with certainty what Jesus said about marriage and divorce, on the basis of our earliest traditions: Paul, "Q," and Mark 10:11-12?
2. Using that tradition, what does Paul say about the question in 54 CE, as he speaks to the situation of the Greco-Roman Christian community at Corinth in 1 Corinthians 7:8-16?
3. How does Mark use that same Jesus-tradition, in the context of the Roman Empire about 70 CE, as he reports Jesus' debate with the Pharisees, and then in his subsequent discussion with his disciples in Mark 10:1-12?
4. Finally, how does Matthew use it, both in his adaptation of his "Q" source, and in his rewriting of Mark 10:1-12 in Matthew 19:3-12, in the latter half of the 80's CE?[15]

Not every word printed in an English translation of the New Testament was actually said by Jesus of Nazareth. Not every deed done by Jesus of Nazareth reported there necessarily happened exactly as it is described. The Gospels bear witness to what Jesus did and said during his lifetime; they also reflect the pastoral and theological agenda of the inspired Scriptures that have been accepted by the Church as its New Testament. The earliest Christian writers (Paul in the 50's, "Q" from 50-70, Mark about 70, and Matthew and Luke in the late 80's) looked back to Jesus. They inform their audience about Jesus of Nazareth, but they go further.[16] They also instruct a Christian audience about what God has achieved for humankind in and through the event of Jesus. One leads to the other, but the latter very regularly develops the traditions that come from Jesus to speak to the needs of the community for which any single author is writing. These "writings" subsequently became part of the Christian Sacred Scriptures because they were recognized as speaking to the ongoing history of the Church as the "Word of God."

This simple affirmation hides a very important principle of interpretation for a Church (like the Catholic Church) that takes the New Testament as part of its inspired Scriptures (see *Dei Verbum* 17-20). The Word of God in the New Testament is not *only* to be identified with the words of Jesus that we can confidently find within its pages. The Word of God is *also* the ongoing interpretation and application of those words developed within the teaching of the earliest and inspired Christian authors to address the Church.

An important example from Christian history shows the truth of this affirmation. It is universally accepted that the Gospel of John, that appeared about 100 CE, is the most theologically developed document in the New Testament. Without hesitation, it proclaims that Jesus of Nazareth was the Christ, the pre-existent Logos of God (John 1:1-2), the only begotten Son of God (1:14), I AM HE (13:19, etc.), the Son of Man, and the Messiah, who was always aware of his oneness with God, and thus made God known in an authoritative and unique fashion (6:25-59, etc.). Having come from a oneness with God that the Logos has occupied since before all time (John 1:1-2, 14), Jesus returns to the Father (20:18), to send the gift of the Paraclete (14:15-17, 25-26; 15:26-27; 16:7-11, 12-15; 19:30; 20:21-

23).[17] The teaching of the Gospel of John, most of which cannot be found in such an explicit way anywhere else in the New Testament,[18] became the backbone for the eventual articulation of the Christian Church's faith at the Councils of Nicea (325 CE), Constantinople (381 CE), Ephesus (431 CE), Chalcedon (451 CE), and again at Constantinople (553 CE).[19] As Christians make their confessions of faith, they do so in a language that has been shaped by the Gospel of John, not simply by what Jesus of Nazareth *actually said* between 28-30 CE.

Beyond the scope of this study, the same could be said for the formative role of the Letters of Paul, written in the 50's of the first Christian century, in the development of the later Christian Tradition. Jesus understood his forthcoming death as in some way "for others," but the inspired writings of Paul the Apostle make the saving significance of the death and resurrection of Jesus Christ so central to his thought and teaching that it has shaped all subsequent Christian teaching—and practice.[20] The revelation of God to the world is not found in *either* the Word of God in the Bible *or* the formal teaching of the Councils. It is found in *both*. Indeed, without John and Paul, there would be very little in the teaching of the Councils. Scripture and Tradition "flow from the same divine well-spring" (*Dei Verbum* 9). "Tradition and scripture make up a single sacred deposit of the word of God, which is entrusted to the Church" (*Dei Verbum* 10). Obviously, therefore, God's revelation is not only found in those words of Jesus that can be reliably traced to the life and teaching of Jesus and Nazareth. What follows will initially trace what Jesus of Nazareth taught about divorce and remarriage. Once that is in place, we must examine what the earliest Church (Paul, Mark, and Matthew) passed on to their own communities in their Letters and Gospels, accepted as an integral part of the Word of God to the Church. As with the example of the use of the Christologies of the Gospel of John and the Letters of Paul in the eventual formation of the Christian Tradition, so too with the Church's understanding and practice of marriage, divorce, and admission to the eucharistic table—we must *see the entire picture*.

Jesus of Nazareth was a Jew who lived and ministered largely in the Galilee of Roman-occupied Palestine in the first half of what is known as the first century of the Common Era. As such, he was a product of traditional Palestinian Jewish thought and practice. This means that he would have been shaped by the teaching of the Mosaic Torah.[21] Adultery was a capital crime. According to Leviticus 20:10 and Deuteronomy 22:22, both offending parties involved must die, and its prohibition is found in the Decalogue (Exodus 20:19; Deuteronomy 4:10; 5:20-21).[22] Surprisingly, however, the question of divorce and remarriage was not a major concern for the Jewish legal tradition. It was taken for granted that divorce and remarriage would take place. The tradition ensured that the male partner was always in command of the situation. There is only one passage in the Torah that deals with the question in any detail: Deuteronomy 24:1-4.[23] The text itself is a long single Hebrew sentence. Its major concern is to ensure that a woman who is dismissed from the household by the male, not be permitted to return to the intimate situation of man and wife by returning to the husband who dismissed her. This is regarded as bringing "sin upon the land" (v. 4). "That, remarkably, is the extent of the divorce laws in the Pentateuch."[24] The same basic approach to the question is found in the Prophets (already part of Israel's Sacred Scripture) and the Wisdom literature (an important pseudo-philosophical reflection reflecting Israel's gradual integration with its surrounding Hellenistic world, but with ancient roots in Israel's tradition).[25]

Recourse is often had, by Christian scholars, to the prophet Malachi 2:10-16. The RSV renders v. 16: "For I hate divorce, says the Lord the God of Israel." The notes of the RSV rightly indicate the speculative nature of this translation. It has come down to us in a corrupted Hebrew text, and does not make sense the way it stands. Using an image found elsewhere in the prophets (e.g., Isaiah, Jeremiah, Ezekiel, and Hosea),[26] Malachi 2:10-16 criticizes Jerusalem and Judah for their unfaithfulness to God by paralleling their behavior with that of husbands unfaithful to their wives. After careful consideration of the Hebrew of v. 16, however, John Meier states categorically that the text does not say: "I hate divorce." The closest he can come to generating a confusing English translation for the confused Hebrew is "For [or: 'if'; or 'when'; or 'indeed'] he hated [or possibly: 'hating'], send away! [or possibly 'to send away']."[27] The same confusion is found in the Greek translations, and the Latin Vulgate for 2:16 is "*cum odio habueris dimitte*" ("when [or: since] you hate [her], send [her] away." Later Christian interpreters and Rabbinic thought have turned to Malachi 2:16 for biblical support for the absolute prohibition of divorce. But this is a misuse of the original text (which remains confused), and would not have influenced Jesus of Nazareth in any way. As we will see, when Jesus comes to discuss divorce, he turns to the Torah texts of Deuteronomy and Genesis. He never mentions Malachi.

There are other witnesses to Jewish thought that come from the same period, notably Philo of Alexandria (20 BCE-40 CE), a Jew who worked strenuously to make Jewish traditions relevant to a Hellenistic world, and Josephus (37-100 CE), a Jewish historian who wrote significant commentaries on the Jewish War and the history of Jewish life and practice. They both demonstrate minimal interest in the matter of marriage and divorce, and repeat the legislation of Deuteronomy 24:1-4. There are obvious minor issues that they attend to, reflecting their particular cultural location.[28]

The texts found at the Dead Sea raise further questions about the attitude of the first-century Jewish sect that produced those documents, generally recognized as the Essenes. Much has been made of two texts that suggest a prohibition of divorce, the Damascus Document (CD 4:20-21) and the Temple Scroll (11QTemple 57:15-19). The former is a difficult text to interpret. It has been widely translated as a condemnation of those who take two wives in their lifetime, but it may be better understood as the prohibition of multiple wives. The second envisions the way things will be when the ideal king rules in the near future. One of the telling arguments against the prohibition of divorce at Qumran is that there is no suggestion of any such practice in the Community Rule (1QS). The Damascus Document was written for Essene communities at large; the Community Rule determines the life of the Essene community at Qumran.[29] Generally regarded as a minority sectarian group that advocated the prohibition of divorce, reflecting a sectarian strain within Judaism to which Jesus also belonged,[30] recent detailed analysis of the situation at Qumran is more reserved. While such a view of divorce and remarriage at Qumran is not ruled out, the majority opinion now is that although "[t]he Essenes did forbid polygamy; their position on divorce remains a question mark."[31]

This is the cultural, religious, and legal setting for Jesus' teaching on divorce. Our earliest witness is 1 Corinthians 7:10-11. The study of the eucharistic passages in 1 Corinthians 10-11 already provided a setting for this enthusiastic early Christian community. Paul finds himself responding to a number of practical, pastoral, and theologically significant problems. Often he opens his reflections with the expression "now concerning ..." (Greek: *peri de*: 7:1, 25; 8:1; 12:1; 16:1), as he responds to queries concerning the Corinthians' state of life, now that they live in new existence generated by the death and resurrection of Jesus.[32] His general principle is that they should stay as they are,[33] and this is what he tells them to do concerning their marital state in 7:1-9. To this point in his argument he is expressing his own opinion. He will resume giving advice on these grounds in vv. 12-16 (see v. 12: "I say, not the Lord"). However, in vv. 10-11 he leaves his own opinion to one side, and gives a word of Jesus on divorce:

> To the married I give charge, not I but the Lord, that the wife should not separate from her husband (but if she does, let her remain single or else be reconciled to her husband)—and that the husband should not divorce the wife.

There are two remarkable aspects to these words that Paul claims come from Jesus. Most significantly, Paul reports that Jesus forbad divorce. The wife was not to leave her husband (v. 10), and if she does, she must return to him (v. 11a). No husband should divorce his wife (v. 11b). Secondly, unlike anything we find in Jewish tradition, Paul takes it for granted that a woman could leave her husband on her own initiative.

There may be a number of possible explanations for the latter element from the teaching of Jesus (the initiative of the woman),[34] but our concern is with the former. Unlike Paul's use of the remembered words of Jesus on the night before he died in 11:23-25, in 7:10-11 we have no verbatim use of the actual words of Jesus of Nazareth. But

Paul's consistent claim that he is teaching on his own authority (vv. 1-9 and vv. 12-16), and the dramatic change to a "charge" that comes from the Lord (v. 10) when he prohibits divorce, is early evidence of Jesus' prohibition of divorce and remarriage.[35] Paul has not provided a setting for this "word of the Lord," but the early evidence of Matthew 5:32, paralleled in Luke 16:18 (and thus "Q" material), provides two different narrative settings for a tradition that looks back to the words of Jesus.[36]

In the Gospel of Luke, Jesus addresses the question of divorce, rather surprisingly, only once: in Luke 16:18. As we have already seen, these words are found in a rather loosely connected series of teachings poised between Jesus' parable on the dishonest steward (16:1-9) and the parable on the rich man and Lazarus (vv. 19-30). Most of these teachings are connected in some way with the theme of wealth and possessions that is present in the two parables (see vv. 10-13, 14-15), while vv. 16-17 touches upon important Lukan concerns: the place of John the Baptist, and the law and the prophets, in God's design. Most surprisingly, v. 18 follows: "Everyone who divorces his wife and marries another commits adultery, and he who marries a woman divorced from her husband commits adultery."[37]

The issue of divorce appears twice in Matthew.[38] In 19:1-12 Matthew reports, in his own way, an encounter between Jesus and the Pharisees originally reported in Mark 10:1-12. As we will see below, although Matthew reports this discussion of divorce between Jesus and the Pharisees by using Mark 10:1-12 as his source, he does so in his own way. However, in a fashion that fits its narrative context more coherently than Luke 16:18, Matthew deals with the question of divorce in 5:32, in the series of ethical instructions located in the antitheses of 5:17-48. Commenting on the words of Decalogue forbidding divorce (Exodus 20:14 and Deuteronomy 5:18), Jesus extends his commentary to the legislation of Deuteronomy 24:1-4. He comments: *"But I say to you that* everyone who divorces his wife, *except on the ground of unchastity*, makes her an adulteress; and whoever marries a divorced woman commits adultery"* (Matt 5:32).

The closeness between the two teachings is clear. Once the Matthean redactional additions—"But I say to you that" and "except on the ground of adultery"—are removed, then the possibility that Luke 16:18 and Matthew 5:32 come from the same source ("Q") is very real.

Matthew 5:32	Luke 16:18
(a) Everyone who divorces his wife	Everyone who divorces his wife
except on the ground of unchastity	*and marries another*
(b) makes her an adulteress	commits adultery
(a) and whoever marries a divorced woman	and the one who marries a woman divorced by her husband
(b) commits adultery.	commits adultery.

Allowing for stylistic and slight changes of content made by the two authors using the same source (Luke clarifies, while Matthew takes the details of divorce between a husband and a wife for granted), the literary structure and the message of this passage indicates that Matthew and Luke are using the same source. The passage (from "Q") points back to a very early record of a word from Jesus that prohibited divorce, prior to Matthew and Luke, but not found in Mark. Unlike Paul's words, which he cites as from the Lord, the "Q" passage makes no allowances for the initiative of the woman. At least in that respect, it continues Jewish tradition.

Calling upon the data provided by 1 Corinthians 7:10-11 (where Paul appears to be paraphrasing a word of Jesus), and Matthew 5:32 and Luke 16:18 ("Q"), scholars are able to suggest the probable "primitive form" of this word of Jesus that had its origins on the lips of Jesus of Nazareth during the course of his ministry.[39] Reflecting a Semitic balance, intricacy, and a density worthy of the importance of the subject being dealt with, a two-part saying emerges:

Part 1a: Everyone who divorces his wife and marries another
Part 1b: commits adultery.
Part 2a: And the one who marries a divorced woman
Part 2b: commits adultery.[40]

Whether or not one accepts this "reconstruction" as words of Jesus himself, there is no doubt that Jesus of Nazareth forbad divorce and remarriage.[41] Our glance at the society and religious practice of Jesus' time indicates that such teaching stands alone. "Jesus the Jew clashes with the Mosaic Torah as it was understood and practiced by mainstream Judaism before, during, and after his time."[42]

Although centuries and worlds apart, there is a certain parallel between the challenge of Jesus' teaching then and now. Modern society is structured, legally and socially, to accept and even encourage (in certain circumstances) the practice of divorce and remarriage. Although the practice of divorce and remarriage was not as widespread at the time of Jesus, Deuteronomy 24:1-4 indicated that a man could dismiss his wife and marry another (see Mark 10:3-4; Matt 19:7).[43] Jesus contradicted this teaching and practice.

In the light of the conclusions reached by his major study of Jesus of Nazareth as a marginal Jew, John Meier indicates how Jesus' prohibition of divorce and remarriage must have appeared to his contemporaries. I will cite his words at length, and come back to them in a reflection on the theological developments found in Mark 10:1-12//Matthew 19:1-12.

> Jesus consciously presented himself to his fellow Jews as the eschatological prophet, performing Elijah's task of beginning the regathering of Israel in the end time while also performing miracles like Elijah's. These miracles were interpreted as signs of the kingdom that was coming and yet that, in a way, was already present in Jesus' ministry. In this highly charged context of future-yet-realized eschatology, the eschatological prophet named Jesus may have inculcated as already binding certain types of behavior that pointed forward, as did his whole ministry, to the final period of Israel's restoration as God's holy people.[44]

1 CORINTHIANS 7:8-16: GOD HAS CALLED US TO PEACE

In 1 Corinthians 7:1, Paul turns his attention to a number of issues related to marriage, with his usual indication of "now concerning these matters …" (Greek: *peri de* …). Writing to his over-enthusiastic new Christians, in vv. 1-7 he informs them that there should not be anything "new" in the way husbands and wives should relate, although expressing his personal support for his own way of life, most likely celibate, admitting that not all have this gift from God (v. 7).[45] He then addresses, in sequence, the issues faced by the unmarried and the widows (vv. 8-9), the married (vv. 10-11), and the situation of a woman married to an unbeliever (vv. 12-16). On the first and the third question he provides his own opinion: "I say" (v. 8); "I say, not the Lord" (v. 12). As we have seen, in dealing with the married, he indicates, "I give charge, but not I but the Lord" (v. 10), taking us back to our earliest record of Jesus' prohibition of divorce.

As he has done in his general discussion of matters sexual (vv. 1-7), in vv. 8-9 he asks that people maintain their current status. But in vv. 12-16 he moves on to discuss what must have been a common enough reality in Pauline Corinth: a man (v. 12) or a woman (v. 13) married to an unbeliever.[46] As throughout this discussion, Paul recommends that they remain in their current marriage. He provides reason for this recommendation: the potential for mutual consecration of a couple through marriage, and the subsequent consecration of the children (see v. 14).[47] Critically, however, "if the unbelieving partner desires to separate, let it be so; in such a case your brother or sister is not bound" (v. 15abc).[48] He again provides good reasons for this decision: there can be no certainty that such a mixed marriage will lead to salvation (v. 16).[49] The fundamental principle of human relationships must be maintained: "for God has called us to peace" (v. 15d). Immediately after reporting Jesus' word that there be no separation between married couples, Paul addresses the difficult situation of couples and families in Corinth where the union of a believer and an unbeliever is damaging an element essential in God's calling (see the Greek of v. 15d: *keklēken*), the call for the Christians to live in peace (Greek: *en de eirēnēi*).[50] He reads that situation in the light of God's call of the Christian to peace and salvation, and instructs the Christians in Corinth that a separation should take place.

Paul sees the necessity to *accommodate* the special circumstances of a mixed marriage between a pagan and a Christian, and *reverses* Jesus' decision to prohibit divorce. However, what must be noted is that Paul does not permit the believing partner, no doubt instructed and committed to the word of the Lord recalled in vv. 10-11, to initiate the process of separation. The initiative must come from the non-believing partner.[51] Jesus has *reversed* the traditional Jewish understanding of the possibility of divorce; Paul now does the same thing with the teaching of Jesus (vv. 10-11) by *allowing* separation between Christian and non-Christian partners. There were no doubt outstanding pastoral reasons for making this decision in support of the God-given peace of Corinthian community.[52] Paul does not appear to be in any anguish over this decision. Juxtaposed with the word of the Lord (vv. 10-11), in vv. 12-16 he gives instructions that are not consistent with vv. 10-11, but which clearly *accommodate* the situation of the Church in Corinth.[53] There is no indication from Paul whether or not the Christian spouse would be permitted to remarry; what he said about remarriage in v. 11 ("remain single") may well continue to apply.[54] Pheme Perkins wisely suggests that Paul might expect them to be guided by v. 7: "I wish that all were as I myself am. But each one has his own special gift from God, one of one kind and one of another."[55]

The summary explanation offered above makes clear that there are a number of puzzles associated with the interpretation of 1 Corinthians 7:12-16.[56] What is crucial for this study, however, is that *within the Sacred Scriptures of Christianity* we find an accommodation of Jesus' absolute prohibition of divorce.[57] But Paul is not alone in instituting an exception.

MARK 10:1-12//MATTHEW 19:1-12 (MATTHEW 5:32 AGAIN)

As we have had occasion to see, Matthew regularly uses Mark as one of his major sources. But he generally has something of his own to say, and does not re-write Mark verbatim. The reporting of Jesus' debate with the Pharisees over divorce is a good example of this.[58]

Mark 10:1-12	*Matthew 19:1-12*
[1] And he left there and went to the region of Judea and beyond the Jordan,	[1] Now when Jesus had finished these sayings, he went away from Galilee and entered the region of Judea beyond the Jordan;
and crowds gathered to him again; and again, as his custom was, he taught them.	[2] and large crowds followed him, and he healed them there.

² And Pharisees came up and in order to test him asked, "Is it lawful for a man to divorce his wife?"

³ He answered them, "What did Moses command you?"

⁴ They said, "Moses allowed a man to write a certificate of divorce, and to put her away."

⁵ But Jesus said to them, "For your hardness of heart he wrote you this commandment.

⁶ But from the beginning of creation, 'God made them male and female.'

⁷ 'For this reason a man shall leave his father and mother and be joined to his wife, ⁸ and the two shall become one flesh.' So they are no longer two but one flesh.
⁹ What therefore God has joined together, let not man put asunder."

³ And Pharisees came up to him and tested him by asking, "Is it lawful to divorce one's wife for any cause?"

[Transposed: ⁷ *They said to him, "Why then did Moses command one to give a certificate of divorce, and to put her away?"*
⁸ *He said to them, "For your hardness of heart Moses allowed you to divorce your wives,*

but from the beginning it was not so.]
⁴ He answered, "Have you not read that he who made them from the beginning made them male and female,
⁵ and said, 'For this reason a man shall leave his father and mother and be joined to his wife, and the two shall become one flesh'? ⁶ So they are no longer two but one flesh.

What therefore God has joined together, let not man put asunder."

⁷ They said to him, "Why then did Moses command one to give a

certificate of divorce, and to put her away?" [8] He said to them, "For your hardness of heart Moses allowed you to divorce your wives, but from the beginning it was not so.

[Transposed: [11] *And he said to them, "Whoever divorces his wife and marries another, commits adultery against her;* [12] *and if she divorces her husband and marries another, she commits adultery."*]
[10] And in the house the disciples asked him again about this matter.

[9] And I say to you: whoever divorces his wife, *except for unchastity* (Greek: *mē epi porneia*), and marries another, commits adultery."

The disciples said to him, "If such is the case of a man with his wife, it is not expedient to marry."

[11] And he said to them, "Whoever divorces his wife and marries another, commits adultery against her; [12] and if she divorces her husband and marries another, she commits adultery."

[11] But he said to them, "Not all men can receive this saying, but only those to whom it is given. [12] For there are eunuchs who have been so from birth, and there are eunuchs who have been made eunuchs by men, and there are eunuchs who have made themselves eunuchs for the sake of the kingdom of heaven. He who is able to receive this, let him receive it."

Matthew 18:1-35 reports Jesus' discourse on the community and its internal discipline. In typical Matthean fashion, the discourse finishes and Matthew moves on to the next episode in 19:1ab, and resumes his use of Mark in v. 2c (see Mark 10:1). From that point on, the parallels laid side by side in the above diagram are clear. Matthew alters Mark's indication that Jesus was teaching large crowds to claim that he was healing them (Mark 10:1-2; Matt 19:1-2). This is not the place for a detailed consideration of the two encounters, but some explanation of the Markan original and Matthew's adaptation of it can be sketched.

Mark 10:1-9 is shaped like a traditional rabbinic discussion. The question of divorce is posed. Mark indicates the hostility of the Pharisees; they asked the question "in order to test him" (v. 2). Jesus responds with a further question, asking the Pharisees to locate their query within the teaching of the Law (v. 3). They respond by citing the general meaning of Deuteronomy 24:1-4 (v. 4), but Jesus counters with a correction of the Pharisees' understanding of Torah by showing that this was not God's original design. It was allowed, through Moses, only because of the hardness of hearts in Israel. The *original* design of God, *from the beginning of creation*, is found in Genesis 1:27 and 2:24 (vv. 5-8). It provides his response to the original question (see v. 2) with the words, "What therefore God has joined together, let no man put asunder" (v. 9).[59] Jesus has answered Torah with Torah, and the Pharisees fall silent. But "in the house," as the disciples ask him about the matter, he shifts the argument from divorce to adultery.[60] Mark regularly uses "the house" as the location in which Jesus instructs his disciples (see 3:20; 7:17-23; 9:28, 33). A man or a woman who divorces and remarries "commits adultery" (vv. 11-12). Although adultery has been introduced in Jesus' discussion with the disciples, there is a logical link with what Jesus has taught the Pharisees. The Torah legislates against adultery (Exod 20:19; Deut 4:10; 22:22; Lev 20:10). Jesus teaches his disciples (and they are the audience for all that is found across 10:1-31) that the practice of the Pharisees leads to a breach of the Torah, as divorce and remarriage is adultery.[61] Jesus' absolute prohibition of divorce in Mark 10:1-12 echoes the earlier record of 1 Corinthians 7:10-11. Writing in the Roman world, Mark addresses the possibility of divorce and remarriage (and subsequent adultery) on the part of both the man and the woman.

Matthew does not have the parrying back-and-forth that shapes rabbinic discussion. The Pharisees test Jesus by asking if it is lawful to divorce one's wife *for any cause* (v. 3).[62] Matthew has Jesus respond immediately in terms of Genesis 1:27 and 2:24 (vv. 5-6). Only when the Pharisees are cornered by Jesus' use of the Torah do they turn to Deuteronomy 24:1-4 (v. 7). Jesus replies in terms of Israel's hardness of heart, picking up his earlier response from Genesis by telling them that "from the beginning it was not so" (v. 8). Mark's location of the link between divorce and adultery (Mark 10:11-12) is used to end the Matthean encounter between Jesus and the Pharisees (v. 9), rather than to the disciples (Mark 10:11-12). Matthew, reflecting a more Jewish tradition, regards the man as the one who might initiate divorce, and thus commit adultery. The woman is not considered. As in Mark (10:10-12), Matthew closes the episode with an explanation to the disciples in 19:10-12, but the discussions are very different. Matthew uses his own special traditions, not found anywhere else in the New Testament.[63] The disciples cannot imagine how such a prohibition could work. If one cannot divorce, then the institution of marriage is to be avoided (v. 10). Jesus responds that the never-failing gift of loyalty in marriage is "a special gift from God" (v. 11; recalling 1 Cor 7:1), and closes with the famous saying about being a eunuch because of the kingdom of heaven (v. 12).[64]

Within these parallel narratives in Mark and Matthew, there are two significant issues that call for closer attention:

1. Matthew reports Jesus prohibiting divorce, "except for unchastity" (Greek: *mē epi porneia, 19:9*), in his encounter with the Pharisees. This exception must have been important for Matthew and his Christian community. It was not present in Mark 10:11-12, which Matthew is using as a source. He also inserts the same sentiment, "except for unchastity," in 5:32 (Greek: *parektos logou porneias*), where the original "Q" passage (see Luke 16:18) did not allow any such possibility (see Luke 16:18).

Remarkably, when Matthew uses two of his major sources—"Q" (see Luke 16:18) and the Gospel of Mark (see Mark 10:1-12)—he *qualifies* the absolute prohibition of divorce found in both of them. What is perhaps more remarkable, for the contemporary interpreter of the New Testament, is that he uses exactly the same expression to describe the motivation for this exception. The Greek word used, *porneia*, is a notoriously difficult word to translate with any precision. This is so because a number of different Greek expressions are used with reference to specific sexually immoral acts, but *porneia* is a more generic word that can refer to any one of them, or to all of them.[65] In his use of "Q" he softens Jesus' absolute prohibition by adding "except in the case of *porneia*," and his rewriting of Mark is similarly softened by the words "except for *porneia*."

Understandably, given the importance of these two exceptions, what Matthew meant by his use of *porneia* has long been the source of debate and discussion.[66] A decision need not be made here, and what I am about to suggest is but one possibility among many. The situation of the early Christian community addressed by the Gospel of Matthew was, as we have seen, marked by the presence of both Jews and Gentiles. No doubt the inner-community marital situation addressed by Paul in 1 Corinthians 7:12-16 would have again been present, even though the cultural and religious settings of Corinth and Antioch were different. In the newly founded Christian community, there would have been marriages that had been entered into by some of the pre-Christian *Gentile* members. For the Christian community, and especially for the Matthean community where an observance of the Law was required (see 5:17-19), these pagan marriages were regarded as *porneia*. We need not decide precisely what that meant, and the generic word used by the RSV, "unchastity," serves well. I suspect that Paul's use of the expression *porneia* to refer to the incestuous relationship between a man and his father's wife in 1 Corinthians 5:1 is a pointer to its meaning in Matthew 5:32 and 19:9.[67] Whatever one makes of that suggestion, Matthew asks that marriages marked by what the Christian community considered *porneia* be ended. In rewriting Mark 10:1-12, he adds vv. 10-12, found only in Matthew, to his Markan source instructing his disciples (again in a way that echoes 1 Corinthians 7:8-9) that, once freed from this unacceptable marriage situation, they should remain single.[68] Such a request, however, is recognized as extremely difficult. It is not possible for everyone to live that way, and only those gifted for such a lifestyle should practice it (v. 12d. See 1 Cor 7:7-9).[69]

Whatever the precise situation addressed by Matthew, and whatever the exact meaning he wishes to give to the word *porneia*, the decisive matter is that he uses two sources that record the memory of Jesus' absolute prohibition of divorce and remarriage ("Q" and Mark), and he modifies *both* of them (Matt 5:32; 19:9).[70] We are clearly dealing with another moment in the developing theological and pastoral consciousness of the earliest Church that quite freely *and consistently* qualifies a teaching of Jesus. This is a further indication *within the inspired pages of our Christian Sacred Scriptures* that shows the need for the Church to rethink Jesus' fiercely eschatological teaching, in the light of the long-term pastoral situation of the developing Christian Church. As Craig Keener has pointed out:

> In practice, the early Christians immediately began to qualify Jesus' divorce saying; other principles of Jesus, such as not condemning the innocent (12:7) or the principle of mercy (23:23), would have forced them to do so in some circumstances. ... Paul and Matthew's exceptions (Mt 5:32; 19:9; 1 Cor 7:15, 27-28) constitute two-thirds of the extant first-century Christian references to divorce.[71]

2. Jesus' use of Genesis in both accounts, and his explanation of the prohibition of divorce, is based upon God's design "from the beginning of creation" (Mark 10:6a) and "from the beginning" (Matthew 19:4b, 8c). The dispute between Jesus and the Pharisees over divorce and remarriage in Mark 10:1-12 hangs upon the use Jesus makes of the Torah texts of Genesis 1:27 and 2:24 to overcome their use of the Torah text of Deuteronomy 24:1-4 as the reason for allowing divorce. Whether or not he succeeds in closing this issue by use of a text that comes "before" the legislation handed down through Moses in Deuteronomy 24:1-4—because of the hardness of heart of Israel—Jesus' explanation of why the Genesis texts close the discussion is provided by the words "from the beginning of creation" (Greek: *apo tēs arches ktiseōs*), which open his citations from Genesis (Mark 10:6. See also Matt 19:8). A crucial theological point needs to be made here, before we turn to a historical question.

Jesus' appeal to texts from Genesis, and his explicit reference to "the beginning," situates Jesus' description of the situation between a woman and a man in the Garden of Eden! Genesis 1:27 and 2:24 describe the situation between a man (Adam) and a woman (Eve) *before* the introduction of sin into the human story (see Gen 3:1-24). Mark (followed by Matthew) presents Jesus' teaching as the reconstitution of God's original design: "from the beginning (*archē*) of creation" (Mark), and "from the beginning (*archē*)" (twice in Matthew). As Joel Marcus has correctly commented, "Jesus and the Markan Christians are people who rejoice in the dawning light of the new age—which is also the recaptured radiance of Eden."[72] But sin has entered the world, and theologically we now claim that only Jesus of Nazareth has embodied the perfect human condition that God intended. That perfection has been represented in the biblical account of Adam and Eve, but such perfection has been lost to the human condition (Genesis 3). The loss of the glory of these beginnings through the sin and disobedience of Adam has been overcome by the universal significance of the obedience of Jesus, revealed in his death and resurrection. But the story of Adam and the story of Jesus Christ continue to run side by side throughout the human story. Nowhere has this been more eloquently stated than in the close contrasting parallels that Paul draws between Adam and Christ in Romans 5:12-21. The Christian must live the in-between-time, called to join the Christ story and reject the Adam story.[73] As history eloquently demonstrates, humankind is "in process": the ideal of God's original creative plan has never been fully present in the ambiguity of that history.[74]

The introduction of Pauline thought on the "new creation" (see Gal 2:15; 2 Corinthians 5:17) raises a further question. Reflecting upon Jesus' bold rejection of Torah in forbidding the practice of divorce, we earlier saw John Meier arguing that Jesus understood himself, and was understood by his followers, as the eschatological prophet.

> In this highly charged context of future-yet-realized eschatology, the eschatological prophet named Jesus may have inculcated as already binding certain types of behavior that pointed forward, as did his whole ministry, to the final period of Israel's restoration as God's holy people.[75]

Both Paul (in the 50's CE) and Mark (about 70 CE) continue to portray Jesus in this fashion. However, they not only continue Jesus' teaching by looking to "the end" as the explanation for the uniqueness of Jesus and his teaching.[76] They also reach back to the beginnings of all creation. This tendency continued as the early Church developed an ever-deepening understanding of Jesus' significance.[77] Paul refers to a pre-existent Christ in Philippians 2:6-11, but this development finds its highest expression in the Prologue to the Gospel of John, where Jesus is described as the Logos of God, who dwelt in a unique oneness of time "in the beginning" (John 1:1-2. Greek: *en archēi*).[78]

Mark 10:1-12 and Matthew 19:1-12 are bearers of this theological tradition.[79] The strength of Jesus' prohibition of divorce comes from his indication that there was no divorce in the Garden of Eden. Christians do not live in the Garden of Eden, but within the ambiguity of the contemporary human story. Contemporary Catholic legislation prohibits divorce on the basis of the fact that Jesus did so. This position misses an important theological truth in its presupposition that the "ideal" of God's original creation is in place from the very first moment of the long, and often complex, "real" journey of Christian marriage. It transfers what was primarily a Christological intuition of the early Church into an essential element of its marriage legislation (Canon 1141). The confusion of the "ideal" with the "real" in the lives of imperfect people, striving (and sometimes failing) in their Christian lives, calls for re-examination by the Church's highest authority.

EXCLUSION FROM THE TABLE

An important feature of all forms of Christian life is the celebration of the Lord's Table. The Roman Catholic Tradition has solemnly described the Eucharist as "the source and summit of the Christian life" (Vatican II, *Lumen Gentium* 11; *Sacrosanctum Concilium* 10), and such a description is happily shared by many Christian communions. At the heart of a Christian community is the call to the authentic celebration of Eucharist. But the Christian life is not limited to its liturgical celebration of the Eucharist. The celebration is the place where the entire "rhythm" of the Christian life can be perceived (its source), and the ideal that challenges the Christian to love more (its summit). The celebration of the Eucharist also demands the living of eucharistic lives: "They offer the divine victim to God *and themselves along with it*" (*Lumen Gentium* 11; emphasis mine). Our study demonstrates that part of the message of the New Testament regarding the celebration of the Eucharist is a message of the Lord's presence to the broken.

The New Testament texts on the Eucharist have been produced by a Christian people aware of their sinfulness, nourished and challenged at the eucharistic table. However, the New Testament also indicates that the earliest communities felt there were situations in which they had the right, and even the duty, to exclude certain members from the community and its life. Particularly important in this regard are 1 Corinthians 5 and Hebrews 6:1-8.[80] There can be no selective reading of the New Testament to argue for a "free for all" admission to the eucharistic table. This study must not be understood in that way. It is important to be aware that the early Church experienced a growing sense of "exclusiveness" that necessarily led to the eventual elimination of certain people from the community, and thus from the Table of the Lord. The exclusion from the community, as it is evidenced in the New Testament, was primarily based in the early Church's developing understanding of the person of Jesus and its response to him as a community of believers.[81] Paul's intervention in Corinth, demanding that the man in an incestuous relationship "be removed from among you" (1 Cor 5:2), is motivated by the theme of the final coming of Christ, "that his spirit may be saved in the day of the Lord Jesus" (5:5). The need for purity in the community is also founded upon a Christological motivation:

> Cleanse out the old leaven that you may be a new lump, as you really are unleavened. For Christ, our paschal lamb, has been sacrificed. Let us, therefore, celebrate the festival, not with the old leaven, the leaven of malice and evil, but with the unleavened bread of sincerity and truth. (5:7-8)

As Murphy-O'Connor has commented: "The presence within the community of an attitude incompatible with Christ puts the freedom of all at risk because the protective barrier against the value system of the 'world' (= 'Sin') has been weakened."[82] Such a flagrant moral disorder cannot be tolerated. A community that is based upon the self-sacrificing love of Jesus—the paschal lamb (see also 11:23-25)—must live in recognition of that fact.[83] What has happened in Corinth is totally unacceptable on these grounds. The Corinthians' tolerance of this situation, rather than showing the quality of their self-giving love in imitation of Christ (5:7; 11:23-25), places them outside the quality of the love of the pagans among whom they live: "There is immorality among you, and of a kind that is not found even among the pagans" (v. 1). The exclusion flows logically from Paul's deepest beliefs concerning the saving event of Jesus Christ's death and resurrection.[84]

Hebrews 6:1-8 also advocates that certain people be separated from the community.[85] Here the Christological basis for such a separation is obvious. The author exhorts the recipients of the tract to accept the duty that they have to progress in their Christian faith and practice (vv. 1-3).[86] They are to go further than "the elementary doctrines of Christ and go on to maturity" (v. 1). The reader is made immediately aware that the teachings of the faith (vv. 2-3) are concerned with "the doctrines of Christ" (v. 1). However, in this journey to a mature Christianity, Christians will encounter the perils of apostasy (vv. 4-8). There is an indication of the nature of the apostasy involved: "They crucify the Son of God on their own account and hold him up to contempt" (v. 6).[87] The general meaning of this difficult passage is that some Christians, who have enjoyed all the privileges of the Christian life (vv. 4-5), can repeat the arrogance and unbelief of the original crucifiers of Jesus. It is impossible to restore such apostates to repentance (vv. 4-6). They are like a well-watered field that has received God's gifts, but has produced only thorns. They will be destroyed by fire (vv. 7-8). The issue at stake is rejection of Jesus Christ, not moral performance.[88] Brooke F. Westcott has suggested: "Perhaps there is the further thought in the image of crucifixion that Christ dwells in the believer. To fall away from the faith is therefore to slay him."[89] Now, as then, there can be no admission to the common union that the Eucharist creates between both Christ and the believer and the celebrating faithful among themselves (see 1 Cor 10:16-17), for those who do not or will not accept Jesus as the Christ, Son of God, and savior (see, among many, Mark 1:1; Matt 16:16; Luke 9:20; John 20:30-31; Romans 1:1-4).

As far as the New Testament evidence is concerned, the reasons for exclusion from the community, and thus from the Eucharist, are issues of belief rather than moral performance.[90] Both 1 Corinthians

5 and Hebrews 6:1-8 indicate that moral faults often arise from a faulty Christology (1 Cor 5, and Heb 6:1-8), or a faulty Ecclesiology (1 Cor 5). Our approach to this central mystery of the Christian life cannot be "free-for-all." The tradition of exclusion from the Eucharist of those who knowingly, willingly, consciously, and deliberately break "communion" with those who believe in Jesus as the Christ, the Son of God and savior must be maintained. Yet, it is of equal concern that the Christian Church recognize the truth of the New Testament's precious insight: the Eucharist is always a gift of the Lord to his failing community. A balance must be maintained between an understanding of the Eucharist as a place where sinners gather to express repentance, to be nourished and challenged by their Lord, and a sacred encounter that must not be cheapened through the admission of those who have no right to such "communion" with its obligation of continual striving to live as Jesus lived.

We have seen the importance of the early Church's understanding of Jesus' presence to his failing disciples, and their obligation to continue that "presence" in the celebration of the Eucharist. We are also aware that those who deliberately and publicly break "communion" (*koinōnia*) have no place at the celebration of our eucharistic "communion." We need to develop better criteria concerning admission to the Table of the Lord. It should look back to the double meaning of the word "communion" (*koinōnia*) found in 1 Corinthians 10:14-22. The "communion" created by genuinely eucharistic lives renders the "body of Christ" present in the Church's eucharistic celebrations.

Those who recognize the imperfection and even the sinfulness of their lives, but have no other options, should not be excluded. One often finds a Christ-like gift of self in these situations. Many suffer deeply in the ambiguity of their situation, yet maintain their loyalty to the Christian Church and its values. Many find themselves in situations where life itself depends upon a choice that excludes them from the Table of the Lord. In such situations a decision may not even be a choice, so much as a response forced upon them by circumstances beyond their control. This can lead to the exclusion of those who commit themselves to a daily following of the crucified Christ. They are regularly found among the poor and suffering in society. The only choices in life available to them are those that currently exclude them from the Lord's Table.[91]

But there are good reasons to exclude from the eucharistic table those who arrogantly reject what God has done for us in and through the person of Jesus. "Those who could not eat with Jesus were those who rejected him, not those whom he rejected: his welcome was for all who would respond to him. He made no exceptions."[92]

CONCLUSION

Division within the Catholic Church over the issues discussed in this study indicate a deepening rift in the "communion" needed for genuine eucharistic celebrations (see 1 Cor. 11:17-34). It is, as Paul has said, a question of correctly "discerning the body of the Lord" (see 1 Cor 11:29). We often ignore the cries of the genuinely suffering and the poor, including outstanding Christians who have divorced and remarried. They have no word in such debates, but bear the consequences of them.

> The full power to be a witness to Christ, which is given to the church and to all its members, has been converted into the claim that the church is the rich and gracious mediator of grace and salvation. Thus the church has become blind to its essential poverty (cf. 2 Cor. 4:8; Rev. 3:17). The glorious baroque church buildings, with their gilded altar walls and lovely angels in the blue skylike ceiling, clearly bear one message: a person who has entered the church has already entered the heavenly kingdom. Thus the church, with its sacraments, seems to have fallen victim to the temptation to represent, if not almost to replace, the glory of God's own kingdom.[93]

As we proclaim the Gospels we recognize that it is not only to the failing and broken disciples of the Gospel stories that Jesus comes in his eucharistic presence. He is present to the failing and broken disciples of all places and all times: his fragile yet grace-filled Church, "at once holy, and always in need of purification" (*Lumen Gentium* 8). However, it is easy to raise a questioning finger to "the institution." We are in touch with a basic injustice of which we are all guilty. We have a tendency, in this matter, to preach one message and live another. To frequent the Eucharist in my own sense of worthiness is to leave no space for the presence of a eucharistic Lord who seeks me out in my brokenness. He challenges me to go on taking the risky and difficult task of the Christian life, in imitation of him.

A response to the questions raised by this study cannot be found by appealing to good pastoral practice, or to the importance of making visible God's mercy and compassion. Pastoral practice, mercy, and compassion are crucial for the Church's mission of reflecting the face of Christ in the world. But the issue at stake is the belief among many that current practice is an essential element of the Catholic *Tradition*. The possibility of admitting divorced and remarried Catholics to a full participation in the eucharistic table must face the fact that the current legislation on this matter is, in fact, founded upon a "distorted tradition" (Ratzinger).[94] It does not reach back to the founding Tradition of the earliest Church, as the understanding and administration of marriage as a Sacrament belongs to relatively recent Catholic Church history.

The Patristic era, especially under the influence of Augustine, saw marriage as a secondary element in the life of Christians, when compared with the riches promised by God's Kingdom. The medieval period was also ambiguous, as the scholastics had difficulty in understanding how marriage conferred grace. Peter Abelard (1079-1142), who groups marriage with Baptism, Confirmation, Eucharist, and the Anointing of the Sick, can still write: "Among them [these Sacraments] there is one that does not avail unto salvation and yet is the sacrament of a weighty matter, namely matrimony, for to bring a wife home is not meritorious for salvation, but it is allowed for salvation's sake because of incontinence" (*Epitome theologiae Christianae* 28; PL CLXXVIII:1738). In 1439 during the attempt to restore unity with the Eastern Churches at the Council of Florence, the *Decree for the Armenians* established for the first time in Catholic history that this Sacrament contains grace and communicates grace to those who receive it worthily (DS 1327).

This position is formally canonized during the Council of Trent (1543-63).[95] In 1520, Martin Luther (in his *De captivitate Babylonica ecclesiae praeludium*) rejected marriage as a Sacrament, as it has no founding moment in the Scriptures. This opinion was endorsed by the subsequent Lutheran creed in the *Augsburg Confession* (1530). The Reformers also approved the practice of divorce as a lesser of two evils. Trent expressly defines that marriage is a Sacrament, instituted by Christ (using Ephesians 5:25, 32), and conferring grace, in its *Doctrine on the Sacrament of Matrimony* of 1563 (DS 1799-1800). The Council Fathers condemned all who rejected this teaching in the first canon attached to this decree (DS 1801). In the fifth of these canons, they condemned as heretical all who claimed that a marriage could be dissolved (DS 1805).

The complex history that led from these formal decisions in 1563 to our current legislation calls for detailed research that is beyond the scope of this project, and the capacities of the author.[96] But the Catholic Church has focused myopically on Jesus' prohibition of divorce and remarriage (1 Cor 7:10-11; Mark 10:1-12), and paid no heed to the truth that *the inspired revelation of God in the Word of its Sacred Scriptures calls for an accommodation of Jesus' prohibition* (1 Cor 7:12-14; Mark 10:6//Matt 19:8; Matt [1:19?]; 5:32; 19:9). Our legislation on marriage, divorce, and admission to the eucharistic table should accept the overwhelming evidence of the eucharistic teaching of the New Testament: the Eucharist is Jesus Christ's presence among us in his *body, broken for a broken people.* Members of the community who have married and subsequently divorced, but who retain their commitment to Christ and his Church belong to those *broken people.*

The Christian Church has never based its teaching and practice only on what can be shown as the authentic teaching and practice of the historical Jesus. As we have seen earlier in our reflections, the foundational Councils that produced much of the Christian Tradition ranged widely across *everything in the New Testament,* and especially the Gospel of John and the Letters of Paul, to establish its rule of faith, and to articulate it in the great Creeds.[97] There should be no "picking and choosing" with the Word of God. These debates are often colored by the suggestion that the Church is selective in what it chooses from the teaching of Jesus, and point to such requirements as cutting off the hand, the foot, and plucking out the eye (see Mark 9:43-47). They are not legislated in Canon law, but Jesus' authority prohibiting divorce (found only in 1 Cor 7:10-11 and Mark 10:1-12) is found in Canonical legislation (see Canon 1055). Such debates can sometimes be superficial, but they contain a challenge. Martin Hengel has devoted detailed attention to a saying of Jesus, found in

"Q," that he argues lies at the heart of Jesus' personal sense of his charism: "Leave the dead to bury their own dead; but as for you, go and proclaim the kingdom of God" (Luke 9:60//Matt 8:22).[98] Living the Word of God in the Christian Church is no easy matter.[99]

An important principle of interpretation has always been at play in the development of Christian Tradition, and in the Church's necessary commitment to play an effective role in an increasingly informed world. It has never been a simple process. It generates tension and misunderstanding, as the story of the Ecumenical Councils, from Nicea (325 CE) to Vatican II (1962-65 CE), indicate.[100] But the Church does not simply look back to the identifiable words of Jesus to establish its doctrinal and moral bedrock truths; it reflects upon its biblical and ecclesial tradition in dialogue with an ever-expanding body of knowledge and experience. As Benjamin Edsall puts it:

> We all have particular areas of expertise and at times the various things you discover or realize may come into conflict with your understanding of some aspect of theology or scripture—or perhaps more likely, with *someone else's* understanding. But we see here that the truth discovered and/or articulated elsewhere can have a *positive* influence on the understanding of scripture and theology. Of course we lack the benefit of hindsight and a canonized affirmation of our interpretative decisions. But if what we find is in fact true, then what we do in times of external influence is to return to our internal resources—in our case scripture and the living traditions of the Church—in order to find ways to negotiate or accommodate the new information. [101]

The Church's treatment of the divorced and the remarried must take into account *the entire picture*. As the early Church recognized that Jesus had begun a "new creation," it challenged believers to resist and overcome sin, guided by the example of Jesus and enlivened by the pardoning and life-giving grace generated by his death and resurrection (see Rom 5:12-21; Mark 10:6; Matt 19:4, 8). Within those same inspired pages the earliest Church began a Tradition recognizing that only Jesus incarnated the "new creation." The rest of humankind must strive to live a Christian life caught in the ambiguity of the ongoing presence of both the Adam and the Christ stories (see Rom 5:12-21), confident that "where sin increased, grace abounded all the more" (Rom 5:20). Consequently Paul and Matthew, without compunction, allowed an exception to Jesus' absolute prohibition of divorce for its fragile members (1 Cor 7:14-16; Matt 5:32; 19:9).

This is the *authentic Tradition* generated within the Spirit-filled formative decades of Christianity. It should direct us as we read the entire New Testament, seeking the guidance that is found there.[102] No one has stated this better, or more authoritatively, than Joseph A. Fitzmyer:

> If Matthew under inspiration could have been moved to add an exceptive phrase to the saying of Jesus about divorce that he found in an absolute form in either his Marcan source or in 'Q,' or if Paul likewise under inspiration could introduce into his writing an exception on his own authority, then why cannot the Spirit-guided institutional Church of a later generation make a similar exception in view of problems confronting Christian married life of its day or so-called broken marriage? [103]

Recognizing this *authentic Tradition* the Church's leadership will see that its current legislation is based on a late, theologically unfounded, *distorted tradition*. The Church must face the confusing challenges of contemporary society through an examination of its Tradition, and not purely on the basis of good pastoral practice or the desire to show more mercy and compassion to those in need, however precious they are to Christianity. That being said, however, a more powerful manifestation of good pastoral practice and a spectacular manifestation of God's mercy and compassion will follow inevitably from an acceptance and implementation of an authentic Tradition that comes from our origins. It is with that sentiment that I conclude.

The puzzling words found on the frontispiece of this book first appeared in the remarkable Italian of Dante Alleghieri's *Commedia*. It is time to return to them. Very early in Dante's passing through Purgatory, the Latin poet Virgil, who accompanies him, assures him that everyone he meets in this place is destined for Paradise. He is astounded to find Manfred, the illegitimate son of the Holy Roman Emperor, Frederick II. Manfred had been killed at the battle of Benevento in 1266, in a failed attempt to restore the authority of the Empire in the Italian peninsula. Manfred had murdered several close relatives to further his career, and was guilty of a host of other sins, including drunkenness and debauchery. It was even claimed that he had killed his father. He had been declared a heretic by one pope, and excommunicated by two others. *But Dante finds him in Purgatory!* Dante is dumbfounded that this man would be saved. Manfred explains how he managed to escape the Inferno:

> ... *io mi rendei,*
> *piangendo, a quei che volentier perdona.*
> *Orribil furon li peccati miei;*
> *ma la bontà infinita ha sì gran braccia,*
> *che prende ciò che si rivolge a lei.*

> "I gave myself up,
> weeping, to Him who willingly pardons.
> My sins were horrible;
> but infinite goodness has such wide arms,
> that it takes what turns to it."
> (Dante, *Il Purgatorio iii* 119-23).[104]

NOTES

1   For a recent attempt to guide believers to a better grasp the importance of the Word of God in the life and practice of the Church, see Moloney, *Reading the New Testament in the Church*.

2   See Moloney, *Reading the New Testament in the Church*, 57-63.

3   For a study of this aspect of the supper, attested across all the traditions, see Léon-Dufour, *Sharing the Eucharistic Bread*, 165-68. He regards it as an authentic memory of something Jesus of Nazareth said on that night.

4   I have deliberately used the generic expression "traditional ritual meal," rather than "a Passover meal," because the New Testament authors are not clear about this, and Luke (Luke 22:15) is the only one to state that it was a Passover meal (but see Mark 14:12//Matt 25:17), and the dating, in relationship with the timing of the death and burial of Jesus, is confusing. For a full discussion of the problem, and attempts to resolve it, see Jeremias, *The Eucharistic Words*, 16-41. For his decision that it was a Passover meal, see his extensive argument on pp. 41-88. For the arguments for and against a

Passover meal, deciding that this setting developed in early Christian liturgical practice, see Theissen and Merz, *The Historical Jesus*, 423-27. Léon-Dufour, *Sharing the Eucharistic Bread*, 52-53, 87-90, 189-93, explores the difficulty, and suggests that whatever the exact nature of the meal, it celebrated *the Passover of the person of Jesus* (see pp. 192-93).

5   As we have already mentioned, some scholars reject this historical link between a meal celebrated by Jesus and the disciples, and the later practice of the Last Supper. See above, p. 38 note 45. At this late stage of our study, a word of warning must be issued. Our close focus upon history, the New Testament, and its reception is directed to uncovering *only one crucial element* in the significance of the Church's celebration of the Eucharist. There is so much more that can and should be said. For example, the cosmic nature of the celebration whereby "the Christian assembly … becomes a community of hope on behalf of all creation" (Hugh O'Donnell, *Eucharist and the Living Earth* [Dublin: The Columba Press, 2007], 94) has not been broached. See especially Martelet, *The Risen Christ and the Eucharistic World*.

6   On this, see Francis J. Moloney, "Jesus Christ: The Question to Cultures," *Pacifica* 1 (1988), 18-21.

7   For Crossan, *The Historical Jesus*, 360-67, it was the hallmark of Jesus' life and ministry. Although not so passionate about this feature in his life, the following insist on table-fellowship with the marginalized: Günther Bornkamm, *Jesus of Nazareth* (London: Hodder and Stoughton, 1963), 80-81; Charles H. Dodd, *The Founder of Christianity* (London: Collins, 1971), 43-47, 75-79; Norman Perrin, *Rediscovering the Teaching of Jesus* (London: SCM Press, 1967), 102-8; Ben F. Meyer, *The Aims of Jesus* (London: SCM Press, 1979), 158-62; Ed Parish Sanders, *Jesus and Judaism* (Philadelphia: Fortress Press, 1985), 174-211, 270-81; idem, *The Historical Figure of Jesus* (London: Penguin Books, 1993*)*, 198-204; Albert Nolan, *Jesus Before Christianity: The Gospel of Liberation* (London: Darton, Longman & Todd, 1977), 37-42; Gerhard Lohfink, *Jesus and Community: The Social Dimension of Christian Faith* (New York/Philadelphia: Paulist Press/Fortress Press, 1984), 18-20, 42, 93; idem, *No Irrelevant Jesus: On Jesus and Christians Today*, trans. Linda M. Maloney (Collegeville, MI: The Liturgical Press, 2014), 37-46; Gerd Theissen, *The Shadow of the Galilean: The Quest of the Historical Jesus in Narrative Form* (London: SCM Press, 1987), 97-108; Meier, *A Marginal Jew*, 3:80-82. See also John P. Mackey, *Jesus the Man and the Myth* (London: SCM Press, 1979), 142-59.

8   Perrin, *Rediscovering the Teaching of Jesus*, 102.

9   Léon-Dufour, *Sharing the Eucharistic Bread*, 53.

10   As we have seen, Paul intervened quite powerfully when he sensed that something along these lines was happening in Corinth. See above, pp. 51-59.

11   This importance is understandably reflected in the interest that scholars and commentators have shown in the question. John P. Meier, *A Marginal Jew: Rethinking the Historical Jesus*, Anchor Bible Reference Library/Anchor Yale Bible Reference Library, 4 vols. (New York/New Haven: Doubleday/Yale University Press, 1991-2009), 4:128-39, provides twelve densely printed pages of what Meier describes as a "a sample of representative works." His investigation is strictly limited to identifying the teaching of Jesus of Nazareth. He does not concern himself with the further interpretation of the words of Jesus by Paul (in 1 Cor 11:10-16), Mark 10:1-12, and Matthew 19:1-12. For the purposes of this study, in order not to overburden the reader, I will limit my consultation of secondary literature to the detailed work of Meier, Raymond F. Collins, *Divorce in the New Testament*, Good News Studies 38 (Collegeville, MN: The Liturgical Press, 1992), and David Instone-Brewer, *Divorce and Remarriage in the Bible* (Grand Rapids: Eerdmans, 2002), as well as classical and recent commentaries on 1 Corinthians, Mark, and Matthew.

12   In the light of the oceans of ink that have been spilt over this question, an apology is required at this stage. I will only survey major questions, taking one possible position among many in interpreting the evidence. The originality of what follows is the hermeneutical step that I will take—that the earliest Church was Spirit-filled and thus inspired when it understood and embraced the teaching of Jesus of Nazareth, yet still choose to qualify it in the face of the real-life problems that divorce and remarriage presented. I will argue that such practice represents an authentic Christian Tradition. It also provides a new perspective on the role the evidence of the New Testament texts has for the life and teaching of the contemporary Church.

13   The recent study of William R. G. Loader, "Did Adultery Mandate Divorce? A Reassessment of Jesus' Divorce Logia," *New Testament Studies* 61 (2015), 67-78, raises a serious doubt about Jesus' absolute prohibition of divorce, as we will see. For Loader, the leading international authority on sexual relationships in the cultures and settings that produced early Christianity, Jesus' prohibition of divorce may only appear to be absolute. As a person of his time and tradition, he took it for granted, on the basis of Genesis 2:24, that adultery *necessarily* led to divorce. He did not need to say it.

14   At this stage of our study, it should be apparent to a reader that Paul stands alone as the earliest written witness to the Christian Tradition. Another

early witness is the so-called "Q" (material common to Matthew and Luke, and thus prior to them, to be dated from 50-70 CE), followed by Mark (70), Matthew and Luke (latter half of the 80's), and John (about 100).

15   An attentive reader will notice that no further questions are posed to Luke 16:18. It is not called for, as Luke's use of this passage from "Q" (see Matt 5:32; less the exception clause), within a loosely arranged series of ethical teaching in 16:10-18, is perched between the parable of the cunning steward in 16:1-9 and the parable of the rich man and Lazarus. As such, it serves as an important witness that takes us back to the oldest recorded tradition from Jesus. This is not the case with 1 Corinthians 7:8-16, Mark 10:1-12, and Matthew 19:1-12.

16   The reader must recall that no document called "Q" is found in the New Testament. As was explained early in the book, it is a sigla used by critics to indicate early material, common to Matthew and Luke, but not found in Mark, that would have been earlier than Mark. See Kloppenborg, *Q, the Earliest Gospel*, 1-40, and Ivan Havener, *Q: The Sayings of Jesus*, Good News Studies 19 (Wilmington, DE: Michael Glazier, 1987). Speculatively reconstructed texts of "Q" can be found in Kloppenborg, *Q, the Earliest Gospel*, 123-44, and Havener, *The Sayings of Jesus*, 123-46. The most complete treatment of "Q," and the reconstruction of its text is James M. Robinson, Paul Hoffmann, and John S. Kloppenborg, *The Critical Edition of Q: Synopsis including the Gospels of Matthew and Luke, Mark and Thomas with English, German, and French Translations of Q and Thomas*, Hermeneia (Minneapolis: Fortress, 2000).

17   These major elements of Johannine Christology, rapidly stated, which form the heart of the Christian Creeds, cannot be found in the earlier traditions of Paul and the Synoptic Gospels. There are many elements that are common (Son of Man, Son of God, God as "Father") but they are different in meaning, and closer to the Church's Jewish roots, in the earlier tradition. Any good dictionary of the Bible, or of biblical theology, will show this. See, for example, Karl H. Rengstorf, "Jesus Christ," in *The New International Dictionary of New Testament Theology*, ed. Colin Brown, 3 vols. (Exeter: Paternoster Press, 1976), 2:330-43. Also useful, and written for the non-specialist, is the study of Earl Richard, *Jesus: One and Many: The Christological Concept of New Testament Authors* (Wilmington, DE: Michael Glazier, 1988), 187-231.

18   This affirmation does *not* reject the possibility that much of the material in the Gospel of John comes from earlier tradition, and that authentic traditions from the words and actions of Jesus are found there. However, these

traditions have been absorbed (and often remodelled) to fit the Johannine literary and theological agenda. The classical work on this remains Dodd, *Historical Tradition in the Fourth Gospel.*

19 Most, but not all, mainstream Christian Churches have continued the use of the pre-Reformation Creeds, originally forged through vigorous debate at the early Councils, as an essential statement of what they believe. See the classic work of John N. D. Kelly, *Early Christian Creeds*, 3rd ed. (London: Routledge, 1982), and the very useful book of Leo D. Davis, *The First Seven Ecumenical Councils (325-787): Their History and Theology* (Collegeville: Liturgical Press, 1983).

20 On Jesus' approach to his death, see Allison, *Constructing Jesus*, 387-433. On the centrality of the saving effects of Jesus' death and resurrection in Paul, among many, see James D. G. Dunn, *The Theology of the Apostle Paul* (Grand Rapids: Eerdmans, 1998), 207-65.

21 For much of what follows, I am indebted to the work of Meier, *A Marginal Jew*, 4:74-181. This fourth volume of Meier's as yet unfinished *magnum opus* is entitled: "Law and Love." For Jesus of Nazareth, the Sacred Scriptures would have been largely the Torah, the first five books of our Old Testament. At that time, the Prophets had been accepted as Sacred Scripture, but were less normative than the Torah. The so-called "Writings" (the rest of our Old Testament) did not become part of the Jewish Sacred writings till early in the second century CE.

22 See the discussion in Elaine A. Goodfriend, "Adultery," in *The Anchor Bible Dictionary*, 1:82-86. See, however, Loader, "Did Adultery Mandate Divorce?" 68. He points out that the Jews no longer had the right to mandate death, and thus "the sentence had to take an alternate form." Divorce "was the obvious alternative and it was mandatory."

23 See Collins, *Divorce*, 89-91.

24 Meier, *A Marginal Jew*, 4:80.

25 See Meier, *A Marginal Jew*, 4:81-86; Instone-Brewer, *Divorce and Remarriage*, 34-58. One anomaly needs attention. Archaeologists have uncovered documents from a Jewish community in Elephantine in Egypt that reflects the thought and practice of a diaspora Jewish military community from the 5th century BCE. The practice of divorce is taken for granted, but the documents indicate, for the first time, that a "bill of divorce" had to be prepared, and that it was not only possible for the man to divorce the woman, but also for the woman to divorce the man. This was a quite unique diaspora situation, and should not be given too much weight in trying to

establish divorce practices in first-century Palestinian Judaism. See Meier, *A Marginal Jew*, 4:83-84.

26 See Instone-Brewer, *Divorce and Remarriage*, 34-58.

27 Meier, *A Marginal Jew*, 2:82. For the discussion, see pp. 81-82, and the associated footnotes on pp. 144-49. The options in the square parentheses generate a translation: "Indeed he hated to send away." Instone-Brewer, *Divorce and Remarriage*, 54-57, among others, is aware of the difficulty of the Hebrew text, but insists that v. 16 "shows that God is against the person who breaks one's marriage vows" (p. 57).

28 See Meier, *A Marginal Jew*, 4:84-87.

29 For excellent treatments of CD 4:20-21 and 11QTemple 57:15-19, and wide-ranging scholarship that surround the interpretation of these texts, see Meier, *A Marginal Jew*, 4:87-93, and the associated notes on pp. 155-62.

30 See, for example, Joseph A. Fitzmyer, "The Matthean Divorce Texts and Some New Palestinian Evidence," *Theological Studies* 39 (1976), 221-23.

31 Meier, *A Marginal Jew*, 4:93. But see Joseph A. Fitzmyer, "Marriage and Divorce," in *Encyclopedia of the Dead Sea Scrolls*, ed. Lawrence H. Schiffman and James C. VanderKam, 2 vols. (Oxford/New York: Oxford University Press, 2000), 1:512, who interprets these same documents as the prohibition of divorce, and not only polygamy. He also claims that in this the Essenes "honored God's words recorded in *Malachi* 2:14b-16." For more detail, see idem, "The Matthean Divorce Texts," 197-226, and more recently, Fitzmyer, *First Corinthians*, 288-90. See also, Collins, *Divorce*, 80-85. Meier's uncertainty is shared by Luz, *Matthew*, 494. William R. G. Loader, *The Dead Sea Scrolls on Sexuality in Sectarian and Related Literature at Qumran* (Grand Rapids: Eerdmans, 2009), 107-19, argues that the availability of all the Qumran material now makes it clear that "the cited prohibition is best taken as referring not to divorce but to polygyny." See idem, "Did Adultery Mandate Divorce?" 71, for the citation.

32 See Edsall, *Paul's Witness*, 99-109; Collins, *Divorce*, 11-13.

33 On this principle, see Fitzmyer, *First Corinthians*, 305-7.

34 The possible remembrance in the tradition of the new world that Jesus created for women could be one of the motivations. Most explain it by indicating the Corinthian situation in the Roman colony of Corinth. See Horsley, *1 Corinthians*, 98-99; Collins, *Divorce*, 13-22; Meier, *A Marginal Jew*, 4:165-66 note 92. Roman law allowed the woman to divorce her husband, and thus Paul takes this into account. For the discussion, see Meier,

A Marginal Jew, 4:99-101. Instone-Brewer, *Divorce and Remarriage*, 24-26, suggests that one can trace evidence of increasing rights for women at this period from information found in rabbinic documents. Meier, *A Marginal Jew*, 139-40 note 5, rejects this suggestion. Instone-Brewer's work is marred by over-optimism about the impact debates recorded in later Jewish documents made upon earliest Christianity.

35   See Collins, *Divorce*, 29-39; idem, *First Corinthians*, 263-65. In a strange assessment of 1 Corinthians 7:1-16 (which he links with Romans 7:1-4), Instone-Brewer, *Divorce and Remarriage*, 189-212, devotes no close attention to the "word of the Lord" in vv. 10-11, and argues that Paul's main concern was to encourage the Corinthians not to divorce, but "if the marriage ends despite the best efforts, he or she is entitled to divorce and is free to remarry" (p. 212).

36   For the discussion of possible links between 1 Corinthians 7:10-11 and Synoptic sayings, see Collins, *Divorce*, 32-38.

37   For a discussion of the problems surrounding Luke's narrative composition at this point of his Gospel, see Collins, *Divorce*, 175-79. See also the very helpful study of Brendan Byrne, "Forceful Stewardship and Neglectful Wealth: A Contemporary Reading of Luke 16," *Pacifica* 1 (1988), 1-14, especially pp. 10-14.

38   In fact, as Dale C. Allison, Jr, "Divorce, Celibacy and Joseph (Matthew 1.18-25 and 19.1-12)," *Journal for the Study of the New Testament* 49 (1993), 3-10, points out, Matthew raises the issue of divorce *three times*: Joseph's decision to divorce his wife "quietly" is recorded in 1:19. Allison's main concern is to show that *porneia* in 19:9 means adultery, and that Joseph's celibacy in 1:24-25 clarifies what is meant by the eunuch saying in 19:10-12. However, he makes an important point when he suggests that the description of Joseph as a "righteous man" (Greek: *dikaios*) demands that there be an exception to Jesus' absolute prohibition of divorce. It is "righteous" to divorce the unfaithful wife. Not to do so would bring "sin upon the land" (see Deut 24:4). Joseph "is to be regarded as a model of behavior in accord with God's will" (p. 5). Coherently, therefore, Matthew *must* add the exception clauses to Matthew 5:32 and 19:9. If divorce was necessary for Joseph, the just man, it must be fine for the followers of Jesus. Loader, "Did Adultery Mandate Divorce?" 68-69, understands Joseph's "righteousness" as a judgment of his decision to divorce his Mary, rather than execute her. But he agrees that this decision is closely linked to the addition of the exception clauses in 5:32 and 19:9.

39   For a fully documented discussion of this research, see Meier, *A Marginal Jew*, 4:104-8, and the notes on pp. 168-71.

40   See Meier, *A Marginal Jew*, 4:107-108, for the reconstructed text, and reflections upon its structure and meaning. This is also the reconstruction of Robinson, Hoffmann, and Kloppenborg, *The Critical Edition of Q*, 470.

41   See also Collins, *Divorce*, 214; Fitzmyer, *First Corinthians*, 290-91. However Loader, "Did Adultery Mandate Divorce?" 67-78, has indicated his serious doubt. Although once convinced of this opinion (see p. 68), he now claims that, on the basis of Genesis 2:24 (see pp. 75-76), Jesus took it for granted that divorce would follow adultery. "[T]he exception now found in Matt 5.32 and 19.9 was already presupposed in Mark 10.11-12, Luke 16.18 and 1 Cor 7:10-11. Matthew, rather than uncharacteristically softening Jesus' demand, simply spelled out what has always been assumed" (p. 74).

42   For an application of the usual "criteria" used by historians to detect the historicity of material found in such sayings, see Meier, *A Marginal Jew*, 4:112-19. The citation comes from p. 114. Not all would be so clear-cut. See, for example, Collins, *Divorce*, 178, who suggests that Moses did not mandate divorce, so therefore there is some "room" for Jesus' hard line in these debates. For a similar case, see also Sanders, *Jesus and Judaism*, 256-60; Hooker, *St Mark*, 235; William Loader, *Jesus' Attitude to the Law: A Study of the Gospels* (Grand Rapids: Eerdmans, 2002), 88-91 (Mark), 174-75, 225 (Matthew), 338-39 (Luke); Marcus, *Mark*, 2:710-11; Gerhard Lohfink, *Jesus of Nazareth: What He Wanted, Who He Was*, trans. Linda M. Maloney (Collegeville, MI: The Liturgical Press, 2012), 202-204. A general comment on Meier's work is called for. He strives diligently to lay bare the *contrasts* between Jesus and his world and culture (using what is called "the criterion of dissimilarity"). Others are less aggressive in this pursuit. See, for example, Lohfink, *Jesus of Nazareth*, 204: "Jesus' prohibition of divorce is not directed against the Torah as such but instead clarifies a particular point in Torah." Of course, for Loader, "Did Marriage Mandate Divorce?" 67-78 (changing his earlier opinion; see earlier in this note), claims that there is no tension: "Matthew is simply spelling out what all would have assumed, namely that adultery mandated divorce" (p. 74). If such was the case, there is nothing surprisingly "eschatological" in Jesus' attitude to divorce.

43   A huge social and legal chasm exists between the time of Jesus and our modern society, in which the practice of "partners" (heterosexual or homosexual), rather than wives and husbands, is commonly accepted.

44   Meier, *A Marginal Jew*, 4:127. See also Collins, *Divorce*, 218-22.

45   The likely background to Paul's insertion of this thought is that some of the Corinthians, who were not able to live such a life (see v. 9), aspire to live

as Paul lives. This would not be appropriate. See Perkins, *First Corinthians*, 109-10.

46　There is no need to associate this issue with the widely touted sexual license of ancient Corinth. This has been shown to be greatly exaggerated, at least for the time of Paul. See, for example, Jerome Murphy-O'Connor, "Corinth," in *The Anchor Bible*, 1:1134-39, and his collection of ancient sources in Murphy-O'Connor, *St. Paul's Corinth*. It was only natural that adult conversion to Christianity (which was the norm in this founding period) brought women and men into Christianity who already had non-Christian spouses. There is nothing licentious involved.

47　On the idea of the mutual "sanctification" of spouses and children in the biblical and Jewish tradition, see Collins, *First Corinthians*, 266-67. While this is helpful, it is also important to notice the suggestion of Barrett, *The First Epistle to the Corinthians*, 164-65, and Conzelmann, *1 Corinthians*, 121-23, that Paul continues to deal with some of the negative ideas about marriage and sexuality of vv. 1-9. His assurance on the "holiness" of the couple of a Christian and a non-Christian, and of their children, indicates that their marriage is "clean": "within the covenant" (Barrett, *First Epistle*, 165). For a good synthesis of the discussion, also suggesting the sanctifying situation of the couple in a mixed union, see Fitzmyer, *First Corinthians*, 299-301. See p. 301: "God's sanctifying power is greater than any unbelief."

48　Will Deming, *Paul on Marriage and Celibacy: The Hellenistic Background of 1 Corinthians 7* (Grand Rapids: Eerdmans, 2004), 145-69, interprets the use of the Greek verb *dedoulōtai* (v. 15b), generally translated as "to be bound" to a partner, as being "enslaved." He finds parallels in Cynic writing that may have influenced Paul. A Cynic with a non-Cynic partner is "enslaved" in a non-Cynic context. Whatever the background, Paul allows the non-believer to leave the marriage.

49　The interpretation of v. 16 concerning a wife or a husband's knowledge of the eventual salvation of their respective partner is divided. A positive interpretation supports the permanence of the union, in the hope that the partner might come to salvation. A negative interpretation suggests that there is no point staying in the marriage hoping that salvation will come to one's spouse. That is beyond anyone's knowledge of control; it belongs to God. See Collins, *First Corinthians*, 272, for the discussion. He accepts the positive interpretation, in the light of the recommendation to common holiness in v. 14. See also Barrett, *The First Epistle to the Corinthians*, 167. For the negative position, see Conzelmann, *1 Corinthians*, 124.

50   I have drawn attention to the Greek verb "to call" (Greek: *kaleô*) as this became a technical expression in early Christianity for God's initiative in calling people to the following of Jesus Christ: "vocation." See Collins, *First Corinthians*, 267. I am also accepting that Paul is addressing what he regards as the unique situation of the Christian community. Following the RSV, I have used the first-person plural pronoun, "you" (Greek: *hēmas*). This is textually doubtful. The original may be the second-person plural, "you" (Greek: *hymas*). Although the "us" is more clearly associated with the inner-group of the Christian community, the use of "you" does not alter the argument. The reference to "any brother" (Greek: *tis adelphos*) in v. 12 makes it clear that Paul is addressing the inner-dynamics of a Christian community. For the textual issue, see Metzger, *A Textual Commentary*, 489; Collins, *First Corinthians*, 272.

51   See, among many, Horsley, *1 Corinthians*, 99.

52   Perkins, *First Corinthians*, 110, points out that Paul is speaking to "the social goal of harmony within the household is the divine intent for all marriages." Instone-Brewer, *Divorce and Remarriage*, 203-4, argues that this invitation to peace indicates that a divorced person is free to remarry. This hardly fits the evidence.

53   Collins, *First Corinthians*, 267-68, tries to lessen the dramatic nature of this reversal of Jesus' instructions by suggestion that it is a "casuistic aside." There is no evidence for this, unless Collins regards dealing with a local Corinthians situation "casuistic." However local, the earliest tradition of the Church, found in 1 Corinthians 7:14-16, *permits divorce* in certain circumstances. For a more aggressive treatment from Collins, see *Divorce*, 40-64. For an awareness of the sharpness of the contrast, see Fitzmyer, *First Corinthians*, 301-2.

54   Collins, *Divorce*, 63-64, rightly claims that there is a lack of clarity in what Paul thinks about remarriage. Meier, *A Marginal Jew*, 174 note 126, suggests that the texts reflect Paul's own lack of certainty as to "what the Christian caught in this difficult situation can or should do." Fitzmyer, *First Corinthians*, 301-2 is more optimistic: "Paul says nothing against further marriages" (p. 302).

55   Perkins, *First Corinthians*, 110.

56   They are expertly dealt with by Collins, *Divorce*, 40-64.

57   The Catholic Church recognizes this "exception" in its law. Naming Paul, it claims that it has the authority to "dissolve" a marriage between two non-believers (not baptized), when one of the parties subsequently becomes

a Catholic. This so-called *privilegium paulinum* (the Pauline privilege), is carefully legislated in Canon 1143-1150 (see *Code of Canon Law*, 357-59). Fitzmyer, *First Corinthians*, 302-3, comments: "That is a development in Canon Law that goes beyond the limits of the case envisaged by Paul." The classical biblical/pastoral approach to this issue by Catholic authorities is reflected in the document of the International Theological Commission to the Holy See. In its "Propositions on the Doctrine of Marriage" (Sharkey, ed., *International Theological Commission: Texts and Documents*), 173, 1 Corinthians 7:10-11 is used to reinforce the absolute prohibition of divorce, but vv. 12-16 are ignored.

58   The following parallel presentation of the Markan and Matthean texts provides the order of the Markan text. Both texts are presented in full, in regular type. However, passages that Matthew has relocated are presented in *italics*, so that the reader will more easily be able to follow the parallels. They also show Matthew's creative freedom with his source. For a good comparison of the two texts, see Collins, *Divorce*, 132-40.

59   There is a crucial distinction drawn between what God (Greek: *ho theos*) has done, and what "man" (Greek: *anthrōpos*) attempts to undo in v. 9.

60   See, for example, Collins, *Mark*, 469-70.

61   On the focus upon teaching the disciples across 10:1-31, see, among many, Moloney, *The Gospel of Mark*, 192-203.

62   It has long been argued that Matthew's addition of "for any cause" reflects the difference of opinion between the school of Shammai, who only allowed divorce on the basis of moral disorder on the part of the woman, and the school of Hillel, who allowed divorce "for any cause." Both argued their case on an interpretation of Deuteronomy 24:1-4. This debate is widely recorded in rabbinic documents. See, for example, Fitzmyer, "The Matthean Divorce Texts," 197-226; Collins, *Divorce*, 75-76; Davies and Allison, *Matthew*, 3:9; Luz, *Matthew*, 2:488-89; Instone-Brewer, *Divorce and Remarriage*, 110-14; Loader, "Did Adultery Mandate Divorce?" 72-73. This position is strenuously opposed by Meier, *A Marginal Jew*, 94-95, 163 note 80. He claims the rabbinic texts are too late (written early in the third century) to be used in the interpretation of a first century document.

63   See Collins, *Divorce*, 119-20.

64   It is beyond our scope to discuss the history and meaning of Matthew 19:10-12. For more detail, see Moloney, "Matthew 19:3-12 and Celibacy," 42-60. In brief, following the intuition of Josef Blinzler, "*Eisin eunouchoi*. Zur Auslegung von Mt 19,12," *Zeitschrift für die Neutestamentliche Wissenschaft*

48 (1957), 254-70, I argue that the saying had its origins on the lips of Jesus. He used the word "eunuch" because that was a form of crude abuse hurled at him as he was known to be unmarried. His response indicated that he was so taken up with the kingdom (thus translating the Greek *dia tēn basileian* as "because of," and not the traditional "for the sake of") that he was celibate. He could do no other. Matthew received this Jesus-saying in his tradition, and applied it to those Christians in his mixed Jewish-Christian community who had been abandoned by former non-Christian partners. He asks them to remain unmarried, "because of the kingdom of heaven," but is aware that such a lifestyle is a gift. 1 Corinthians 7:7 is again close at hand. See also Quentin Quesnell, "Made Themselves Eunuchs for the Kingdom of Heaven (Mt. 19:12)," *The Catholic Biblical Quarterly* 30 (1968), 335-58. On the traditional nature of v. 12, see Collins, *Divorce*, 119-20.

65   For the many possible meanings, see BDAG, 854, s.v. *porneia*. The following possibilities are listed and documented: unlawful sexual intercourse, prostitution, unchastity, fornication, participation in prohibited degrees of marriage, and immorality of a transcendent nature (i.e., participation in orgiastic cultic rituals). For a very good survey, see William R. G. Loader, *The New Testament on Sexuality* (Grand Rapids: Eerdmans, 2012), 244-50.

66   For a survey of this discussion until 1979, see Moloney, "Matthew 19:3-12 and Celibacy," 44, and notes 13-14. For the discussion since then, see Meier, *Law and History*, 140-50; Collins, *Divorce*, 184-213; Davies and Allison, *Matthew*, 1:529-31; 3:16; Luz, *Matthew*, 1:250-59. Instone-Brewer, *Divorce and Remarriage*, 167-71, without any analysis of the history of the tradition, claims that these are further radical words of Jesus teaching that being married and having children were not necessary.

67   As we have seen, Loader, "Did Adultery Mandate Divorce?" 67-78, challenges this suggestion. He claims that *porneia* certainly meant adultery, and that it was taken for granted, even by Jesus, that divorce would follow adultery.

68   This case is argued at length in Moloney, "Matthew 19:3-12 and Celibacy," 44-60. In support of the meaning of "incestuous relationship," see also Meier, *Law and History*, 140-50; Fitzmyer, "Matthean Divorce Texts," 221.

69   The Pauline teaching of 1 Corinthians 7:7-9 is again present. The verb used by Matthew in 19:12d, translated in the RSV in the command "He who is able to *receive* this, let him *receive* it," is *chōreō*. Its primary meaning is not "receive," but "make space" (see Mark 2:2). See BDAG, s.v. *chōreō*, p. 1094. It thus carries the idea of being open to a gift, and thus "accept."

70   For up-to-date commentary on these passages, see Davies and Allison, *Matthew*, 1:527-32, 3:4-30; Luz, *Matthew*, 1:249-59, 2:405-3.

71   Keener, *Gospel of Matthew*, 191. See also Collins, *Divorce*, 230-31: "[T]he first generations of Christians experienced a need not only to pass along Jesus' teaching on divorce but also to adapt it to ever new circumstances. To pass along the tradition, while all the while adapting it to the circumstances of later times, is the perennial challenge to those who want to be faithful to Jesus' prophetic witness and to a teaching that concerns not only the lives of specific individuals but also the very existence of the Church itself."

72   Marcus, *Mark*, 2:710.

73   On Paul's concept of the Adam story, and the "new creation" of Jesus' death and resurrection, see Moloney, *Reading the New Testament in the Church*, 97-102, and further discussion there.

74   Some may query this statement in the light of the saints, and especially the Mother of Jesus, in Catholic teaching. Such holiness, which is a restoration of God's original design, is only possible because of a positive response to the gift of God's grace. It is not *natural*. This truth lies at the heart of the Catholic doctrine of the Immaculate Conception: the saving efficacy of Jesus' death and resurrection—by special privilege—is applied to Mary at conception. She is the recipient of God's grace. Simeon's words about a sword piercing her heart, recorded in Luke 2:34-35, are an indication that she still had to suffer the ambiguities of the human condition.

75   As cited above, from Meier, *A Marginal Jew*, 4:127. See above, p. 218. He does not develop the theme, as he is totally focused upon the historical question. However, on p. 177 note 143 and p. 178 note 147, Meier indicates the possibility that these Jewish and early Christian themes may be present.

76   Jesus' looking to "the end" as the basis for an understanding of his person and message has been splendidly shown by Allison, *Constructing Jesus*. One of the clearest indications of the early Church's further development of Jesus' eschatological importance is found in the rendering of the expression "the Son of Man" more and more eschatological as the Jesus-tradition grew. See Francis J. Moloney, "*Constructing Jesus* and the Son of Man," *The Catholic Biblical Quarterly* 75 (2013), 719-38.

77   There is considerable contemporary interest in the relationship between Pauline and Markan theology, initiated by Joel Marcus, "Mark—Interpreter of Paul," *New Testament Studies* 46 (2000), 473-87. See also the provocative essay of Brendan Byrne, "Paul and Mark Before the Cross: Common Echoes of the Day of Atonement Ritual," in *Transcending Boundaries*, 217-29, and

the recent important collection of Oda Wischmeyer, David C. Sim, and Ian J. Elmer, *Paul and Mark: Comparative Essays: Two Authors at the Beginnings of Christianity*, Beihefte zur Zeitschrift für die neutestamentliche Wissenschaft 198 (Berlin/Boston: de Gruyter, 2014). I do not accept a "literary" connection between Paul and Mark (i.e., Mark was not reading and copying Paul), but a sharing of fundamental early Christian beliefs. See Moloney, *The Gospel of Mark*, 348-54.

78   There is no questioning the Johannine presentation of the pre-existent Logos. However, a number of Pauline scholars have denied that Paul taught Jesus Christ's pre-existence. For the discussion, and a convincing exegetical and theological argument in defense of a Pauline notion of pre-existence, see Brendan Byrne, "Christ's Pre-Existence in Pauline Soteriology," *Theological Studies* 58 (1997), 308-30.

79   This affirmation raises the question of the "historicity" of Mark's report of the discussion of divorce between Jesus and the Pharisees. A literary form used regularly in the Gospels is called a "controversy dialogue" (scholars use the technical German word *Streitgespräch*). They reflect the discussions, generally conflictual, that went on between the early Church and the contemporary Jewish leadership, and beyond, often reflecting a more Greco-Roman setting. As such, they are the bearers of the expanding theology of the early Church. The best guide is still found in Rudolf Bultmann, *History of the Synoptic Tradition*, trans. John Marsh (Oxford: Blackwell, 1968), 39-54. This does not deny that behind the discussion one cannot find an authentic memory of an experience of Jesus. However, what has been said above indicates the growing association of Jesus with the restoration of God's original creation that developed in the early Church. For full detail, see Meier, *A Marginal Jew*, 4:119-24, who accepts that the conflict reflects the theology of the later Church, but remarks: "I find it a strange presupposition that a noted Jewish teacher who preached for over two years to his fellow Jews, would never cite or argue from the Jewish scriptures, especially the Mosaic Torah" (4:180 note 151). Collins, *Divorce*, 70-71, 77-80, agrees on the nature of the conflict, claiming that Mark 10:11 ("whoever divorces his wife and marries another, commits adultery against her") may be pre-Markan, while the rest of the saying developed in a Hellenistic setting (pp. 71-103).

80   It is sometimes suggested that Matthew 5:23-24 (reconciling oneself with one's brother before offering sacrifice) is pertinent to this discussion. The text is not eucharistic. The passage may be dominical; it presupposes the sacrificial system in Jerusalem, not the Christian Eucharist (see Davies and Allison, *Matthew*, 1:516-18; Luz, *Matthew*, 240; Keener, *Matthew*, 185). The message of Matthew 5:23-24 is further indication of the centrality of

the case I have argued. As John P. Meier, *The Vision of Matthew* (New York: Paulist Press, 1979), 245, remarks: "In a sense, Jesus' basic teaching on the union of the love of God and love of neighbor is summed up in this parable. An alienated brother alienates us from God, no matter how splendid be the liturgy we perform." See also Schweizer, *Matthew*, 119.

81   See also Matthew 18:8-9, 15-20; 2 Thessalonians 3:6-15; and 1 John 5:16-17. For a comprehensive exegetical study, see Goran Forkman, *The Limits of Religious Community: Expulsion from the Religious Community within the Qumran Sect, within Rabbinic Judaism, and within Primitive Christianity*, Coniectanea Biblica New Testament Series 5 (Lund: Gleerup, 1972), 115-17. For some indications of the Christological process that inevitably led to some form of "exclusion" in early Christian communities, see James D. G. Dunn, *Unity and Diversity in the New Testament: An Inquiry into the Character of Earliest Christianity* (London: SCM Press, 1977), especially 262-63, 306-7, 378-79. The early patristic tradition also based its admission to the Eucharist on the faith of the participant. See, for example, *The Didache* IX:5 (K. Lake, ed., *The Apostolic Fathers*, Loeb Classical Library, 2 vols. [Cambridge, MA: Harvard University Press, 1912] 1, 1:323) and Tertullian, *De Praescriptione*, 41 (PL 2:68-69). Catechumens, non-baptized, unbelievers, and heretics are excluded. No mention is made of sinful believers. Matthew 7:6 (not casting pearls before swine) is used in both of these passages.

82   Murphy-O'Connor, *1 Corinthians*, 43. See also Barrett, *The First Epistle to the Corinthians*, 120-30.

83   See Perkins, *First Corinthians*, 89-90; Horsley, *1 Corinthians*, 80-81; Fitzmyer, *First Corinthians*, 236-37.

84   Forkman, *The Limits of Religious Community*, concludes his detailed study of 1 Corinthians 5 (pp. 139-51): "The community has gone over from the sphere of death and flesh, the old context, to the new context of life and the spirit. The consequences ought to be: He who does not want to walk in the new context has by this himself chosen to stay in the old" (p. 149). See also Conzelmann, *1 Corinthians*, 97-99; Barrett, *The First Epistle to the Corinthians*, 127-30; Fitzmyer, *First Corinthians*, 229-30.

85   The harshness of vv. 4-8 has generated a complex history of interpretation. See the survey of Craig R. Koester, *Hebrews*, The Anchor Bible 36 (New York: Doubleday, 2001), 318-21.

86   I say "author," "recipients," and "tract" in deference to my erstwhile teacher, a world authority on Hebrews, Albert Vanhoye. He opened his lectures on Hebrews in 1972 with the words: "The Letter of Saint Paul to the Hebrews is not a letter, or written by Saint Paul, or addressed to the

Hebrews." These questions are expertly presented by Harold W. Attridge, *The Epistle to the Hebrews*, Hermeneia (Philadelphia: Fortress, 1989), 1-13, and Brown, *An Introduction to the New Testament*, 691-701.

87   Forkman, *The Limits of Religious Community*, 176: "It is a question of open, intentional and voluntary apostasy. There is no recommending of measures from the community's side."

88   See the commentaries of Koester, *Hebrews*, 321-23, and Attridge, *The Epistle to the Hebrews*, 167-73. See Attridge's excursus on the impossibility of repentance on pp. 168-69: "What our author has in view is clearly the extreme sin of apostasy" (p. 169).

89   Brooke F. Westcott, *The Epistle to the Hebrews: The Greek Text with Notes and Essays* (London: Macmillan, 1889), 151. See his helpful treatment on pp. 142-53.

90   Forkman, *The Limits of Religious Community*, 217, concludes his comprehensive study of this question by claiming that neither Jesus nor the early Church saw the holiness of the community as the important issue. It was "the individual's standpoint in face of the message about the kingdom of God."

91   Words from Gilbert Keith Chesterton's *Orthodoxy* (New York: Doubleday, 1959), 100, come to mind: "The church announces terrible ideas and devouring doctrines, each one of them strong enough to turn into a false religion and lay waste the world … Thus, if some small mistake is made in doctrine, huge blunders may be made in human happiness." A powerful witness to this can be found in John Feighery, "Street People's Mass," *The Tablet* 243 (1989), 347-48. For some further reflections, see William F. Stolzman, "Communion for Repenting Sinners?" *The Clergy Review* 65 (1980), 322-27.

92   Patrick Considine, "Remarriage and the Eucharist," *Priest and People* 3 (1989), 226-27.

93   Barth, *Rediscovering the Lord's Supper*, 54.

94   See Ratzinger, "Transmission of Divine Revelation," in *Commentary on the Documents of Vatican II*, 3:392-93.

95   On the influence that the *Decree for the Armenians* had on discussions at Trent, see John W. O'Malley, *Trent: What Happened at the Council* (Cambridge, MA: Harvard University Press, 2013), 119.

96   For an overview, see Instone-Brewer, *Divorce and Remarriage*, 238-67. A synthesis of Catholic history can be found in Waldemar Molinski, "Marriage," in *Encyclopedia of Theology*, ed. Karl Rahner, trans. John Griffiths

(London: Burns & Oates, 1975), 905-10. For a concise (although somewhat dated) history of Catholic marriage thought and practice from the beginnings to Trent, see also Edward Schillebeeckx, *Marriage: Secular Reality and Saving Mystery*, trans. N. D. Smith, Stag Books, 2 vols. (London: Sheed & Ward, 1965), 1:3-182. On the Council of Florence, see pp. 166-67. It is generally thought that in signing off on the decisions of the Council of Florence on the seven Sacraments, the Eastern Churches were not aware that they had accepted all the implications for the sacramentality of marriage.

97 See above, pp. 211-12.

98 Martin Hengel, *The Charismatic Leader and His Followers*, trans. James C. G. Greig, Studies of the New Testament and Its World (Edinburgh: T. & T. Clark, 1981). This study rightly points to the importance of Jesus' intense eschatological understanding of his mission, shared by his followers.

99 This statement could lead to a discussion of the need for all the Christian Churches to reflect a "shared wisdom and experience" when they face such difficult questions. This is not the place for such a debate, but the Catholic Church stands alone among the Christian Churches, which also look to the Word of God for their founding and formative Traditions, in the matter of divorce and remarriage. This calls for some self-examination. Commenting on Matthew 19:1-12, Ulrich Luz suggests "that the Catholic divorce law, close as it is to the substance of Matthew's position, does not do justice to the New Testament at an essential point." It does not reflect "Jesus' spirit of unlimited forgiveness" (Luz, *Matthew*, 3:496).

100 The tensions surrounding Vatican II have been graphically documented by Yves Congar, *My Journal of the Council*, trans. Denis Minns, et al. (Adelaide: ATF Theology, 2012).

101 Edsall, "Watching Jesus do Theology," 9-10.

102 This hermeneutic (principle of interpretation) was hesitatingly proposed to the teaching authority of the Church thirty-five years ago by Pierre Benoit, "Christian Marriage According to Saint Paul," *The Clergy Review* 65 (1980), 309-21. See especially pp. 320-21.

103 Fitzmyer, *First Corinthians*, 298. Fitzmyer first made this suggestion in 1976 ("The Matthean Divorce Texts," 224-26). Loader, "Did Adultery Mandate Divorce?" 73 note 31, acknowledges this hermeneutical stance, but rightly points out that his interest is in "historical reconstruction."

104 Dante's text, the translation, and the background information on Manfred, is taken from Prue Shaw, *Reading Dante: From Here to Eternity* (New York/London: Liveright Publishing, 2014), 57-60. The presentation

of the translation to match Dante's verse structure is mine. Shaw interprets Dante's thought thus: "This is a fundamental principle which governs one's destiny in the afterlife" (p. 59). I agree with Dante.

BIBLIOGRAPHY

BIBLICAL COMMENTARIES

Attridge, Harold W. *The Epistle to the Hebrews*. Hermeneia. Philadelphia: Fortress, 1989.

Barrett, C. Kingsley. *The First Epistle to the Corinthians*. Black's New Testament Commentaries. London: A. & C. Black, 1971.

_____. *The Gospel According to St John*. 2nd ed. London: SPCK, 1978.

_____. *The Second Epistle to the Corinthians*. Black's New Testament Commentaries. London: A. & C. Black, 1973.

Bauer, Walter. *Das Johannesevangelium*. 3rd ed. Handbuch zum Neuen Testament 6. Tübingen: J. C. B. Mohr (Paul Siebeck), 1933.

Beare, Frederick W. *The Gospel According to Matthew*. Oxford: Blackwell, 1981.

Bernard, John H. *A Critical and Exegetical Commentary on the Gospel According to St John*. International Critical Commentary. 2 vols. Edinburgh: T. & T. Clark, 1928.

Blomberg, Craig. *Matthew*. The New American Commentary 22. Nashville: Broadman Press, 1992.

Bovon, François. *Luke*. Hermeneia. Translated by Christine M. Thomas, Donald S. Deer, and James Crouch. 3 vols. Minneapolis: Fortress, 2002-2012.

Brown, Raymond E. *The Gospel According to John*. Anchor Bible 29-29A. 2 vols. Garden City, NY: Doubleday, 1966-70.

Bruner, Frederick B. *The Gospel of John: A Commentary*. Grand Rapids: Eerdmans, 2012.

Byrne, Brendan. *A Costly Freedom: A Theological Reading of Mark's Gospel*. Collegeville, MN: The Liturgical Press, 2008.

_____. *Life Abounding: A Reading of John's Gospel*. Collegeville, MN: The Liturgical Press, 2014.

_____. *Lifting the Burden. Reading Matthew's Gospel in the Church Today*. Collegeville, MN: The Liturgical Press, 2004.

_____. *Romans*. Sacra Pagina 6. Collegeville, MN: The Liturgical Press, 1996.

_____. *The Hospitality of God: A Reading of Luke's Gospel*. Collegeville, MN: The Liturgical Press, 2000.

Carroll, John T. *Luke: A Commentary*, The New Testament Library. Louisville: Westminster John Knox, 2012.

Collins, Adela Y. *Mark*. Hermeneia. Minneapolis: Fortress, 2007.

Collins, Raymond F. *First Corinthians*. Sacra Pagina 7. Collegeville, MN: The Liturgical Press, 1999.

Conzelmann, Hans, *1 Corinthians: A Commentary on the First Epistle to the Corinthians*. Hermeneia. Translated by James W. Leitch. Philadelphia: Fortress Press, 1975.

Culpepper, R. Alan. *Mark*. Smith & Helwys Bible Commentary. Macon, GA: Smith & Helwys, 2007.

Davies, William D., and Dale C. Allison Jr. *A Critical and Exegetical Commentary on the Gospel of Matthew*. International Critical Commentary. 3 vols. Edinburgh: T. & T. Clark, 1988-1997.

Ellis, E. Earle. *The Gospel of Luke*. New Century Bible. London: Oliphants, 1974.

Ellis, Peter. *The Genius of John: A Composition-Critical Commentary on the Fourth Gospel*. Collegeville, MN: The Liturgical Press, 1984.

Evans, Christopher F. *Saint Luke*. New Testament Commentaries. London: SCM Press, 1990.

Evans, Craig A. *Mark 8:27-16:20*. Word Biblical Commentary 34B. Nashville: Thomas Nelson, 2001

Fenton, John. *Saint Matthew*. The Pelican New Testament Commentaries. Harmondsworth: Penguin Books, 1963.

Fitzmyer, Joseph A., *First Corinthians*. The Anchor Yale Bible 32. New Haven: Yale University Press, 2008.

_____. *The Gospel According to Luke*. The Anchor Bible 28-28a. 2 vols. New York: Doubleday, 1981-1985.

France, Richard T. *The Gospel of Matthew*. The New International Commentary on the New Testament. Grand Rapids: Eerdmans, 2007.

Garland, David E. *Reading Matthew: A Literary and Theological Commentary.* Macon, GA: Smyth & Helwys, 2001.

Gundry, Robert H. *Matthew: A Commentary on His Literary and Theological Art.* Grand Rapids: Eerdmans, 1982.

Hagner, Donald. *Matthew.* Work Biblical Commentary 33-33A. 2 vols. Dallas: Word, 1993-1995.

Hill, David. *The Gospel of Matthew.* New Century Bible. London: Oliphants, 1972.

Horsley, Richard A. *1 Corinthians.* Abingdon New Testament Commentaries. Nashville: Abingdon Press, 1998.

Hoskyns, Edwyn C. *The Fourth Gospel.* Edited by Francis N. Davey. London: Faber & Faber, 1947.

Johnson, Luke T. *The Gospel of Luke.* Sacra Pagina 3. Collegeville: The Liturgical Press, 1991.

Keener, Craig S. *A Commentary on the Gospel of Matthew.* Grand Rapids: Eerdmans, 1999.

_____. *The Gospel of John: A Commentary.* 2 vols. Peabody, MA: Hendrickson, 2003.

Koester, Craig R. *Hebrews.* The Anchor Bible 36. New York: Doubleday, 2001.

Kysar, Robert. *John.* Augsburg Commentary on the New Testament. Minneapolis: Augsburg, 1986.

Lagrange, Michel-Joseph. *Évangile selon Jean.* Etudes Bibliques. Paris: Gabalda, 1927.

Lane, William L. *Commentary on the Gospel of Mark.* The New International Commentary on the New Testament. Grand Rapids: Eerdmans, 1974.

Léon-Dufour, Xavier. *Lecture de l'Évangile selon Jean.* 4 vols. Paris: Seuil, 1988-1996.

Lincoln, Andrew T. *The Gospel According to Saint John.* Black's New Testament Commentaries. London/New York: Continuum, 2005.

Lindars, Barnabas. *The Gospel of John.* New Century Bible. London: Oliphants, 1972.

Luz, Ulrich. *Matthew.* Translated by James E. Crowe. Hermeneia. 3 vols. Minneapolis: Fortress, 2001-2007.

Macgregor, George H. C. *The Gospel of John*. Moffatt New Testament Commentary. London: Hodder & Stoughton, 1928.

Marcus, Joel. *Mark*. The Anchor Yale Bible 27-27A. 2 vols. New York/New Haven: Doubleday/Yale University Press, 2000-2009.

Marshall, I. Howard. *The Gospel of Luke: A Commentary on the Greek Text*. The New International Greek Testament Commentary. Grand Rapids: Eerdmans, 1978.

Matera, Frank J. *Romans*. Paideia Commentaries on the New Testament. Grand Rapids: Baker Academic, 2010.

Meier, John P. *Matthew*. New Testament Message 3. Wilmington, DE: Michael Glazier, 1980.

Moloney, Francis J. *Glory not Dishonor: Reading John 13-21*. Minneapolis: Fortress, 1998.

_____. *Signs and Shadows: Reading John 5-12*. Minneapolis: Fortress, 1996.

_____. *The Gospel of John*, Sacra Pagina 4. Collegeville, MI: The Liturgical Press, 1998.

_____. *The Gospel of Mark: A Commentary*. Grand Rapids: Baker Academic, 2012.

Murphy-O'Connor, Jerome. *1 Corinthians*. New Testament Message 10. Wilmington, DE: Michael Glazier, 1979.

Nolland, John. *The Gospel of Matthew*. The New International Greek Testament Commentary. Grand Rapids: Eerdmans, 2005.

Orr, William F., and James A. Walther. *1 Corinthians*. The Anchor Bible 32. Garden City, NY: Doubleday, 1976.

Patte, Daniel. *The Gospel According to Matthew: A Structural Commentary on Matthew's Faith*. Philadelphia: Fortress, 1987.

Perkins, Pheme. *First Corinthians*. Paideia Commentaries on the New Testament. Grand Rapids: Baker Academic, 2012.

Pesch, Rudolf. *Das Markusevangelium*. Herders theologischer Kommentar zum Neuen Testament II/1-2. 2 vols. Herder: Freiburg, 1977.

Radermakers, Jean. *Au fil de l'évangile selon saint Matthieu*. 2 vols. Bruxelles: Institut d'Etudes Théologiques, 1974.

Schnackenburg, Rudolf. *The Gospel According to St John*. Translated by Kevin Smith, Cecily Hastings, et al. Herder's Theological Commentary on the New Testament IV/1-3. London/New York: Burns & Oates/Crossroad, 1962-82.

Schnelle, Udo. *Das Evangelium nach Johannes*. Theologischer Handkommentar zum Neuen Testament 4. Leipzig: Evangelische Verlagsanstalt, 1998.

Schürmann, Heinz. *Das Lukasevangelium*. Herders theologischer Kommentar zum Neuen Testament. Freiburg: Herder, 1969.

Schweizer, Eduard. *The Good News According to Luke*. Translated by David E. Green. London: SPCK, 1984.

_____. *The Good News According to Matthew*. Translated by David E. Green. London: SPCK, 1976.

Senior, Donald. *Matthew*. Abingdon New Testament Commentaries. Nashville: Abinbgdon Press, 1998.

Talbert, Charles H. *Matthew*. Paideia Commentaries on the New Testament. Grand Rapids: Baker Academic, 2010.

_____. *Reading Luke: A Literary and Theological Commentary on the Third Gospel*. New York: Crossroad, 1982.

Tannehill, Robert C. *Luke*. Abingdon New Testament Commentaries. Nashville: Abingdon Press, 1996.

_____. *The Narrative Unity of Luke–Acts: A Literary Interpretation*. 2 vols. Foundation and Facets. Philadelphia: Fortress Press, 1986.

Taylor, Vincent. *The Gospel According to St. Mark*. London: Macmillan, 1966.

Westcott, Brooke F. *The Epistle to the Hebrews: The Greek Text with Notes and Essays*. London: Macmillan, 1889.

_____. *The Gospel According to John*. London: John Murray, 1908.

Zumstein, Jean. *L'Évangile selon Jean*. Commentaire du Nouveasu Testament IVa-b. 2 vols. Geneva: Labor et Fides, 2007-2013.

OTHER STUDIES CITED

Abrams, Meyer H. *A Glossary of Literary Terms*. 5th ed. New York: Holt, Reinhart and Winstone, 1985.

Aletti, Jean-Noël. *L'art de raconter Jésus Christ*. Paris: Seuil, 1989.

Alexander, Loveday. *The Preface to Luke's Gospel: Literary Convention and Social Context in Luke 1.1-4 and Acts 1.1.* SNTS Monograph Series 78. Cambridge: Cambridge University Press, 1993.

Allison, Dale C. Jr. *Constructing Jesus: Memory, Imagination, and History.* Grand Rapids: Baker Academic, 2010.

_____. "Divorce, Celibacy and Joseph (Matthew 1.18-25 and 19.1-12)." *Journal for the Study of the New Testament* 49 (1993): 3-10.

Anderson, Paul N. "The Community that Raymond Brown Left Behind: Reflections on the Johannine Dialectical Situation." Pages 47-93 in *Communities in Dispute: Current Scholarship on the Johannine Epistles.* Edited by R. Alan Culpepper and Paul N. Anderson. Early Christianity and Its Literature 13. Atlanta: SBL Press, 2014.

Ashton, John. *Understanding the Fourth Gospel.* Oxford: Clarendon Press, 1991.

Banks, Robert. *Paul's Idea of Community: The Early House Churches in Their Historical Setting.* Exeter: Paternoster Press, 1979.

Barr, James. *Fundamentalism.* London: SCM Press, 1977.

_____. *The Scope and Authority of the Bible.* Explorations in Theology 7. London: SCM Press, 1980.

Barth, Markus. *Rediscovering the Lord's Supper: Communion with Israel, with Christ, and Among the Guests.* Atlanta: John Knox Press, 1988.

Benoit, Pierre. "Christian Marriage according to Saint Paul." *The Clergy Review* 65 (1980): 309-21.

_____. "The Accounts of the Institution and What They Imply." Pages 71-101 in *The Eucharist in the New Testament: A Symposium.* Edited by Jean Delorme, et al. Translated by E. M. Stewart. London: Geoffrey Chapman, 1964.

Betz, Hans Dieter. "Apostle." Volume 1, pages 309-11 in *The Anchor Bible Dictionary.* Edited By David N. Freedman. 6 vols. New York: Doubleday, 1992.

Beutler, Johannes. "Psalm 82/83 im Johannesevangelium." *New Testament Studies* 25 (1978-79): 34-37.

Bienert, David C. *Abendmahl im johanneischen Kreis: Eine exegetische-hermeneutische Studie zur Mahltheologie des Johannesevangeliums.*

Beihefte zur Zeitschrift für die neutestamentliche Wissenshaft 202. Berlin: de Gruyter, 2014.

Black, C. Clifton. *The Disciples According to Mark: Markan Redaction in Current Debate*. Journal for the Study of the New Testament Supplement Series 27. 2nd ed. Grand Rapids: Eerdmans, 2012.

Blinzler, Josef. "*Eisin eunouchoi*. Zur Auslegung von Mt 19,12." *Zeitschrift für die Neutestamentliche Wissenschaft* 48 (1957): 254-70.

Bockmuel, Markus. *Simon Peter in Scripture and Memory*. Grand Rapids: Baker Academic, 2012.

Boomershine, Thomas E. "Mark 16:8 and the Apostolic Commission." *Journal of Biblical Literature* 100 (1981): 225-39.

Boomershine, Thomas E., and Gilbert L. Bartholomew. "The Narrative Technique of Mark 16:8." *Journal of Biblical Literature* 100 (1981): 213-23.

Borgen, Peder. *Bread from Heaven: An Exegetical Study of the Concept of the Manna in the Gospel of John and the Writings of Philo*. Supplements to Novum Testamentum 10. Leiden: E. J. Brill, 1965.

Bornkamm, Günther. *Jesus of Nazareth*. London: Hodder & Stoughton, 1963.

_____. "Lord's Supper and Church in Paul." Pages 123-60 in *Early Christian Experience*. London: SCM Press, 1969.

Bovon, François. *Luke the Theologian*. Translated by Ken McKinney. 2nd ed. Waco, TX: Baylor University Press, 2006.

Bradshaw, Paul F. *The Search for the Origin of Christian Worship*. Oxford/New York: Oxford University Press, 2002.

Brown, Raymond E. *An Introduction to the Gospel of John*. Edited by Francis J. Moloney. The Anchor Bible Reference Library. New York: Doubleday, 2010.

_____. *An Introduction to the New Testament*. The Anchor Bible Reference Library. New York: Doubleday, 1997.

_____. "Critical Biblical Exegesis and the Development of Doctrine." Pages 26-53 in *Biblical Exegesis and Church Doctrine*. New York: Paulist Press, 1985.

_____. *The Community of the Beloved Disciple: The Life, Loves and*

Hates of an Individual Church in New Testament Times. London: Geoffrey Chapman, 1979.

_____. *The Death of the Messiah: A Commentary on the Passion Narratives in the Four Gospels*. Anchor Bible Reference Library. 2 vols. New York: Doubleday, 1993.

_____. "The Eucharist and Baptism in John." Pages 77-95 in *New Testament Essays*. London: Geoffrey Chapman, 1967.

_____. "The Johannine Sacramentary." Pages 51-76 in *New Testament Essays*. London: Geoffrey Chapman, 1967.

_____. *The Virginal Conception and the Bodily Resurrection of Jesus*. London: Geoffrey Chapman, 1973.

Brown, Raymond E., and John P. Meier. *Antioch and Rome: New Testament Cradles of Catholic Christianity*. New York: Paulist Press, 1983.

Brown, Raymond E., Karl P. Donfried, and John Reumann, eds. *Peter in the New Testament: A Collaborative Assessment by Protestant and Roman Catholic Scholars*. Minneapolis/New York: Augsburg/Paulist, 1973.

Bultmann, Rudolf. *History of the Synoptic Tradition*. Translated by John Marsh. Oxford: Blackwell, 1968.

Burridge, Richard A. *Imitating Jesus. An Inclusive Approach to New Testament Ethics*. Grand Rapids: Eerdmans, 2007.

Byrne, Brendan J. "Christ's Pre-Existence in Pauline Soteriology." *Theological Studies* 58 (1997): 308-30.

_____. "Forceful Stewardship and Neglectful Wealth: A Contemporary Reading of Luke 16." *Pacifica* 1 (1988): 1-14.

_____. "Paul and Mark Before the Cross: Common Echoes of the Day of Atonement Ritual." Pages 217-29 in *Transcending Boundaries: Contemporary Readings of the New Testament: Studies in Honor of Francis J. Moloney*. Edited by Rekha M. Chennattu and Mary L. Coloe. Biblioteca di Scienze Religiose. Rome: LAS, 2005.

_____. *Paul and the Christian Woman*. Homebush. St Paul Publications, 1988.

_____. *Reckoning with Romans: A Contemporary Reading of Paul's Gospel*. Good News Studies 18. Wilmington, DE: Michael Glazier, 1986.

Canon Law Society of America. *Code of Canon Law: Latin-English Edition.* Washington, DC: Canon Law Society of America, 1983.

Cadbury, Henry J. *The Making of Luke–Acts.* London: SPCK, 1927.

Carnazzo, Sebastian A. *Seeing Blood and Water: A Narrative-Critical Study of John 19:34.* Eugene, OR: Pickwick Publications, 2012.

Charlesworth, James H. *The Beloved Disciple: Whose Witness Validates the Gospel of John?* Valley Forge, PN: Trinity Press International, 1995.

_____. *The Old Testament Pseudepigrapha.* 2 vols. London: Darton, Longman & Todd, 1983.

Chenderlin, Fritz. *"Do This as My Memorial."* Analecta Biblica 99. Rome: Biblical Institute Press, 1982.

Chesterton, Gilbert K. *Orthodoxy.* New York: Doubleday, 1959.

Coleridge, Mark. *The Birth of the Lukan Narrative: Narrative as Christology in Luke 1-2.* Journal for the Study of the New Testament Supplement Series 88. Sheffield: JSOT Press, 1993.

Collins, Raymond F. *Divorce in the New Testament.* Good News Studies 38. Collegeville, MN: The Liturgical Press, 1992.

Congar, Yves. *My Journal of the Council.* Translated by Denis Minns, et al. Adelaide: ATF Theology, 2012.

_____. *Tradition and Traditions. A Historical Essay and a Theological Essay.* London: Burns & Oates, 1966.

Considine, Patrick. "Remarriage and the Eucharist." *Priests and People* 3 (1989): 226-29.

Cross, Frank L., and Elizabeth A. Livingstone, eds., *The Oxford Dictionary of the Christian Church.* 2nd ed. Oxford: Oxford University Press, 1974.

Crossan, John D. *The Historical Jesus: The Life of a Mediterranean Jewish Peasant.* Edinburgh: T. & T. Clark, 1991.

Cullmann, Oscar. *Early Christian Worship.* Studies in Biblical Theology 10. London: SCM Press, 1953.

Culpepper, R. Alan. "Setting the Stage: Context for the Conversation." Pages 3-15 in *Communities in Dispute: Current Scholarship on the Johannine Epistles.* Edited by R. Alan Culpepper and Paul N. Anderson. Early Christianity and Its Literature 13. Atlanta: SBL Press, 2014.

_____. "The Johannine *hypodeigma*: A Reading of John 13:1-38." *Semeia* 53 (1991): 133-52.

_____. "The Relationship Between the Gospel and 1 John." Pages 95-118 in *Communities in Dispute: Current Scholarship on the Johannine Epistles*. Edited by R. Alan Culpepper and Paul N. Anderson. Early Christianity and Its Literature 13. Atlanta: SBL Press, 2014.

Dahl, Nils A. "Anamnesis. Memory and Commemoration in Early Christianity." Pages 11-29 in *Jesus in the Memory of the Early Church*. Minneapolis: Augsburg, 1976.

Davies, William D. *The Setting of the Sermon on the Mount*. Cambridge: Cambridge University Press, 1966.

Davis, Henry. *Moral and Pastoral Theology*. Heythrop Series 11, 4 vols. London: Sheed and Ward, 1959.

Davis, Leo. *The First Seven Ecumenical Councils (325-787): Their History and Theology*. Collegeville, MN: The Liturgical Press, 1983.

de Aldama, I. A., F. A. P. Solá Severino Gonzales, and J. F. Sagüés. *Sacrae Theologiae Summa*. Biblioteca de Auctores Christianos II/73. Madrid: La Editorial Catolica, 1953.

de la Potterie, Ignace. "Principles for the Christian Interpretation of Sacred Scripture." Pages 182-90 in *The Hour of Jesus: The Passion and Resurrection of Jesus According to John: Text and Spirit*. Slough: St Paul Publications, 1989.

Delebecque, Édouard. *Évangile de Jean: Text traduit et annoté*. Cahiers de la Revue Biblique 23. Paris: Gabalda, 1987.

Deming, Will. *Paul on Marriage and Celibacy: The Hellenistic Background of 1 Corinthians 7*. Grand Rapids: Eerdmans, 2004.

Dequeker, Luc, and Willem Zuidema. "The Eucharist and St Paul: 1 Cor. 11.17-34." *Concilium* 4 (1968): 26-31.

Dettweiler, Andreas. *Die Gegenwart des Erhöhten: Eine exegetische Studie zu den johanneischen Abschiedsreden (Joh 13:31-16:33) unter besonderer Berücksichtigung ihres Relecture-Characters*. Forschungen zur Religion und Literatur des Alten und Neuen Testaments. Göttingen: Vandenhoech & Ruprecht, 1995.

Dewey, Joanna. "The Survival of Mark's Gospel: A Good Story?" *Journal of Biblical Literature* 123 (2004): 495-507.

Diederich, Everrett A. "Reflections on Post-Conciliar Shifts in Eucharistic Faith and Practice." *Communio: International Catholic Review* 12 (1985): 223-37.

Dillon, Richard J. *From Eye-Witnesses to Ministers of the Word: Tradition and Composition in Luke 24.* Analecta Biblica 82. Rome: Biblical Institute Press, 1978.

Do, Toan. *Rethinking the Death of Jesus: An Exegetical and Theological Study of* Hilasmos *and* Agapē *in 1 John 2:1-2 and 4:7-10.* Contributions to Biblical Exegesis and Theology 73. Leuven: Peeters, 2014.

Dodd, Charles H. *Historical Tradition in the Fourth Gospel.* Cambridge: Cambridge University Press, 1965.

_____. "The Appearances of the Risen Christ: An Essay in Form-Criticism of the Gospels." Pages 102-133 of *More New Testament Studies.* Manchester: Manchester University Press, 1968.

_____. *The Founder of Christianity.* London: Collins, 1971.

_____. *The Interpretation of the Fourth Gospel.* Cambridge: Cambridge University Press, 1953.

Donahue, John R. *Are You the Christ? The Trial Narrative in the Gospel of Mark.* SBL Dissertation Series 10. Missoula: Scholars Press, 1973.

_____. *The Gospel in Parable.* Philadelphia: Fortress Press, 1988.

Donaldson, Terrence L. *Jesus on the Mountain: A Study in Matthean Theology.* Journal for the Study of the New Testament Supplement Series 8. Sheffield: JSOT Press, 1985.

Doyle, B. Rod. "Matthew's Intention Discerned by his Structure." *Revue Biblique* 95 (1988): 34-54.

Dumm, Demetrius R. "Luke 24:44-49 and Hospitality." Pages 230-39 in *Sin, Salvation and the Spirit: Commemorating the Fiftieth Year of the Liturgical Press.* Edited by Daniel Durken. Collegeville, MN: The Liturgical Press, 1979.

Dunn, James D. G. *Unity and Diversity in the New Testament: An Inquiry into the Character of Earliest Christianity.* London: SCM Press, 1977.

Duplacy, Jacques. "A propos d'un lieu variant de 1 Cor 11,24: 'Voici mon corps (-, rompu, donné etc.) pour vous." Pages 27-46 in *Le Corps et le corps du Christ dans la Première Epître aux Corinthiens.* Congress de l'ACFEB, Tarbes, 1981. Lectio Divina 114. Paris: Cerf, 1983.

Dupont, Jacques. "The Meal at Emmaus." Pages 105-21 in *The Eucharist in the New Testament*. Edited by Jean Delorme. London: Geoffrey Chapman, 1985.

Dunn, James D. G. *The Theology of Paul the Apostle*. Grand Rapids: Eerdmans, 1998.

Edsall, Benjamin A. *Paul's Witness to Formative Early Christian Instruction*. WUNT 2.365. Tübingen: Mohr Siebeck, 2014.

_____. "Watching Jesus do Theology: Debating the Sadducees over Resurrection." Unpublished paper delivered to the Seattle School of Theology and Psychology. June 2, 2014.

"Einspruch und Bekräftigung. Schreiben der Glaubenskongregation und Brief der Bischöfe von Freiburg, Mainz und Rottenburg-Stuttgart zu wiederverheiraten Geschiedenen." *Herder-Korrespondenz* 48 (1994): 565-71.

Eriksson, Anders. *Tradition as Rhetorical Proof: Pauline Argumentation in 1 Corinthians*. Coniectana Biblica New Testament Series 29. Stockholm: Almqvist & Wiksell International, 1998.

Esler, Philip. *Community and Gospel in Luke–Acts: The Social and Political Motivations of Lucan Theology*. SNTS Monograph Series 57. Cambridge: Cambridge University Press, 1987.

Feighery, John. "Street People's Mass." *The Tablet* 243 (1989): 392-93.

Fitzmyer, Joseph A. "Marriage and Divorce." Volume 1, pages 511-15 in *Encyclopedia of the Dead Sea Scrolls*. Edited by Lawrence H. Schiffman and James C. VanderKam. 2 vols. Oxford/New York: Oxford University Press, 2000.

_____. "The Matthean Divorce Texts and Some New Palestinian Evidence." *Theological Studies* 39 (1976): 197-226.

Flannery, Austin, ed. *Vatican Council II: Constitutions, Decrees, Declarations: A Completely Revised Translation in Inclusive Language*. Northport, NY: Costelloe, 1995.

Fleddermann, Harry. "The Flight of a Naked Young Man (Mark 14:51-52)." *The Catholic Biblical Quarterly* 41 (1979): 412-18.

Forkman, Goran, *The Limits of Religious Community: Expulsion from the Religious Community within the Qumran Sect, within Rabbinic Judaism, and within Primitive Christianity*. Coniectanea Biblica New Testament Series 5. Lund: Gleerup, 1972.

Fotopoulos, John. *Food Offered to Idols in Roman Corinth: A Social Rhetorical Reconsideration of 1 Corinthians 8:1-11:1*. WUNT 2.151. Tübingen: Mohr Siebeck, 2003.

Fowler, Robert M. *Let the Reader Understand: Reader-Response Criticism and the Gospel of Mark*. Minneapolis: Fortress, 1991.

_____. *Loaves and Fishes: The Function of the Feeding Stories in the Gospel of Mark*. SBL Dissertation Series 54. Chico: Scholars Press, 1981.

Francis, Pope. *Evangelii Gaudium*. Città del Vaticano: Libreria Editrice Vaticana, 2013.

Frend, William H. C. *The Rise of Christianity*. London: Darton, Longman & Todd, 1984.

Gaventa, Beverly. "'You Proclaim the Lord's Death': 1 Corinthians 11:26 and Paul's Understanding of Worship." *Review and Expositor* 80 (1983): 377-87.

George, Augustin. *Études sur l'Oeuvres de Luc*. Sources Bibliques. Paris: Gabalda, 1978.

Gignac, Francis T. "The Use of Verbal Variety in the Fourth Gospel." Pages 191-200 in *Transcending Boundaries: Contemporary Readings of the New Testament: Essays in Honor of Francis J. Moloney*. Edited by Rekha M. Chennattu and Mary L. Coloe. Biblioteca di Scienze Religiose 187. Rome: LAS, 2005.

Goodfriend, Elaine A. "Adultery." Volume 1, pages 82-86 in *The Anchor Bible Dictionary*. Edited by David N. Freedman. 6 vols. New York: Doubleday, 1992.

Grabowski, John S. "Divorce, Remarriage and Reception of the Sacraments." *America* (October 8, 1994): 20-24.

Gray, Timothy C. *The Temple in the Gospel of Mark: A Study in Its Narrative Role*. Grand Rapids: Baker Academic, 2010.

Gregg, Robert C., ed. *Athanasius: The Life of Antony and the Letter to Marcellinus*. The Classics of Western Spirituality. London: SPCK, 1980.

Hamilton, Neil Q. "Resurrection, Tradition and the Composition of Mark." *Journal of Biblical Literature* 84 (1965): 415-21.

Hanges, James C. Paul, *Founder of Churches: A Study in Light of Evidence for the Role of "Founder Figures" in the Hellenistic-Roman Period.* WUNT 292. Tübingen: Mohr Siebeck, 2012.

Harner, Philip B. *The "I Am" of the Fourth Gospel: A Study in Usage and Thought.* Facet Books Biblical Series 26. Philadelphia: Fortress, 1970.

Harvey, William J. *Character and the Novel.* London: Chatto & Windus, 1965.

Havener, Ivan. *Q: The Sayings of Jesus.* Good News Studies 19. Wilmington, DE: Michael Glazier, 1987.

Heilmann, Jan. *Wein und Blut: Das Ende der Eucharistie im Johannesevangelium und dessen Konsequenzen.* Beiträge zur Wissenschaft vom Alten und Neuen Testament 204. Stuttgart: Kohlhammer, 2014.

Hengel, Martin. *Die Johanneische Frage: Ein Lösungsversuch mit einem Beitrag zur Apokalypse von Jörg Frey.* WUNT 67. Tübiingen: J. C. B. Mohr (Paul Siebeck), 1993.

——————. *Saint Peter: The Underestimated Apostle.* Translated by Thomas H. Trapp. Grand Rapids: Eerdmans, 2010.

——————. *The Charismatic Leader and His Followers.* Translated by James C. G. Greig. Studies of the New Testament and Its World. Edinburgh: T. & T. Clark, 1981.

——————. "The Titles of the Gospels and the Gospel of Mark." Pages 64-84 in *Studies in the Gospel of Mark.* Philadelphia: Fortress, 1985.

Henrici, Peter. "'Do this in remembrance of me': The Sacrifice of Christ and the Sacrifice of the Faithful." *Communio: International Catholic Review* 12 (1985): 146-57.

Howard, William F., and C. Kingsley Barrett. *The Fourth Gospel in Recent Criticism.* London: Epworth Press, 1955.

Huels, John M. *One Table, Many Laws: Essays on Catholic Eucharistic Practice.* Collegeville, MN: The Liturgical Press, 1986.

Hurtardo, Larry W. "Oral Fixation and New Testament Studies? 'Orality,' 'Performance,' and Reading Texts in Early Christianity." *New Testament Studies* 60 (2014): 321-40.

Instone-Brewer, David. *Divorce and Remarriage in the Bible.* Grand Rapids: Eerdmans, 2002.

Iser, Wolfgang. *The Implied Reader: Patterns of Communication in Prose Fiction from Bunyan to Beckett*. Baltimore: Johns Hopkins University Press, 1978.

Iverson, Kelly R. "Performance Criticism." Volume 2, pages 92-105 in *The Oxford Encyclopedia of Biblical Interpretation*. Edited by Steven McKenzie. Oxford/New York: Oxford University Press, 2013.

Jeffrey, David L., and I. Howard Marshall. "Emmaus." Pages 236-37 in *A Dictionary of Biblical Tradition in English Literature*. Grand Rapids: Eerdmans, 1992.

Jeremias, Joachim. *Jesus' Promise to the Nations*. Translated by Samuel H. Hooke. Studies in Biblical Theology 24. London: SCM Press, 1964.

—————. *The Eucharistic Words of Jesus*. London: SCM Press, 1966.

John Paul II, Pope. *Apostolic Exhortation* Familiaris Consortio (Città del Vaticano: Editrice Vaticana, 1981).

Johnson, Luke T. *Prophetic Jesus, Prophetic Church: The Challenge of Luke–Acts to Contemporary Christians*. Grand Rapids: Eerdmans, 2011.

Juel, Donald D. *Messiah and Temple: The Trial of Jesus in the Gospel of Mark*. SBL Dissertation Series 31. Missoula: Scholars Press, 1977.

Jungmann, Josef. *The Mass of the Roman Rite: Its Origin and Development*. Translated by Francis A. Brunner. Christian Classics. New York: Thomas More Publishing, 1986.

Käsemann, Ernst. "The Pauline Doctrine of the Lord's Supper." Pages 108-35 in *Essays on New Testament Themes*. Studies in Biblical Theology 41. London: SCM Press, 1964.

—————. "Thoughts on the Present Controversy about Scriptural Interpretation." Pages 268-85 in *New Testament Questions of Today*. London: SCM Press, 1969.

Kasper, Walter. *Mercy: The Essence of the Gospel and the Key to Christian Life*. Translated by William Madges. New York/Mahwah, NJ: Paulist Press, 2014.

Karris, Robert J. "God's Boundary-Breaking Mercy." *The Bible Today* 24 (1986): 24-29.

—————. *Luke: Artist and Theologian: Luke's Passion Account as Literature*. New York: Paulist Press, 1985.

Kee, Howard C. *Community of the New Age: Studies in Mark's Gospel*. London: SCM Press, 1977.

Kelly, John N. D. *Early Christian Creeds*. 3rd ed. London: Routledge, 1982.

Kingsbury, Jack D. *Matthew as Story*. Philadelphia: Fortress Press, 1986.

_____. *The Christology of Mark's Gospel*. Philadelphia: Fortress, 1983.

Kloppenborg, John S. *Q, the Earliest Gospel: An Introduction to the Original Stories and Sayings of Jesus*. Louisville, KY: Westminster John Knox, 2008.

Kodell, Jerome. *The Eucharist in the New Testament*. Zacchaeus Studies: New Testament. Wilmington: Michael Glazier, 1989.

Kosmala, Hans. "Das tut zu meinem Gedächtnis." *Novum Testamentum* 4 (1960): 81-94.

Kugler, Robert A. "Testaments." Volume 2, pages 933-36 in *Encyclopedia of the Dead Sea Scrolls*. Edited by Lawrence Shiffman and James C. VanderKam. 2 vols. Oxford/New York: Oxford University Press, 2000.

_____. "Twelve Patriarchs, Testaments of the." Volume 2, pages 952-53 in *Encyclopedia of the Dead Sea Scrolls*. Edited by Lawrence Shiffman and James C. VanderKam. 2 vols. Oxford/New York: Oxford University Press, 2000.

Kümmel, Werner. *Introduction to the New Testament*. London: SCM Press, 1975.

Kurz, William S. "Luke 22:14-38 and Greco-Roman and Biblical Farewell Addresses." *Journal of Biblical Literature* 104 (1985): 251-68.

Kysar, Robert. *The Fourth Evangelist and His Gospel: An Examination of Contemporary Scholarship*. Minneapolis: Augsburg, 1975.

Labahn, Michael. *Offenbarung im Zeichen und Werke*. WUNT 2.117. Tübingen: Mohr Siebeck, 2000.

Labahn, Michael, and Manfred Lang. "Johannes und die Synoptiker. Positionen und Impulse seit 1990." Pages 443-514 in *Kontexte des Johannesevangeliums: Das vierte Evangelium in religions- und traditionsgeschichtlicher Perspektive*. Edited by Jörg Frey and Udo Schnelle. WUNT 175. Tübingen: Mohr Siebeck, 2004.

Lake, Kirsopp, ed. *The Apostolic Fathers*. Loeb Classical Library. 2 vols. Cambridge, MA: Harvard University Press, 1912.

Laurance, John D. "The Eucharist as the Imitation of Christ." *Theological Studies* 47 (1986): 286-96.

Laverdiere, Eugene, and William G. Thompson. "New Testament Communities in Transition." *Theological Studies* 37 (1976): 567-97.

Léon-Dufour, Xavier. "Les miracles de Jésus selon Jean." Pages 269-86 in *Les Miracles de Jésus selon le Nouveau Testament*. Edited by Xavier Léon-Dufour. Paris: Seuil, 1977.

_____. "Présence du Seigneur Ressuscité (Mt 28:16-20)." Pages 195-209 in *A Cause de l'Évangile: Études sur les Synoptiques et les Actes offertes: au Père Jacques Dupont, O.S.B. à l'occasion de son 70e anniversaire.* Lectio Divina 123. Paris: Editions du Cerf, 1985.

_____. *Sharing the Eucharistic Bread: The Witness of the New Testament.* Translated by Matthew J. O'Connell. New York: Paulist Press, 1987.

_____. "Towards a Symbolic Reading of the Fourth Gospel." *New Testament Studies* 27 (1980-81): 439-56.

Lightfoot, Robert H. *History and Interpretation in the Gospels.* London: Hodder & Stoughton, 1935.

Loader, William R. G. "Did Adultery Mandate Divorce? A Reassessment of Jesus' Divorce Logia." *New Testament Studies* 61 (2015): 67-78.

_____. *Jesus' Attitude to the Law: A Study of the Gospels.* Grand Rapids: Eerdmans, 2002.

_____. *The Dead Sea Scrolls on Sexuality: Attitudes Towards Sexuality in Sectarian and Related Literature at Qumran.* Grand Rapids: Eerdmans, 2009.

_____. *The New Testament on Sexuality.* Grand Rapids: Eerdmans, 2012.

Lohfink, Gerhard. *Jesus and Community: The Social Dimension of Christian Faith.* New York/Philadelphia: Paulist Press/Fortress, 1984.

_____. *Jesus of Nazareth: What He Wanted, Who He Was.* Translated by Linda M. Maloney. Collegeville, MN: The Liturgical Press, 2012.

_____. *No Irrelevant Jesus: On Jesus and Christians Today.* Translated by Linda M. Maloney. Collegeville, MN: The Liturgical Press, 2014.

Lohse, Eduard. "Miracles in the Fourth Gospel." Pages 64-75 in *What About the New Testament?* Edited by Morna Hooker and Colin Hickling. London: SCM Press, 1975.

Luz, Ulrich. "The Disciples in the Gospel according to Matthew." Pages 98-128 in *The Interpretation of Matthew*. Edited by Graham Stanton. Issues in Religion and Theology. London: SPCK, 1983.

Mackey, John. *Jesus the Man and the Myth*. London: SCM Press, 1979.

Maddox, Robert. *The Purpose of Luke–Acts*. Studies in the New Testament and Its World. Edinburgh: T. & T. Clark, 1982.

Magness, J. Lee. *Sense and Absence: Structure and Suspension in the Ending of Mark's Gospel*. Semeia Studies. Atlanta: Scholars Press, 1986.

Malatesta, Edward. "Blood and Water from the Pierced Side of Christ." Pages 164-81 in *Segni e Sacramenti nel Vangelo di Giovanni*. Edited by Pius-Ramon Tragan. Studia Anselmiana 66. Rome: Editrice Anselmiana, 1977.

Malbon, Elizabeth S. "Characters in Mark's Story: Changing Perspectives on the Narrative Process." Pages 45-69 in *Mark as Story: Retrospect and Prospect*. Edited by Kelly R. Iverson and Christopher W. Skinner. Resources for Biblical Studies 65. Atlanta: SBL, 2011.

_____. *In the Company of Jesus: Characters in Mark's Gospel*. Louisville: Westminster John Knox, 2000.

Manson, Thomas W. *The Sayings of Jesus*. London: SCM Press, 1971.

Manzoni, Alessandro. *I Promessi Sposi: Storia Milanese del Secolo XVII*. Edited by Fausto Ghisalberti. Milano: Hoepli, 1973.

Marcus, Joel. "Mark—Interpreter of Paul." *New Testament Studies* 46 (2000): 473-87.

Martelet, Gustave. *The Risen Christ and the Eucharistic World*. London: Collins, 1976.

Massyngbaerde Ford, Josephine. *Bonded with the Immortal: A Pastoral Introduction to the New Testament*. Wilmington, DE: Michael Glazier, 1987.

Masuda, Sanae. "The Good News of the Miracle of the Bread: The Tradition and Its Markan Redaction." *New Testament Studies* 28 (1982): 191-219.

Matera, Frank J. *God's Saving Grace: A Pauline Theology*. Grand Rapids: Eerdmans, 2012.

_____. "The Plot of Matthew's Gospel." *The Catholic Biblical Quarterly* 49 (1987): 233-53.

McGowan, Andrew B. *Ancient Christian Worship: Early Church Practices in*

Social, Historical, and Theological Perspective. Grand Rapids: Baker Academic, 2014.

Meier, John P. A Marginal Jew: Rethinking the Historical Jesus. Anchor Bible Reference Library/Anchor Yale Bible Reference Library. 4 vols. New York/New Haven: Doubleday/Yale University Press, 1991-2009.

_____. Law and History in Matthew's Gospel. Analecta Biblica 71. Rome: Biblical Institute Press, 1976.

_____. The Vision of Matthew. New York: Paulist Press, 1979.

Menoud, Philippe H. "The Acts of the Apostles and the Eucharist." Pages 84-106 in Jesus Christ and the Faith: A Collection of Studies by Philippe H. Menoud. Pittsburgh Theological Monograph Series 18. Pittsburgh: Pickwick Press, 1978.

Metzger, Bruce M. A Textual Commentary on the Greek New Testament. London/New York: United Bible Societies, 1971.

Meyer, Ben. The Aims of Jesus. London: SCM Press, 1979.

Minear, Paul S. "A Note on Luke 22:36." Novum Testamentum 7 (1964-65): 128-34.

_____. "Some Glimpses of Luke's Sacramental Theology." Worship 44 (1970): 322-31.

Molinski, Waldemar. "Marriage." Pages 905-10 in Encyclopedia of Theology. Edited by Karl Rahner. Translated by John Griffiths. London: Burns & Oates, 1975.

Moloney, Francis J. A Body Broken for a Broken People: Eucharist in the New Testament. Melbourne: Collins-Dove, 1990.

_____. A Body Broken for a Broken People: Eucharist in the New Testament. 2nd ed. Peabody, MA: Hendrickson Publications, 1997.

_____. Beginning the Good News: A Narrative Approach. Biblical Studies 1. Homebush: St Paul Publications, 1992.

_____. "Constructing Jesus and the Son of Man." The Catholic Biblical Quarterly 75 (2013): 719-38.

_____. "Eis telos (v. 1) as the Hermeneutical Key for the Interpretation of John 13:1-38." Salesianum 86 (2014): 27-46.

_____. "Jesus Christ: The Question to Cultures." Pacifica 1 (1988): 15-43.

_____. "Johannine Theology." Pages 1417-26 in *The New Jerome Biblical Commentary*. Edited by Raymond E. Brown, Joseph A. Fitzmyer, and Roland E. Murphy. Englewood Cliffs: Prentice-Hall, 1989.

_____. "John 6 and the Celebration of the Eucharist." *The Downside Review* 93 (1975): 243-51.

_____. *Love in the Gospel of John: An Exegetical, Theological, and Literary Study*. Grand Rapids: Baker Academic, 2013.

_____. "Luke 24: To be Witnesses of the Forgiveness and Compassion of Jesus." Pages 183-95 in *Apostolic Passion "Give me Souls."* Edited by Rafael Vicent, and Corrado Pastore. Bangalore: Kristu Joti Publications, 2010.

_____. "Mark 6:6b-30: Mission, the Baptist, and Failure." *The Catholic Biblical Quarterly* 63 (2001): 663-79.

_____. *Mark: Storyteller, Interpreter, Evangelist*. Peabody, MA: Hendrickson Publications, 2004.

_____. "Matthew 5:17-18 and the Matthean Use of *dikaiosunē*." Pages 33-54 in *Unity and Diversity in the Gospels and Paul*. Edited by Christopher W. Skinner and Kelly R. Iverson. Early Christianity and Its Literature 7. Atlanta: SBL, 2012.

_____. "Matthew 19:3-12 and Celibacy: A Redactional and Form Critical Study." *Journal for the Study of the New Testament* 2 (1979): 42-60.

_____. "Narrative Criticism of the Gospels." *Pacifica* 4 (1991): 181-201.

_____. *Reading the New Testament in the Church: A Primer for Pastors, Religious Educators, and Believers*. Grand Rapids: Baker Academic, 2015.

_____. "The Eucharist as the Presence of Jesus to the Broken." *Pacifica* 2 (1989): 151-74.

_____. "The Function of John 13-17 within the Johannine Narrative." Pages 43-66 in *"What is John?" Volume II: Literary and Social Readings of the Fourth Gospel*. Edited by Fernando F. Segovia. Symposium 7. Atlanta: Scholars Press, 1998.

_____. "The Function of *Prolepsis* in the Interpretation of John

6." Pages 129-48 in *The Interpretation of John 6*. Edited by R. Alan Culpepper. Biblical Interpretation Series 22. Leiden: Brill, 1997.

_____. "'The Jews' in the Fourth Gospel: Another Perspective." Pages 20-44 in *The Gospel of John: Text and Context*. Biblical Interpretation Series 72. Leiden/Boston: Brill, 2005.

_____. *The Johannine Son of Man*. 2nd ed. Eugene, OR: Wipf & Stock, 2007.

_____. "The Literary Unity of John 13,1-38." *Ephemerides Theologicae Lovanienses* 91 (2015): 33-53.

_____. *The Living Voice of the Gospel: The Gospels Today*. Melbourne: John Garratt, 2006.

_____. *The Resurrection of the Messiah: A Narrative Commentary on the Resurrection Accounts*. New York/Mahwah, NJ: Paulist Press, 2013.

_____. "Synchronic Interpretation." Volume 2, pages 345-54 in *The Oxford Encyclopedia of Biblical Interpretation*. Edited by Steven McKenzie. 2 vols. Oxford/New York: Oxford University Press, 2013.

_____. "Vatican II and 'The Study of the Sacred Page' as 'The Soul of Theology' (*Dei Verbum* 24)." Pages 19-40 in *God's Word and the Church's Council: Vatican II and Divine Revelation*. Edited by Mark O'Brien and Christopher Monaghan. Adelaide: ATF Theology, 2014.

_____. "When is John Talking about Sacraments?" *Australian Biblical Review* 30 (1982): 10-33.

_____. "Whither Catholic Biblical Studies?" *The Australasian Catholic Record* 66 (1989): 83-93.

Moore, Stephen D. *Literary Criticism and the Gospels: The Literary Challenge*. New Haven: Yale University Press, 1989.

_____. "Luke's Economy of Knowledge." Pages 38-56 in *Society of Biblical Literature Seminar Papers 1989*. Edited by David J. Lull. Atlanta: Scholars Press, 1989.

Moran, Stuart. *A Friendly Guide to the Gospel of Luke*. Melbourne: Garratt Publishing, 2013.

Morrison, Gregg S. *The Turning Point in the Gospel of Mark: A Study in Markan Christology*. Eugene, OR: Pickwick Publications, 2014.

Moxnes, Halvor. *The Economy of the Kingdom: Social Conflict and Economic*

Relations in Luke's Gospel. Overtures to Biblical Theology. Philadelphia: Fortress, 1988.

Müller, Dietrich, and Colin Brown, eds. "Apostle." Pages 128-37 in *The New International Dictionary of New Testament Theology.* 3 vols. Exeter: Paternoster Press, 1975.

Murphy-O'Connor, Jerome. *Becoming Human Together: The Pastoral Anthropology of St. Paul.* Good New Studies 2. Wilmington: Michael Glazier, 1982.

_____. "Corinth." Volume 1, pages 1134-39 in *The Anchor Bible Dictionary.* Edited by David N. Freedman. 6 vols. New York: Doubleday, 1992.

_____. "Eucharist and Community in First Corinthians." *Worship* 50 (1976): 370-85, and 51 (1977): 56-69.

_____. *St. Paul's Corinth: Texts and Archeology.* Good News Studies 6. Wilmington, DE: Michael Glazier, 1983.

_____. "The Structure of Matthew XIV-XVII." *Revue Biblique* 82 (1975): 360-84

Neirynck, Frans. "The Anonymous Disciple in John 1." *Ephemerides Theologicae Lovanienses* 66 (1990): 5-37.

Neudecker, Reinhard. *Moses Interpreted by the Pharisees and Jesus: Matthew's Antitheses in the Light of Early Rabbinic Literature.* Rome: Gregorian and Biblical Press, 2012.

Neusner, Jacob. *Ancient Israel after the Catastrophe: The Religious World View of the Mishnah.* Charlottsville: University Press of Virginia, 1983.

Neyrey, Jerome. *The Passion According to Luke: A Redaction Study of Luke's Soteriology.* New York: Paulist Press, 1985.

Niemand, Christoph. *Die Fusswaschungerzählung des Johannesevangeliums. Untersuchungen zu ihrer Enstehung und* Überlieferung *im Urchristentum.* Studia Anselmiana 114. Rome: Pontificio Ateneo S. Anselmo, 1993.

Nineham, Dennis. *The Use and Abuse of the Bible: A Study of the Bible in an Age of Rapid Cultural Change.* Library of Contemporary Philosophy and Religion. London: Macmillan, 1976.

Nolan, Albert. *Jesus Before Christianity: The Gospel of Liberation.* London: Darton, Longman & Todd, 1977.

Odeberg, Hugo. *The Fourth Gospel: Interpreted in Relation to Contemporaneous Religious Currents in Palestine and the Hellenistic-Oriental World.* Uppsala: Almqvist, 1929.

O'Donnell, Hugh. *Eucharist and the Living Earth.* Dublin: The Columba Press, 2007.

O'Malley, John W. *Trent: What Happened at the Council.* Cambridge, MA: Harvard University Press, 2013.

_____. *What Happened at Vatican II.* Cambridge, MA: Harvard University Press, 2008

O'Toole, Robert F. *The Unity of Luke's Theology: An Analysis of Luke–Acts.* Good News Studies 9. Wilmington, DE: Michael Glazier, 1984.

Painter, John. "The Farewell Discourses and the History of Johannine Christianity." *New Testament Studies* 27 (1980-81): 525-43.

Paul VI, Pope. *Encyclical Letter* Ecclesiam Suam *with a Discussion Aid Outline.* Homebush: St Paul Publications, 1964.

Perrin, Norman. *Rediscovering the Teaching of Jesus.* London: SCM Press, 1967.

_____. "The Christology of Mark: A Study in Methodology." *Journal of Religion* 51 (1971): 173-87.

_____. *The Resurrection Narratives: A New Approach.* London: SCM Press, 1977.

Perrot, Charles. "Lecture de 1 Co 11:17-34." Pages 87-101 in *Le Corps et le corps du Christ dans la Première Epître aux Corinthiens.* Congress de l'ACFEB, Tarbes, 1981. Lectio Divina 114. Paris: Cerf, 1983.

Piolanti, Antonio. *The Holy Eucharist.* New York: Desclée, 1961.

Pongratz-Lippitt, Christa. "Remarried Divorcees a Test Case for Church's Credibility, German Bishops Convinced." *National Catholic Reporter,* December 29 (2014): 1.

Powell, Mark Allan. *Introducing the New Testament: A Historical, Literary, and Theological Survey.* Grand Rapids: Baker Academic, 2009.

Power, David N. "The Holy Spirit: Scripture, Tradition, and Interpretation." Pages 152-78 in *Keeping the Faith: Essays to Mark the Centenary of Lux Mundi.* Edited by Geoffrey Wainwright. London: SPCK, 1989.

"Propositions on the Doctrine of Christian Marriage." Pages 163-83 in

International Theological Commission: Texts and Documents. Edited by Michael Sharkey. San Francisco: Ignatius Press, 1989.

Pryke, E. J. *Redactional Style in the Markan Gospel: A Study of Syntax and Vocabulary as Guides to Redaction in Mark*. SNTS Monograph Series 33. Cambridge: Cambridge University Press, 1978.

Quesnell, Quentin. "Made Themselves Eunuchs for the Kingdom of Heaven (Mt. 19:12)." *The Catholic Biblical Quarterly* 30 (1968): 335-58.

Rahner, Karl. *The Practice of Faith: A Handbook of Contemporary Spirituality*. Edited by Karl Lehmann and Albert Raffelt. New York: Crossroad, 1984.

Ratzinger, Joseph. "Sacred Scripture in the Life of the Church." Volume 3, pages 262-72 in *Commentary on the Documents of Vatican II*. Edited by Herbert Vorgrimler. London: Burns & Oates/Herder & Herder, 1969.

——————. "The Transmission of Divine Revelation." Volume 3, pages 181-98 in *Commentary on the Documents of Vatican II*. Edited by Herbert Vorgrimler. London: Burns & Oates/Herder & Herder, 1969.

Rengstorf, Karl H. "Jesus Christ." Volume 2, pages 330-43 in *The New International Dictionary of New Testament Theology*. Edited by Colin Brown. 3 vols. Exeter: Paternoster Press, 1976.

Rensberger, David. *Johannine Faith and Liberating Community*. Philadelphia: Westminster Press, 1988.

Rhoads, David. *Israel in Revolution 6-74 C.E.: A Political History Based on the Writings of Josephus*. Philadelphia: Fortress, 1976.

——————. "Performance Criticism: An Emerging Methodology in Second Temple Studies." *Biblical Theology Bulletin* 36 (2006): 118-33, 164-84.

Rhoads, David, Joanna Dewey, and Donald Michie, *Mark as Story: An Introduction to the Gospel as a Narrative*. 2nd ed. Minneapolis: Fortress, 1999.

Richard, Earl. *Jesus: One and Many: The Christological Concept of New Testament Authors*. Wilmington, DE: Michael Glazier, 1988.

Robbins, Vernon K. "Last Meal: Preparation, Betrayal, and Absence." Pages 21-40 in *The Passion in Mark: Studies on Mark 14-16*. Edited by Werner Kelber. Philadelphia: Fortress Press, 1976.

Robinson, James M., Paul Hoffmann, and John S. Kloppenborg. *The Critical

Edition of Q: Synopsis including the Gospels of Matthew and Luke, Mark and Thomas with English, German, and French Translations of Q and Thomas. Hermeneia. Minneapolis: Fortress, 2000.

Ruether, Rosemary Radford. *Sexism and God-Talk: Towards a Feminist Theology.* London: SCM Press, 1983.

Sanders, Ed Parish, *Jesus and Judaism.* Philadelphia: Fortress, 1985.

_____. *The Historical Figure of Jesus.* Harmondsworth: Penguin Books, 1993.

Schillebeeckx, Edward. *Marriage: Secular Reality and Saving Mystery.* Stag Books. 2 vols. London: Sheed & Ward, 1965.

Schmithals, Walter. *Gnosticism in Corinth: An Investigation into the Letters to the Corinthians.* Nashville/New York: Abingdon Press, 1971.

Schnackenburg, Rudolf. "Die Funktion der Exegese in Theologie und Kirche." Pages 11-36 in *Maßstab des Glaubens: Fragen heutiger Christen im Licht des Neuen Testaments.* Freiburg: Herder, 1978.

Schneider, Gerhard. *Das Evangelium nach Lukas:* Ökumenischer Taschenbuchkommentar zum Neuen Testament 3/1-2, 2 vols. Gütersloh/München: Gerd Mohn/Echter, 1977.

Schneiders, Sandra M. "Symbolism and the Sacramental Principle in the Fourth Gospel." Pages 221-35 in *Segni E Sacramenti Nel Vangelo Di Giovanni.* Edited by Pius-Ramon Tragan. Studia Anselmiana 67. Rome: Editrice Anselmiana, 1977.

_____. "The Footwashing (John 13:1-20): An Experiment in Hermeneutics." *The Catholic Biblical Quarterly* 43 (1981): 76-92.

Schweizer, Eduard. "Matthew's Church." Pages 129-55 in *The Interpretation of Matthew.* Edited by Graham Stanton. Issues in Religion and Theology 3. Philadelphia: Fortress, 1983.

Segovia, Fernando F. "John 13:1-20: The Footwashing in the Johannine Tradition." *Zeitschrift für die Neutestamentliche Wissenschaft* 73 (1982): 31-51.

_____. "John 15:18-16:4a: A First Addition to the Original Farewell Discourse." *The Catholic Biblical Quarterly* 45 (1983): 210-30.

_____. *Love Relationships in the Johannine Tradition: Agapē/Agapan in 1 John and the Fourth Gospel.* SBL Dissertation Series 58. Chico, CA: Scholars Press, 1982.

_____. *The Farewell of the Word: The Johannine Call to Abide.* Minneapolis: Fortress, 1991.

Senior, Donald. "The Eucharist in Mark: Mission, Reconciliation, Hope." *Biblical Theology Bulletin* 12 (1982): 67-72.

_____. *The Passion Narrative According to Matthew: A Redactional Study.* Bibliotheca Ephemeridum Theologicarum Lovaniensium XXXIX. Louvain: Leuven University Press, 1975.

_____. *The Passion of Jesus in the Gospel of Mark.* The Passion Series 2. Wilmington: Michael Glazier, 1984.

_____. *The Passion of Jesus in the Gospel of Matthew.* The Passion Series 1. Wilmington: Michael Glazier, 1985.

Senior, Donald, and Carol Stuhmueller. *The Biblical Foundations for Mission.* New York: Orbis Books, 1983.

Shaw, Prue. *Reading Dante: From Here to Eternity.* New York/London: Liveright Publishing, 2014.

Shepherd, Thomas. "The Narrative Function of Markan Intercalation." *New Testament Studies* 41 (1995): 522-40.

Shiner, Whitney T. *Proclaiming the Gospel: First Century Performance of Mark.* Harrisburg, PA: Trinity Press International, 2003.

Sim, David C. *The Gospel of Matthew and Christian Judaism.* Studies in the New Testament and Its World. Edinburgh: T. & T. Clark, 1998.

Simoens, Yves. *La gloire d'aimer: Structures Stylistiques et interprétative dans la Discours de la Cène.* Analecta Biblica 90. Rome: Biblical Institute Press, 1981.

Skinner, Christopher W., and Matthew Ryan Hauge. *Character Studies in the Gospel of Mark.* Library of New Testament Studies 483. London: Bloomsbury/T. & T. Clark, 2014.

Smith, Barry. "The Problem with the Observance of the Lord's Supper in the Corinthian Church." *Bulletin of Biblical Research* 20 (2010): 517-44.

Smith, D. Moody. *John Among the Gospels.* 2nd ed. Columbia: University of South Carolina Press, 2001.

Spicq, Ceslaus. "*Trōgein*: Est-il synonyme de *phagein* et de *esthiein* dans le Nouveau Testament?" *New Testament Studies* 26 (1979-80): 414-19.

Stendahl, Krister. *The School of St. Matthew.* 2nd ed. Philadelphia: Fortress, 1968.

Stock, Klemens. *Boten aus dem Mit-Ihm-Sein. Das Verhältnis zwischen Jesus und den Zwölf nach Markus.* Analecta Biblica 70. Rome: Biblical Institute Press, 1975.

Stolzman, William F. "Communion for Repenting Sinners?" *The Clergy Review* 65 (1980): 322-27.

Streeter, Burnett H. *The Four Gospels: A Study of Origins.* London: Macmillan, 1924.

Stuhlmacher, Peter. *Historical Criticism and Theological Interpretation of Scripture.* London: SPCK, 1977.

Tannehill, Robert C. "The Disciples in Mark: The Function of a Narrative Role." *Journal of Religion* 57 (1977): 386-405.

Taylor, Vincent. *The Passion Narrative of St Luke: A Critical and Historical Investigation.* Edited by Owen E. Evans. SNTS Monograph Series 19. Cambridge: Cambridge University Press, 1972.

Theissen, Gerd. "Social Integration and Sacramental Activity: An Analysis of 1 Cor 11:17-34." Pages 145-74 in *The Social Setting of Pauline Christianity: Essays on Corinth.* Philadelphia: Fortress Press, 1982.

_____. *The Shadow of the Galilean.* London: SCM Press, 1987.

Theissen, Gerd, and Annette Merz. *The Historical Figure of Jesus: A Comprehensive Guide.* Translated by John Bowden. Minneapolis: Fortress, 1998.

Theobald, Michael. "Eucharist and Passover: the two 'loci' of the liturgical commemoration of the Last Supper in the early Church." Pages 231-54 in *Engaging with C. H. Dodd on the Gospel of John: Sixty Years of Tradition and Interpretation.* Edited by Tom Thatcher and Catrin H. Williams. Cambridge: Cambridge University Press, 2013.

Thisselton, Anthony C. *New Horizons in Hermeneutics: The Theory and Practice of Transforming Biblical Reading.* London: Harper Collins, 1992.

Thomas, John C. *Footwashing in John 13 and the Johannine Community.* Journal for the Study of the New Testament Supplement Series 61. Sheffield: Sheffield Academic Press, 1991.

van Cangh, Jean-Marie. *Le Multiplication des Pains et l'Eucharistie,* Lectio Divina 86. Paris: Editions du Cerf, 1975.

van Iersel, Bas. "Die Wunderbare Speisung und das Abendmahl in der synoptischen Tradition (Mk VI 35-44 par., VIII 1-20 par.)." *Novum Testamentum* 7 (1964): 167-94.

von Wahlde, Urban C. "Raymond Brown's View of the Crisis in 1 John: In the Light of Some Peculiar Features of the Johannine Gospel." Pages 19-45 in *Communities in Dispute: Current Scholarship on the Johannine Epistles*. Edited by R. Alan Culpepper and Paul N. Anderson. Early Christianity and Its Literature 13. Atlanta: SBL Press, 2014.

Wansbrough, Henry. *The Use and Abuse of the Bible*. London: T. & T. Clark, 2010.

Wasserman, Tommy. "The 'Son of God' was in the Beginning (Mark 1:1)." *The Journal of Theological Studies* 62 (2011): 20-50.

Watson, Francis. "I Received from the Lord: Paul, Jesus, and the Last Supper." Pages 103-24 in *Jesus and Paul Reconnected*. Edited by Todd Still. Grand Rapids: Eerdmans, 2007.

Weeden, Theodore J. *Mark: Traditions in Conflict*. Philadelphia: Fortress, 1976.

Willis, W. L., *Idol Meat in Corinth: The Pauline Argument in 1 Corinthians 8 and 10*. SBL Dissertation Series 68. Chico, CA: Scholars Press, 1985.

Wischmeyer, Oda, David C. Sim, and Ian J. Elmer, eds. *Paul and Mark: Comparative Essays: Two Authors at the Beginnings of Christianity*. Beihefte zur die Zeitschrift für die neutestamentliche Wissenschaft 198. Berlin/Boston: de Gruyter, 2014.

INDEX OF AUTHORS

Fowler, R. M., 92, 94

France, R. T., 125

Francis, Pope, 6, 9, 11, 19, 26, 31, 34, 37, 209

Frend, W. H. C., 25, 37

Garland, D. E., 124, 126

Gaventa, B., 67

George, A., 154, 164

Gignac, F. T., 201

Gonzales, F. A. P. S. S., 61

Goodfriend, E. A., 241

Grabowski, J. S., 35

Gray, T. C., 97

Gregg, R. C., 37

Gundry, R. H., 125

Hagner, D., 121, 124, 125, 126, 127

Hamilton, N. Q., 93

Hanges, J. C., 62

Hansen, L., 11

Harner, P. B., 200

Harvey, W. J., 73, 75, 93

Hauge, M. R., 92

Havener, I., 240

Heilmann, J., 192, 194, 195, 196

Hengel, M., 91, 122, 197, 234, 253

Henrici, P., 54, 66, 67

Hill, D., 125, 127

Hoffmann, P., 240, 244

Hooker, M. D., 244

Horsley, R. A., 63, 64, 242, 246, 251

Hoskyns, E. C., 193, 195

Howard, W. F., 192

Huels, J. M., 33, 34

Hurtado, L. W., 96

Instone-Brewer, D., 239, 241, 242, 243, 246, 247, 248, 252

Iser, W., 197

Iverson, K. R., 92, 95

Jeffrey, D. L., 154

Jeremias, J., 29, 38, 67, 124, 125, 159, 196, 237

John Paul II, Pope, 33

Johnson, L. T., 157, 158, 159, 160, 162, 163, 164

Juel, D. H., 97

Jungmann, J., 32

Karris, R. J., 157, 158, 163, 164

Käsemann, E., 37

Kasper, W., 19, 35

Kee, H. C., 95, 96, 160

Keener, C. S., 121, 124, 128, 194, 195, 199, 226, 249, 250

Kelly, J. N. D., 241

Kingsbury, J. D., 97, 122, 123, 127

Kloppenborg, J. S., 12, 240, 244

Kodell, J., 38, 67, 68, 158, 159, 161, 192

Index of Scripture and Other Ancient Sources

Jewish Sources

Ancient Christian Authors

About the Author

Professor Francis J. Moloney, SDB, AM, FAHA, is an Australian Salesian Priest. Educated in Rome (STL, SSL) and at the University of Oxford (D. Phil.), he has taught widely, in Europe, Israel, Australia, East Asia, and the USA. Most recently he was the Professor of New Testament and the Dean of the School of Theology and Religious Studies at the Catholic University of America (Washington, DC) (1999-2005), and the Provincial Superior of the Salesians of Don Bosco in Australia and the Pacific (2006-2011).

He is the author of many significant books and studies, especially regarding the Gospel of John, including: *The Johannine Son of Man* (1976, 2nd edition 2007); the 3-volume *Belief in the Word: Reading John 1-4* (1993), *Signs and Shadow: Reading John 5-12* (1996), and *Glory not Dishonor: Reading John 13-21* (1998); *Reading John: Introducing the Johannine Gospel and Letters* (1995); *The Gospel of John* (Sacra Pagina series, 1998); *The Experience of God in the Johannine Writings* (with Anthony J. Kelly, 2003); *The Gospel of John: Text and Context* (2005); *Love in the Gospel of John: An Exegetical, Theological and Literary Study* (2013); and, as editor, Raymond E. Brown's *Introduction to the Gospel of John* (Anchor Bible Reference Library, 2003).

Other New Testament studies include: *Beginning the Good News: A Narrative Approach* (1992), *The Gospel of Mark: A Commentary* (2002), *Mark: Storyteller, Interpreter, Evangelist* (2004), *The Resurrection of the Messiah: A Narrative Commentary on the Resurrection Accounts in the Four Gospels* (2013), and *Reading the New Testament in the Church: A Primer for Pastors, Religious Educators, and Believers* (2015). He is also the author of *Mary: Woman and Mother* (1988), *Disciples and Prophets: A Biblical Model for the Religious Life* (1980), *A Life of Promise: Poverty-Chastity-Obedience* (1984), and *Life of Jesus in Icons from the "Bible of Tblisi"* (2008).

He is currently a Professorial Fellow at Australian Catholic University, and a Senior Fellow of Catholic Theological College, within the University of Divinity, Melbourne. A member of the International Theological Commission of the Holy See from 1984 to 2002, he is a Member of the Order of Australia, and a Fellow of the Australian Academy of the Humanities.

Praise for *A Body Broken for a Broken People*

"These pages show why close attention to Scripture matters and why Scripture in itself is not enough. Francis Moloney demonstrates that individual texts, however unambiguous they may seem, need to be set within a larger context of ongoing interpretation found in the New Testament itself. But he shows as well that an essentially unfinished Bible needs to be set within the still larger context of the Church's interpretation of Scripture through history, the never-ending reading that we call Tradition. Not all will agree with all the assumptions or conclusions found here, but it is hard to deny the soundness of Moloney's approach or the timeliness of what he offers."

The Most Reverend Mark Coleridge, BA DSS,
Archbishop of Brisbane, Australia

"Francis J. Moloney's *A Body Broken for a Broken People* offered a beautiful meditation on the presence of Christ in the Eucharist through careful and lucid interpretation of the relevant New Testament texts some 25 years ago. This new edition thoroughly updates and revitalizes that work as Moloney brings a lifetime of contemplative study to bear on the texts through which the 'earliest Church looked back to a Tradition of Jesus' sharing meals with the broken and the marginalized' and provided ongoing interpretation and application of Christ's words for the faithful who live 'within the ambiguity of the contemporary human story.' The Eucharist is indeed the place where God's broken yet faithful people gather for a sacred encounter with Christ that nourishes and challenges body and soul. Moloney likewise faithfully summons the Church to engage this Tradition anew in the 21st century and reflect upon its call to openness and balance in sacramental life. Christians of all traditions will be both challenged and supported by this new offering for them."

Sherri Brown, Ph.D., Assistant Professor of New Testament,
Department of Theology, Creighton University

"I rejoice to see an exegete taking a courageous look at a pastoral problem. He has performed a task too often abandoned by the specialist who imagines that he has completed his work when he thinks that he has determined the meaning of the texts. The exegete should do more. The specialist should always be concerned with the pastoral impact of scholarly affirmations, particularly when explaining the contexts within which the most important actions of Jesus of Nazareth took place. ... Exegetical endeavor is indispensable to prevent the Church from resting sleepily on past practices. ... Francis Moloney invites us not to settle for acquired positions of strength. They must always be challenged with the demands of the Gospel message."

Xavier Léon-Dufour, SJ, author of *Sharing the Eucharistic Bread:
The Witness of the New Testament*

"Francis Moloney is both a biblical exegete and theologian of international standing within the Academy and Church. From within the heart of the Church he is thus able to ask critical questions about Jesus' table practice and the Christian Churches' current eucharistic practice. With an eye to the Synod within the Catholic Church on the Family, this book looks directly at the exclusion from the eucharistic table of those who have been divorced and remarried. What wisdom can the biblical accounts offer for pastoral practice today? In examining significant eucharistic texts across the Gospels and Paul's letters, Moloney points to the earliest perception of Eucharist as Jesus' self-gift to disciples who betray, deny, misunderstand, and fail. Eucharist in Moloney's words is 'a body broken for a broken people.' This New Testament theology of Eucharist is Moloney's gift to the Church, and especially her Bishops, in pondering issues of worthiness in the brokenness of *all* our lives. I highly recommend this for all Christians seeking a richer understanding of the Eucharist in today's communities."

Associate Professor Mary Coloe, PBVM, Head of the Department of Biblical Studies, Yarra Theological Union, University of Divinity, Melbourne